THE SOFTWARE HANDBOOK

Dimitris N. Chorafas

PETROCELLI BOOKS
Princeton, New Jersey

© 1984 Petrocelli Books, Inc.
All rights reserved.

Designed by Diane L. Backes
Typography by Backes Graphics

Printed in the United States of America.
1 2 3 4 5 6 7 8 9 10

Library of Congress Cataloging in Publication Data

Chorafas, Dimitris N.
The software handbook.

Includes index.
1. Computer programming management—Handbooks, manuals, etc.
2. Computer programs—Handbooks, manuals, etc.
I. Title
QA76.6.C4555   1984   001.64'2'068   84-1169
ISBN 0-89433-248-1

CONTENTS

PART ONE
THE ART OF PROJECT MANAGEMENT

1 The Management of Projects
Introduction 3 / A Project Management Strategy 4 / Setting the Goals 6 / The Personnel Issue 9 / Organizational Standards 13

2 Conditions for a Successful Project
Introduction 17 / Planning Premises 18 / A Systems Development Methodology 20 / The Comprehensive Effort 24 / Project Control 26

3 The Systems Specialists
Introduction 31 / The Quality of a Project Manager 32 / A System Specialist Looks at Software Development 35 / Critical Regions and Semaphores 39 / Keep It Small and Simple 42

4 Model of an Information System Study
Introduction 49 / Management Approval 50 / Using a Valid Methodology 54 / Characteristics of a Valid Documentation 58 / Testing Premises 62

5 Medium Range Planning
Introduction 67 / Planning as an Agent of Change 68 / The Concept of Software Standards 72 / Restructuring Analysis and Programming 78 / Following Documentation Standards 84

PART TWO
THE ART OF SOFTWARE IMPLEMENTATION

6 The Software Challenge
Introduction 89 / What Is Meant by Software Engineering? 90 / A Program Is Not a Personal Object 93 / The Life Cycle Solution 96 / Fault Tolerant Approaches 100

7 Software Developments for Personal Computers
Introduction 105 / Product Quality and Productivity 106 / Revamping the Management Information System 111 / The Software Industry and its Problems 116 / Programming Practices 120

8 Organizing for Efficient Software
Introduction 127 / Attention to the Fundamentals 128 / Taking a Systems View 132 / Growing Software Endowment 137 / The Microsoftware Industry 141 / Protecting Proprietary Software 145

9 System Analysis for Myriaprocessors
Introduction 147 / Cost Trends in Hardware/Software 148 / The Systems Study 153 / Evaluating the Application 157 / Study of the Workplace 161

10 Structured System Analysis
Introduction 167 / Structuring Around the Data Component 168 / Rules to be Observed 172 / The Merits of a Structured Systems Analysis 175 / Logical Paths in Playback 179

11 Tools for a Structured Approach
Introduction 185 / What is Meant by the Right Tool? 186 / Critical Characteristics of Structural Analysis 196 / The Development Database 200 / Fringe Benefits? 203

PART THREE
THE ART OF LANGUAGE SELECTION

12 Interactive Languages
Introduction 211 / Which Level Language? 212 / Greater Efficiency in Programming 217 / A User-Oriented Language 221 / Programming Workstations 225

13 Developing Portable Programs
Introduction 231 / The Programming Product 232 / Conditions for Portability 236 / Algorithmic Characteristics 240 / Software Procurement 243

14 "C", Pascal, and the Lisp Languages
Introduction 247 / Computer Literacy 248 / Positioning the "C" Language 251 / Pilot and Logo 254 / A "C" and Pascal Comparison 257

15 Pascal, Cobol, and the Microcomputer Environment
Introduction 261 / Pascal and the Alternatives 262 / Cobol vs. Pascal 265 / The Longer Term 270 / Critical Tests 273

16 Betting on the Operating System
Introduction 277 / Developments in Basic Software 279 / The Evolution of Layered Solutions 282 / Memory Management 287 / Bringing into Action the MicroDBMS 291

17 An Overview of Unix
Introduction 295 / The Making of Unix 297 / The PDP 11/45 Versions at Bell Labs 302 / The File System 306 / Functions of the Shell 310 / Character Set 312 / Strengths and Weaknesses 314 / Unix System V 317 / Paying for Unix 318

PART FOUR
THE ART OF PROGRAM ADMINISTRATION

18 Evolving Microsoftware Industry
Introduction 323 / The Visicorp Story 325 / Visicalc 327 / Desktop/Plan and Micro/DSS Finance 330 / TK Solver 336

19 Integrated Software
Introduction 343 / What is Integrated Software? 344 / A Broader Range of Software 346 / An Applications Network Architecture 348 / Software for Executive Workstations 350 / The Horizontal Tools 353 / Telesoftware 355 / Videotex Services 358

20 Software Costs, Efficiency, and Programmer Productivity
Introduction 361 / Cost and Benefit 362 / The Shifting Impact of Knowhow 366 / A More Classical Look at Productivity 370 / The Merit of Structured Approaches 374

21 Fourth Generation Languages
Introduction 381 / New Images with Very High Level Language 383 / Adopting a Policy with VHLL 386 / A VHLL Classification 390 / The ADF Example 393 / Database Programming Languages 398 / IBM's DB 2 400

22 Computer-Based Documentation
Introduction 405 / The Contributions of a Documentation System 406 / What are the Alternatives? 410 / Coordinating Software Development and Documentation 414 / Focus on Efficiency 416

23 Reliability and Quality Assurance
Introduction 421 / Software Reliability 422 / Certification Criteria, Correctness, and Robustness 426 / Japanese Answers to Software Quality 430 / Structural Testing Approaches 433 / Reliability with Online Systems 438

24 New Thinking About Software Maintenance
Introduction 441 / Facilitating the Maintenance Task 443 / Testing as a Prerequisite to Successful Maintenance 446 / Prediction Techniques 451 / The Role of Remote Diagnostics 456

PREFACE

Computers and the communications systems promoted by an advancing technology may be powerful, but they are useless until the user specifies what he or she wants. The advent of computers on the financial and industrial scene has greatly accelerated the pace of operations, but with deep implications on how best to utilize both the electronics and the human resources.

While the efficiency of machines has improved, the skills of systems analysis, design, programming, testing and documentation have advanced at a much slower pace—and human knowhow has been threatened with rapid obsolescence. At no other time in history has there been more need to devise appropriate methods of project management to take advantage of the facilities the cutting edge of technology provides.

At the same time, personal computing is changing the way we look at data processing, databasing, datacomm, and software development. The wealth of libraries available through personal computers is altering our concept of programming. This is true both of vertical and of horizontal software.

We learn how to exploit computers and communications more skillfully when we encounter their limits, evaluate how to behave against these limits, and stay slightly ahead of the state of the art in exploiting them. Rather than asking for larger systems, more computer time, and greater bandwidth, we must do a better analysis of the job and of what it entails.

This is the aim of *The Software Handbook*. It is written in a direct, easy-to-follow language, without jargon, and with specific examples. It is addressed to the computer professional who wants to sort out techniques and methodologies used in project management, systems analysis, programming, testing, documentation, and software quality assurance—from large machines to microcomputers.

Part One presents to the reader "The Art of Project Management." Chapter 1 discusses how to manage projects, the strategic objectives to follow, and the organizational prerequisites. From planning to project control, the conditions for a successful project are at issue in chapter 2. Chapter 3 reviews the skills necessary for up-to-date system specialists. It underlines the reason this rule holds: the higher our knowhow, the simpler and smaller we will keep the software engine we develop. Chapter 4 presents a model of information systems duty, and chapter 5 underlines the merits of medium range-planning premises.

Project management is a vital discipline and it is still widely misunderstood. When it comes to software development, anything that takes longer than 6 to 9 months to build will run up against problems. Budgets are overrun, timetables skid, knowledge wasted. A new philosophy is necessary, and that's why I have stressed concepts rather than parading known tools.

The issue of Part Two is "The Art of Software Implementation." Introducing the breadth of the software challenge, chapter 6 discusses what is meant by software engineering. Emphasis is then placed on life cycle solutions and the need for fault-tolerant software. Personal computers enter the discussion in chapter 7, which is devoted to software development for that level of engines. This chapter also addresses the problems being faced by the software industry. By paying attention to the fundamentals, chapter 8 suggests organizational approaches for efficient software. The trend in personal computers is toward interconnecting through a local area network. This is the sense of a *myriaprocessor,* which implies its own system analysis perspectives. Chapters 10 and 11 treat the evoluting concept of a structured systems analysis. Chapter 10 emphasizes the data component of a structural system. Chapter 11 presents the reader with the tools now available for a structured approach, suggesting the wisdom of a development database as a systems analysis tool.

Part Three addresses itself to "The Art of Language Selection." This is one of the critical issues which will see great debates in this decade. First of all, the language to be chosen for personal computing and for online systems at large must be interactive—an issue not yet appreciated in all quarters. Chapter 12 speaks of interactive languages, recommending user-oriented solutions and the employment of programming workstations. Chapter 13 tells why the development of portable programs is a wise policy and how to go about it. In chapter 14 computer literacy is judged through the knowledge of "C", Pascal, and the Lisp languages. Then Pascal is compared to Cobol as the programming language to be adopted in a microcomputer environment. The operating system has obviously to be brought under focus. This is done in chapter 16. The overview of Unix in chapter 17 aims to elaborate an example and to emphasize one of the foremost OS available today.

"The Art of Program Administration" is described in Part Four. Both the industry perspective and the user views are supported. The former is done in chapter 18; the latter in the following chapters. Chapter 19 is devoted to integrated software: its meaning, range, functionality, and applications, down to the executive workstation level. Then the issue of telesoftware is introduced, particularly through videotex services. Software costs, efficiency, and programmer productivity are discussed in chapter 20.

Chapter 21 discusses fourth generation languages, a subject which is rapidly evolving. Chapter 22 tells why computer-based documentation is inseparable from a neat programming effort. Our awareness of reliability and quality control for programming products may be recent, but as chapter 23 demonstrates, software verification, certification, correctness, and robustness are changing our way of looking at product quality. The Japanese have some answers, and they are discussed in some detail. Finally, the reader does not need to be reminded of the high cost of software maintenance and its consumption of human resources. But there is some new thinking in this area, and this is shown in chapter 24.

Inevitably, some key issues are cross-indexed between the different chapters and parts. This is the case of thorough testing, which is just as vital with quality assurance as with an orderly maintenance. The same is true of structured approaches, project management techniques, and without doubt documentation. Such concepts are critical not only on their own merits but also in order to renew the meaning of *hardware* and *software.*

While creating new problems, technological changes offer improved ways of approaching the solutions to issues that have been facing us for years. We must profit from the new tools in systems analysis and project management. But we also must not forget that the fast-developing field of building software engines is still an art.

Let me close by expressing my thanks to everybody who contributed to making this book successful: from my colleagues, for their advice; to the organizations I visited in my research, for the insight; and to Eva-Maria Binder, for the drawings, typing, and index.

Valmer and Vitznau   Dimitris N. Chorafas
January, 1984

PART ONE

THE ART OF PROJECT MANAGEMENT

1

THE MANAGEMENT OF PROJECTS

1 INTRODUCTION

A *Project* is a well-defined activity set up to produce predetermined results. It involves resources:

- *Knowhow,* hence personnel
- *Money,* therefore budgets
- *Time,* projected in timetables
- Other resources, such as *computers* and *communications* support.

As an organizational unit, the project is dedicated to the attainment of a precise, short-to-medium term goal. It aims to create a product, service, or process by using the brainpower of its men and women—professional specialists in their field.

Results may be produced at a properly agreed upon point in time; budgets should not be overrun; human resources kept steady and never distracted from the objective they are set to reach. Record should be kept of every activity. Small, spirited, and knowledgeable working groups are the preferred solution.

The lines of responsibility have to be clear and frequently reinforced. If these lines start to blur, it is an indication that problems have developed and people are trying to avoid them. The main reason projects fail is that no one cares enough about them to avoid failure.

A project must be committed to a goal. Such commitment must be visible. Nothing should be allowed to shift the focus from what is needed to get the project done. Responsibility must be personal. If not knowing who is responsible is the root of the evil, lack of control is one of the most obvious ways this root cause manifests itself.

Regular design reviews help to ascertain responsibility. Every project should have interim control points built right into the project plan. Design reviews are a decision instrument and they should be implemented as such.

2 A PROJECT MANAGEMENT STRATEGY

Projects are found in business and industry as unique, well-defined efforts to produce specified results at a particular point in time. Such efforts typically cut across many functional and organizational lines. They may be called programs, task forces, teams, projects and ad hoc committees.

The design of information systems; new product introduction; plant expansion, relocation, or construction; urban renewal; aerospace research and engineering; capital investments and acquisition are just a few of the many, diverse types of project-like endeavors that display common management problems.

Projects must be managed. The assignment of responsibility for results is assumed by the manager. The ability to recognize the project nature of the task enables the manager to support the project effort through management concepts and techniques.

Project management is based on three basic concepts:

1. *The Project Manager:* A single point of authority and responsibility is designated.

2. *Planning and Control:* Exerted by the project manager.

3. *Organizing, Staffing, Directing:* Organizational perspectives; staffing requirements involving the best of the available personnel; and day-to-day activities; interest management; the leader of the project and its members.

The project manager's mission is to create a *product* or *service*, as specified in his or her job description. The primary tool available is the brainpower of men and women who are professional specialists in diverse fields. The manager uses this tool in all phases of the creation of the product, from concept through the initial test operation and subsequent *production* stages.

Organization-wise, a project is a unit dedicated to the attainment of a goal: generally the successful completion of a developmental product on time, within budget, and in conformance with predetermined performance specifications. The project staff itself will be a mix of brainpower varying with the project's mission.

A project involving a high degree of development will have a higher proportion of theoretically inclined personnel. This is another way of saying that projects are typically organized by task (diagonal structure) instead of by function performed by established departments.

Projects must bring professionalism to the job being done through skilled management able to assume complete responsibility for the entire requirements regarding job performance. With information systems projects, this includes the design, installation, and operation of the entire IS. The requirements range from system analysis and software development to providing guidance to the end user.

The obvious organizational goal is to seek the advantages of (1) The *vertical structure* in which the control and performance associated with autonomous management are maintained for a given project, and (2) The *horizontal structure* in which better continuity, flexibility, and use of scarce talents may be achieved in a technical group.

A study of the project manager's function must examine what one does, what one must be, and what training one needs. How does advanced technology management differ from the picture of the conventional manager? First, the project manager runs a higher proportion of professionals. Therefore, such a manager needs a different attitude regarding the classic functions of planning, coordinating, communicating, controlling, and setting performance standards.

The project manager knows that his basic responsibilities are to deliver his end product in accordance with performance requirements, within the limitations of his budget, and within the time schedule that has been specified. Success or failure may well hinge on the project manager's ability to discern fine variations in emphasis among performance, budget, and time schedule needs. The project manager must resolve the continuous apparent conflicts that occur among these three responsibilities. During the life of a typical project, the relative importance of each may change several times. The skillful project manager will aim for a balanced emphasis; one will try to stay flexible so one can shift and adapt to new circumstances as they occur.

A project manager often depends on top management to provide a continuity of work on successive missions. The record in achieving this continuity affects the peace of mind, if not the performance, of the project manager and the entire staff. Continuity is relatively easier to achieve on a project organization, than in a classic department. A unique aspect of the project manager's job is that the task is finite in duration. One cannot see a reasonably long line of repetitive or similar functions stretching ahead as the management counterparts in, say, engineering, manufacturing, or sales do.

The project leader is managing a specific group of advanced specialists. The professional mix of his group is tailored specifically for the accomplishment of an assigned mission. If manager and group are successful performers, they will complete all facets of their job in the best possible manner.

Like the line manager, the project manager should be a person of action, a person of thought, and a front person. As to managerial action, the most important function is the establishment and the preservation of a sense of momentum throughout all layers of the project. What one strives hardest to avoid is deadlock situations in which general inertia seems to become overpowering, and the technical people momentarily see no direction in which to advance. Thus, the usual management function of trouble shooting or of unravelling the knots occupies a great deal of time.

3 SETTING THE GOALS

We said that a project is set up to reach specific goals. These must be explicit, precise, and set in writing. Goals should not be changed midterm in a project, but a project with these characteristics should be closed down:

Fails to reach its milestones,

Overruns its estimated costs,

Misuses its human resources by periodically diverting them to secondary issues, and

Goes out of control.

It will never become a success and failure will be very expensive. Many projects drift aimlessly because no one knows what the goals are. A related problem is continually adding new goals to the same project.

The notion that the whole is a function of who is viewing it introduces another issue. Having received in writing the project's goals, its managers should define the boundaries between the whole and its environment. Diversion is what happens when this requirement is not fulfilled.

Banks, business, and industry look towards project management solutions because the project method has proved to be an effective way of utilizing the available brainpower. Since the days of the famed Manhattan Project, many projects have piled up a fine record of accomplishment. Not all projects are, however, that successful.

One of the weakest subjects in project management is the deadlines. Milestones and deadlines are an integral part of the goal. If they are often weak, it is because of the bad practice of amending them all the time. Yet management rarely understands the gravity of this situation.

Even when goals and milestones are easily met, a project would fail if top management is looking for easy ways out. Correctly, management wants results, but it does not always understand that it also needs to get involved.

The goals which are set and the resources allocated for meeting them will help distinguish between low-risk and high-risk projects. Risk can be defined by

- size, hence investment,
- technology, and
- degree of certainty about what the output should be.

Progress toward a given goal can be significantly enhanced if management, users, and designers have a common understanding of how risky a given project is. Good planning will deliberately strike a balanced agenda between the low and the high risks. In a certain sense, that is a hedging stategy involving both frontier and well-worn paths.

Project managers must be cognizant of and compensate for risk. As a project goes on toward fulfilling its goals, it also gets riskier. Formal controls are therefore at a premium, but controls should be established during the planning stage. The more unstructured a project is, the more unknown elements there will be. The better it is planned and controlled, the less is the uncertainty.

Uncertainty can be properly reduced through the clear definition of responsibility. Project management must accept in writing responsibility for these activities:

1. Planning and meeting contractual requirements on programs assigned to it.

2. In cooperation with the operating departments, preparing schedules for the execution of all tasks in accordance with program requirements.

3. Preparing budgets and negotiating them with operating departments.

4. Monitoring technical progress with a frequency sufficient to ensure the timely detection of problem areas.

5. Working with operating department managers to provide corrective action on any problem areas.

6. Bringing serious or unresolved problems to the attention of senior management.

7. Being the main contact point for the customer (end user), handling requests for information, and furnishing status reports.

Because goals are difficult to define and, once defined, difficult to contain; because available cost and time standards are not always reliable; and because technological and economic forces effect unanticipated changes—for all these reasons the project should be subjected to greater not lesser control action. Success requires integration of thousands of minor decisions and of elements that may lie outside the manager's direct control.

From goal setting to the final design review, a formal, planned action helps in reducing uncertainty and in eliminating the failure reasons. Such action will typically involve those activities able to produce a tangible product, starting with the indispensable written and signed-off analysis of what the user wants.

The preliminary analysis must be immediately followed by written, user-accepted, functional specifications regarding how to do the project; the breakdown into subsystems; the analysis and design of each subsystem; component and aggregate testing; all the way to an installed and user-accepted system. A thorough documentation should be included at each step, the whole being computer supported.

These are notions to which we will return on several occasions to assure proper understanding. For the moment let's keep with the broader view of the subject, which often helps distinguish how successful a project can be.

4 THE PERSONNEL ISSUE

A project manager is selected during the proposal phase of an undertaking. Following the assignment, the manager plays a major role in determining the project organization's functions and responsibilities. He also selects the personnel needed to accomplish the job. The project manager's proposals must get top management's approval. In the baseline, top management makes the relevant decisions about the project, including naming the project manager. It is essential that the project manager have superior leadership ability. He must have administrative experience, and he must be skilled in planning, budgeting, scheduling, and control techniques.

A weak project manager cannot be made strong and effective by creating additional controls or a top-heavy project organization structure. Furthermore, one of the most serious problems that the project manager may face is the reluctance of specialists to join a project organization because they fear that at the completion of the job they may be transferred to other, less desirable assignments.

A man with a record of good progress and an established reputation in a functional department is likely to turn down an offer to join a project unit. Another factor affecting his decision is the division of responsibilities between a functional organization and its counterpart in the project organization.

To attract good people in a project organization, salary and promotion issues must be settled in an able manner. Yet, the employee who becomes a part of the project organization often finds that the project manager has little or no control over pay increases and promotions.

Management can do a number of things to encourage valid people to transfer to project organizations.

- Salary increases can be offered to employees as inducements to accept carrier risks.

- A number of proportional opportunities can be outlined; they will usually result from forming a project organization, since additional management structure is being created.

- Special efforts can be made to reassign personnel phasing out of existing project organizations, and thereby create an atmosphere of security.

If senior management and the project leader don't look after the staff during phase-out of a project, they may not get them back on another project.

Job rotation is an important characteristic in a project management activity. The project team brings personnel from affected departments together with specialists, to contribute to and to coordinate the accomplishment of the objectives of the system. The composition of the project team must be such as to keep departmental involvement in line with the actual progress of the systems effort.

Since the members of this team come from different backgrounds, project management must be keen in enforcing the employment of established standards, ensuring that the appropriate person(s) are made responsible for formal quality control. Results will be so much better when the most capable personnel is made available to participate in the sytems effort, relieved from other duties, and given suitable training. It is important to ensure that personnel comprehend their place in the total project picture:

- All team members have a clear understanding of the purpose and scope of their assignment.

- They are familiar with the schedules and constraints of the systems effort which are applicable to their work.
- They know how their team is organized, its relationship to other teams.
- They are aware of the manner in which they are expected to contribute.
- They observe the standards of documentation to be applied and the methods of progress reporting.

Effectiveness and output are significantly reduced if personnel is transferred to and from the project while the work is in process. The same is true if the organization does not have the caliber of men required to make project management a viable effort.

Next to the brainpower under his control, the project manager's most important tool is the authority given by management to cut red tape. In principle:

- Projects must never be permanently structured: they must be dismantled upon completion.
- Projects should be organized by task (diagonal structure) rather than staff or line.
- In a diagonal structure the control of performance rests on management capabilities.
- As already stated, a project manager runs a higher proportion of professionals than any other manager in the organization.

The men working on the project do not fit the frame of a pyramidal organization; they are concentrated around the project as required. Authority and responsibility patterns are important, but let's not forget that a significant portion of the project manager's authority depends on his ability to resolve conflicts, build alliances and reciprocity, and maintain the integrity of the project team.

For this reason, his sensitivity, motivation, and persuasion must be high. The project manager must have clear ideas, he must communicate, and he must dispose direct channels of information. *Selling* is a never-ending job of a project manager, as it is of most other senior managers in the corporate organization.

In the matters of acquiring scarce funds, people, and systems support, the project manager must always be able to make an effective presentation, often on short notice. Many project managers have suddenly found themselves, in midcourse, fighting for the very existence of their project.

In pursuing the objective of maintaining momentum, the project manager must be constantly aware of the apparent disdain for time commitments which prevails on the part of the more theoretically inclined systems specialists. While this attitude is a rather deep study in itself, one part of it that must be understood is the drive for perfection that so often characterizes the professional mind. The tendency to finish the job to perfection, if allowed to run rampant, can result in continuous postponements of outputs, thus reducing the productivity of the project as a whole. Such practice often erodes the good will of users and of top management and puts in doubt the project's ability to meet its goal.

Confidence comes with results. Deadlines can be maintained through organizational planning, that is, the correct tailoring of organization structure to available individuals. In advanced technology, sound organization requires adroitness in recruiting scarce talent. It also involves the ability to utilize men, who, in some cases, do not measure up to reasonable levels for the project—the ability to shape a team which can "play over its head" when it has to.

Valid organization planning in a project cannot be done without a thorough understanding of the personalities, the characteristics, and the attitudes of all the technologists, both as individuals and as members of the particular profession. Advance planning is an important duty of the project manager, and it can make the difference between failure and success.

The project manager is an integrator. One of the important characteristics of effective integrators is that their orientation and ways of thinking strike a good balance between the extremes of the members of the team whose efforts they are integrating. Differences in ways of thinking are part of what makes it difficult for people to collaborate effectively. The fact that an effective integrator has a balanced orientation means that he shares more ways of thinking and more behavior patterns with the members of the team than these members normally do with each other. In a sense, he speaks the language of each of the specialists, and thus he is able to work at resolving conflicts.

Some of the qualifications that a successful project manager must possess proceed logically from the preceding discussion:

A working knowledge of many fields.

A career molded in the systems technology environment.

A good understanding of general management problems.

Familiarity with the concept of profitability.

A strong, continuous, active interest in teaching, training, and developing subordinates.

In reviewing these qualifications, we can observe the emphasis on the integrative function in the operations of the project manager. There is an ever-present requirement for the joining of many parts into a systematic whole. Describing the processes depending on the integrative mind is of course difficult: they are largely indefinable, just as the requisite qualities for managerial personnel are not subject to scientific definition.

The integrative mind must deal with intangible factors as well as tangible. At times there is also need for an intuitive process in the formulation of judgment and decision, especially where men's reactions are an important factor. It is perhaps in this respect that the outlook of a good project manager differs most sharply from that of the researcher. The analytical mind will not draw its hypothesis until all relevant data have been observed and interpreted. If a hypothesis must be drawn before this, it must be thoroughly qualified and hedged in the interest of scientific accuracy.

In project organizations, it is recognized that the analytical mind produces the concepts by which the project advances towards its goal. Yet, without the integrative function, nothing would be done with the concepts originating in the analytical function. The sound manager of a technology project must be capable of both integration and analysis, and must understand that the rigorous training of professional technologists, with its emphasis on analysis, sometimes impairs their integrative ability.

5 ORGANIZATIONAL STANDARDS

Since so much rests on the project manager and the results he can obtain, the first basic standard to observe regards his person. The profile of the project manager can be described through the following qualities:

> ability to foretell, plan, and estimate trends
>
> analytic penetrating mind
>
> knowledge to appraise alternative approaches
>
> ability to quantify and qualify user needs
>
> willingness to put in writing all project documentation
>
> appreciation of qualities, yields, costs, and human reaction
>
> an iron hand in implementing an orderly discipline
>
> ability to make up his or her mind when faced with difficult decisions as to the course to follow.

In terms of organizational perspectives, the project manager must embrace such functions as planning, organizing, staffing, directing and controlling.

Organizational standards are necessary to perform the project mission in an able manner. Such standards would typically concern the products to be developed in terms of hardware, software, performance, quality, reliability, and maintainability. Standards are necessary for management purposes: to allocate funds to all groups performing the tasks and services for the project; to coordinate analyses of capabilities, capacities, and efficiencies; to develop project schedules and coordinate requirements with affected company organizations; and to establish status reporting and to continuously monitor project expenditures, task completion, and delivery.

An important activity for which standards are necessary is project change control. This is needed to exercise control over all project changes, including design changes, keeping them to a minimum. For this and all other purposes, the project manager's authority must be defined through an organizational description.

There are no definite ground rules for determining the extent of such authority. It must be decided after consideration of project requirements and organizational/managerial strengths. The goal is delineating the extent of the manager's authority both over the project and in dealing with the functional organizations (whose support the project manager needs to enable him to exercise authority).

Authority and responsibility must be written in a job description, and the relation between a given project and the staff/line departments must be properly documented:

> The functional departments are doing the day-to-day work.
>
> The project(s) address themselves to new undertakings, specific in aims and time scales.
>
> In either case, skills should be transferable: the skills developed on one project can be applied to current and succeeding projects.

Some of the project support functions such as financial control and administration can be performed by the existing departmental staff.

Coordination between the existing departmental structure and the projects to be undertaken is one of the reasons why, before establishing a project organization, a company should assess the nature of the job and its requirements. Management should evaluate the existing structure to pinpoint any organizational weaknesses that might inhibit successful accomplishment of the project. The project organization should be assigned any functions needed to compensate for known or probable organizational deficiencies, its scale being determined by the kind and scope of the organization functions assigned to it.

The organizational decisions to which we make reference will impact the cost of the project. The cost of project organization varies according to

> its size,
>
> its duration
>
> extent of personnel and
>
> equipment needed.

How much cost control a project manager has, or should have, is sometimes difficult to determine, but guidelines do assist. Financial institutions and industrial companies have suffered unwarranted cost resulting from failure to reduce manpower levels in functional units when tasks are transferred to the project group. Most companies have also found unpleasant surprises as they failed to control in a steady manner:

1. budgets,
2. timetables,
3. personnel, and
4. equipment to be acquired.

All four issues call for exercising better cost control. Winners include:

applying more management to the project;

tasks and budgets being better defined;

changes more rigidly controlled;

performance more closely watched; and

management initiating action sooner to prevent or correct problems.

A valid way to initiate corrective action is the institution of *design reviews*. They should be held at regular intervals (bi-weekly, monthly) and regard both the managerial aspects and the technical details.

Hence, while cost control is a key part of managerial supervision of a project, it is not the only one. The control of timetables is very important and so is emphasis on the necessary technical detail.

2

CONDITIONS FOR A SUCCESSFUL PROJECT

1 INTRODUCTION

All projects should integrate into a plan, the latter being properly conceived and documented. Systems projects should involve both users and analysts, and their management assigned to the best people available. These should be computer assisted throughout the life of the project and subjected to steady design-reviews.

Management support calls for an able definition of what a project group is, how it should be structured; who should participate, and the role of the project manager. It is necessary to spell out the manager's responsibility for the establishment and the observance of timetables; for quantifying the productivity of analysts and programmers; and for the employment of tools in assisting a project's group performance.

Information system analysis and design is *par excellence* a multidimensional discipline. Hence, the project manager must have a broad horizon and the clearest perspective on his or her own views and thoughts. The messages to be transmitted to the users also must be clear. The same is valid for any orders the manager gives to subordinates.

He or she must have done work of distinction and have at least ten years of hands-on experience with information systems. A main criteria of excellence is the robustness of the codes he writes, their documentation, his team's productivity, and the able use of the available computer resources. An equally important criterion is program life cycles.

Robustness, documentation, and life cycles have not characterized computer systems work in years past. The state of most applications libraries justifies this reference. The problems arising from existing bits and pieces of information systems are an important reference. They can be used as an opportunity to flesh out past failures, improve performance, and improve the quality of the new systems.

The planning premises for systems studies rest on relatively simple rules: First, the necessity to establish and follow the appropriate milestones. Second, the study and implementation of quantitative standards. Third, the following up of a control methodology—both for quality assurance and for swamping costs.

Management must manage. A project manager must be put in the position to critically evaluate the capabilities of the available manpower, to review results obtained, and to suggest ways and means of bettering the cost effectiveness, based on:

> the standards which have been established in planning the project, and
>
> the experience acquired in the course of the subject work.

For this, he needs the proper tools. The following are tools which have been used, tested, and found to be valid.

2 PLANNING PREMISES

A planning system for analysts and programmers necessarily starts with the identification of the work to be done. Then this work is divided into milestones. There are seven major phases within a life cycle:

1. *The initial planning of systems and procedures.* This is a largely procedural study, aiming at the mapping of the current status in systems processing, including the main phases of data handling: output, storage, throughput, and input. This initiation phase is aimed at the identification of project requirements. It should take place before the project is approved.
2. *Logical System Design.* This step identifies what the system is to accomplish. It puts into motion the process of chang-

ing organization and structure. It regards organizational responsibilities, information flow, and capabilities for bettered service.

Solutions require choices in which the user should have a major role. Systems choices must be given a precise description. The logical system design examines both the requirements to be answered by module and the linkages between the different modules.

3. *Physical System Design.* Its aim is to establish characteristics of the facility on which the logical system will run. This is the job of the system specialist, not for the user. The user should be primarily concerned with the logical design. The physical system design must not only account for but also resolve the demands posed by the logical system.

4. *Construction.* Programming is part of the construction effort. In summary, this phase includes database design, datacomm capabilities, protocols, choice of personal workstations, choice of memory supports, and programming interfaces to noncomputerized parts of the IS.

5. *Evaluation.* This phase includes tests, conversion, and installation. The tests comprise those of individual program tests and the integration (system) test. The planning of the administration and the development data for program tests and file tests; the execution of the tests; and the evaluation of the results represent part of this phase. A test analysis report should be prepared upon completion.

The conversion and installation phases include a great deal of organization studies needed for the transition from the old to the new system, as well as the parallel runs and their supervision.

6. *Operation.* This should be divided into two parts: preparatory work and actual operation. The former involves the completion of the user's, operations, and maintenance manuals, as well as the test and implementation manual.

The documentation issue should address itself to the functional description, the text/data requirements, and all matters relating to the logical system design.

The actual operation of the information system concentrates on the day-to-day production issues. It calls for training of the end users and for assisting them over a period of time to make sure that timely production is not handicapped by missing data, by errors, and by delays in the periphery.

> 7. *Maintenance.* The maintenance procedures and tools to be used must be outlined at the very beginning, if they are to serve as the standard references in all modifications the system will undergo in its life cycle from analysis to programming. Maintenance can be both logical and physical. The developing policy for the latter is *after failure* maintenance. For the former, the wise way is to keep it to the bare minimum.

Maintenance can be divided into repair and enhancement. The latter concerns itself with Logical System Design; the former with Physical System Design. Starting from these two concepts, maintenance projects go through a number of phases in the programs' life cycle. Maintenance projects may consist of activities similar to those of development projects. In both cases there is an existing applications system which has to be improved either through repair of the software which is already available or by providing totally new applications programs.

3 A SYSTEMS DEVELOPMENT METHODOLOGY

The first step in evaluating the future structure of an MIS through project management is the defining of company goals and the methods to reach those goals. This step is not complete until top management clearly understands what the objectives are and knows how it can accomplish those objectives. Only then can management be prepared to evaluate potential information systems applications in an able manner.

Conditions for a Successful Project

Based on these goals, an information systems strategy can be defined. Development and implementation are the order of business for the project group. Implementation requires a step-by-step procedure for each application and the development of programming specifications. Criteria to be considered are costs, user-friendly solutions, the employment of advance technology, response time, local intelligence by workstation, databasing, datacomm, protocols, and the predominant use of software packages.

One of the elements for a successful information systems implementation is documentation. Proper documentation enables the users of the system to learn how to perform the necessary procedures and eases the problems resulting from systems change.

There are countless problems that may and usually do emerge during a project. The greatest number of them lie in three areas, each posing documentation requirements of its own:

- *Organizational level.* Because management information systems generally involve computers, there has been a tendency to try to implement programs for interactive systems through the same techniques commonly used for conventional data processing.

Information systems projects have too frequently been left chiefly to batch-oriented personnel for conception, design, and development. When this happens, the system which goes into operation will probably not deliver the results which top management wants. The user learns, too late, that he has been given an engine designed to answer somebody else's ideas of what the user's problems are.

Nobody knows what information is needed to run a company except the people living with the everyday pressures and responsibilities. Therefore, if the end user is not ready to make a commitment about the information he wants and to establish value criteria, he is better off not trying to implement a computers and communications solution.

- *Scope and Cost of the Projects.* Those who initiate information systems projects tend to aim for a scope which is beyond the budget envisaged by the sponsoring organization. They also tend to give results which are too little/too late.

Furthermore, once projects get started, information systems appetites tend to get out of hand. Users may want too much, too soon, or the original requirements are not well defined and spread like an oil spot. This upsets costs estimates and changes the scope of the project.

In many cases, cost overruns are directly related to lack of management commitment. Failure to delineate the exact scope of a system to be developed leads to a looseness of control which lets costs get out of hand. Cost problems are usually related to ignorance or insecurity on the part of people making final commitments and exercising ultimate control. Formal budgetary documentation and plan/actual follow-ups can be of great help.

- *Analysis and Design.* The prerequisite to an able information systems implementation is that management knows what it wants in the way of analytical information and is able to put a realistic value on the acquisition of this faculty.

Such values should be firm. Information availability must be evaluated in terms of its impact on running the bank or the company. Managers unwilling to establish values for acquired information should not be given the information support they might otherwise have needed or deserved.

It is advisable to begin the information analysis on needs and requirements through the identification of the quantitative elements that are critical. It is not enough merely to show the flow of documents and the existence of files. It is essential that volumes of documents, sizes of files, and interactive requirements be pinpointed as closely as feasible. Every task connected with the development of the new information system should be responsibility oriented.

A number of critical questions are associated with this last reference. Is the project local or remote? What is the volume and frequency of database interaction? Of text and data processing? Are extensions of system anticipated? Will there be a need to interface existing software? What are the system size constraints?

Answers have to be precise both in a qualitative and in a quantitative sense. What are the specific processing needs: resource facilities, interactive reports, formats, frequencies, response times?

Conditions for a Successful Project

How much memory is required? What are the cost trade-offs among software packages? How do they impact on hardware choices?

In making studies of information flow and file content, data gathered on volumes of documents and file sizes should be certified in writing by the responsible head of the user department. After management objectives, information values, and data source/destination have been established, the project manager is ready to authorize his systems analysts to proceed with the design of the system. This study should start with a survey of available software packages (applications programs) and all major cost incurring commitments.

We have spoken of milestones. Any and every information systems project should have previously designated work checkpoints. In this way, exposure is limited to a series of controllable steps. For each milestone, costs and the assignment of responsibilities for meeting objectives must be firm and irrevocable.

One of the evident milestones is the point where the preliminary design has been completed. The information system tentatively designed by the technicians must be measured against the initial stipulations of management objectives and values. Among veterans of system design wares, this is frequently referred to as "tradeoff time." It is the moment of truth: broad management stipulations are measured against the realities of costs and operating characteristics.

Tradeoffs that can be applied at the stage of system development include changes in deadlines or format of delivery. Most frequently this involves weighing the extent of online inquiry capabilities, particularly in regard to memory size and response time.

Depending on the scope of the projected information system, communications facilities, protocols, software, equipment, and implementation must be evaluated in terms of end objectives, available knowhow, developmental expenses, and operating overhead—as well as the urgency of delivering specific types of information.

A valid principle to keep in mind throughout this evaluation phase is that information systems projects are vital to the competitiveness of organizations. But information systems alone, though necessary, are not enough. The other pillar of the effort is the steady training of the bank's or industry's human resources on how to make the best use of technology.

Every executive today wants to stand higher and to see more. But the majority has not been trained on how to see through the shape of things. Hence, they may see more, but they do not know what they are looking at. They cannot benefit from this "further-out" sight.

4 THE COMPREHENSIVE EFFORT

The need for a progressively greater understanding of the control elements essential to financial and industrial operations goes hand in hand with the wisdom to couple information systems design with a thorough, well studied training program. Matching computer software and hardware to functional needs is no easy business. It is becoming impossible when met by apathy or lack of understanding.

The applications that a director of engineering would have for his computer-aided design equipment are as varied as the creativity of his engineers and the company's product line. The controller's applications can be just as varied, but even the most straightforward, such as receivables and payables, become laborious when processed in a manual way.

Not only new concepts should characterize the approaches followed in system design—concepts making full use of software and equipment capabilities. But these systems also must be *simple*. One often discarded principle is that systems can be simple and effective at the same time.

Along this line of thought, information systems must be designed for exception reporting and other approaches of relief for the nearly chaotic world of text/data acquisition, retention, and dissemination. They must also be designed for the control of people, costs, and time.

The needs of management probably require the most sophisticated approaches, but sophistication is no end in itself when effectiveness is a goal. The new technology makes available new means such as:

1. personal, intelligent workstations

2. local area networks

3. the handling of voice, text, data, and image

Conditions for a Successful Project

4. effective database applications
5. instantaneous long haul communications
6. the beginning of standardized protocols
7. color and graphics exchange between men and machines.

These tools offer a new dimension to the system designers and the end users who know how to employ them wisely. The major failure is in understanding how to use them.

If from the several hundred thousand information system projects around the world today only a few are considered to be well managed, this is because most organizations lack the tools to

coordinate projects,

check the impact of the new or proposed systems on the existing structure,

understand the implications,

and plan in advance the life cycle before committing vital resources to a project.

Organizations are condemned to rediscover the wheel because of basic failures in the work of their specialists. Unavoidably, time and again they discover that systems don't do what they were initially promised to do, specifications are steadily decreased to meet the falling standards of achievement, and costs exceed the levels promised when the system started being studied.

While attacking these problems in a competent fashion, the system designer and the end user must:

1. Train people, enabling every participant to the project—analyst/designer or user—to comprehend what's done. That is, avoid using people who are *not* adequately trained.

2. Improve procedures. Streamline them, primarily by focusing on management procedures, systems specifications, work conditions, and the like.

3. Provide better tools but only in a user-friendly manner.

Pencil, paper, and a programming language are archaic means by present-day standards. Becoming computer aided is a goal, but its implementation brings into evidence a great deal of preparatory steps, starting with the study of project requirements.

As cannot be repeated too often, the design goal of the system, from the procedural analysis onwards, should be influenced by the timetable for development; system flexibility considerations; program and algorithmic accuracy to be observed; maintainability of software and hardware throughout the life cycle of the system; and production run efficiency. Such criteria should be considered right from the drawing board. The key to a successful development, meeting the stated requirements, is to assure the participation of users who will ultimately benefit from the information system when it is complete and operational.

Let's recapitulate the basic steps that enter in the information systems study. The aim of the procedural analysis is to define the objectives concerning services and information contents of input, output, and throughput (both volume and frequency). This requires a listing and description of interactive output (reports) faculties, input specifications (data collection, formats), text and databasing, and handling procedures to which the input must be submitted in order to obtain the defined results.

A number of distinct steps will need to be taken in the course of the work in reference: a feasibility study; user interviews in writing, preferably through a personal computer; a collection of basic operational statistics; a review of organizational procedures as to their suitability; the establishment of intermediate and final reports and exhibits reflecting the conclusions, strong/weak points, and the new procedural systems proposal.

5 PROJECT CONTROL

The project manager should coordinate the use and maximize the effectiveness of resources under his control. To do so, he must be armed with reliable cost and time standards and be able to monitor and control with precision.

A valid strategy is based on well structured forecasts specific to the project's area of expertise. The scope of everybody's efforts in the project team must be predictable; their targets well defined; degrees of success (or failure) readily measured. These are matters a valid practice would recommend, while also acknowledging that managing a project means planning in the context of an unknown which can present itself during implementation.

All activities with their beginning events must be identified. They should be reported as to status at each updating. Calendar dates representing the base reference points must be set. These are also subject to subsequent updating. Meaningful, specified accomplishments should be recognizeable at a particular instant in time. Without this organization, there is no sense of control.

The heart of the project control system must reflect in summary form the contents of the program plan. It should be designed simultaneously to present data on

cost,

schedule,

and technical status for a given project.

This will enable management to make an assessment of progress quickly and give a sound basis for determining which projects require special attention.

Each project manager should be required to make an objective evaluation and appraisal of whether the project is meeting its technical performance requirements, is running on schedule, is staying within the planned cost, and is receiving adequate funding. The necessity of giving a *yes* or *no* answer seems to minimize much of the subjectivity in the evaluation made in the progress of a given project.

Once the project manager has given *yes/no* responses, he or she should be expected also to color code the status of critical parameters. For instance, green coding might be used when performance is proceeding in accordance with objectives (green is normally coupled with a *yes* response). Amber could be used when warning of potentially serious trouble, suggesting that careful attention is warranted. Red might reflect out-of-control situations (cost overrun, schedule delinquency, or technical problems).

Amber and red indicators should require written explanation beyond the program highlights. Furthermore, each project manager must update his status reports monthly. Each month, the green, amber, and red indicators for technical, schedule, cost, and funding status must be posted on large, permanent, summary display boards that are maintained in an executive chart room.

A graphical presentation helps in the

- appraisal of performance;
- the execution of plans in accordance with the established standards, and
- the initiation of corrective action if required.

Examples of cases in which project control should ensure that corrective actions are taken are change detected in cost figures, slippage of schedules, and deviations from accepted working standards. Control is not a process that may be accomplished once and then forgotten; to be effective, it must be a dynamic, continuing process. Planning and control should be done early in the project. The schedules developed should be progressively refined to take advantage of the knowledge gained during the course of the project. The schedules and needs of resources should be evaluated in each design review. The teams assigned to perform the activities in a systems effort should participate in drawing up the schedules relevant to its project and should be aware of the costs of the effort.

Since we are talking of projects in computers and communications it will be quite proper to implement computer supported management techniques. These should be designed to optimize planning and control in every aspect of project delivery.

An interactive graphic analysis can be quite helpful in project control. The same is true about documentation of program alternatives, a database for ongoing management evaluations, historic trends and unit price, and a creative cost management during design and execution. The project manager must have at his disposal:

A management information system for planning, scheduling, and control of time and money throughout the project.

Financial modeling capabilities for financial management and life cycle cost analysis.

The ability to reach early and informed compromises among conflicting aims.

Frequently, conflicting aims have differing priorities among sections of the project. High-quality decisions depend on careful analysis of alternatives from each point of view, leading to a blend of options able to provide an appropriate level of satisfaction in reaching the objective.

High-quality decisions involve priorities. Given the project's goals, timetables, budget, and human resources, the manager should know what to work on first, before beginning to work on it.

The setting of priorities is the first fundamental step in developing guidelines for project control. The next step is the establishment of a relatively simple tracking mechanism.

1. Milestones must be identified to provide management with major points to monitor the project's progress.
2. Each milestone must be divided into the tasks and subtasks required to complete the milestone.
3. Each task must be assigned to a specific individual, related to a computer file or program, and given start and anticipated stop dates.

This allows to issue a weekly report of those tasks due to start or stop during a particular period. Each individual must be given a copy of those tasks assigned directly to him, with the corresponding dates, and asked to return this copy at the specified milestone. It is still better to have this activity interactively handled by computer.

Estimates must be made on tangible and measurable issues. Aspects such as size, technology, and structure must be considered. An interactive approach should be followed to track estimates relative to actual figures, reviewing them in order to learn from possible errors.

Each project must be evaluated according to its characteristics, and each should track its own data and improve in relation to itself. But this evaluation should follow a standard procedure and be based on units which enable easy and meaningful comparisons between projects.

This reference is particularly valid for cost control. A cost algorithm and set of statistics must address the costs of project development through implementation and postimplementation reviews. Once a project estimate is established in terms of man hours and budgets, the project manager will be in a position to establish a master project schedule. The study of prior projects can reveal the distribution of resource consumption over project duration, though these statistics may require some refinement in order to be applicable to a new environment. If each project task is treated as a separate entity and the rule is made that subsequent tasks cannot be initiated until the current one is completed, then the project manager can establish a schedule for each task. The estimated hours for each resource must be steadily compared to the current consumption (plan/actual), deviations flashed to the project manager's attention, and from there to the senior management.

Computer-based scheduling can help resolve conflicts and achieve solutions to the project's needs. They will also see to it that the planning and control process is not rigid, but rather outlines a general approach to successful project completion. This is important as each project is unique. Its management must respond with a thoughtfully tailored program to meet exact requirements. With this as with management activities, the basic principle is that we are able to achieve results only through careful and extensive planning. Carefully evaluate the resources and requirements and formulate a detailed, comprehensive plan of action.

Let's recapitulate. A project organization is responsible for completing an assigned objective on schedule and within cost. The objective is usually one requiring special management attention and emphasis. Projects lasting only a few weeks or months can be accomplished with a minimum of disruption by teams organized with the purpose of bringing these projects to completion. Faster decision making is required on a new project, and the project organization should provide the arrangement, emphasis, and control necessary to counteract any weaknesses, functional or otherwise, that could impair successful completion of the objectives.

3

THE SYSTEM SPECIALISTS

1 INTRODUCTION

Change occurs all the time in the system world. People, technology, and companies change. Engineers and scientists are designing bombs to kill easier, medical instruments to save lives more efficiently, vehicles to move people faster, computers and communications to handle increasing amounts of text and data in more sophisticated ways. From one day to the next, our lives and the world itself are changing.

The systems specialists are *par excellence* the agents of change. The successful agent in this process sees himself or herself as both the animator and the catalyst. One knows that people find change difficult and that they accept it at varying rates. One realizes that systems can become distorted and ineffective because of too much change. But one also appreciates that change that is too slow causes stagnation and loss of the objective.

As an agent of change in the computers and communications environment, the project manager is a subordinate dependent on the director of information systems. What might be the distinguishable characteristics of the boss? The ideal information systems director should be able to lead the development of the third generation online system. His functions include the organization and management of development projects based on microcomputers, local area networks, long haul networks, and distributed processing, databasing, and data communications.

The systems that the director designs (or has others design) must be end-user oriented, bringing computer power to the workstation level. They will substitute for the currently employed centralized, realtime, and batch processing.

To do his job in an able manner, the director of information systems should be imaginative, decisive, and forceful. He should possess at least 10 years of experience in information processing with direct involvement as project manager with distributed information systems.

He should have a university degree (engineering, mathematics, physics, or economics), a demonstrated capability as a *doer*, and the will to accept change as a way of life. Above all, he should be able to prove that he is a hard worker and a good manager.

Knowhow should be a mark of excellence for the information systems director and the project managers. As an integral part of their career they will be responsible for following up, studying, examining, evaluating, testing, and implementing new software and hardware experiences.

Experiences relating to software development will include operating systems (supervisors, I/O monitors, database management routines, loaders, editors, communications programs), applications software, associated documentation, and the unavoidable maintenance chores. The director and managers should be able to lead or at least adapt to the hardware revolution, to test for reliability the new approaches being adopted, and to take the steps necessary for personnel training purposes.

Nothing becomes obsolete faster than knowhow. The personnel in an information systems division have the right to expect that their management be keen in keeping them trained in the latest technology. Top management has the right to demand that the company move ahead of the competition in information systems implementation, sharpening the advantages the cutting edge of technology can offer.

Success, like happiness, is basically a state of the mind. Online systems analysis, computer-aided programming, higher quality-standards, a structured methodology, and means for better productivity are tools. And while tools are necessary, without the right philosophy the best tools will remain ineffective.

2 THE QUALITY OF A PROJECT MANAGER

The foremost quality of a project manager involves the active role taken in fostering ideas and creativity. The next most important quality is selecting qualified people, motivating them, and promot-

The System Specialists

ing their efforts to attain the project's objectives. There is evidence that highly knowledgable people are much more productive than the average analyst and not just incrementally so. Therefore, there are big gains to be made by identifying them, training them, and organizing to use them effectively.

Identifying the ablest team members in original recruitment and in subsequent selection for development and assignment poses certain problems. One of the challenging is how to structure teams so as to accommodate the immense variety of personalities, talents, and working styles found in highly productive people.

One of the salient problems which the project manager must address is how to provide incentives and rewards so as to keep the members of the team happy, productive, and growing. This is second only to the challenge of how to educate and develop.

The project manager will find the needed assistance inside and outside the organization. To do so, he must identify the people who in fact establish the technical philosophies and set the directions in each of the many software technology areas. Here he should be getting a direct hand from senior management, with the latter continually asking middle and lower management "Who are the high performers? How are you maximizing their output? How can we best use them?"

To flesh out such qualities and keep good people, both carrot and stick should be used. There is an imperative need for a reward system for technical leadership and productivity just as for management and articulation skills. Such a reward system must encourage people to do what they do best, and it should be balanced by a scheme of penalties (affecting safety and promotion) for poor performers. In the reward side, the organization will be well advised to plan the training and development of high performers. Expose them to an every broadening domain of software technology by careful assignments. Bring to them the best current thought and creative minds in their fields *outside* their own environment. Encourage them to publish and to travel, both to develop outside recognition and to build technical competence.

Subsequently come the technical issues. At the top of the list is the ability to recognize that software knowhow encompasses specific high-technology skills, just as much as does semiconductor or disc head design. And the systems skills are the lifeblood of the systems project.

To help develop the system skills it is necessary to provide a continuous, consistent performance evaluation so as to detect possible lags and do monitoring and correction. Promoting technical skills by example is a valid policy. Productive software experts are attracted to places where other outstanding specialists exist.

The availability of challenging work, the ability to expand experience by exposure, the increase of knowledge through seminars, the opportunity for peer recognition, as well as the ability to participate in advance technology projects are critical considerations in attracting good people. Management must work out development plans and tailor them to individual needs and goals to obtain the best balance of work experience and exposure.

Next are the organizational challenges. A company that restructured its information systems operations to give more authority and responsibility to the project teams, that thoroughly trained their members, and that assured a valid system of rewards reported significant results. The number of steps programmed per working hour doubled; the number of database handling errors decreased by a third; other types of analysis and programming errors decreased by two thirds; the average length of a bug find-and-fix cycle was reduced to less than half the conventional statistics.

Within the organizational perspectives, the project manager must see to it that the system being developed can be implemented within schedules and budget, both of which are usually preset before the "go ahead" is given. Timetables and budgets must be maintained without cutting corners. The information system to be accomplished must be not only technically competent but also elegant, clean, and simple.

A quality manager will observe these prerequisites, and he will be keen to show how and why. Given a mission, he will specify for the members of his team objectives, criteria, the nature of elements, and representation schemes. He will outline problem statements, constraints, and operational requirements. He will pay attention to the systems environment, the operational management, and characteristics such as reliability, transferability, and maintainability.

The design he will present to the end user for his authorization will be charactertized by modularity. It will use recursive processes, avoid duplications, and be open to quality control. Such design will show clarity, a control of complexity, and a respect for priorities—

without abandoning the search for efficiency and the employment of advanced technological factors.

At the heart of this last reference is the realization that the presently available application programs have aged and they no longer serve competitive information needs. This is not surprising since computer programs are usually written at different time periods without benefit of an overall system design and intersystems coordination. But simply the fact of writing new programs is no condition for success.

3 A SYSTEM SPECIALIST LOOKS AT SOFTWARE DEVELOPMENT

One of the characteristics that helps distinguish the good from the average system specialist is the ability to avoid repeating past mistakes. In the 1960s and 1970s, as analysts experimented with a new idea, they were gradually led to develop very complicated systems without much conceptual basis.

Not too surprisingly these systems soon become unreliable and *software crisis* was coined to express their state. Conversely, examining successful projects we learned that, once the essence of the problem was understood, a notation was advanced for the basic concepts. A notation makes it possible to precisely define concepts prior to implementation.

Similar challenges face analysts and designers today. We are undergoing major systems change from mainframes, midis, and minis to local area networks, personal computers, and distributed databases. The intellectual challenge of this technological revolution is formidable. For the first time fairly complex programs become small and manageable and hence able to be understood completely by the simple programmer.

It is the irony of this profession that a complicated business is easier appreciated than a simple one. Nobody in his right mind would think that analysts/programmers would reject simplicity, as if it were an insult to their skills. Yet this strange phenomenon of rejection does happen almost daily in the computer centers where management assigns the best of its systems people to work on personal computers and local area networks.

The specialization of functions is the very basis of the tremendous industrial advance which we experienced at the beginning of this century. It is also the basic ingredient of the microcomputer-based workstation solution. This brings a new perspective to computers and communications relieving the well known strains from the simultaneous execution of several tasks on one computer.

No computer professional should permit himself to forget this lesson. We all know the serious problems that took so long to solve: programming errors could cause a concurrent program to behave in an erratic, time-dependent manner, and operating systems ended by absorbing a greater part of the available hardware resources than was left to do the applications job.

The resulting errors were extremely difficult to find and the constraints difficult to relieve. Their effect varied from one execution to the next even when the input data remained the same. It has taken 20 years to cope with this problem of concurrency, and still it is not totally resolved.

Another challenge today is to master the complexity of the hardware innovations that were introduced 2 decades ago. By comparison microcomputers are simple engines. Their numerous possibilities for new applications are far reaching, and they have not, so far, posed new programming problems of significant difficulty.

Among the lessons to be learned from the experience of the last 30 years on pitfalls to be avoided is the coordination of functioning between electronic and electromechanical units. The slowness of peripheral devices made asynchronous operation essential for efficient computer usage. But concurrency made it equally important to present the user with a simple, sequential interface to the machine. This was the basic mission given to the operating systems.

Early operating systems provided the basis for learning, and this led to a conceptual evolution. The price has been complexity and a horde of errors. In 1969, 3 years after the initial release of OS 360, one of its designers was to comment: "We face a fantastic problem in big systems. In OS 360 we have about 1,000 errors in each release and this number seems to be reasonably constant."

For a good part of a decade it had become common for large operating systems to fail daily, and it was doubtful whether they were achieving their original aim of ensuring efficient, reliable computer operation. The concept of *releases* was invented to lead toward a more polished system.

What this concept meant to the computer professional at the user side? One of the issues which even today consumes considerable time is the difficulties presented in implementing new OS releases on mainframes and minicomputer equipment. These crises occur because computer manufacturers are in a steady process of successive releases of their operating system, characterized by five main issues:

- the correction of the errors and omissions in the preceding release,
- a greater sophistication in the supported functions,
- the new functions added to the preceding release,
- a greater precision on the work that is executed, and more recently
- the adoption of a layered approach, which is the right way of running the system.

However, in a practical sense the professionals of the user organization not only must learn and implement the new release (which often changes the semantics of that preceding it) but also face the reemergence of faults in the programming of their own applications. Typically such faults are filtered through the preceding releases, but they are usually caught by the new release, which refutes them, causing the computer to fail (abort).

It is beyond doubt that new releases create work for the user's software experts, since they require a special effort till they are introduced and stabilized. But, after all, that's why we have the software experts around. Let's not forget this argument when we discuss the architectural routines of the local area networks (LAN).

If the user has, say, two mainframes in the same installation that are compatible hardware-wise (of the same make) but run on two different releases, this is tantamount to having systems incompatible among themselves. Such incompatibility, which should be avoided, is an example of the impact of software on hardware.

With this background in mind, let us talk of the frequency of the new OS releases. One particular mainframer that I have in mind introduced the following OS releases in the short span of four years:

2H, in November 1976

3I, in mid 1977

4J, at the end of 1978

4JS1, in mid 1979

4JS2, in the beginning of 1980

4JS3, at the end of 1980.

Every time a new release has been introduced the user's software experts had problems to solve in order to apply it. They solved them, but in doing so they found that the system was aborting (there are a hundred reasons why the system may fall, and all of them have to be overcome). There are several inconveniences, and there were some problems with the job control language.

The importance of the problems associated with operating systems have by now become clear to software specialists (and some of the management) who were forced to depend on these systems in their computer centers. To face these challenges, a conceptual basis proved to be necessary, and many experts think that by now we have found it.

The best approach to a better understanding of the problem is the modularization of a concurrent program into smaller asynchronous units with time-independent behavior. This divided a large OS into sequential processes executed asynchronously. Such program modules typically consist of a data structure and a sequence of statements that operate on it. Once again, let's recall this particular reference when we talk of local network architectures.

The basic point that the new generation of mainframe OS and of the modern LAN share is this: if each process only operates on its own data, then it will behave in a completely predictable manner each time it is executed with the same data. Hardware protection mechanisms can prevent processes from referring to each other's data structures—and this takes care of another serious problem.

Where this discussion leads the knowledgeable mind is the realization that the now evolving solution makes it possible to perform unrelated tasks almost simultaneously without time-dependent interference. Only when processes share computer resources or cooperate on common tasks do they need to work in a system-wide controlled manner.

4 CRITICAL REGIONS AND SEMAPHORES

The reason why we spend time on the concepts discussed in the preceding section is the dramatization of two facts. First, today it is unconceivable to talk of software specialists without them mastering the subjects we are discussing and beyond. Anything less than that does not make a man an expert. He is only able to perform some second class maintenance. This is most important to underline as many organizations are kidding themselves into thinking that just because they designate a man a "software expert," he is. Expertise comes from leadership in the field, and this has to be demonstrated through hard facts.

Second, the asynchronous type operation to which we are referring will become the standard of this decade. That OS for mainframes and minis are being rewritten to observe this principle is very interesting. But even better note should be taken of the fact that the asynchronous mode of operation* will find its fulfillment in the implementation of local area networks with personal computers (workstations).

To understand why, we must introduce the notion of a *critical region* for operations on common variables that take place one at a time. If one process operates on common variables, then the whole system must delay further operations on the same variable till the going operation is completed. The result is interlock.

Logically, this leads to the strategy of trying to avoid interlock by minimizing the common variable dependence. Taking advantage of the nearly zero cost of the microprocessor, we can distribute intelligent workstations at the very place the work is being done. By executing locally the processing functions, we minimize the extent of the critical region. That's a great change from the concepts of the last three decades. Software experts and

---

*Not to be confused with asynchronous type (start/stop) communications, which is a different issue and a rather obsolete means for datacomm.

data processing management who fail to appreciate the wisdom and resist change are not worth their grain of salt.

A different way of making this statement can be even more radical. No new project should be undertaken in information systems with dumb terminals online to a mainframe or mini. Even mainframes and minis should not be the focal point of a study. Let the old software do its life cycle and die peacefully. The new information systems projects should:

1. Employ intelligent workstations based on personal and handheld computers.
2. Be interconnected within the office area through local area networks.
3. Feature local databases run through file servers on the LAN.
4. Communicate with other networks and remote databases (text and data warehouses) through long haul disciplines.

But let nobody imagine this is a free lunch. We have to observe rules and protocols and establish a policing station. The concept of the critical regions of which we spoke is the first to come to mind —and with it the *semaphores*.

Mainframe experience with concurrent processes suggests that critical regions only prevent competing processes from using common variables simultaneously. But they do not help in transmitting data correctly from one process to another within the broader problem of interprocess communication. Hence, something more is necessary.

This something more, as every systems expert should understand, is the system of traffic lights for regulation purposes. With computers and communications we can emulate it through timing signals sent from one process to another. That's the object of the semaphores. Their operation permits a process to transmit a timing signal through a semaphore variable to another process which recevies the signal by performing a wait operation.

Speaking in systems terms, in a concurrent operation the programmer cannot predict the relative speeds of asynchronous processes. It is therefore impossible to know whether one process will try to send a signal before another process is ready to receive it or vice versa.

Such constraint can be removed by defining the semaphore operation. It doesn't matter in which order processes are initiated:

- If a process tries to receive a timing signal before it is available, the wait operation will simply delay the process until another process sends the next signal.
- If signals temporarily are being sent faster than they can be received, they will simply be stored in the semaphore variable until they are needed.
- Not only semaphore operations make process synchronization time dependent, but critical regions (and message buffers) can be implemented through their presence.

These references bring us to the critical issue of this discussion: a valid systems specialist is one whose mind and knowhow are in a constant evolution. He or she must be adapting to the new technology as it develops, must use the tools available in the most efficient way, and must not only plan work but also improvise as problems develop—all of which requires ingenuity.

When involved in an information systems project, the specialist has to study its complexity—both the apparent and the underlying. He or she must put the best effort forward to simplify, dividing the aggregate into manageable parts.

It is almost a law with information systems that complexity decreases by defining the variables, their behavior, and interaction. Hence one of the first tasks of the systems expert is to properly determine the number of variables, the degree of their interdependence, the databases accessed and updated, the logical functions, the needed degree of flexibility, and the required response time.

Structure will be defined to a great extent through the answers to be given to these challenges. It can *then* be enhanced when experience from similar systems is available. Environmental factors can also have a great influence on the definition process, the most important being the end user's understanding of his own needs.

Typically, the able and willing user will define the procedural terms the type of system he is after. His basic interest is functionality. The project manager and his systems experts must express this functionality in a technical sense, identifying the type of system to be projected.

Chances are the project they are asked to perform will be of a transactional, online nature. Transaction processors and reporting systems have the advantage of being functionally specific, finite, and tangible and hence well-definable. This eases the task of evaluating the size of the system.

Like performance size is measured in several ways: the number of functions to be done; its subsystems, components, and interfaces; but also

> the workplaces to be served (hence, the number of workstations),
>
> the text and data files to be handled,
>
> the datacomm protocols to be employed and the supported interconnections.

The answers to be given to these challenges can vary from black to white depending on the system philosophy to be employed. That's why the discussion on critical regions and semaphores was so critical. The system experts who understand them will be prone to suggest distributed resources.

5 KEEP IT SMALL AND SIMPLE

In the expanding field of microcomputer applications, there is a class of information systems which used to be implemented through mainframes or large minicomputers. These systems often involve control functions with reliability and availability demands. A distributed environment reduces the complexity of the technical problems. Let's see why.

The first critical reference of interest to the system specialist is the ability to improve functional understanding. This has a direct impact on project staffing and simplifies the communications requirements between end users and analysts.

The significance of such simplification is that much greater since, as we will see in Part Two, we still lack formal languages in systems analysis to aid in explanation and understanding. Such lack is all the more felt in analysis and design as language concepts have a dramatic impact on the structure of systems and programs.

Had there been an efficient but user-friendly systems analysis language, it would also have been possible to define all the meaningful operations on a data structure, studying and testing the modules one at a time. The capabilities now being developed, as we will see in a later chapter, lead toward a concept of program modules that combine data representations and procedures into integrated units. The concern for clarity and the desire to make program verification simpler can also be served.

Small size and simplicity eases the issues behind the underlying concept as it becomes possible to refine the module further and get a more formal understanding of its properties. This is of primary importance to the systems specialist who should also understand that distributed information systems at the workstation level have other reasons supporting simplicity.

This leads us to the second critical reference characterized by the trend of decreasing hardware costs and increasing software prices for mainframes and minis. Such trend is likely to continue due to miniaturization and better production methods at the hardware side, without comparable software advances.

Analysis and programming for large scale systems is therefore faced with a meaningless choice among cost, reliability, and efficiency. The solution is quite obvious: we must build computer architectures that escape these constraints. This logically suggests LAN and personal computers, the concept of *myriaprocessors.*

Systems specialists who keep up with the state of the art should easily understand that the microprocessor technology makes it possible to build computers and communications architectures that directly support the concepts we are discussing. In such distributed environments, each workstation has a local memory dedicated to a single process. The stations share a common database that contains the monitors but also the text and data of interest to all of them.

The myriaprocessor has practically no interrupts and does not multiplex its workstations among several processes. It is therefore ideal for realtime applications. And it is economical to specialize the hardware.

These are two good reasons why the systems specialist who knows his job should be the first to suggest a myriaprocessor implementation when new information systems are contemplated. It has taken two decades to design reliable computer systems in which concurrent processes share storage. Now semiconductor technology provides a new challenge: microcomputer networks in which processes communicate by input/output only, thus opening new vistas to realtime applications in which distributed functions must be coordinated.

A third critical reason for a myriaprocessor implementation should be immediately underlined: Personal computer software is bending the ever increasing curve of programming costs. Not only are the modules smaller and the programming simpler—which would have been enough of a reason by itself—but also a rich library of microcomputer packages are now offered at incredibly low prices as compared to their mainframe and minicomputer oriented counterparts. A 2% to 5% ratio between similar programs, for instance DBMS, is a proven statement.

Developed programming products offered on the market by microcomputer software manufacturers as independent vendors are very well adapted to the workstation-level applications that involve a unique microprocessor and a limited volume of code. Nothing similar has been seen in the development of large programming systems.

What the system specialist should expect from a programming product starts being well understood for microcomputer software development. Since this has to do mainly with the way the user sees the information system and gains access to it, there is no reason not to follow this road. After all, the project manager and his system specialists have to be dearly concerned with

1. *Project length.* The long project leads to blind alleys; it also gives the end user more time to change his mind.

2. *Schedules.* Project control decreases when inadequate time is allowed for the project, but long timetables have many ills.

3. *Budgets.* Money allocated to a project translates into available man hours and from there to time for analysis, design, programming, testing, training, and software aids. The demands are many; and when budgets are overrun, this leads to management stress.

4. *Management stress.* User pressure, project invisibility, extent of expectations for system results, and the time and budget allowed for an applications system are all subject to management scrutiny. With slippages in any reference, stress develops.

Greater project visibility helps all involved, from senior management to first line supervision, to do a better job in information systems definition and implementation. As such, it reduces corporate stress. Table 1 presents an appreciation of roles and responsibilities in this field.

These are good reasons the project manager and his system experts should be keen in keeping the information system they design simple and small. The myriaprocessor technology provides them with a concrete frame of reference.

- The users can see how their definition has been interpreted by the system experts.
- The time lag between system definition and system demonstration is minimized.
- Experience data gained during the stage of workstation development can favorably influence the design of the myriaprocessor as a whole.

Other qualities have to do with ease of use and access, the overriding consideration being that the system is workstation oriented, bringing computer power to the user's site. The problems associated with testing are of a lesser order of magnitude than those relative to realtime operations on mainframes or minis. Workstations dedicated to word processing can be used during systems development as the myriaprocessor's documentation center.

TABLE 1
ROLES AND RESPONSIBILITIES IN INFORMATION SYSTEMS

Management Level	Primary Roles	Problems	Requirements	Effective Control
TOP	*Provide 1. Corporate Strategy for Technology 2. Guidelines for Investments in Information Systems 3. Evaluation of Organizational Performance.	Few Information Systems Scientists and Practioneers Versatile on Business Issues and vice versa	1. Understanding of the Implication of Software Development on the Organization 2. Capability to Delegate to the Specialists while Keeping Overall Control.	1. Assuring Information Systems Development Conforms to Corporate Strategy 2. Guaranteeing that Key Resources: Money, People, Time, are Properly Used. 3. Evaluating Capitalization and Return on Investment.

MIDDLE	1. Formulate the Direction of Advancement by Department 2. Communicate Effectively on Needs and Requirements 3. Assure Project Management	Difficulty in Communicating Problems, Requirements, and Specifications of the Job	1. Technical Background 2. Ability to Choose and Control the Members of Project Teams	Evaluating Productivity of Project Team and Quality Assurance of Result
FIRST LINE	Direct Responsibility for Software Product Development, Testing, Documentation, Implementation and Maintenance.	Accelerated Obsolescence on Technical Skills	Ability to Lead Team Members, Combining Diverse People into a Coherent Whole	Estimating Product Development and Taking Corrective Action

4
MODEL OF AN INFORMATION SYSTEM STUDY

1 INTRODUCTION

Let's start with the hypothesis that the information system to be developed has been defined and divided into discrete parts. A time period corresponds to each part. This is fundamental if we wish to manage the project well, which essentially means being able to answer in a documented manner questions such as:

What is the Plan vs. Actual?

Did we spend more or less money than was projected?

Are we in time, ahead of time, or delayed?

By identifying the object of project planning, more than half the battle is won. A project is nothing other than the framework in which the system is commissioned, defined, constructed, and implemented. The planning of the project creates the framework within which the project will gain its identity. Such identity involves project definition and organization, problem analysis, and system specification.

Problem Definition addresses itself to the following questions: Who wants the system? (the user) Why does he want the system? (problem) What does he want the system to do? (goal) How will the system benefit the user? (objectives) **Project Organization** aims to respond to queries such as: Who will authorize the project? (management) Who will manage the project? (project manager) Who will participate in the project? (project team)

Problem Analysis addresses itself to the issues: What is the real problem? What is the cause? Can the problem be eliminated or mitigated? Do we have to construct a system to handle it? **Systems Specifications** help define: What's the environment? (real world) What are the inputs, database, text/data flows, report structure, interactivity, graphic means, rules and procedures? What are the facilities? (software, hardware)

Each one of these references should be subject to management review and approval. This calls for a formal process of reviewing the requirements and specifications against proposed capability to ensure a good match. The focal point is documentation and the project's turning point is here.

2 MANAGEMENT APPROVAL

Management review and approval closely concern themselves with the question of how to improve project organization for better quality results, cost control, and timely completion. The answer is found in structuring the information environment:

> Developing methods that can last longer, i.e. be useful when conditions change.
>
> Looking for something in the organization more stable than the individual people.
>
> Developing a flexible method to get the text/data in and out of the database—the word *flexible* interpreted to mean independent of format, user, and frequency.
>
> Putting the documentation in an easily accessible, comprehensive form.

As a general rule, a good part of the development methodology consists of finding out and defining the text, data, and images that must go into the system, the ways of accessing them, and the authorization for doing so. In the base line, an information system is a set of computer programs, hardware components, documentation, and training of both the users and the specialists. That's what the system design is all about.

A valid approach would guarantee that obstacles will not be hidden but fleshed out and faced as encountered. The hidden or forgotten obstacles are a reason for project failure. An information system may:

1. never get completed through lack of cooperation
2. never get implemented because of lack of consent by required contributors
3. never get off the ground because basic challenges have been kept in the background
4. never be faced head on. Hence, the inherent difficulties remain unresolved.

The role of systems documentation thus comes into perspective. To be worth its salt, it must show in writing what the system will do, what the system will *not* do, why it will *not* offer some services, the frequency with which it will work, how it will work, who must support it and at what capacity, who will specifically benefit from it, and how the total organization will get results, cover expenses, and derive profits.

Every user participating in the system must have the opportunity to see what he or she is buying, to determine whether the *merchandise* is good, and to propose design modifications to better meet requirements before being locked into an inflexible system. This, however, should be accomplished during the procedural analysis phase and not after the system design is done.

The timing of the procedural analysis as of all other operations is primarily conditioned by the skill of those men who perform the work and the quality of the project leadership. Secondarily it is influenced by the complexity of the job. Two well-trained procedural analysts or organizational experts, for instance, should be able to complete the feasibility study in between 1 and 2 months.

This time estimate allows for a fair amount of interviewing and the collection of relevant and accurate statistics, although more time may be necessary for the preparation of the reports and exhibit. It is advantageous to keep the overall time short, as this first phase will detetermine whether or not the system work is to be continued. Management approval is generally given after the procedural design review.

Within the framework of the logical system design, which follows the written approval on the procedural analysis, we distinguish:

1. file structure
2. database and datacomm protocols
3. new input/output methodologies
4. formats for interactive applications
5. processing runs
6. logs, recovery, and security mechanisms.

The structuring of files and, therefore, of the database should reflect a user orientation but should also be designed for homogeneous program access. It should be thought out from input to output. Reports must be generated directly from the database. In terms of design, the system must be straightforward except for internal relationships.

For each subsystem file, the passages through the different processing runs must be indicated with reference to the operations being handled. Each file must be specified as to field/record allocation and relative data volume. The structure of files and their uses must be defined.

Workstations and local area networks will communicate with each other and with the text and databases through protocols. A protocol is a formalism; it defines a standard procedure or term of exchange, agreed upon, understood, and observed by everybody with communications requirements.

Protocols become the more important as computers move out of the private and impersonal enclosure of the air-conditioned computer room toward the workplace and into the field. A computers and communications system will only work as long as the protocol is observed correctly by all devices attached to it—whether human or mechanical.

A new input/output methodology is developing in the communication between man and information which is, to a large extent, the negation of what was so far known with computers. This information flow is bidirectional and it can become that much more effective if a few, properly defined, standard formats are used.

The phase of system analysis should specifically consider the cause and effect relationship between the source or sending device (man or machine) and the receiver (*idem*). Such relationship defines the direction of the transfer and is itself subjected to formalisms. Hence it obeys a protocol.

Hardware has long ceased being central to the study of man-information communications means and requirements. The role of software is more important than that of hardware, but it is not the most crucial issue either. *The central component of a computers and communications system is the protocol.*

The processing of text and data also has rules to follow. At the current state of the art it must be specified exactly as a sequence of steps called the *program*. Processing runs define the computer-handling activities, indicating for each:

memory support(s)

input/output media

links with other processing runs

short description of the activity functions

estimates on memory use for programs and data buffers

processing time.

An integral part of the processing study is the design of the programs and the actual organization and coordination of the programming job. Programs must be designed to adhere to the principles of structural design. They must be kept small, easy to handle, and functional. Large programs should be divided into modules.

As far as possible, a module should be projected for general use, so that it is reusable in other parts of the system. In this way, repetitious coding is eliminated. Each module should be physically separate from any other module. Each should be as small as its function allows. Each module must have a limited and precise function, and its environment must be well defined.

In terms of man-information communication, the reporting structure must be interactive and use graphics and color. Graphic media are very helpful for the input of information and not only for engineering applications but also for business functions.

Reporting formats must be structured as much as possible. For each report to be furnished by the system, the following specifications must be supplied: title, destination(s), updating, frequency of presentation, use of standard generators, test procedures, authentication/authorization.

Furthermore, logical system design must always reflect the data load, the amount of preparatory work, the streamlining of procedural organization and structure, the status of the available classification/identification systems in use, the difficulty experienced in cutting through red tape to get the job done, and, conversely, the spirit of open-mindedness and collaboration shown by the user department.

A computer-based simulation study can be of assistance by flashing out persistent weak points. A major objective in system design should be to make more use of the computer itself. Record initial data as close to the source as possible because this is cheaper and involves fewer errors.

3 USING A VALID METHODOLOGY

Without a valid methodology even the best intentions will have a negligible effect. It must be once again underlined that one should follow the agreement of the user services (offices, departments, divisions) on the procedural outline. No alterations should be made on the input, throughput, and output, regarding information type or form. This is valid throughout system development and implementation.

Furthermore, any demand for modifications after the information system is in operation must be formally registered with the office responsible for logical maintenance. Such demand must be accompanied by estimates on cost/benefit, submitted for approval, and (if approved) paid for by the demanding department.

The last reference is most important and should be properly understood. During the procedural system analysis, user department(s) should be requested to participate in both the periodic and the final design reviews to make suggestions and to propose alterations. They should be given the written documentation to make comments. User departments should be invited to do the same for the logical design, provided that their remarks are kept within the general outlines, standards, and procedures already agreed upon and provided that no deviations occur.

However, once the software construction phase begins, user departments should not be allowed to interfere with the systems work. Any such intervention will upset the work schedule, increase costs, delay development, and, instead of improving, impair the results.

To keep productivity under control, from the study of the systems specifications to flow charting, coding, compilation, program and system testing, the time required should be counted on the basis of the number of instructions per hour to be produced by the analysts and programmers. Productivity is also conditioned by the programming language to be used.

Ten even 20 years ago the dominant language was Cobol. With personal computers and local networks, this is no longer the road to coding. The solution is Pascal, with Basic an alternative possibility.

Programmers' productivity can be measured through two criteria:

the number of statements written per hour

the faults (bugs) found during the test (and subsequent implementation) together with the time spent in correcting them.

The former can constitute a system of *merits;* the latter of *demerits.* At Cobol times, able programmers could make as many as 18 statements per hour; but this is exceptional. Twelve statements per hour is a very good performance; 8 to 9 statements per hour an acceptable average; 4 to 5 represents a very poor speed. Pascal makes feasible a 20% to 25% better productivity than Cobol.

The quality of a programmer's performance depends on

- The training given to the programmers, both in language proficiency and in performance ethics.
- The planning and control tools being used.
- Management's determination to achieve results and to put a premium on efficiency.

- The carrot-and-stick (reward and penalty) policies management employs.

Programming productivity can be enhanced if a support group dedicates itself to basic software expertise, database design, and datacomm. The logical system should cover the preparation of preliminary database layouts: files, records, and structure. Table 2 presents in a comprehensive manner the different activities involved in the procedural analysis and logical system design phase.

Programming is the construction phase and the passage into this stage is a point of no return. From this moment on, it is no longer allowed to change the specifications that have been written. Maintenance will be carried out long after the system has come into operation.

TABLE 2

PROCEDURAL ANALYSIS AND LOGICAL SYSTEM DESIGN
A COMPREHENSIVE OUTLINE

Activities	*Collaborators*
1. *Presentation and Agreement with Management on the Procedural Analysis*	• Experts in the area concerned
Details and Results Presentation of Report and Exhibits Discussion and Approval by General Management; Directors of Services (division, department); the Personnel of the Services	• Organization Specialists • Analysts • Management
2. *Logical System Design* Definition of Interactive Input/output, Databasing, Datacomm, and Processing Activities	• Analysts • Organization Experts • When necessary, specialists of the area concerned
3. *Presentation and Agreement with Management and User Services concerning the Logical Design*	

The following elements must be systematically kept in perspective: Definition of the layout of records for the input/output files and for storage; identification of the data flow, including data origin and destination; detailed description of the text/data fields; control of the fields and description of the systematic tests which will be necessary; projection on the way computing algorithms are flashing out possible conflicts or incompatibilities; establishment of test cases and of necessary text/data for a simulated dry run on the projected files. After these specifications have been drawn, no further change shoud be allowed.

Moreover, if the programs are to be farmed out, the basic steps which we outlined should not only serve for the completion of the specifications but also as main references for the quality control that must be done in the course of the test phases. It must not be forgotten that a good number of the tests that are to take place will concern the structure of the programs. Quality is built at the drafting board, and by now the systems analysis work is leaving the drafting board. Thus, prior to handling the project to the programmer, the analyst must

> verify the principal logic of the programs, including the sequence,
>
> review input/output formats and the design of the main files down to the byte level,
>
> examine the use of parameters and of switches,
>
> play the role of the devil's advocate in flushing out possible logical errors,
>
> correct such errors and update documentation,
>
> assure that this documentation is complete, comprehensive, and non-contradictory.

Great attention should be directed toward the building of a workable system. Once the system requirements are met, consideration will be given to run-time efficiency. There is no time to make such considerations during babysitting, after the cart has been put on the tracks.

Yet *systems optimization* means nothing until and unless one states what the criteria are. This job can be best accomplished through experimentation in early production time. The project manager and his anlaysts must invest time in this particular phase of work. If allowed to occur, errors and ambiguities will happen. On-and-off error correction takes a considerable time and is responsible for poor software results.

4 CHARACTERISTICS OF A VALID DOCUMENTATION

Evaluation of the quality built into a product can take a variety of aspects and approaches. Some are quite comprehensive; others are limited to a specific end. A broad evaluation perspective is the formal process of measuring how well the capabilities of both product and service match the requirements. Part of this task is the subsequent fine tuning of the system to accomplish a good match.

Preoccupation with a built-in quality must manifest itself early in project planning. Without this essential ingredient a framework for conduct is not possible. To estimate, schedule, or control proves impractical. To analyze the deviation from the *quality plan* is likewise unfeasible. Similarly, a broad issue that filters through every step of the project is the preoccupation with the organization of the documentation accompanying this project.

Among the problem areas we distinguish the following.

How is this documentation stored?

Much of the information is stored in the minds of the systems personnel. If the employee goes, the information is *not* recoverable. A computer based solution gives a better control. It records the information and, depending on the analyst, enriches it.

Is the documentation capable of being used both by people and by machines?

Computer-aided documentation is a good answer, because it can accommodate both requirements. However, it should be kept in mind that information is assimilated by people in a *far* different

Model of an Information System Study 59

way than by machines: people work with a natural language; machines with a formal machine language.

Is the documentation organized to serve different types of use?

This is a background reason why manuals are soon redundant. But redundancy has its price. If a change is made, then either the documentation is inconsistent or a large number of updatings must also be done.

The computer can be of assistance: updating only once, keeping this update current, and storing the data in a nonredundant manner. The computer should therefore be called into play—a process only recently awakening major interest.

Streamline the inherently complex documentation as retrieval-oriented information.

Information systems tend to be complex and heavily interrelated during development, during usage, and across system boundaries. Retrieval must consider these facts of life. Retrieval keys should be built-in from the start. To help retrieval, it is recommended to

Distinguish different data types: basic data (what's really necessary), derived data (for different types of use).

The analyst and his computer-supported system should store only the basic data, which is a very small part compared to derived data. But to be easily retrievable, such basic data should be properly classified and identified.

One way of looking into classification is between text/data describing the target system and those recorded in reference to interfaces. Furthermore, the systems analyst should remember that

If the documentation is large, he or she should be selective and also be prepared to handle changes and exceptions.

This reference is applicable both to fields and formats. Being selective essentially means *standardize* and *simplify*. It is wise to study how data must be recorded in terms of content, format, natural/formal languages, tables, graphs, charts, figures, and color presentation. A valid approach is to consider the formats and charts the user wants to see. A further question is this:

When should the documentation be produced? Define the timing.

One possibility is *after* the systems project is completed; another *during;* a third, *before.* A preliminary documentation should definitely be made before; the other during, through computer assistance. "After" is the most frequent, but also the worst solution, because it means that (1) the analyst has the least control, (2) encounters the most problems, and (3) at any time few people work in the documentation.

The *"before"* and *"during"* documentation provide the focal point for project estimation. The quantifiable components for estimating are the numbers of each functional type of module or program that will be required to construct the system. The following sections can be constructed beforehand and updated as one goes ahead with the project

1. *Data definition:* File, record, and transaction layouts that are stored in a library; formats, graphs, and colors for user-oriented outputs.
2. *Needed utilities:* Programs to create files, generate test data, simulate processing, and conduct tests; programs to convert or reformat data files; modules to perform repeated functions (date conversions, table lookups, and the like).
3. *Database/datacomm interfaces.* Interfaces between application programs and most database management systems provide a higher degree of data independence. (*Idem* for data communications capabilities.)

Such programs are necessary to assure the physical integrity of the database. This is done by auditing, deleting, and updates. The programs also are needed to provide file content and utilization statistics. Interfaces will relate functional entry points for application modules to technique-oriented entry points and commands supplied by database management packages.

4. *Edit modules.* Programs that assure the logical integrity of data entered into the system and that provide error listings or alerts.
5. *Update modules.* Programs that update the database. A function to be performed within or outside the editing function.
6. *Processing modules.* Programs that do extensive calculations, analyses, and manipulations of data, resulting in possible additional file maintenance, and that can be reasonably standardized.
7. *Database extracts.* Programs that select data from the database for subsequent (or simultaneous) analysis and reporting —such as is demanded by interactive videotex.

To the latter class belong programs that report the results of major extracts, processing control breaks, and totals; row and column formatting; controlled accesses to the text and database; as well as graphical and color presentation.

In conclusion, the following can be stated by way of recommendations: start preparing the documentation on a given project (new or revamped) at the earliest posssible time—during the procedural systems analysis. Keep this practice as you go along. Don't abandon the effort. The logical systems design, for example, will provide a very significant part of the documentation.

Every time you return to a subsystem, file, processing run, or message exchange completed in a preceding phase of the work, write down all instructions necessary for updating. Don't update at that very moment, as more finishing work may follow. Only after the final design review (of the project or of a good chunk of a very large project) should you go ahead with integrating and updating all of the documentation that has been developed so far.

Instructions relative to program maintenance and data on the tests, resulting from the actual testing of the programs, are part and parcel of the documentation. The same is true of errors found in the programs, the reasons for these errors, and the correction of same. Notes relative to the tests of the subsystems and of the systems, (including the data of the tests, the results, and corrections) should be part of the total.

Finally, instructions for the attention of the operator and/or end user, including messages at the workstation and the parameters, should be carefully recorded and explained. This is equally valid for procedures relative to recovery, restart, dump, description of what the user should (or should not) do with reference to the program in question, and so on. Properly established recovery procedures help simplify the user interfaces.

5 TESTING PREMISES

Software robustness rests on two pillars: attention at the drawing board and thorough testing. Costs and delays increase exponentially when tests are not done at the proper phases, when errors are not flashed out, then corrected and when the programming product is not made dependable. Such dependency must be assured by every means technology puts at our disposal.

The following subphases of testing must be distinguished.

- *Test Data.* One of the weak points in most programming projects is the development of test data. Yet the performance of tests is the most vital phase of any programming job.

The array of errors in subsequent use will be unlimited, unless the correct tests have been made. These tests should take place on two levels: single programs and subsystems. The outcome of the tests will determine whether or not the subsystem can be released for production runs.

Tests must be preplanned. The preparation of the tests to take place after compilation should preceed the coding phase. Test files should be built in parallel to this activity. Test proper will thus concern the applications content of the programs. Its aims are not only to detect and correct errors but also to show up the quality characteristics (robustness) of the programs.

The test files to be used should as far as possible represent not simulated but real data, if necessary enriched with additional information to perform a complete and thorough evaluation of the programs. The test files should as far as possible reflect the real situation in data processing, datacomm, and databasing—that is, the situation the program (or system) will be required to handle after it enters into production.

Incidently, in the case of a purchased package or farmed-out software, this test will be the basis for the acceptance test that must be performed. Even if an organization develops programs internally, it is advisable to prepare a second file for an independent audit or acceptance test of the programs. A valid procedure will focus on 3 levels: Unit testing, Integration, and Acceptance testing.

The acceptance test to which we make reference will not be at the single program level but rather at the subsystem level. The test data will therefore start at input and will serve through the consecutive phases. But they must be thoroughly controlled after each phase.

In this process of testing, all the individual possibilities established at the time of definition of the programming specs should be covered. Namely:

1. The verification that all controls have been executed.
2. The assurance that all prescribed error routines are functioning.
3. The specified applications requirements and man-information interfaces.

The errors detected in the course of these tests and the correction that takes place should be carefully recorded.

Acceptance test is a good policy to ensure that the programs have no handicaps which will show up in subsequent processing. Acceptance tests should be done by the operating personnel, eventually by the end user who will have to use the programs for production purposes

Parallel runs should not be confused with acceptance tests. They comprise the functioning of the subsystem with effective data as well as the testing of results and passage to the production stage. This period of parallel functioning of the old and new programs and of the verification of the results prior to employment of the new ones for production proper involves several areas of responsibility.

At this time, user departments must offer their full collaboration. Parallel processing is often complex, as it tries to reach every corner of the application. The completion of the parallel runs should take at least 1 whole month, with the passage to production delayed if errors are unearthed, until such errors have been corrected and a new parallel test has been made.

Baby-Sitting is a follow-up procedure on the production runs at the user site. It is made to assure that the last errors have been weeded out and that the queries of the user have been answered in a comprehensive, timely manner. This period may vary with the problems uncovered during baby-sitting—a 3 to 6 month period being a reasonable average. It should be assured by a senior analyst, preferably the designer of the system.

Maintenance is a continual process in every project. It can be relatively easy or difficult depending on whether or not the original programmers have followed standards, avoided distorted instructions, and supplemented each program with the correct documentation. The need for more effective and realistic control of software maintenance is reflected in

> the increased unit cost of maintenance and therefore in the resulting investments,
>
> the use of larger program libraries that augment the mass of work to be done,
>
> the growth of interactive but also integrated information systems where an interruption of a vital software component can close the whole system down.

The financial aspects of software maintenance must be given the correct perspective. A set of procedures must be provided to assure effective maintenance control. The principal tools are the correct scheduling of programming manpower and the availability of cost data on individual jobs.

The cost of software maintenance is by far outstripping the cost of writing software. At the April 1976 Symposium on Sofware Engineering, the DOD stated that the cost of Cobol instruction for weapons systems stood at $75. But the maintenance cost per instruction over a 10 year period reached $4,000 or $400 per year.* Since then, costs have nearly doubled.

The test phases which we have described can help reduce the subsequent maintenance costs by assuring the inherent quality of the programs. Proper documentation will further assist the maintainability of the program and make it independent of the person or persons who wrote the subject programs in the first place.

Software engineering is moving far out, preplanning its formal phases. The practice of calling-in the original programmer to assure the maintenance of a program should be forbidden—for the sake of good management. It is also proper to remember that any maintenance can be complicated if the preceding work did not abide by standards. This job should be accomplished by specialized maintenance programmers, supported by adequate, well organized, and updated maintenance documentation—not by trainees.

In conclusion, many specific issues can be raised within the framework of a precise analysis and programming methodology. The choice of a programming language and the quantification of the programmer's results are examples. But within each choice both the quality and the quantity of the results will often depend upon the determination, preparatory steps, and work practices of both the management and of the analysts and programmers.

That is the reason the best way to control the quality of the outgoing product is the introduction of *life cycle costing,* tying into it the direct accountability of the person or the organization responsible for the development of the software. This procedure has been successfully used in connection with hardware projects, particularly weapons systems. It can also be implemented with applications systems.

The other side of the coin is timing. The observance of budget requires both the control of the timetable and improvements in analysts/programmers' productivity. In turn, the latter calls for the right planning and control methodology, including the review of qualitative milestones and quantitative standards. The adoption of control procedures is a prerequisite.

Brainstorming sessions should be held to critically evaluate the functional capabilities of the established system on the basis of

---

*Such colossal costs and the need for better software management were instrumental in introducing the DOD "Life Cycle Costing."

obtained results. These sessions also should suggest ways and means of bringing this experience on data processing/databasing/datacomm standards to other applications. Any methodology can be improved, but to start with we need to have a sound approach.

5

MEDIUM RANGE PLANNING

1 INTRODUCTION

A typical information systems project today runs between 6 months and 2 years, with 1 year being a good average. As we move from mainframes to minis and from there to personal computers with local area networks, the time range necessary for project completion is reduced. The median starts being counted in months rather than years.

Yet even if timescales are accelerating, projects must fall within an overall plan like the stones in a mosaic. The overall plan will typically be medium range: from 3 to 5 years. But it will also be subordinate to a long range plan running into 10 years and reflecting the information systems policy of the financial or industrial organization.

New areas of information system implementation subject to a medium range plan will typically include:

- Electronic mail and message services
- Electronic news delivery including newsletters
- Financial data communications for banks, brokerage houses, and other financial institutions
- Educational services addressed to all levels in the organization
- Software distribution, downloading, maintenance, and database updating.

The methodology for making valid planning premises for information systems development involves several actions. The first and most basic is the identification of the activities that have to be performed to obtain a defined result. This invariably leads to a list of tasks applicable to a specific project.

The next issue where attention should be paid is the identification of the relationships among the specified activities. The organization and structure of project management dictates the logical relationships among the activities. Planning and scheduling help to identify which activities or steps are critical in the execution of the project(s) and thus provide a means to direct management attention.

The following basic component of a medium range plan is the determination of the type and magnitude of the resources required for the performance of each activity. Examples are knowledge, skills, timetables, equipment, software, and budget. Though there are no hard and fast rules for estimating the magnitude of the resources required for the performance of the activities and phases in the systems effort, experience often dictates the rules.

One of the most valid rules in establishing and maintaining a medium range plan on information systems is to swamp requests for changes. A change control procedure must establish a standard method of initiating, evaluating, and monitoring change requests after the systems effort. Changes can be avoided through proper planning. The alternatives to be considered and the requirements from different areas that must be satisfied should be evaluated and incorporated in the procedural analysis phase—not during or after programming. Design decisions should be made in a systematic manner.

Within the medium range management perspectives an orderly approach should also be followed in regard to adding new capabilities to the information system, expanding it to other areas in the organization than those originally covered, solving possible inconsistencies, allowing a more economical use of equipment, and accelerating the development of a subsystem to accomodate a rapidly increasing workload. Whenever such interventions are needed, they must be executed in an orderly and able manner.

2   PLANNING AS AN AGENT OF CHANGE

The research projects I conducted during the last 3 years among leading financial institutions, industrial concerns, and computer manufacturers document the need to focus on planning several years in advance the information systems structure and the software development(s). They also emphasize on program robustness, quality assurance, documentation, and maintainability.

We should be looking in a responsible, coordinated way towards moving out of the current illogical situation where nearly three-quarters of our system specialists are tied down to software maintenance procedures. This situation may not change overnight, but we should definitely plan for a change. The best transition to an orderly change is to plan ahead for all eventualities.

Data processing, datacomm, and databasing are the offspring of computer-based, formal procedures. During the formative years of the information sciences, we learned to think in terms of man-machine interfaces and people who can be adapted to system needs. Within this harness we attempted to make our machines more user-friendly by introducing

1. The use of nearly zero cost microprocessors to assure a user-friendly operating environment
2. Flexible database management systems, with the machine taking care of the storage and retrieval requirements
3. Distributed processing, bringing the computer to the user's side
4. An integration of voice, text, data and image in communications
5. And, eventually the implementation of natural languages: the user will program the machine in a non-computer language and be able to obtain the required results.

Medium range planning becomes so much more of a prerequisite as the change in our way of managing computers and communications starts to manifest itself. Yet few people are conscious of this fact even if they do realize that administrative systems are mainly human communication tools.

At the operational level of our society—in industry, banking, and government or in any organized community—it is people communicating with one other that provide the cohesion necessary to realize the goals of the community as a whole, including those regarding business transactions. The more this organized community is computer-based, the more we need formalisms to run its communications requirements and quality assurance to guarantee the machines and programs that we are using are dependable and robust.

Project management often works under pressure; the better the tools we put at its disposal, the better the results to be expected. Medium range planning is one of these tools. But are the personnel familiar with the various problems and opportunities? What is the degree of planning direction taken by the organization?

A number of queries show up once we try to define the direction of the planning effort: What is the size of the projects? Their requirements? Their number? What will the user (scheduler) do? What tasks must the specialist personnel perform? What's the ability of management to schedule work with computers? Work with people?

Unless one is clear about the management philosophy that prevails, one can never be sure of the results to be obtained. A valid management philosophy starts with strategic planning. Information systems faculties are an integral part of the long range business plan, which must also discuss future computers and communications objectives.

The business plan of the organization must address specific questions such as:

What is the planned change over the next five years?

What is the forecast in terms of the expected rate of change?

What are the lead times needed to serve the market through computer-based services?

What degree of vertical and horizontal integration is projected for information systems?

What is the expected impact of quality control on the information production and distribution process?

These considerations, along with many other questions, describe how management expects the organization to look and function in the future. They forecast expected change and growth, and their impacts will most immediately be felt in the facilities structure of the business.

Medium Range Planning

Most essential in the references that are being made is the concept that in many industries, such as banking and insurance, systems automation has a direct impact on competitive position. Hence, the business plan must address issues such as market size and growth rate, market share relative to major competitors, price relative to competition, percent of sales stemming from new product areas, lead times to introduce new products, and degree of marketing intensiveness of the industry.

The able identification of these factors will permit an orderly transition to new systems to substitute for the fire brigade approach which has classically characterized projects in information systems. The essential message in this connnection is that the IS plan should be part and parcel of the organization's overall business plan. It should answer the latter's requirements.

Both plans should be the subject of an acid test in terms of *profit* and *loss,* and this calls for measurable objective along with quantifiable results. The translation of these measurable objectives and results into financial data should be undertaken in close cooperation with, and under the responsibility of, the financial director and the controller of the organization.

In this connection, collecting cost and benefit items and arranging them according to the breakdown of the projected calculation for evaluation purposes becomes the direct responsibility of project management. A major consideration is the timetable. For an adequate cost evaluation, the timespan chosen should fall in line with the business practices of the organization.

A project life cycle is also very important. The economic life time of the new system is of special interest when the impact of the system on the user organization is expected to manifest itself gradually, not directly in the first year of operation. Cost calculation should take into account the initial or nonrecurring costs connected with

the systems effort,

the installing of new software/hardware,

the implementation of new procedures,

and the user level handling benefits.

This method permits an integrated evaluation of all costs and benefits concerned. But it also poses the requirement of keeping accurate records of all cost and benefit items for each project.

Recurring costs must be properly monitored with particular emphasis on maintenance and the implementation of necessary changes throughout the system's life cycle. This is the more necessary as, against all rationality, the forementioned expenses are now consuming an estimated 75% of the human resources available in an organization for work on information systems.

Benefits will come from system performance. In this connection, the development of performance ratios from detailed quantifiable objectives is a wise step. Such ratios serve to measure the influence of the improvement in organizational control arising from the implementation of the new information system. The benefits to be quantified range from market position (with market share a specific quantitative result) to the better use of corporate resources (inventory control, turnover, capital investments, shorter delivery times).

The perpetual record keeping on cost and benefit should be assured by computer. This suggests the development of a properly organized database section enabling management to reflect on cost incurred and obtained results. This would also assure the administration of issues associated with transition. Wherever this has been done, it has improved the level of control and helped swamp requests for changes.

Changes in information systems content and structure have two detrimental results on the quality of the computers and communications services enjoyed by the organization. The first is an increase in cost not equalled by benefit since alterations in the software mean upsetting and destabilizing it. The second is a direct result of the fact that changes in the information system's software reduce its robustness, quality, and performance.

3   THE CONCEPT OF SOFTWARE STANDARDS

Any medium range plan for information systems should promote the concept of software standards. Software is deferred hardware design. It is more flexible than hardware; but when changes affect it, it tends to be destabilized.

Particular attention should be paid to software handling since software helps companies manage data and assists executives in generating their own reports. Among the critical questions to be asked in this connection we distinguish:

- Is the software suitable? Will this solution do the job? Will it remedy the situation completely or only partially? Is it permanent or stop-gap?
- Is it feasible? Will it work in actual practice? Within the perspective of the going information system? Can we afford this approach?
- Is it acceptable? Will the president, the management, and the personnel go along with the changes required by this plan?
- What's the effect on objective? What effect will it have on personal, financial, professional, or other type of status sought? What might be accomplished?
- What's the effect on costs relating to acquisition, ownership, life cycle? Would it be financially acceptable? What kinds of costly breakdowns might occur? Could it be easily replaced? What is the life expectancy?

A most fundamental issue is the acceptance of the concept of Software Quality Assurance (SQA), the goal being to assure that software developed, acquired, or otherwise provided under the contract complies with specific quality requirements. Whoever is given the responsibility to develop software should be responsible for compliance with all provisions of the specs and for furnishing software that complies with the quality requirements.

This has become a much more important issue than it was during the first 30 years of computing. Though with mini- and microcomputers the complexity of programming at the single machine has decreased, networking and communicating databases see to it that complexity goes again up (Figure 5-1). We should counter this turn through formalisms and standards.

For any project to be undertaken, project management must plan, develop, and implement a SQA program that includes practices and procedures to assure compliance with software requirements.

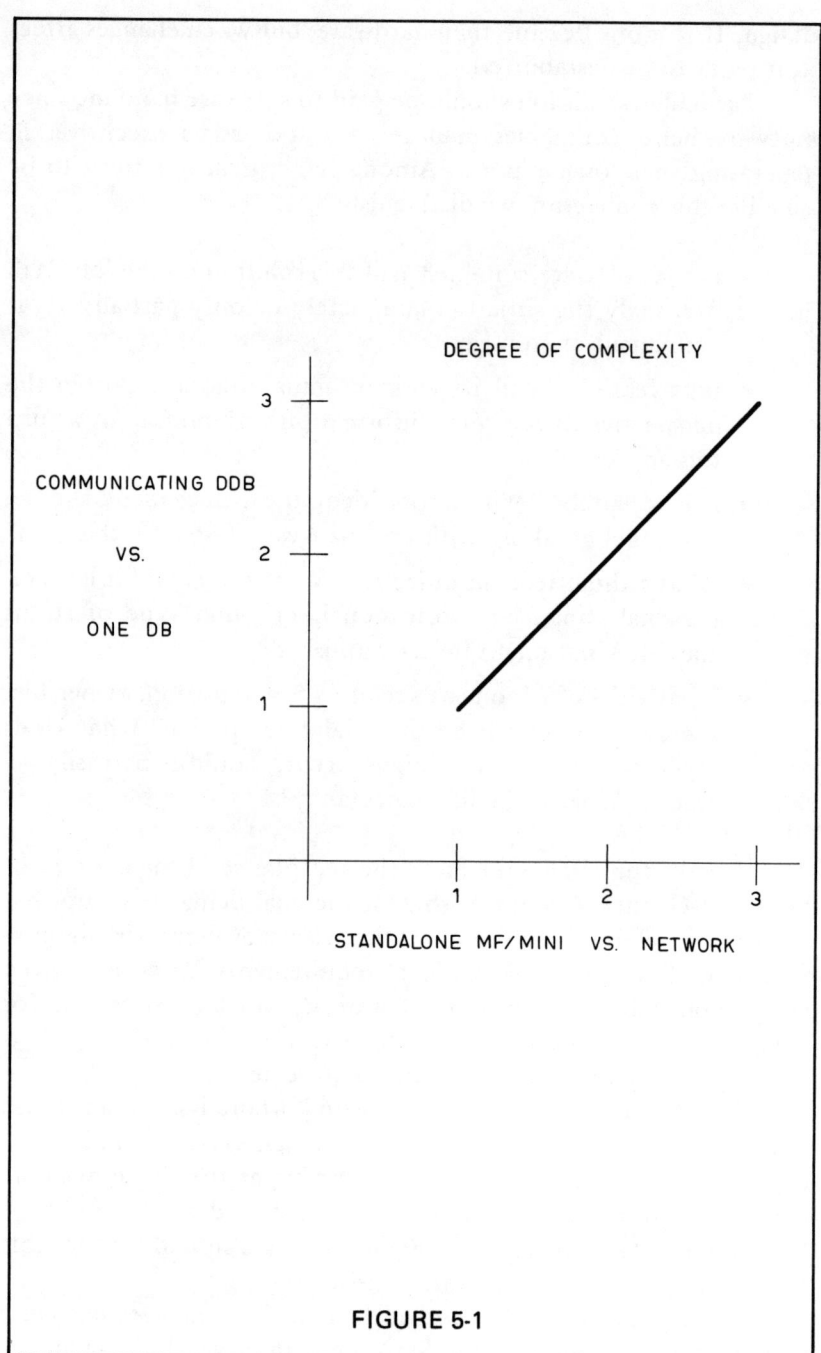

FIGURE 5-1

Development activities shall be a part of the management reporting system throughout the life of the product.

Project management shall document the work being done in the form of a SQA plan that meets the requirements of the specification: Identify organizational responsibilities for its execution and the events critical to its implementation. Product management shall also identify and make timely provisions for:

- controls,
- tools,
- facilities,
- skills

These are required for reporting, analysis, and correction of software problems and deficiencies. Personnel performing quality functions shall have the responsibility, authority, and organizational freedom to evaluate software activities, identify problems, and initiate or recommend corrective action.

Project management shall reference the procedures by which design documentation is reviewed in order to evaluate design logic, fulfillment of requirements, specification tracing, completeness, and compliance with established standards. Design documentation shall be subjected to critical review prior to its release.

Whether internal or external (contractual) development procedures are chosen, project management shall follow established procedures and controls for the handling of source code and object code and related data in their various forms and versions. The objective of these controls is to ensure that

> different computer programs are accurately identified and documented,
>
> no unauthorized modifications are made,
>
> all approved modifications are properly incorporated, and
>
> software submitted for testing is the correct version.

Project management shall follow the established procedures for preparation and execution of reviews and audits, for establishing the traceability of initial requirements through the successive baselines, and for ensuring that the reviews and audits are conducted in accordance with the prescribed procedures. Project management is the responsible authority for the accomplishment of

1. A careful examination of software specifications to guarantee the answer to the user's needs.
2. Assurance that design is flexible enough, modular, and provides for user exits.
3. Analysis of software requirements to determine testability.
6. Review of test requirements and criteria for adequacy, feasibility, traceability, and satisfaction of requirements.
5. Review of test plans, procedures, and specifications for compliance.
6. The assurance that all authorized and only authorized changes are implemented.
7. Verification that tests are conducted in accordance with approved test plans and procedures.
8. Certification that test results are the actual findings of the tests.
9. Review and certification of test reports.
10. Ensuring that test-related media and documentation are maintained to allow repeatability of tests.

These steps have been written in terms of their increasing impact on time and cost. Their wisdom must be appreciated and the proper action taken as it should.

For the purpose of corrective action, project management shall reference procedures that assure the prompt detection, documentation, and correction of software problems and deficiencies. Such procedures must include:

Documenting and reporting problems and deficiencies to appropriate management levels.

Analysis of data and examination of problem and deficiency reports to determine their extent and causes.

Analysis of trends in performance of work to prevent the development of noncompliant products.

Review of corrective measures to ensure that problems and deficiencies have been resolved and correctly reflected in the appropriate documents.

Management and its technical experts advising on design, analysis, programming, testing, and quality control reserve the right to review, at their sources, all products or services to determine the conformance of software products with specifications. Such evaluation and auditing will be based on discreet development specifications and a companion product specification. Senior management approval is necessary for changes over the configuration or identification governing a given software product—and possible modification actions.

Computer-supported documentation should be relied upon for providing traceability of detailed design for follow-on activity, including historical data and individual status information as well as investigations, failure analyses, and so on.

Individual design review activity should always be undertaken during development, leading to individual qualification testing and reporting. Physical and functional audits will be conducted at the conclusion of development.

Particular attention shall be placed on the maintenance of software qualification records to assure that no administrative red tape results. Emphasis will be placed on

- status reporting

- control over time and cost

- the identification of an inefficient design early in the development cycle

- the need for maintaining coordination without unnecessary generation of paperwork.

Full view will be kept of the life cycle cost and management impacts associated with such a designation. Reporting systems will be evaluated through the crucial question: "What does program/project management need to know and control?" in light of cost/benefit tradeoffs.

4 RESTRUCTURING ANALYSIS AND PROGRAMMING

A new attitude is necessary in tackling system design, analysis, and programming projects. In a nutshell, this attitude suggests the wisdom of always involving the user directly in those parts of the system work that affect him.

We should employ techniques, checks, reviews, and promoting, that encourage the user to get involved and committed to the system's success. During implementation and regularly thereafter, we should review with the user to ensure the system is being utilized and explore ways of developing the system so that effectiveness, in relation to cost, can be maximized.

These guidelines have the virtue of being widely accepted by practioners. But we should also assure our designers are working in a climate that promotes such approaches, increases their effectiveness, and permits the development of a modular, layered, and robust software.

System design must be keen in integrating people and information into a common structure. This is an issue to be settled at the top level of a system architecture and is not connected to the programming chores that will follow.

An often made mistake is to relate information requirements to computer programming and management information needs to what computers can do. To have a leading edge in information systems we must match the means to our requirements.

Neither computer programming nor any structured methodology is going to replace thinking. We have to think ahead, evaluate what we are doing, and provide for a structure that answers our goals in an able manner. If we wait for a given "structure" to support *our* requirements on its free will, nothing is going to help us.

- Our first and foremost responsiblity is to define in a sound manner our information requirements: both present and projected.
- Our next most important responsibility is to use the best technology can offer in order to remain competitive.

The software can be looked up in two ways (Figure 5-2): mainly routine or imaginative. And either way can be either one-shot or repetitive in terms of usage. Packages are the best answer to routine requirements, while internal skill must be put to work on new solutions and applications that have not been done before. In the decade of the 1980s, we will all be searching for a way to cope with the inevitable integration of computers and communications with all the information-processing disciplines that are evolving.

Our systems search will be oriented towards obtaining simple, cost/effective, friendly, reliable, communicating systems, with shared logic, memory, and, generally, resources. And we have to think in both operational and financial terms. Prior to being distributed, text and data must be stored somewhere—this "somewhere" costs money. As systems experts we know that money can't buy everything; a system study must be done with the best of knowhow. It must cover:

procedural documentation

work priority and scheduling

maintenance and servicing

catastrophe planning

physical file storage

file security

document/file naming conventions and controls

backup.

The information systems of the 1980s will work online, and online systems eventually involve personnel at all levels. They are

	USER SOFTWARE	
	<u>REPETITIVE</u>	<u>ONE SHOT</u>
<u>ROUTINE</u>	PACKAGES	TS
<u>IMAGINATIVE</u>	INTERNAL DEVELOPMENT	BEST FIT

FIGURE 5-2

much more than "another modification of established work patterns;" they can even bring a certain amount of resentment. Unless the users are properly involved from the start, they lead toward confusion and resistance.

In any system designed for a broad audience, it is the user base who is going to make it work. That is why discussions on language resemble medieval debates about the sex of the angels—until the system perspectives are fixed.

This being done, we will be well advised to look into the tools that can assist and ease the programming job. We all know that there are problems with current programming languages, resulting from the very nature of the von Neumann computer:

- pumping single words back and forth through the bus connecting the memory and the CPU.

That is, the von Neumann computer picks up individual words from memory and combines them by some expression, a practice which doesn't permit you to look at text and data as a whole entity.

- providing an inordinate amount of code for interprogram linkage.

This is a practice which has classically inhibited the effective breaking of a big program into smaller but integral parts.

- avoiding recursive definitions, with which a function is defined in terms of itself.

What we should have till natural language programming comes around is languages that allow us to state the properties the desired program must have and which say what we would like to do without saying how. Needed is a system that can bring:

- a radical reduction in physical code

- performance or major rewrites when the processing requirements change
- reduction of compilation as a result of an interface with the computer's operating system
- access to an easy to use DBMS and assurance of data independence
- dynamic, relational database accessing rather than cross reference indexes
- a language code comprising a wide range of powerful non-procedural verbs with natural language syntax
- flexible distributed database processing using a single non-procedural verb
- data dictionary interface with host computer system
- easy conversion to online interactive graphics display
- statistical analysis capability
- interactive file editor, permitting online, interactive update and retrieval.

In general, the desideratum is a 4th generation language able to tap a large new pool of programming talent, without prior programming experience or technical training as prerequisites for use.

Our eyes should definitely be on the nonspecialist users. All the tools of the trade are made for him: the requirements definition document; data entry forms; interactive video solutions; program commands; validation messages; report formats; graphic output; training seminars; and so on. In program development we should assure that interactive solutions, the custom tailoring, the reports, and whatever support we are assuring calls for minimal effort. Graphical output should be handled as a routine operation. Integrated DB access approaches give the manager his needed information all on one table or graph.

Finally, we should be paying due attention to the quality assurance of our software products. The organizational approach to implementing a software quality assurance program starts with the definition of the roles and responsibilities of the project organization in terms of program robustness and dependability.

We need a methodology to assure that all requirements in terms of product quality specifications are satisfied in the software design specifications. This evidently implies the need for setting up a verification of all requirements. There is a need also for the application of a quality related software engineering methodology.

To ascertain software quality, formal reviews are necessary. We should establish a clear definition of the reviews to be conducted. The methodology to be applied must assure readiness and robustness. A test program should specify the measures for review and testing. Compliance with described testing standards must be assured.

In short, the proper mechanism should be developed to assure that quality assurance requirements have been met. Yet review and test procedures can be no better than the capabilities built into the software in the first place. We must appreciate the need to put into place the means for producing the high-quality software product: processing code, database files, and documentation. In any product, quality is build into the design phase or not at all. Quality cannot be assured through test unless it is designed into the specifications. Software is no exception to this rule.

Observing what experience dictates calls for the definition of what high product quality is. But to properly understand specifications the software development division must run training sessions on the content and application of quality assurance standards. It must even certify that each designer, analyst, and programmer participates in this training activity.

Before the detailed design of a software module begins, each analyst and programmer must have a precise and detailed definition of what the module is to do, how well it must perform, the environment in which it must operate, and its external interfaces.

Auditability is a key reference: from auditing design projections to auditing the specifications, code development, file structure, review accomplishments, program robustness, and compliance to the documentation standards. The quality of a software product is strongly dependent on the ability to test it. During the development process it is necessary to look ahead and assure testability.

The design of a software test program must follow organization-wide standards to be developed and certified by management—including the definition of the test environment. As cannot be too often repeated: "Quality must be built in; it can't be just tested in."

5 FOLLOWING DOCUMENTATION STANDARDS

Documentation standards and programming conventions and practices shall be used for all software. Each individual project shall reference the procedures to be applied to assure compliance with standards, practices, and conventions. Delivery of correct documentation is a prerequisite to the completion of any phase of a project.

Though we will dedicate to this subject a whole chapter, I would include in this section the managerial and auditing viewpoints. Management (which constitutes the approval authority) should provide for the independent review of documentation. The documentation to be produced must be defined to assure formal, controlled communication among project organizational elements. Standards for the preparation of the documentation and the measures to be applied to assure compliance with the standards must be defined. Formality is that much more necessary as several, successive releases characterize the life cycle of a package (or any other piece of software). Such releases put more stress on an astute documentation support.

Documentation is not only necessary; it is inevitable. Computer users that realized this in the past are far ahead of those that didn't. But if one's documentation closet is a mess, lack of foresight may be only partly to blame.

Many organizations are caught in the situation that arose between 1965 and 1980, when development outstripped the ability of users to keep up. Audits on programs that lack robustness and coherence have invariably revealed patchwork written in the mid- to late-1960s. Such programs have these characteristics:

A mixture of languages and styles of programming

A great deal of duplication of processing, and

A labyrinth of processing routines that could be reduced by 75%

In all these cases, systems seem to have grown by themselves and have large areas of their data handling unknown to everybody in the organization, including the specialists. Yet the responsible managers don't want to admit that they don't know exactly what their systems do.

Medium Range Planning

As mistakes in processing proliferate, the excuse is easily found on everybody's lips. "The computer made a mistake," is an excuse often heard by management.

A great deal of the mess is management's own fault, as it has failed to insist on the proper documentation. Poor practices see to it that some applications software systems have been years in the making, encompass hundreds of modules, and huge sections of the organization's total data processing capability. Yet documentation is nearly non-existent.

All there is available is a bunch of hand-scribbled pages, often not numbered, and in large measure also illegible. In a sense, so much the better, since they have not been updated and are largely obsolete:

> The maintenance guide has never been put together.
>
> The operator's manual is just a skeleton.
>
> The user guide had been promised in 2 months' time, but no one worried when it was not produced.

Yet in this and other typical cases, DP management repeatedly assured top management that the applications software run beautifully—and "if it wasn't for the mistakes the computer makes there would have been no errors at all..."

Such excuses may carry a day or two, but lies have short legs. It soon becomes evident that inadequacies inhibit good operations. Documenting such a system *after* the need arises is a well-known *real* problem because any design concept has been lost.

Influenced by a lot of nonsense about their real mission, programmers often fail to provide even elementary documentation support. This is not only counterproductive but also eventually works against their own interest. Without documentation, it takes twice as long to figure out WHY

> someone has done something a certain way when at the top of the page it was done differently
>
> on the preceding page the task is accomplished with ten instructions instead of four
>
> one-line patches are inserted without comment, when they can lead the maintenance programmer onto a totally wrong

path and the patchwork compounds the problem, multiplying by an order of magnitude the time necessary for program maintenance.

Even debugging such monstrosities means set-up costs for the programmers. Things get worse as applications systems approach breakdown. Programs and machines no longer have much contact. No documentation is available for dealing quickly with crisis: the only evidence that exists is one of real sloppiness.

Things get still worse, of course, with online systems where users are going to be able to update files. Furthermore, when major files and processing are shared, there must be proper departmental interface. Processing cycles must be set up for interdepartmental use, reports organized, and files standardized and laid out.

In conclusion, an integrated information system is an important goal. It uses computers and communications to solve problems for an entire organization instead of attacking problems on a piecemeal basis. It aims to serve the objectives of management. But such promises remain largely unfulfilled unless the system is well projected, properly managed and financed, able to cope with operations subject to rapid change, and part of an overall strategic plan.

PART TWO

THE ART OF SOFTWARE IMPLEMENTATION

6
THE SOFTWARE CHALLENGE

1 INTRODUCTION

Software is information and therefore essentially intangible. Software can be transferred over telephone lines, so its physical state is inconsequential. The value of software is not in the physical support on which it is stored but in its ability to answer the user's need. This ability reflects the information and skill put forward in the development of the software.

Programs for computers and communications include operating systems, assemblers, compilers, interpreters, transaction processors, data management routines, utility programs, sort/merge and maintenance/diagnostic programs, as well as applications programs. Billing, invoicing, inventory control, payroll, the handling of current accounts, satellite navigation, and engineering analysis are examples of applications software. Such programs may be machine independent; they may be general purpose in nature or projected to satisfy the requirements of a specialized process or a particular user.

In the most frequently used sense of the word, *software* embodies every aspect of using the hardware components of computers and communication equipment for specific applications areas. Software is far more than just lines of code, it includes all of the

- planning
- design
- operating procedures
- language conventions
- encoding

Encoding is translation into machine-processable form in terms of agreed-upon semantics and syntax. To increase understandability, we standardize and simplify the logical flow. We also provide documentation and commentary to explain coded instructions, process patterns, and mnemonics.

To develop applications programs and basic software in an able manner, it is imperative to start with the definition of system objectives and scope and to involve the end user in the design process. Documentation should be prepared during the analysis and design phase. It not only helps clarify the subject but also provides an important training tool, one both analysts and users can understand.

In Part One, when talking of project management for information systems, we underlined the wisdom of monitoring project progress and costs. We have also made reference to the need to include in the team both system-builders and users. Failure to involve user personnel can be fatal to the end results.

One of the foremost challenges in software development is the ability to exchange information among people who speak different languages. Good involvement implies good communication. An inadequate communication between analysts and end users can be the single biggest reason why information systems projects fail.

Two issues come into perspective in this last reference. The first is timing; we spoke of it in Part One. It is only natural that users get impatient for delivery and pressure to get the project done quickly. To meet unrealistic deadlines, corners are cut and with them goes the quality of the product.

Software quality is the second vital issue, and we will speak of it in this chapter. It has many angles. First of all the software product must be usable. A programming product that upon installation passes to maintenance is not a useable one.

An equally important reference on software quality is its documentation. When documentation is cut down for the sake of expediency, there is reason to believe the results will be regrettable. These are the key issues that we will consider in this and the following chapters. But first we should take a good look at the notion of the software.

2 WHAT IS MEANT BY SOFTWARE ENGINEERING?

Software engineering is a broad area of activities related to computers and communications. It comprises several classes of problems (and of professional interest), the most important being programming languages, processors (assemblers, compilers, generators), operating systems (from the classical OS to DBMS and datacomm), applications programs, libraries, and documentation.

As a discipline, software engineering is directed to the production of computer programs that are correct, efficient, flexible, maintainable, and understandable. The programs should also execute in reasonable time spans at acceptable costs. The aims to be assured are that

the work is done on time

the end product is reliable

the programs are robust

the software is maintainable

the object programs are reasonably efficient

there exists the maximum possible transferability (portability) of the resulting software

While these aims are known and everybody agrees with them, software quality often leaves much to be wanted. Among the general manifestations of sloppiness are the excessive number of errors (better known as bugs), the ever increasing maintenance costs, the low level standardization, the often impossible transferability, and the incompleteness of the documentation.

Poor results have background reasons. Among the predominant failures we distinguish inadequate cost estimates; poorly studied timetables; easygoing work schedules; and little understanding of the role of individual routines within a program. The most fundamental reasons for total failure is the inadequate tracking of user requirements and the failure to consider the cost factor of skill.

The latter reference underlines a known but little appreciated principle in technology: *The lowest cost is obtained through the highest trained individual.* A large, poorly coordinated group will produce a fraction of what can be obtained through few knowledgeable and spirited persons.

A spirited, properly directed, and coordinated project group will be keen in exploring the means software engineering puts at its disposal: figuring out the problem to be solved, determining the solution prior to committing resources in blind alleys, implementing the solution to be chosen, creating the programming product, caring for quality assurance, and giving due importance to documentation and user training.

Making the program comprehensible to the user is one of the foremost tasks software engineering should accomplish. Like the other steps outlined in the preceeding paragraph this one is a creative effort that changes programs into products.

As with every engineering discipline, software products should be designed for the end user. The users of computers and communications facilities must be educated to know what they really need (as opposed to perceived needs) and to use what they need. Computers are a people intensive job.

Another aim of software engineering is a reasonable level of standardization. Software standardization makes it possible for software products to talk to each other. That is an added value, and more users are asking for it as they are faced with the integration of formerly diverse phases. These phases include data processing, word processing, electronic mail, query capabilities, management graphics, financial modeling, project planning, and a variety of control schemes.

With the users becoming more knowledgeable about the computer gear, software engineering should not only assure the programming values of the last decade but also aim to provide the final user with useful, specific messages, short and consistent response times, well-organized command languages, lucid menu selection, and powerful graphics approaches. This calls for standards on the comprehensible display of information-messaging systems as well as standards for reliability.

User-centered participatory methodologies should be at a premium. The establishment of interactive system specifications; the development of tools for rapid prototype testing; guidelines for conducting pilot studies; and strategies for collecting and responding to user feedback should also be at a premium. Efforts have to be taken to limit the consequences of software crises: definitely convincing results, new conceptual tools suggested, and tools provided to automate many aspects of software production.

New rules must be established

providing computer support to software development,

fully utilizing life cycle costs and studying detailed cost breakdown,

developing manufacturing engineering methods in software production,

making steady design reviews to insure visibility.

These areas of concern are compatible with a software engineering discipline. The term *engineering* implies the entire development of a product from initial conception through testing and maintenance, organized in an orderly way. Similarly, an engineering *discipline* implies that the quality, performance, and cost of the product must be predictable and appropriate compromises should be achieved.

Software must be reliable. In this connection *reliability* means fully operational programs, properly tested, written for maintenance, with a documentation that is both complete and able to flash-out the crucial factors. Like any engineering development, this work will typically proceed through a series of stages: product planning, specifications, design, documentation, fabrication, and testing. The development of software may pass through this sequence several times, as model, prototype, and in the final implementation of the programming product.

3   A PROGRAM IS NOT A PERSONAL OBJECT

One of the origins of the troubles that are usually associated with computer software is that analysts, programmers, and some users have come to think of programs as their personal objects. By consequence, what they produce or obtain:

Is handled in a way that is difficult to reuse

Is often treated as a throwaway item

Is poorly documented, requiring for maintenance an extraordinary amount of time

What's more, some programmers can become psychologically attached to their programs, looking at them as extensions of themselves. Errors in programs sometimes become damaging to the programmer's self-image. By discouraging "the ownership of code," making it clear, understandable and usable by others, we promote more than the sharing of scarce resources. We can impact on the analyst/programmer's personality.

The point most professionals only slowly come to appreciate is the need to direct their attention toward sharing, saving, and revising software. This means designing robust routines and making them transportable (as the preceeding section underlined). It also calls for a decision to get rid of biases characterizing the last decades (such as programming from scratch) since these biases point in the wrong direction.

We must learn to use software tools effectively. This brings into perspective the need for standards and for a systems methodology. Such requirements become the more vital as computers and communications play so much of a vital role everywhere in our daily lives and are being used extensively in business and industry.

Advances in hardware technology are

1. decreasing the cost, size, weight, and power requirements while
2. increasing the speed and reliability of the computer gear.

VLSI and VHSIC are promising several orders of magnitude improvement in these areas over the next decade. Yet we should never forget that, unless major advances are made in the development and maintenance of software, our society will be unable to take full advantage of the computers and communications technology.

To keep up with the rapidly expanding applications programming requirements, major new software technology initiatives are necessary. The aim must be to achieve an order of magnitude improvement in software productivity, reliability, portability, and maintainability during this decade. Unless we find ways to make such major advances we will be sorely limited in our ability to build sophisticated computers and communications systems.

The way to a valid solution starts with an efficient organization: establishing the proper perspective on the computer network, within, say, the automated office system; identifying the needs and requirements of diverse end users; and providing a cost/effective implementation. The total systems picture must be kept in perspective in every step.

The major subsystems for which the proper software should be made are

The user workstation

The text/database organization and access

The text/data communications component

The processing requirements and tools

The specific applications processes

Hardware and software design should aim to provide the largest possible number of users with an economical and efficient mechanism for moving text and data back and forth between themselves and the system equipment as distributed elements. A highly modular automated system design can be achieved by using an approach that assumes all subsystems are distributed, are modular in nature, and compatible among themselves—and must be served in that manner.

This implementation philosophy must properly examine how available software components fit in organizationally, what the relationship to corporate products and processes is, how management looks at the capitalization of software development, and what the corporate strategy for technology is. The policy to be followed with computers and communications must be consistent with corporate goals and practices.

Senior management must play a major role in the establishment and maintenance of policies that look at software as a product. Even in organizations that already have models and disciplines for software development, the existing policies and procedures may become inflexible, resulting in tailoring for mediocrity, hence stifling innovation.

Firms with developed standards are, however, a small minority. The most frequent situation is represented by organizations that have little experience in software product policies and often employ tools, methodologies, or facilities which are inappropriate to their actual needs. Here the first vital step is to establish an explicit mode and discipline for a software development process. This discipline should be

- usable by the working level of operations and
- enforceable by the appropriate management.

Such discipline must be both flexible and adaptable to technology changes; tailored to both the product and the people involved; and subject to a continuous management education concerning the software development, policies, and disciplines.

This education should be based on experience rather than being theoretical. Hence, it should involve company case studies, successes and failures, and so on. It should also be coupled to systematic reviews and the establishment of an upgradeable state-of-the-art approach.

As I had the opportunity to underline, computer assistance is a *must* in software development. Computers should be used both in improving the analysts/programmers' productivity and in other chores. Though software is basically labor intensive (and the effective utilization of people is paramount) there are a number of other issues rather independent of people management.

In the latter category fall computer-based tools to aid in better planning and controlling the cost of the process, evaluating progress against the plan, helping in relating the expense to return on investment, experimenting in order to determine how and in what form the concept of portability can be utilized to significantly reduce software costs, and so on. What these references suggest is that computers enhance methods and attributes to assess this evolving product and can assist in evaluating its quality, reliability, maintainability, and cost.

4 THE LIFE CYCLE SOLUTION

A concept of a *life cycle* approach for software products has been evolving during the last 10 years. In several ways it resembles a similar practice that has been implemented since the early 1960s with hardware, particularly weapons systems.

The software life cycle is that time period in which the software is conceived, developed, and used. As stated, it can be typically divided into phases: Initial planning (conceptual); logical system design (requirements definition); physical system design; construction; evaluation; operation; and maintenance. The conceptual phase encompasses the problem statement, preliminary systems analysis, and identification of alternative solutions.

The requirements definition phase consists of producing the project objectives, functional specifications, and design constraints. Interfaces and data definitions are generated and verified against the requirements. Implementation involves the actual program code production, unit testing of the programs, and documentation. Operation is the use of the system. Maintenance involves the detection and correction of errors and the incorporation of modifications to add capabilities and improve performance.

The early life cycle solutions for software have been handicapped mainly due to five reasons:

- For nearly three decades, software development projects have demonstrated *no* specific, well-knit sequence of events.
- Progress monitoring is difficult during development and in production.
- Maintenance practices are often ill-structured and deficient in terms of management control.
- Oneshot programming products offer a poor basis for life cycle evaluation. Yet they are still the majority of cases.
- Costing methods make sense when quantitative tools exist for planning and control, while software developers resisted such tools for years.

Till the internal software development methodology is well-structured, life cycle cost makes more sense when we talk of acquisition and implementation of packages. The characteristics of software packages can be brought under close attention, particularly regarding dimensions, efficiency, reliability, cost, and life expectancy.

As with well-established hardware procurement, one approach to encourage the software package bidder to offer programming products with low life cycle costs is to provide an incentive reward in the procurement. This procedure could be applied to all measurable factors, such as efficiency, reliability, and maintainability, provided we care to properly:

1. Define the critical factors and method of measurement.

2. Specify minimum acceptable values for the critical factors and state objective values.

3. Require the package bidder to document in the proposal the basis of his or her claim(s) properly specifying that the ability will be evaluated.

4. State incentive rewards such as credit points for further purchases of software packages if the claimed performance levels are upheld through benchmark and practice.

5. Include as contractual requirement the performance improvements for which a retainer's maintenance fee will be allowed.

This approach creates a positive incentive to develop and take the risk of offering worthwhile improvements in life cycle cost reduction. It should be clear that pursuit of maximum cost effectiveness in the life cycle is a more sound philosophy than an evaluation limited to the procurement level. Its successful application demands a precise and rational evaluation of the areas to be included; these must be clearly defined and subject to absolute measurement.

While these references primarily concern the procurement of software packages, similar approaches could be taken with internal developments of programming products, if the following phases are properly identified and treated as discrete areas of a unified system:

Initial Planning

Logical Systems Design

Physical Systems Design

Construction

Evaluation

Operation

Maintenance.

A rational organization into modules able to promote life cycle perspectives necessarily regards the new products, not the old. We all know that a significant portion of our current large software investment will be with us for a long time. These systems have been expanded, repaired, and patched over a long period, often in a haphazard fashion.

Our chance with personal computers, intelligent workstations, and local area networks is to adopt a new methodology while learning from what we did in the past. This calls for viewing the old programs as manifestations of a large number of interconnected functions, which is an important asset.

The procedures and data structures embedded in the old software are the result of many years of experience. They can become the basis of critical analysis, out of which broadly usable components of future systems can be predicted—thus answering the systems planning and logical design prerequisites.

With careful analysis, we can identify software components that occur frequently within a given application area or across applications. Then we can use the new capabilities embodied in microprocessor-based systems and move from the logical to the physical design. Gradually, the evolving program components must become the building blocks of our future software, replacing the ones constructed earlier without a definite system plan.

Although with the coming systems the main emphasis will be placed on the horizontal interconnection of the building blocks across the functional boundaries in the organization, we should not forget the need of looking at depth at each function. Most existing functions can be gradually mapped onto the set of distributed hardware through an allocation function: the smooth relocation of software components along the network.

In each of these phases of system evolution, due appreciation should be given to the fact that computer programming is an exact procedure that requires a solid definition of the problem. This takes time. Additional time is required to do the logical and physical design code, test, debug, again test all this before the implementation can take place.

The baseline is formalisms to be understood and observed by everybody in the organization—computers and communications professionals as well as users. If we continue to deal in the simplistic way we have to date, we will be plagued by high costs and the reversed priorities, unnatural hierarchy, and isolation that have characterized solutions in the past. Such experiences are haunting computer professionals and management alike. Why not look for a change?

5 FAULT TOLERANT APPROACHES

The references made in the preceding section underline the fact that both management and the analysts should be brought to appreciate the need for change—and for rational thought oriented toward the systems realities of tomorrow. There are both administrative and creativity aspects to consider. We may obtain commendable results

- If we establish a realistic schedule
- If we formalize every phase that must be accomplished
- If we don't change our mind in the middle of the project
- If our staff is trained and provided adequate facilities
- If we keep distractions away and everyone motivated
- If we manage sympathetically but firmly.

The system analyst and the designer are, *par excellence*, creative elements—a fact that is rarely appreciated. Therefore, most organizations fail to provide them with the proper knowhow and incentives. At the same time, because of poor practices of the past designers, analysts and programmers often fail to appreciate timetables, budgets, program portability, and fault tolerance.

Let's then establish some definitions. An *error* results in the software containing a fault. It is made because of an omission or misinterpretation of user requirements in the software subsystem specification. It may also be due to incorrect translation of a requirement in the design. A major source of headache is programming errors. The latter include:

1. Algorithmic, hence failures of proof of correctness.
2. Approximation, giving results accurate for some inputs, inaccurate for others.
3. Due to structure: dimensions, linkages.
4. Semantical and syntactical.
5. Logical or due to interfaces.
6. Of a timing nature (execution time of instruction sequence) and
7. Typographical.

Contrasted to an error, a *fault* is a manifestation in program code of an error made by the program designer, analyst, programmer, or any other person responsible for interpreting the system specification, preparing the software design, or projecting the program or support software. The fault is usually evoked by some input that results in the program failing to compute the function it was designed to produce. (In this sense, fault and bug are synonymous.)

We have not spoken much of fault-tolerance, and the concept involves much more than two words can say. On the theoretical side, the reference means software tolerant of faults in an individual element. This implies a structure strong enough to sustain a fault in a routine without breakdown. No significant piece of fault tolerant software is available today. But ways exist for getting there. One of the keys to fault tolerance is concurrent diagnosis—response to codes established for correctness. In hardware this is done through redundant spares. In software a redundant copy of a faulty program can get us into more trouble. Rollback is an answer. Another more elegant answer for the future is converting the software into firmware and hardware, casting it into silicon. We will return to this notion.

One of the issues we must appreciate is that fault tolerance provision of the software are not themselves fault tolerant. This can still be admitted as long as the control structure is completely checked. Yet the latter is not necessarily supported by the current state of the art. Among the limitation of the existing methods we distinguish:

- No definitive theory on the termination of software tests (*when* to stop testing).
- No definitive assurance of correct execution—hence need for auditing.
- No provision for correctness under bad data situations.
- No principles for limited retest after a software change.
- The best existing methods are very costly, hence scarcely used.

Detection, correction, and rollback were the classical ways of dealing with a software system malfunction. Then came the concept of a microprogrammable machine to develop software in advance of hardware, workout the specs for the hardware, and serve as a debugging aid. But silicon technology now permits us to go much further than that.

It will probably be 10 years before the semiconductor industry (computer makers, software developers, silicon firms, universities) comes up with a process that lets us cast our software into silicon. But this is sure enough to happen. When it happens, software will be ten times cheaper than today, but it will also be reliable, reusable, and fault tolerant.

The first software functions on a chip will be at the modular subroutine level: converse, display, inquiry, update, add, replace, delete, scan, and execute. They will be followed by generator capabilities most like the newer functions in demand, such as the definition of videograms, elementary elaboration of data structures, basic applications definition (by the user), the conversion of tables into graphs, or some sort of online validation.

Slowly, as these developments materialize, the broader software design and programming practices will change. The aim will be reducing software costs per instruction, but in effect also making the product more controllable and better verifiable.

An example of the reference just made is the "sneak circuit analysis" where a program logic structure is reduced to a hardware circuitry representation. This circuitry is examined for a predefined set of faults: open-logic, infinite loops, bypass of desired logic, unnecessary logic, missing logic, unused logic, incorrect addressing, procedural errors, and corrective action is taken.

There should be no great difficulty in microcoding, then writing in silicon the functions that until now have belonged to the software world. But the process will go well beyond this stage, producing small, self-contained, and independent program portions that can be integrated into a larger procedure or changed without affecting the latter.

After the best known utility routines (conversion, I/O operations, data move, sort/merge) have been put on a chip, will come the turn of language compilers and operating system primitives. Operating system software is necessary as a bridge between the hardware and the user programs. Proven and stable OS programs should find themselves next in the list.

But the most significant impact of casting software into silicon will be in the applied programming activity itself. Two areas of impact are safe enough to forecast. The first, least recognized yet highly important, is the conversion of current applications programs into chips. The gained speed of execution can be partly used to pay for bridges and interpreters that can enhance the program's portability. Special silicon-based routines may be added to promote its fault tolerance.

The second area of impact is more evident: it is the development of new applications software. This will be a merger of the currently available packages and of silicon technology, albeit with a time gap between the availability of technology and its insertion into an equipment-level solution for a computer system. This gap is primarily the result of caution exerted in the application of the new technology to system level functions. But it is also a measure of our own inability to exploit, without undue delays, the possibilities technology can offer.

7

SOFTWARE DEVELOPMENTS FOR PERSONAL COMPUTERS

1 INTRODUCTION

Software has become the battleground for many PC makers whose nondifferentiated hardware leaves room for added value. Applications software is a particularly critical issue to users. A common misconception among nonspecialists is that a computer program is a static product. This misconception exacerbates the difficulty.

Software development is dynamic. Management visibility tools are necessary to enable project managers to control the status throughout the software's life cycle. Such tools can provide a means for

enhancing progress,

improving quality, and

reducing costs.

In order to reach such results, we have to move away from current methods and processes for developing software systems that are unstructured and undisciplined. A process discipline must be established and enforced in every development organization.

The structuring of the development process must be performed with the objective of providing measurable means easily accessible for viewing by management personnel. This calls for designing and structuring the development process and its environment so that they are easily observed. The assumptions and problems under which progress data are collected should be well defined, and such data must be controllable.

The generation of a requirements-oriented database should be viewed as a calibration process where a given set of tools and methods can be evaluated within an application environment. In turn, this requires a project planning and control methodology. The second section of the present chapter addresses this issue.

The third section treats a case study on the conversion of a first generation online management information system to a third generation online system structure. This will help demonstrate how the principles of product quality and productivity can be put into effect.

Since emphasis has often been placed on the wisdom of using packaged software, the next to the last section of this chapter addresses itself to problems related to this subject. Finally, the last section treats the same issue but under the viewpoint of internally developed programs.

2   PRODUCT QUALITY AND PRODUCTIVITY

The methodologies and tools at our disposal should aim at improvements in product quality and in productivity. The study and management of productivity in systems analysis and programming calls for a valid measurement discipline. Measurement is as fundamental to programming as it is to any other area of engineering. Its implementation cuts across different areas of concern, including management, motivation, understanding, training and the methodical solutions to be adopted.

Usually productivity models concentrate on a ratio of output to input, such as lines of code per man-month. Another useful notion of economic productivity expresses a ratio of values to costs. For instance: an increase in results attributable to the product or a cost reduction resulting from the use of the product.

Just as important is the understanding of the factors underlying productivity. Such fundamental issues in measurement open new areas of investigation while crystalizing our thinking about existing areas. They also lead to evaluation. Currently the most valid evaluation of productivity is within a given environment over time, rather than across different types of programming environments.

By definition a software environment consists of the sum of the physical facilities, social structures, and intelligent skills dedicated to the system analysis and programming products.

- *Physical facilities* include office space, common areas (libraries, classrooms), sources (journals, books, video tape), capital equipment, different tools and support software, social amenities (recreation areas, sports equipment).
- *Social structures* refer to formal organizational units (departments, programming teams), peer relationships, access to external professional groups and universities, and the placement of software production units within larger institutional units.
- *Intellectual skills* relate to both the factual knowledge and subjective opinions of the software-producing employees in the firm, including new lines and skills we wish to disseminate to existing employees through education.

To express the influence of physical facilities in productivity and quality, the units of physical attributes must be established. These typically include capitalization per software engineer and m^2 of floor space, ratio of conference rooms to software engineers, library size and contents (volumes/journals per software engineer), computer-based storage capacity for listings, formal training expenses per software engineer per year, and ratio of terminals to software engineers, including home terminals.

Social attributes involve sensitive issues of privacy and employee/management relations. Examples include number of employees per project manager or per steady department manager, number of professionals per product, managerial appraisal factors, structural placement of software units; ratio of and facilities of technology transfer (user training, handholding), organizational policies and standards; and critical mass, that is, the percentage of the people who must know a technology to use it.

The measure of intellectual skills involves sensitive issues that may range from ethical concerns such as the respect of property to tangible factors regarding skill and knowhow. Some of the measures of intellectual skills include academic background, intellectual aptitudes, number of days of training per year during employment, recycling for experienced personnel, measurable productivity, and the quality of production. Other criteria are the number of published papers, inventions, and copyrights.

The evaluation of such attributes is a well-established practice. Industrial psychology and organizational behavior often count heavily on them. Psychology also contributes screening media such as intellectual aptitude tests for programmers.

Indeed, with the exception of aptitude tests, software engineering has not capitalized on the findings and guidelines of experimental psychology. Only recently have software production activities emphasized this issue, and the same is true about investments per productive worker. Only few and rather recent cases suggest that it is entirely appropriate to compute the capitalization per programmer. Software engineering as a profession is probably undercapitalized when compared to other fields of economic and industrial activity.

It is important to determine whether or not optimum values exist and whether they are functions of other factors. Among the relevant questions we distinguish the typical patterns of usage of a computer service by programmers, the short and consistent response time for interactive computing functions, the software life cycle, and progress measurements and milestones. Management should establish standard-phase definition activities.

Project management should identify work activities and their associated products for project planning, creating a structure for tracking progress against budget and schedule. Within this framework, a good deal of work needs to be done to identify criteria and suitable measurements to assist in the valuation and selection of technologies—as, for instance, to compare architectures.

Techniques and tools should be used for allocating and controlling resources from the design process:

Evaluating performance and cost.

Establishing rigorous definition of the information elements.

Adding the appropriate levels of explanation.

Identifying multiple criteria, then selecting the most appropriate.

Processing with inspections and audits.

Implementing design reviews.

Testing programs and systems.

Providing baseline and configuration control.

Assuring software quality.

Prototyping helps reduce risk in major software developments. Its purpose is to validate the user requirements prior to implementation. Models can be constructed quickly and at low cost. Subsequently, they help set the project in the right direction, thus eliminating a significant risk that the wrong system gets implemented. Extensive modifications during the system's early operational use are also eliminated in this manner.

Project research programs address the key issues of system design. The problems of concurrency, decentralized controls, distributed databases, and distributed communication are fields where a fundamental understanding must be defined. The issue of high-level specification in a myriaprocessor architecture, which should be layered, helps in performance assessment of hardware alternatives and later on in testing and verification of the distributed system.

Prestudy increases the subsequent flexibility of program implementation. It is wise to use generalized parametric approaches that can be customized through the selection of values. It is also a good idea to subdivide the application into a series of subtasks, selecting for each a module and parameters, and producing an interface for the selected modules.

Complexity should be properly identified and reduced in all steps of development: requirements, specification, and design. In this field modeling can be identified as a powerful tool to combat complexity. Difficulties do exist, however, in identifying the right abstractions and testing to determine what is proper and effective.

The methodology should use abstraction to identify the constraint and boundary conditions that impact the approaches used to refine detail. The mechanism to represent abstraction must be oriented and graphical. A graphical representation of information should be studied to enhance the understanding of interrelated data.

With WS at the desk of each analyst and programmer, attention should be paid to incorporating graphical displays and forms interfaces into all projects. Interactive color and graphics capabilities should be extended to support more efficient representation of design information.

In turn, the functional capabilities to be incorporated in the WS for software development should enhance testing. Most currently used methods ignore the need for testing until the integration and testing phase. To the contrary, we should look at system testability in the formative stages of a project. The facility of program and system testing should become a major criterion during

> requirements analysis,
>
> overall system design, and
>
> detailed design.

Hence, it should become a normal practice to create test specifications at each design stage. Their existence is a quality assurance item, while the test specifications themselves are a vital part of the project and its subsequent success or failure.

The same is valid of maintenance support tools. Maintenance should be a software development preoccupation from the beginning—not just for system modification and regeneration. This concept runs contrary to current practice: maintenance today consists primarily of code patching.

Changes to the system are made at the assembly code level. After a sufficient number of these are accumulated, the system is recompiled. But we all know that this is error prone. Our methodology should allow the maintenance process to begin at the requirements phase:

> Defining changes of system capability.
>
> Assessing impact upon the system.
>
> Assuring traceability and visibility into the development process.

In other words, program and system maintenance should be planned from system conception, viewed as a set of system specifications regarding revisions that will occur late in the development and implementation cycle. As an example on the application of these principles we will follow a case of redesigning an information system originally projected for management use.

3 REVAMPING THE MANAGEMENT INFORMATION SYSTEM

The case study in this section reflects the work done in redesigning and modernizing the management information system of an international bank. In its initial phase of implementation, 10 years ago, this MIS was installed and operated in fifteen countries selected for

Level of systems ability

Volume of work (these countries represented the 80% of total load), and

Requirements for MIS implementation.

Each country's operation had its own data processing production center. The common programs that were then developed did the extraction and formatting operations after the normal DP handling was finished. The selected information elements regarded loans, deposits, and similar activities. This information was stored on a tape airmailed to New York.

Data processing at headquarters devoted a large mainframe to manage the corporate level MIS, both for domestic and for international data. This application grew with experience, and by 1980 it represented four report-generating systems. Their output was made available to management in printed form:

1. *The Country Risk System.* It portrays the risk exposure, country by country.

2. *The Global Relationship System.* It reflects the worldwide position of the bank with any of 800 multinationals.

3. *The Tax System.* It reports the foreign withholding taxes due to loans and other operations under foreign jurisdiction.

4. *The Profit and Loss System.* It's aim is to present to management both the internal profitability by department and the external profitability: for instance, shipping versus auto-manufacturing industry branches.

System design represents 3 years of negotiation with decision makers about what they need in decision support to run the business. However, as experience grew with implementation, changes and alterations were suggested to improve system efficiency. There were two difficulties associated with changes.

- One was the difficulty in predicting the design ramifications of a downstream requirement change and
- The other, the difficulty to trace back to the requirements the effect of a design change.

Both these problems inhibited the ability to make effective design tradeoffs and to proceed with radical alterations on the same old structure. Then a methodology was tried by encapsulating design decisions. This made a significant improvement in changeability since it provided a set of coherent approaches from which project specifications could be constructed.

The design of homogeneous data streams was a major step. In the past, incompatibilities made mandatory reliance on the tape transmission system. By placing the same personal computer at each country DP site, it became possible to use the same data line to transmit after the processing hours. Furthermore, by reversing the line at daytime, management had available online video access.

This first application of PC was consolidated, and standalone engines started spreading in the bank. At management's request the specialists studied PC implementation in business and industry and identified the hold microcomputers were taking in the professional market. The specialists also guaged the interest in making the PC communicate through local area networks.

Another significant finding of the research was the ability of interactive Videotex to answer in a more effective way than tabulated reports the information requirements of management. The three subjects PC, LAN, and Videotex could be nicely brought together on the same system to be designed for management.

The mainframe-based programs were already available to

trace information to the customer level,

then evaluate the facilities, and

finally present management with facilities and customer mirrors.

Why not bring this information to the responsible manager's desk online, interactively and support it at the desk level through a PC connected to the LAN?

The original preparation of programs able to handle the customer mirror and tell the bank about profit and loss was a massive process. The implementation of the myriaprocessor was a necessary refinement.

The creation of such a methodology, however, demanded that formal structured models be used to describe each phase of the development. Automated text and data transformations had to be provided. By adopting methodology that looked at the entire system life cycle, the analysts escaped from the past, which essentially isolated the discrete steps of the software development.

Maintenance for the available software was performed on three different levels:

1. The general approach was to regenerate the system.
2. If major modifications were required, a remodeling effort was in order.
3. Not recommended, but still sometimes necessary was *patching*, which implied all the problems of current day maintenance.

An investigation was made into providing standardization for component parts from which the new system could be built. Based on this, the generalization of process construction concepts was used to develop modules for parametric programs.

Such modules extended available facilities, for instance, by providing not only customer mirror by borrower but also customer parental hierarchy—up to several levels of customers for upper-most parentage. Interactive software improved the identification of the ultimate risk level.

The following is an example of the facility. A bank officer approves a level of credit for the customer under some umbrella arrangement. Below that level the system presents all the details:

letters of credit,

overdrafts,

loans,

guarantees.

Each component part has a ceiling, and no individual ceiling can exceed top level of approval. The sophistication of the system however implies a constant need to monitor the situation and to update the management database.

There are also other levels of risk to be accounted for. Long-term loans are riskier than short-term loans. Hence, qualifying information elements must be contained in the database, and along with them:

compensating balance,

fees collected,

guarantees, and so on.

These are examples of floating elements that can apply to any level in the hierarchy of the customer mirror presentation.

To facilitate better man-information interaction, nontextual forms of communication were investigated: a picture is worth a thousand words. Graphics were used in place of text to convey information between the human and the PC. Furthermore, design-wise, all phases of the development process were linked so that the evolution of any part of the product could be traceable from the initial to the final phase.

This required that verification of completeness, consistency, and correctness had to be facilitated. It also implied that changes made had to be more effectively managed. In an effort to standardize, the user interfaces, support tools, and database facilities at each phase were common in structure and available via a single common language.

In turn, such policy helped minimize training and specialization, improved control, and assured that design and implementation met the problem specifications, requirements, and objectives. It also enhanced the designers' and analysts' ability to identify product attributes that should be tracked for control purposes during the software development cycle.

In short, the following end results were obtained:

1. A truly management-oriented information system, available interactively.

2. The incorporation of integrated subsystems.

3. The implementation of WS based on PC and video presentation—and linked through LAN.

4. Color graphics capability.

5. The provision at the WS not only of computational ability but also the flexibility to integrate text, image, and (eventually) voice.

A side object of the work being done was the development of an office automation strategy for the bank, with the ability to integrate local area and long-haul datacomm both for the bank's own operations and for online client service.

As a cognizant executive was to suggest: "The expense of running dedicated data lines is very high, and you are left with a star network. We don't want that. Our interest is to implement packet switching—and can be done long-haul as well as locally."

Said another senior executive: "Customer access is the wave of the 1980s in banking. Cash management, information services, instant banks are examples. Financial institutions have to offer the facility, inviting the customer to use their network." The design of the new, PC-based information system is indeed assuring these prerequisites. Standards, gear, nodes, control center, protocols are chosen with this in mind, and being components of the new technology, they are nicely integrating together.

4 THE SOFTWARE INDUSTRY AND ITS PROBLEMS

A valid advice to all users is "when you find a suitable package, buy it; don't reinvent." This is particularly true for CP where an impressive number of applications programs now exist to fit the user's needs. This industry, however, is not without its problems.

Both horizontal and vertical software has given rise to a new, wide-scattered industry. But judging from the mainframe and minicomputer experience, there is going to be a concentration in the hands of a few strong survivors. The following is a reference to software products and markets currently prevailing for larger computers.

Among mainframers, only IBM made impressive software sales in 1982, to the tune of an estimated $1.7 billion. Univac, DEC, CDC, Honeywell, and Burroughs sold between $150 million and $100 million each. The largest independent software and professional service vendors in the United States have been (in approximate million dollars in sales)

1. Computer Science ($500 M)
2. EDS ($250 M)
3. PRC ($100 M)
4. CACI ($80 M)
5. MSA (software products only, $75 M)
6. SYSCON ($70 M)
7. Systems Computer and Technology ($65 M)
8. Informatics (software products only $60 M)
9. ADR (software products only, $50 M)
10. CINCOM (software products only, $45 M)

11. Cullinane (software products only, $45 M)
12. Pansophic (software products only, $35 M)

GEISCO, ADP, and CDC generated about half the money of the service bureau market in 1980, but their share slipped to 42% in 1982. Among the top European service bureau and software companies we distinguish:

1. CISI—France BNP ($165 M)
2. SCICON—UK BP ($160 M)
3. SG 2—France Société Generale ($156 M)
4. GSI—France CGE ($150 M)
5. CAP/GEMINI—France Indep. ($145 M)
6. SEMA METRA—France Paribas ($135 M)
7. FINSIEL—Italy IRI ($130 M)
8. Thomson Informatique—France Thomson ($110 M)
9. DATEV—Germany Indep. ($95 M)
10. SLIGOS—France Credit Lyonnais/Tymshare ($85 M)
11. DATEMA—Sweden Johnson ($80 M)
12. CCMC—France Indep. ($75 M)

Among microsoftware manufacturers no company has yet reached these levels in sales, but Visicorp, Digital Research, and Microsoft seem well launched in the horizontal software line. The production of vertical programs is still a cottage industry and will remain so for some time till consolidation takes hold, following an inevitable shakeout—which will impact the computer base.

Looking at marketshares among software publishers for PC, we should appreciate that an estimated 94% of 1983 revenues were made by less than 20 firms while 60% of the revenues were earned by 6 firms:

Independents	Million Dollars
1. Microsoft	70
2. Visicorp	52
3. Micropro (wordstar)	50
4. Digital Research	48
5. Lotus	42
6. Ashton-Tate	35
7. Peachtree	21
8. Software Arts	12
9. Software Publishings, Sorcim, Continental, BPI, Perfect Software, State of Art, Sierra Online, Brøderbund	60
10. Other Independents*	50
	500

*By one account, there are more than 3,000 software firms, mostly 1-man businesses.

A large share of the market loss, however, been commanded by computer reviews—more precisely the top three PC manufacturers:

Computer Makers	
1. IBM	130
2. APPLE	90
3. Radio Shack	80
	300

Finally let's take notice of the conservative estimate on the expected 1984 growth—60%! The optimistic projections foresee that this market will quickly double.

To help the users with the myriad of programs available in the market, leading PC manufacturers prepare "yellow pages editions" with programs marketed by add-on firms and applicable to their equipment. At the same time software manufacturers do their best to protect their products from piracy—that is, from unauthorized copying of programs.

This task is challenging. Quite often, as fast as they can think up a new code, someone else can break it. Finding a way to defeat the pirates is a top priority for the software manufacturers, who are competing fiercely for a share of the emerging, multibillion-dollar market in programs for personal computers. One estimate is that the industry loses 30% of its revenue to pirating.

Some PC companies such as Tandy attempted and quickly dropped copy-protection codes. Scripsit, its popular word processing program, was first marketed with a program that prevented users from making more than two electronic copies. Yet the code was easily broken. Tandy also found that copy-protection codes annoy legitimate users, many of whom make several backup copies of software they purchase in case the original becomes damaged or worn out.

IBM and Apple Computer say they rarely use copy-protection codes on their software, and when they do it is only at the insistence of the company or individual who developed the program. "There are bootleg copies all over," concedes Apple's manager of applications software. "We know that the protection is just a Band-Aid."

Software makers are battling two kinds of code-breakers: the computer buff who makes a copy for a friend and the merchant who runs a mail-order business from his basement and sells thousands of illegal copies at prices substantially below retail. They readily acknowledge that they can do little to stop users who trade copies of programs informally, but they have tried to bring pressure on some computer-user groups that allow trading of copied programs. They are also cracking down on school districts that purchase one copy of an educational program and make reproductions for member schools.

One of the protection steps is placing serial numbers on the software, refusing to offer help to any user who cannot identify his number and where he purchased the program. Also a good policy for keeping ahead of pirates is regularly releasing improved versions of the software in the product list.

Hardware/software protection schemes are also feasible, embossing a computer program with the machine's serial number the first time the program is used. The computer user could make legitimate copies for his or her own use, but they would not work on a machine that bears a different serial number or some other specified characteristics.

Horizontal software firms sometimes employ a printed circuit board in conjunction with the software they sell on diskette; the latter would not work without the former. Telesoftware programs sold through Videotex incorporate a counter mechanism that would automatically destroy the routine after, say, 10 uses. They price their wares on a 10 times run basis, after which they will have to be purchased again. This has been employed with relatively simple programs.

A far better protection is, of course, casting the software into silicon so that it can be supported by patents. Solid state software offers numerous other advantages such as the lack of ability to tamper with the routines and a much faster execution by the computer on which it runs. This will eventually make it the way for answering the horizontal and some of the vertical software requirements of the end user.

Finally, in connection with myriaprocessors the subject of software licensing for PC groups must be faced. PC groups may

- start with, say five WS on the LAN and end with twenty more

- start with one LAN and then proceed with several identical copies.

Most of the PC software sold today is projected and priced for standalone machines. Experience with myriaprocessor pricing is still thin, and so pricing will be most likely the means for policing the number of workstations on a LAN.

One approach, particularly for horizontal software, would be to have the LAN vendor collect the fees. He is the nearest to the myriaprocessor implementation; such a solution also allows a unified maintenance. Another possibility is to price the software usage by threshold of, say, five machines. A PC by PC accounting on a LAN will be an unattainable solution.

5 PROGRAMMING PRACTICES

While the user will be well advised to buy packaged software, it is unavoidable that he or she will also write some of the programs—hopefully only a few and in a decreasing frequency. For this activity it is quite important to install and observe sound programming practice, which is nearly synonymous with implementing a policy radically different from what is usually done today.

At the current state of the art, both programming education and programming practice contain strong biases in the wrong direction. Few courses require analysts and programmers to find and use modules in libraries. As a result, with every mission they tend to start from scratch.

Another deficiency of current policies in software development is that collaboration is strongly discouraged. Analysts and programmers get no permanent shareable file storage on the computer. Lesson: programs are personal. Furthermore, once a project is handed in, it serves no further purpose. Lesson: programs are throwaways.

To reverse these biases, we need to provide ourselves with programming environments embodying these concepts:

- Cooperation
- Save and reuse.

We also need a new policy of instruction that encourages practitioners to

avoid programming from scratch,

construct modules intended for use by others, and

maintain documentation permitting reuse of their own software.

Logic and code reuse are closely associated with efficiency principles. Dividing new program assignments in a way that facilitates code reuse among newly written programs can greatly increase programmer productivity. Even when a program's requirements prevent direct reuse of code from another module, employing the other module's processing logic can result in significant time savings. Various systems such as IBM's ADF (Application Development Facility) capitalize on this principle by reducing coding requirements for logical functions common to many programs.

Most particularly, we must see to it that the rising interest in personal computers does not perpetuate the software problem by encouraging programmers to regard the entire computer as a personal object that seldom interacts with anything else. A critical step in this mission is the implementation of local area networks because of the WS interactivity which they imply.

To better appreciate our professional obligation to change current images for newer and more efficient ones, we can look back to the history of programming. We will then see that current images in software development are deeply rooted in the 1950s. They did not evolute with technology.

1. At first, programs were written in machine code.
2. Then assembly languages arrived.
3. By the mid-to-late 1950s, higher-level languages such as Fortran and Cobol were developed.

But the pressure continued for more abstract ways of stating the procedural steps to be followed by the computer. As a result of this drive, programs were developed able to structure other programs. Report writers are an example. Furthermore, with online systems the idea of providing the program instructions interactively rather than batch took hold. A long list of interactive query products has been introduced to the market.

Table 3 lists a number of design, programming, and interactive end-user tools that are available today. To this could be added the DBMS written for maxi-, mini-, and microcomputers.

The background for packaged software products is both cost reduction and the drive for making the development of software libraries progressively easier. A common limit to the expressiveness and ease of use of programming languages has been our lack of images on how to exploit them in an effective manner. Packages substitute for the need to program the computers; they also provide a way to higher software quality at lesser cost.

Like programming languages, the software packages are tools. Tools by themselves do not, however, make a system. A new philosophy is needed in software development. But we should not forget that programming languages, classical OS, transactional routines, and database management systems are now emerging into an aggregate that intends to be user-friendly and surely leads toward *integrated software* (Chapter 19).

TABLE 3
Design, Programming and Interactive Tools Which Are Available Today

1. Nomad
2. Online English
3. QBE
4. Focus
5. Mantis and T/ASK (Cincom)
6. Easytrieve (Pansophic)
7. ADF and DMS (IBM)
8. Natural (Software A6)
9. Ramis
10. ADRS (an APL Generator)
11. SAS, SPSS (statistical packages)
12. ADI (APL + DB Access)
13. SAS–Graph, Visitrend Plot and others
14. Datatrieve (DEC)
15. Use.It (Sysmode, Paris)
16. Visicalc and the Visi-Clones
17. Minimodel, Target, T-Maker, Microfinesse, FPL, Micro DSS/Finance, Desktop/Plan II
18. IIS (Interactive Inst. System)
19. Logo (for Instructional Approaches); Pilot
20. SQL (Structured Query, IBM)
21. Quest (SQL on Apple II, III Subset)

The integrated software approach will act as a logical bus to which will be attached other logical products. Such a solution will necessarily integrate the operating system that has acted for 20 years as the logical bus of the computer. In turn, this places emphasis on the able selection of an OS to run on the PC.

The best advice is to keep with *commodity OS*. Some commodity OS are the de facto standards in the industry. For instance: CP/M 80 and 86, MS DOS, UNIX, and way down the line USCD Pascal, Pick, Oasis. Most software developments efforts center around the first three OS.

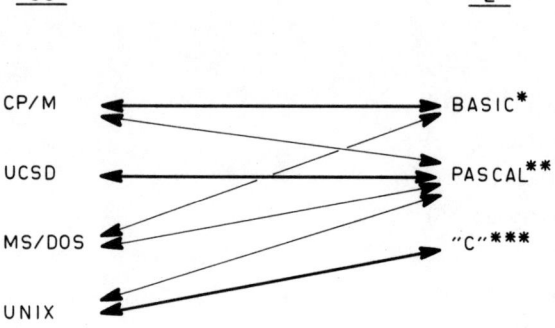

* FOR HOBBY STANDALONE, NON-SOPHISTICATED APPLICATION
** MAIN LANGUAGE FOR PC, LAN AND DIS ENVIRONMENT
*** FAST DEVELOPING AS CHALLENGER TO PASCAL. POWERFUL, PORTABLE.

FIGURE 7-1

Intel realized the CP/M in firmware. Including the Digital Research license, it sells for $90. Intel has also contracted with Digital Research to port Unix System V to the 80286. These considerations are vital as the new generation of PC presents a complete hardware/software package with a database management system, word processing, and a host of other functions.

As Figure 7-1 demonstrates, there is a close correspondence between the choice of a programming language and the OS to be used on a PC. The degrees of freedom available on a LAN allow us to attach devices with different OS, languages, and applications. But there still exist some restrictions particularly related to the way a language/OS looks at file organization on the disc. It is therefore wise to establish a well thought-out policy on this subject.

Finally, the issue of documentation must be given the attention that it deserves. The policy to be established should direct the analysts/programmers to have remark statements at the beginning of the program to identify and describe it. External documentation may be lost, so it is proper that a program contain its own.

Identification statements should contain information on program name, online description of the program, computer for which the program is written, minimum amount of memory (in KB) required to run the program—including also memory needed for variables, language version, OS release, peripherals needed, files used, author, controller, and author's organization.

Other identification data may involve address of author and author's organization, date written, release, special annotations, copyright statement or statement on permission to copy, modifications, author of modification, and date of last modification. Organization-wise, it is advisable to double space the text so that it is easier to read, to limit instructions to three screen pages in length, and to use diagrams whenever possible.

Sound policy with workstations suggests the wisdom of including prompting and reminders throughout the program. For example, if the user is to enter a given operation, the program might remind him to enter two numbers separated by a hyphen. If the user proceeds through menu selection, the program may advise him how to turn back a page or do browsing.

8

ORGANIZING FOR EFFICIENT SOFTWARE

1 INTRODUCTION

The Japanese have proved themselves master manufacturers of cars, cameras, and computers. But that seems to be only the beginning. It is time to discard the myth that the Japanese are good at producing hardware but out of their depth in software.

A massive amount of software is now being developed by Japanese hardware manufacturers and software vendors as part of the Third Five Year Plan in Information Systems (IS). The quality of this software is, for the moment, of secondary importance; its merits or demerits are of little consequence, compared with the efficiency of the techniques that may be deployed to produce its successors. The important fact is that the same dedicated logic is being applied to the processes of software production that has enabled Nissan to achieve six times the output of British Leyland with only half the work force.

Japan reaches an aggressive position in the software industry through a coordinated national effort that is evident in a consistent pattern of work. The top priority of this group effort is to establish an efficient method of development, not a superior product per se. That paves the way for superior products.

The industrialization of software production comes as an absolute necessity at a time when the economics of computing have turned around: the total costs for an application is rising because of the cost of personnel. By 1990, a programmer's annual salary will equal the cost of a computer with the power of an IBM 3033.

There are other aspects to be considered. Marketing is the key to the success of any company in a competitive business environment; this is especially true for the computer industry. Not unexpectedly, a fair proportion of the success of personal computers is due to superior marketing skills. Apple, Tandy, and Commodore positioned themselves in the marketplace with the image of being the product to own if one is going to own a personal computer; this results from the status associated with the way they promoted their product. Most importantly, though, and of greater lasting value, is the emphasis on the part of the company's management regarding the development of software for use with the available product line.

2 ATTENTION TO THE FUNDAMENTALS

Software and not hardware will be the business opportunity but it will also be the limiting factor of this decade. It is therefore understandable that we talk of paying attention to the fundamentals: to the salient issues toward which we must focus our efforts.

But software, particularly applications software, is not being made in a vacuum. It is built to answer user needs. Which are the broader areas to whose requirements we must respond through information system implementation? They divide into three main classes:

- Top Management Decision Making
- Middle Management Allocation/Optimization, and
- Operational Control of day-to-day activities.

Top management decision making has largely to do with strategic planning. Long term in nature, it rests on unstructured problems and requirements. Each issue faced by top management tends to be different. The common thread is the process of identifying objectives, creating the resources needed to attain those objectives, and establishing the policies to govern the product, prices, and financial and human assets of the organization.

Middle management assures the effective deployment of the available resources. Semistructured, it focuses on a monthly or annual timespan. Its operating horizon is cyclic and one of its basic prerequisites is the observance of the actual vs. budget standards.

Day to day, operational direction and control carries out specific tasks in the best possible way. But because these tasks are predefined, operations are structured and repetitious, with different information requirements as the result.

Design-wise, the functional requirements are different at each level, but the underlying system structure need not be. This is just as valid of the physical gear as of the basic logical supports: the OS, DBMS, and datacomm software. Let's always recall that the AP integrates between these information systems resources and the end user. We will return to this issue.

Besides cutting across organizational lines, information systems must be considered generic for another reason: their cost. Data resources often exceed the cost of people and material associated with them, and they have a tendency to grow with time.

Does anyone really know how much it will cost to sustain information resources over the next year? Three, 5, 10 years ahead? Many financial and industrial organizations today try to bring some sense on future cost determinations based on manpower, product, and service cost trends. But the awareness of this need is rather recent.

To be efficient in this effort, an organization has to provide the needed understructure. A key issue is to give information the status that it deserves: consider it a basic resource of business. Technology has been instrumental in all that. Control of data is now more feasible, and lack of it may oblige a company to close doors.

Since it is a resource, information must be managed as one. That means planning, measurement, and control for the near and the longer term along with the ability to measure variations from plan.

Able resource management rests on basic premises. One of them is flexibility. How quickly, how easily can the information system be reconfigured if necessary? Can the applications perspectives be changed locally by use area or must they also be altered system-wide?

Implementing the change at all levels not only costs extra time, trouble, and money, it also increases the chance of error resulting from misunderstood instructions. This often reaches unacceptable proportions and violates the principle that we should always look for a system that is easy to comprehend, adjust, and operate.

Design-wise, of all components the user interface is the most delicate. Often a system fails because it is thrown upon end users who have no idea what is going on at particular locations, or because the designer of the network was not sufficiently aware of the needs of all those involved with the new system.

Thus the levels of experience of those who will use the information system should be determined. Are they already familiar with equipment such as terminals, or are we just replacing a manual system without caring for the results? Talking directly to those who will be using computers and communications will help keep them from seeing it as a threat. Whether users will like the new system or be alienated from it greatly depends on this approach.

Years of experience with online systems help demonstrate that we can deploy resources more effectively if we establish a pay-as-you-go implementation. To do so, user cooperation must be established, a valid timetable worked out, and basic faculties supported and product promises kept.

Since information is a resource, it must be managed effectively. This means tools able to do cost tracking, follow schedules, handle coming events, provide time reminders, and so on. One of the key housekeeping means should be an interactive statistics package able to handle a variety of administrative applications with simple graphical output.

In an interactive system, for instance, it is quite important to know how the use of the computer messaging facility increases over time. An example from such statistics is given in Figure 8-1. Users start by sending an average of three messages a day. The 50th week saw an average of thirty-four messages a day per user.

By the end of the first year, the system had stabilized. Memos, letters, and one-way telephone calls were converted to electronic mail, with messages ranging from a few words to a page long—some 30 words on the average. A statistically documented growth implied the need for system expansion. The key phrase became *control and service.*

Like the preceding references, this one stresses the user-oriented implementation. Let's recapitulate: If we are going to develop a releasable product, we should plan the support tools and requirements from the beginning. To effectively support the system, we must use the same tools during development as in the subsequent upkeep. These means should be computer based.

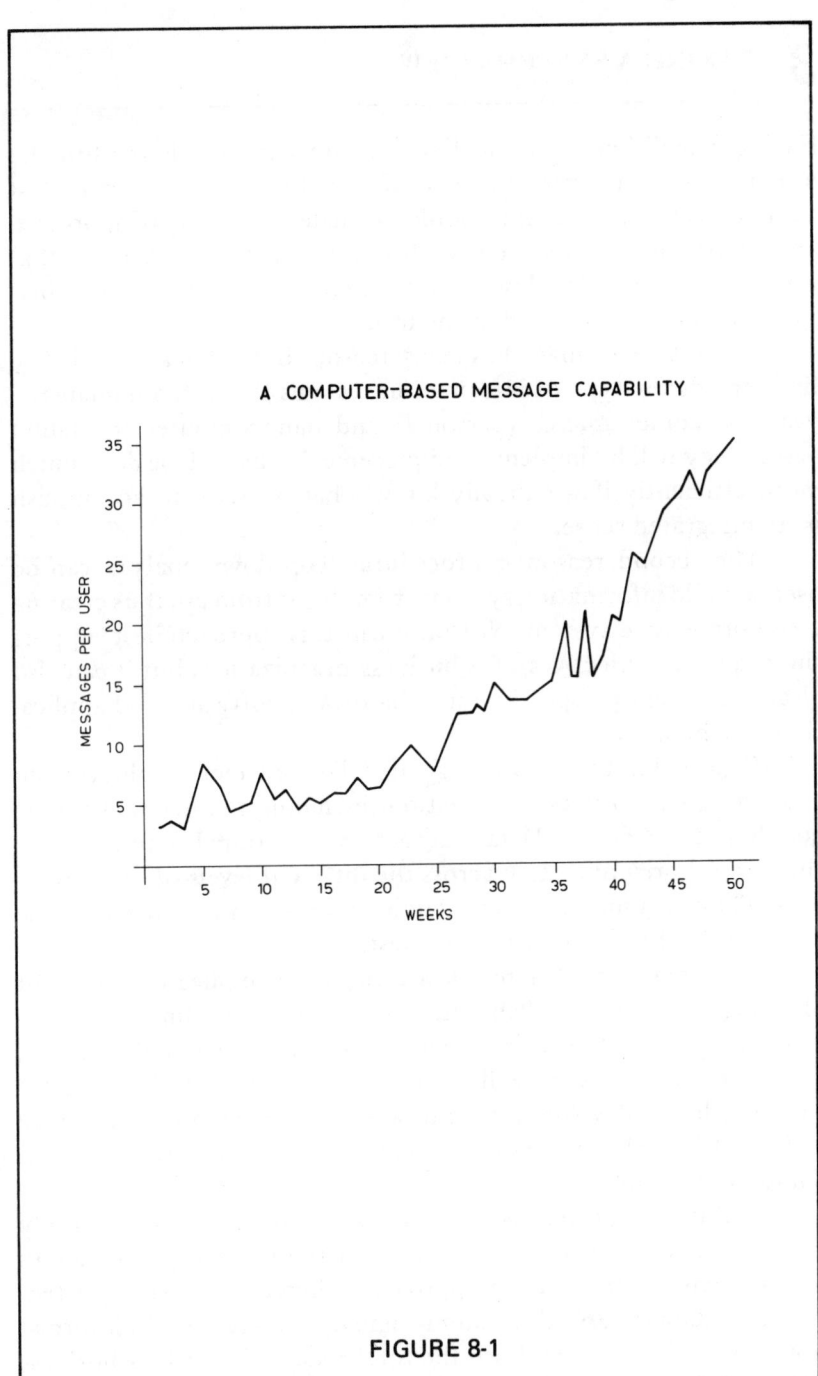

FIGURE 8-1

3 TAKING A SYSTEMS VIEW

Having established that the first fundamental step is the broader orientation perspective and right after it the effective user-analyst communication, a decision should be made on the way of approaching the problem in a system analysis sense. A basic premise is that we can better develop lower-level systems if we have the right perspective of what is needed at the top.

The reference made has many reasons in the background. The first regards the type of information systems that will dominate the years to come: micro- (personal) and nanocomputer (portable) based, they will be implemented piecemeal. This will be done much more efficiently if we already know what we wish to accomplish in an integrated sense.

The second reason is procedural. Top down analysis can be used to build information systems from the bottom up, thus creating a comprehensive system. Not only can this approach best support the goals and objectives of a business organization, but it can also clear the design perspectives in a hardware, software, and applications oriented sense.

Figure 8-2 presents a suggested layered methodology from strategic goals to database creation, including the necessary data-handling procedures. Data cut across functional lines, passing through a horizontal flow across the different levels of doing business. They accumulate in the database and then become available to all levels of management at request.

The adoption of a top-down approach implies management planning and expert collaboration in defining, funding, and managing the project. Once again, when this is done in an able manner, the bottom-up sequence will mean implementation, the package of tools needed to develop, integrate, and maintain computer software and to keep aligned with changing business requirements and computer technology.

In this sense, top-down and bottom-up dimensions are closely tied to one another, each depending on the other to ensure an integrated environment. Both approaches, however, must pay attention to databases and datacomm—being, by consequence information driven. Focusing on both the total perspective and the business unit, an information-driven system must be done within the context

Organizing for Efficient Software

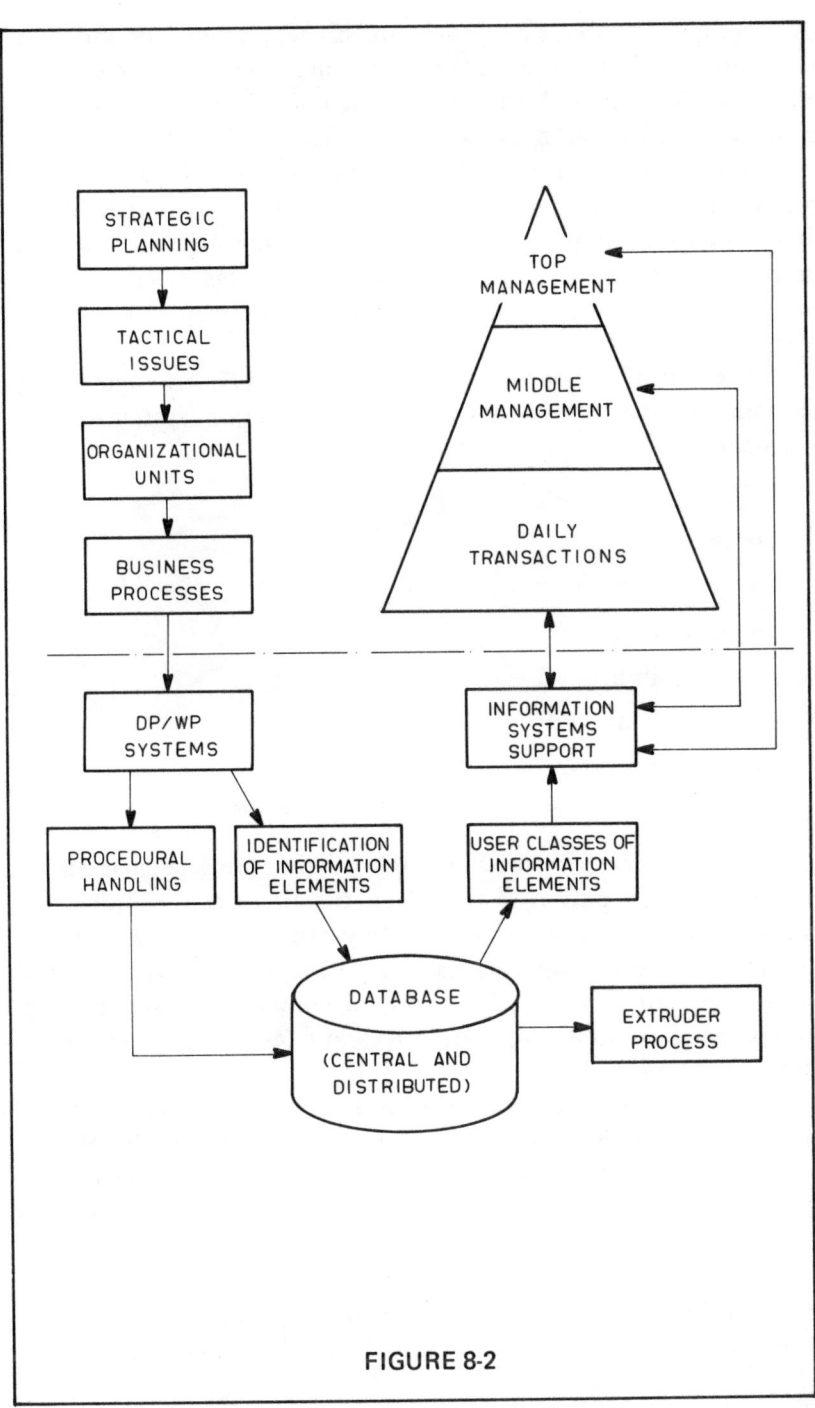

FIGURE 8-2

of a complete systems approach. In this way computer and communications will be consistent with the management logic used for planning and control. Furthermore, alignment between automation strategies and capital investments is crucial.

Important systems concepts must be underlined. One of them regards the *common data.* Databases are meant to be shared, so they should not contain private data, that is, information with only one user. These can be stored on standalone microcomputers and used for private purposes, communicating when necessary with the database.

The next vital issue is logical dependability. Users come to rely on common data. This will happen if and when the system specialists assure

- quality,
- consistency,
- accuracy,
- accessibility,
- availability, and
- completeness.

Still another critical issue is the programming language to be chosen. Though packages should be the first basic option—it is estimated that by 1985 approximately 80% of all software package sales will be for applications—some programming will still need to be done. In this case, it is wise to employ programming languages that insulate the operating system from problems in the applications software.

Applications at the workstation level will be increasingly implemented through personal computers and local networks. Hence, precautions must be taken. If one user tries applications software that totally blows up, none of the other users in the system should be affected.

The choice of languages is evidently critical. Spreading like brushfire in small sites, Pascal is surprisingly strong in large sites, although it is presently used in less than 2% of them. Low as this

Organizing for Efficient Software 135

percentage may be, it compares favorably to IBM's PL/1 which after 15 years of hard sales is only used in 8.4% of large sites and only 2.1% of small ones.

Planning premises should take into account the speed and elegance with which new programming languages can work on personal computers. The following cost data reflect software development and concern a classical billing type program necessary to a certain firm because of equipment change:

Custom-made program on mini: $30,000

Package on micro: $700

Same custom-made program on micro: $6,500

Cost of HW for the micro: $3,500

The savings are impressive, but costs however vital only tell part of the story. Successful implementation requires that responsibility is identified from design through coding, text, documentation, and maintenance. The same is valid of the needed full feedback in the development process assuring user participation and comprehension.

After the top-down organization is done and agreed by all concerned, AP development tasks must be broken into independent units for concurrent implementation. Integration reviews assure that these developments play together, and that both management and the analysts see clearly the progress of the overall project.

Productivity requires timetables; it also calls for identification and construction of new tools to aid the development process. Able solutions also must be provided to the bottleneck caused by insufficient programming talent and lack of turnkey software.

Applications software strategies must be elaborated to meet the needs in key areas such as

standards,

databases,

interactive processing,

operations recovery,

performance optimization,

network interconnection,

man/machine interaction,

program portability,

hardware compatibility through communications solutions.

During the last 20 years, these issues have been steadily downplayed, partly because of misinformation and partly because of fear. Many computer system personnel and their managers live in fear of the technology passing them by. As a result, a good deal of them have already fallen behind. To keep up requires steady training that many organizations are unable or unwilling to provide.

There are many reasons in the background of falling behind the profession. One of them is lack of information on the latest developments and on alternative means and possibilities for doing the systems business. Another is habitual thinking and resistance to change.

Traditionally, resistance to change adds up to being a major cost factor. When "time honored" methods and approaches are followed, lower efficiency is almost always the result. Another reason for falling behind is the line of thinking that "my problem is unique." It leads to generally negative attitudes toward challenge of the future.

The references we just made identify a kind of thinking that is defensive in its essence and most often leads to a source of trouble. Reluctance to seek advice and getting the wrong advice are other common pitfalls contributing to higher costs and lower efficiency.

Rather than trying one's hand at stopping progress, which is a hopeless enterprise, it is much wiser to join it. As a research project demonstrated quite recently, stopping the natural development technology makes possible is also the wrong personal policy. Many American DP managers are being let go or forced into early retirement because the systems they manage no longer serve the strategic plans of their employers.

For the coming years management is after a solution that can bring computer power to every workstation. This means directly to the user level and is, as such, a deviation from policies of the past. This very reference has another aspect: the business opportunity of companies concentrating on personal computer software.

4   GROWING SOFTWARE ENDOWMENT

Software has always been a key component in the sale of computer hardware. This is essentially true in the personal computer marketplace: a number of systems are available among which a user can buy off-the-shelf for an outlay of a few thousand dollars. Under these conditions software makes the difference.

The successful companies in the industry, such as Tandy and Apple, got an early lead in market share and have since expanded that lead by the reinvestment of profits into the development of software packages. Additionally, because of the large population of their machines in the field, most independent software producers have first developed their software products for the more popular machines.

At this point in time, especially when taken in the light of the entrance into the market of new competitors, the software lead enjoyed by the front runners in the personal computer market grows with each passing day. Furthermore, software portability has become an important issue in the personal computer industry. Many feel that given

> standard operating systems, such as CPM and UNIX,
>
> the de facto standard of the S-100 bus, and
>
> the Z-80 microprocessor base

it is possible to benefit from the growing software endowment characterizing the earlier and more successful personal computer systems.

This brings up another point in regard to the purchase of personal computers. First-time users are generally novices relative to the computer gear. How do they go about buying the product? Generally speaking, prospective users look to associates who have these systems for advice on what hardware and software to purchase. Under these circumstances, the new user is likely to purchase the product that exists in the office of an associate and is equipped with a valid software endowment.

This reference is just as valid for the smaller as for the bigger outfits. Many FORTUNE 1000 companies have data-processing departments which are beginning to establish requirements that permit only one or at most two kinds of hardware—so that management, updating, and communications can be easily done. In addition, these DP departments wish to provide support services for personal computers at a minimum of cost.

Furthermore, once users have learned all the commands for Apple Visicalc, Apple Writer III, or Apple PFS database management system, for example, then they will probably not want to relearn each of these application packages for the different systems when, in years to come, they buy their next generation of hardware. In other words, there is a sort of systems lock-in for PC companies as far as future purchases are concerned, be they first-time users or second-generation buyers. And the difference is due to the early applications support.

Let's repeat this last reference. Products are successful because they satisfy the needs of the people who buy them. The more people with needs satisfied by a given product, the larger this product's market will be.

But computer-based products and services can be useless without applications software. That's why the manufacturer and the user are partners in this last count. They should both be highly interested in software development and in the machine's endowment resulting from it.

Before trying to sell a computer product, the manufacturer will be well advised to list all the possible needs or desires it might fill at the user side. Then comes the search for customers who believe they have these needs. Hardware sells software, and this can be much more efficiently done if every care is taken around the software product. Implicitly, this means

- the observance of standards
- quality acceptance tests
- diagnostics and maintenance, and
- a complete documentation.

Readily packaged applications software will determine the difference between micro- and picocomputers that sell well and those that fall behind and disappear. Whatever the application, the purchase decision is even now heavily impacted by the proliferation of AP that tie into it and can answer requirements.

Along with file management schemes, questions of access and data security may one day predominate. But the overriding demand is different. It centers on down-to-earth programs that help keep costs low and answer basic applications requirements, thus enlarging the use perspectives.

New companies try to fill this need and in the process develop better mousetraps than the computer industry ever had. *Personal Software* is a San Jose, California, firm that became well known because of Visicalc and the "Visi" series which followed it. Visicalc was introduced in June 1979 with a price tag of $100, the following January the price was increased to $150, and in March 1981 an enhanced version came out at $200. By the end of 1981, some 200,000 Visicalc programs had been sold—more than most other computer programs so far.

The product was conceived by a Harvard student, Dan Bricklin, who approached his professor with the idea, but the faculty is said to have been unimpressed. To provide a second opinion, the professor called in an upperclassman named Dan Fylstra, who thought it was a great idea. Credit for the implementation goes to Bob Frankston, in charge of sales and merchandising for Fylstra's company, *Personal Software*.

When the company moved to California in mid 1979—there were five employees, including the two cofounders and their wives. Now there are more than 110. *Personal Software* had revenues of less than $4 million in 1980. They grew to nearly $20 million in 1981.

Personal Software now produces Visicalc, Visiplot, Visitrend/Visiplot, Visiterm, Visidex, Desktop/Plan II, Visifile, and Visipack—which for the price of $710 offers Visicalc, Visifile, and Visitrend/Visiplot all in one package. In an easy to use, friendly manner, the packages support

forecasting and projecting

planning

analysing

computing

exploring alternatives

preparing graphs and charts

perceiving complex business interactions

following business trends

communicating over networks

accessing databases

performing a host of DP functions.

Just as successful is a similar firm, *Digital Research* of Pacific Grove, California. It was started by Gary Kildall, a consultant to Intel Corp. who developed an operating system to run under the Intel 8080 microprocessor chip. When Kildall attempted to get Intel interested in this product, they turned him down, so he decided to sell it himself to hobbyists.

That product, CP/M, is now said to be running on 300,000 microcomputers. The company has some 80 employees and is anticipating revenues in 1982 of $20 million, three times that of 1981. Most importantly, CP/M became a microcomputer industry standard, with a number of other software companies growing around it.

A number of Independent Software Vendors (ISV) currently participate in the ISV Support Plan of *Digital Research:* These estimated 500 firms geographically range from coast to coast in the United States, to London and Tokyo, and each writes CP/M compatible software. *Digital Research* also produces:

CP/NET, a logical network operating system

MP/M II, a multi-user OS

CP/M-86, a 16-bit micro OS

PL/1-80 applications programming language

MAC macroassembler

TEX text formatter

SID and ZSID symbolic instruction debuggers

DESPOOL background print utility

BT-80 record retrieval system.

In turn, the ISV vendors provide ready applications programs such as data entry, order entry, job estimating, invoicing, sales ledger, purchase ledger, payroll, job costing, stock control, work in progress, retail inventory, accounts payable, debtors and creditors master files, financial projections and budgeting, and fund accounting. They also provide service rountines such as communications packages, 3780/2780 emulators, data dictionaries, screen editors, and tool programs for software development.

Another significant reference is *Micro Database Systems* of Lafayette, Indiana. It specializes in the development of DBMS software for personal computers. Its MDBS is a network-oriented DBMS featuring variable length records, multiple levels of read/write protection, and recursive ownership. It handles 254 record types.

Optional features are also offered with MDBS. For instance: Dynamic Restructuring System (DRS); Query/Report Writer System (QRS); and Recovery Transaction Logic (RTL). The HDBS is a subset of MDBS supporting hierarchical data structures. Both MDBS and HDBS are available for most Z-80, 8080 and 8086 based microcomputers and CP/M, MP/M compatible OS.

Though CP/M appeals particularly to the 8-bit PC, Digital Research has been diversifying its product line as demonstrated by its 1984 agreement with AT&T to develop application software for Unix.

A fourth example is *Microcomputer Products* of San Jose, California, a manufacturer of broad-level products for the S-100 and Apple II computer. It recently entered the software market with the Transend communications software packages for the Apple II.

Another case of a successful PC software company is *MicroPro International* of San Rafael, California. It makes the WordStar word processing program for microcomputers. Unlike *Personal Software* (Visicorp) and *Digital Research, MicroPro* is also into hardware, having recently formed a division to produce single- and multi-user micros for commercial applications: the PBM-1000.

5 THE MICROSOFTWARE INDUSTRY

The foregoing discussion spells out the reasons companies specializing in microcomputer software are in for a good future. The explosive growth in personal computers and the entry into the marketplace of IBM, DEC, and Xerox has persuaded venture capitalists to take another look at the tiny firms that write the application software programs. Lured by optimistic predictions of an annual market for microcomputer software of about $2 billion by 1985 and soaring to $25 billion by 1990, venture companies are investing in the potentially high-growth firms of this industry. This is a comparatively early stage in a growth area. Aftertax profit margins for microcomputer software companies seem to average 16%, roughly double that for hardware vendors.

Investments in the software business are further leveraged because these companies require significantly less capital than hardware makers, which need considerable amounts of investment money to build manufacturing plants. Most deals so far have been for less than $1 million in venture funding. A software house needs only one third as much investment capital as a hardware company to reach the same dollar level of sales. The software companies may also be better positioned with respect to Japanese competition.

While most microcomputer makers are looking over their shoulders for an expected wave of low cost/high potential products from the Far East, software companies are more confident. But the picture may change if the Japanese thrust ahead with high-productivity solutions in software, as stated in the introduction.

Still looking at the facts as they stand today, one cannot but be puzzled that the small to very small microsoftware companies are doing so well while the larger firms—whether users or computer manufacturers—are doing poorly in software. After all, it is hard for all companies to produce on schedule, within budget, and without flaws and bugs. All are exposed to a practice of "piracy," stemming from the ease with which computer software can be used to copy one of its own programs in less than 4 minutes. Why should the risk be bearable for the small firm, not so for the bigger one? At the current state of the art, one might think that productivity would be about the same everywhere. But it is not so.

Let's examine the facts one by one, starting with the ingenuity of the analysts. In the small software joint the analyst is also the entrepreneur. He projects the application and does the analysis and the programming. He is motivated; he is also typically a young man who has not been exposed to the bureaucracy and the "do nothing" attitude of a large organization.

All this is instrumental in shaping the way that the individual looks at the job, the approaches followed, and the results obtained. Furthermore, he has a self-imposed freedom to fail. Most microsoftware entrepreneurs started working in their living room, just like the earlier personal computers were developed as a part-time assignment in a garage.

This is atypical of the large organization where the constraints are legion and where conformity usually kills imagination. The larger organizations, whether computer manufacturers or users, have had mainframe experience; and that has a very bad influence both on software productivity and on the things the microsoftware can and cannot do.

There is of course the possibility to overcome some of the constraints of the larger firm with microsoftware developments. This may not assure the best of both worlds, but it is a valid approach which has been adopted by IBM. Looking into its developing lower end of the line, IBM is designing itself the basic tree structure: the main body of software support. Then it farms out to software houses and other willing parties (such as its own employees) the branches of the tree and the ornaments to put on the branches.

The hinge here is that if the software development is orderly and goes according to the systems plan, IBM may market it and pay royalties to the developer. This does not leave much room for brilliant ideas by the independent microsoftware firms, but in exchange it protects IBM's ability to manage the software development base. If I had the possibility to choose among the two alternatives, I would have taken the freedom to be imaginative. IBM surely has its reasons for following the structured approach.

IBM is not the only firm engaging in what might be considered "joint software venture." Other firms explicitly recognize that, with computer makers selling to large numbers of smaller and less experienced customers, the availability of ready-to-run software is often more important in making a sale than the computer itself.

Even the larger concerns whose personnel are pinned down with software maintenance costs are looking for vendors able to provide applications software. Therefore, it does not come as a surprise that computer manufacturers are rushing to cultivate partnerships with third-party software houses that write applications programs, even setting up joint marketing arrangements with independent software companies.

The belief among mainframers and mini- and micro- manufacturers is spreading that, as the industry moves to smaller customers, it has to provide a total systems solution, not just a computer. This is a key strategy if a company wishes to be successful over the next 3 to 5 years.

In this sense, the makers of large mainframes and minicomputers are following the lead of the personal computer manufacturers, collaborating with outside suppliers. This way they can expand their product offerings more quickly and economically than they could on their own. This finally confirms the policy of key users: "It makes more sense to buy a good package than to spend time to build one."

Already an estimated 20% of the 500 programs in IBM's small computer software portfolio are written by outsiders, and the company is considering the use of outside software suppliers for its larger machines. Besides helping manufacturers sell more hardware, the new partnerships are also providing the computer makers with a new profit stream: They keep anywhere from 15% to 95% of the sale price of the software, with the rest going to the software house.

Though such deals reduce their profit margins, the software houses welcome the joint ventures. The nationwide sales forces of the hardware manufacturers help them reach new markets that they could not afford to penetrate. And there are other incentives too.

Hewlett-Packard, for example, offers a 28% discount on computers bought for software development, and it trains the software company's staff on the intricacies of its machines for half price. Other computer makers add business advice, mapping out a business and marketing plan that a small software company would have to spend thousands to develop. Such policy makes sense for the immediate future, but for the longer term a far-looking strategy must be developed. The key issues range from software product planning to design, manufacturing, and sales.

As more software is sold jointly, both hardware and software vendors could face problems of conflict of interest. To prevent this from happening, IBM will not consider programs that duplicate its own. And while computer makers sell the alien software under their own name, once it is installed they leave its support up to the software company that created it.

Quality control being a major issue, hardware vendors are hoping to prevent problems by checking the software thoroughly before marketing it. They establish criteria for accepting programs and a level of quality they want to maintain.

Part of this strategy is not to slacken but to increase the pace on internal software development. Hewlett-Packard aquired two software companies to gain additional in-house expertise. Yet the computer makers do recognize that they can not cover all industry applications. Without joint ventures they would need to buy dozens of companies to offer customers the necessary spectrum of packages.

Equally appreciated by the manufacturers is the fact that the smaller applications-programming companies are very focused. That is why they are so successful. As a result, partnerships appear certain to become a big part of the computer business. Over the next few years, Burroughs expects 50% of its small computer sales to be generated by the software discovered in its applications exchange program.

6 PROTECTING PROPRIETARY SOFTWARE

In terms of ways and means for protecting the microsoftware, two solutions come to mind:

1. A microprocessor-based board to be inserted in one of the slots.
2. A self-destructive algorithm included in the software.

The first alternative is used effectively in some cases, as for instance with the KRAM micro-DBMS of U.S.A. (New York City). This has two evident advantages: First, by "firmwarizing" part of the software, it makes its execution faster. Second, since hardware is patentable and the balance of the software cannot do without it, protection seems assured.

There are two drawbacks with this approach. One has to do with the number of slots in the microcomputer. As we will see in the proper chapter, slot availability risks becoming a critical issue. The other is the fact that it's always possible to overcome a barrier. Busybodies seem to have been able to copy the KRAM micro-DBMS, bypassing the firmware.

We said that there is another method for approaching the software protection problem. It has been tried with the telesoftware marketed by Prestel (the Interactive Videotex system) in England. It consists of incorporating a counter into the leased software so that when it has been used, say, 5 times, it destroys the program. Typically, telesoftware concerns small programs; hence this approach has not been widely experimented.

A combination of the two solutions will also seem to make sense. For instance, the incorporation of an algorithm able to destroy the program if an attempt is made to copy it or to use it without the firmware board. This may even enable a two tier pricing: one for one machine usage only, with self-destruction characteristics; the other at a much higher price for multiple use.

Solutions must be properly thought out and their aftermaths examined since software is the microcomputer's most crucial component. The range of software support must be the object of a careful study. Choice may, for instance, include CP/M (control program for minicomputers) as the OS and excellent applications libraries, including games. Let's never forget that over 60% of microcomputers sold play games also.

Clearly enough, these subjects interest both the computer manufacturer and the user. While software and hardware are the moving gears of an information system, return on investment (ROI) can only be justified through proved and properly documented improvements in the quality of information. Experimental and practical results will be a welcome substitute for the vague and often destructive "armchair evidence."

It is nevertheless quite surprising that factual presentations are the hardest to obtain. They do require intellectual effort. This happens in spite of the evidence that, with the development of distributed information systems (DIS), in 95% of all cases applications packages make the difference in ROI.

The same is true of easy portability through planned media compatibility both from the human engineering perspective and in the sense of a hardware/software reference. Due attention must also be paid to product evolution. Good application-oriented systems are usually designed for a specific user group.

9

SYSTEM ANALYSIS FOR MYRIAPROCESSORS

1 INTRODUCTION

The implementation of PC and LAN solutions in a financial, business, or industrial environment calls for a significant amount of attention to systems engineering. Not only are the technologies involved new, but we must also be providing a deeper analysis and wider use of text and data capabilities. This is particularly true as

- office automation and telecommunications proliferate,
- microcomputers present possibilities we never had before,
- database access becomes a critical design reference,
- a new concept, information resource management, struggles to life
- the literacy about information management becomes as vital in organizations as literacy about personnel and financial management.

Coordination is of utmost importance. We cannot have office automation in one department and MIS in another. We also must look after the elimination of information redundancy through the appropriate System Analysis (SA), providing applications the user can agree on—thus opening up a possibility for successful implementation.

Information architecture assures a common conceptual framework for communications. A key aspect of the architecture must be its ability to deliver information to those who need it, when they need it. There are two parts to this:

1. We have to be sure to maintain control over the database and ensure its integrity.

2. We have to provide user-friendly ad hoc query and report generators, as well as modeling packages.

To these two issues relate technical questions to be answered by the systems analysis: Does it make sense to attach more than one database server to a single LAN? If the objective is simply to add capacity or increase reliability, this might be accomplished by putting two discs on the database server so that they can be shared or switched among them. But first this must be supported by the LAN architecture, and second the need must be established by the SA.

System engineering for myriaprocessors gets more interesting when the LAN includes a gateway: the communications server allows nodes in the LAN to link with computers or terminals that are external to the LAN as well as to other LAN. The responsibility of the system analyst is to account for these external links and translate messages between the LAN protocol and the protocols native to the remote hosts or networks.

A great deal of systems work also has to be done in terms of bringing the end user into the picture. We either put the user-friendly capabilities in place or we take the chance that uncontrolled computers will proliferate in an uncontrolled manner and at the same time the applications perspective will become more tangled than ever before.

2 COST TRENDS IN HARDWARE/SOFTWARE

It is common knowledge that hardware prices have been dropping for the best part of the last 2 decades, that in recent years this trend has accelerated, and that increased density per chip is mainly responsible for this trend. This has been feasible not only because of very high level integration at the design stage but also because the manufacturing technology has made giant steps toward process automation.

Without advances in manufacturing automation and robotics we would not have obtained such favorable results in price cutting nor would we have generated the enthusiasm about the advanced solution the PC can offer at the workstation level. At the same time, however, we can observe that the growth curve in semiconductor integration is bending, *as if* we are approaching an asymptote somewhere above the 1 megabit per chip level (which was announced by Japanese manufacturers in San Francisco, in February 1984).

Such an asymptote is not yet seen at the applications side, and for the time being the greatest enthusiasm is reserved for the hot area of office management costs:

- About 80% of U.S. executives think it likely that their companies will invest in devices to cut essentially white-collar labor costs.
- Some 76% like investments in labor-saving equipment on the factory floor.
- 71% believe investments in labor-saving devices affecting sales and clerical functions are coming.

These three areas identify where the greatest interest lies in terms of system studies, but to be successful these studies should be conducted with the proper methodology. A proper methodology implies standards. Good standards have the effect of increasing the analyst's productivity. They reflect the result of calculated judgment concerning their impact on efficiency. They tend to limit bureaucratization of work situations and lead to identifiable purposes and justified rationale.

We are going to look at standards such as project control, design reviews, computer-assisted documentation, and auditing in the following sections. But we should immediately elaborate on one standard: the observance of the principle of Cost/Effectiveness both in terms of hardware and in regard to software implementation.

As already noted, the cost of hardware has gone down to the extent that the PC start having more computational power, central memory, and auxiliary storage than the mainframes that originally executed today's operating systems. However, the fact that the cost of application development continues to go up is often forgotten. It goes up particularly as a proportion of the total data-processing costs.

Let's look first at the hardware side. The critical question is: Are we taking advantage of what technology can offer? Let's compare a myriaprocessor solution to a minicomputer-based small business system. Each has seven workstations on it, a comparable disc storage, and video (softcopy) presentation. But there are also major differences.

The first is in functionality.

The SBS solution provides the end user with nonintelligent workstations. PC and LAN offer microprocessor support at the WS level. The difference can be significant. With the latter we can develop most useful approaches in making the man-information communication user-friendly, as we will see in a case study.

The second is in reliability.

In a myriaprocessor we can easily substitute a PC processor through rollout and rollin of a spare unit, bootstrapping from the disc. To the contrary, if the processor of the SBS fails, the whole system is down and the workstations are no longer operational.
In the LAN case, bootstrapping of the inserted PC is automatically done by the disc. Recovery/restart with the SBS is already a more complex undertaking.

The third is cost.

The cost advantage is clearly at the PC and LAN side. Furthermore, with the LAN the incremental cost of the workstation is about $2,000 while the chosen SBS (small business system) configuration is saturated with 7 terminals. The next one could lead to greater overhead and significant central memory increase—or doubling of the machine. Neither alternative is too attractive.
More significantly, the nature of the LAN allows different applications in each WS on the LAN. Different applications on an SBS of the chosen dimensions will be unthinkable, short of obtaining unacceptably long response times. Minis able to execute two or more applications typically sell at the $150,000 level. In that case the cost comparison to PC and LAN is no longer 1:2.5 but 1:5 or 1:6.

The reference to different applications brings another interesting factor into perspective:

The distance of the WS connection with PC and LAN is greater by order of magnitude as contrasted with the SBS alternative.

This is an issue not to be taken lightly. Backpanel connections with mainframes have traditionally kept below 3 meters and even the connection of central memory (CM) to central processing unit (CPU) and peripherals is not much greater. With minis, the distance between the CPU and the video units stands at the 30 meter level.

On a baseband LAN the minimum supported distance is 300 meters, more typical is 700 meters and with broadband we talk of several kilometers. Apart from the flexibility these greater distances provide in terms of applications, we should never forget that the distances in reference vary by orders of magnitude. Whenever we have an order of magnitude variation we have a totally different system and should engage in totally different systems thinking.

Quite evidently, there are also the software costs to consider. Such costs have been rising since the first program was written; and as a result, easier ways of programming computers have been sought. We will return to this issue when we talk of programming, but it is the proper time to add that the best solution is nonprogrammable machines. The software should be bought in packages—like we buy a manufactured computer rather than making our own.

A commercial software package, particularly a mature one, will often have additional capabilities that other organizations have found useful as their operational needs have evolved. A firm initially acquiring the software package may not be able to use all of these capabilities at once, but they provide an experience-based set of growth options.

As packages become polyvalent to enhance their appeal in the market, they tend to include the organization's operational philosophy and certain implementation issues. But a package should be accepted "as is." Modifying a software package is generally a bigger job than just putting in a few frontend or backend fixes.

Particularly for personal computers and de facto standards in OS, such as CP/M, there is a significant range of software packages available in the market. Just as important is the advent of silicon software with which some PC are now equipped.

Indeed, a good policy toward the end-user is to say:

1. If you find the software *you* want on the micro, we immediately buy the micro for you.

2. If not, first collaborate in establishing the procedural system analysis; see to it that it is fully documented; read it and sign it.

Subsequently, this should become a contract between data processing and user and should be respected in its full extent.

Short of using packaged software, and in appreciation of the fact that at the PC level software can end up costing more than hardware, it is wise to employ one of the developing models for software cost estimation. One model estimates the cost of a proposed software product in the following manner:

- A nominal development effort is projected as a function of the product's size in *delivered* source instructions (in thousands).
- Effort multipliers are determined from the product's ratings, based on cost driver attributes.

The estimated development effort is obtained by multiplying the nominal effort estimate by the product's effort multipliers. Life cycle perspectives must be taken, thus involving analyst/programmer dollar costs, computer costs, test costs, annual maintenance costs, and other cost elements.

Cost drivers are given a rating scale indicating by how much the nominal effort estimate must be multiplied. A project with low tools rating may require 1.25 times the nominal project effort to complete; a project with high tool rating may require on the order of 80% of the nominal project effort. Tools do therefore play a key role. They are computer based and employ data dictionary assistance.

Natural language programming tools will eventually allow a computer user to interact with the machine in English. Such programs should accept as inputs the normal grammatical conventions and respond in accordance with the expectations of the processing job. Natural language will at a later day provide a way of programming a computer while remaining far removed from technical detail.

This will offer the potential to reduce software development and maintenance time. Such solutions, however, are not currently available. The reference to software tools is basically limited to computer-assisted means for easing the analyst's and programmer's job, thus improving quality, increasing productivity, and reducing both development time and software costs.

3 THE SYSTEMS STUDY

A carefully developed systems study will see to it that organizational factors and the technologies interact favorably. This is most important since information costs that were once hidden are becoming more visible. Management is getting excited over these expenditures.

As organizations look at how much is spent on information, in the broad sense of the word, they find that many of the costs are submerged. When clerical and secretarial workers and their equipment are included, DP and telecommunications are only a small part of the total.

After identifying the expenditures, an organization can see where there are advantages to developing structures for managing them—in terms of cost avoidance if not savings. In some cases, the organization will determine where increased spending will bring savings over time.

One leading firm found:

It was spending about 18% of its sales revenues on information;

MIS, DP, and telecommunications came to about a tenth of that total.

But economics is not the only issue. When we propose something in an organization, we are playing with other people's power. Even when we think the executive group will be responsive, we are taking the risks associated with any new approach.

We must have a strategy and we must educate the user group. The concept of managing information as an asset applies across the board. Here the way we approach the systems study is most critical in the subsequent success of the effort.

The purpose of a systems project comes first, followed by criteria and specifications. This leads to design evaluation and project control.

If the beginning of the life cycle should be characterized by feasibility studies, a steady attribute to any subsequent phase of software development should be the design control reviews. Reviews require experience, often considerable experience, in systems analysis and design.

The acceptance testing of a new system before installation is just as critical. Testing is related to skills in quality assurance and in program maintenance. The testing premises should be established at an early design phase and only implemented after the coding statements have been written and compiled.

A similar reference can be made to the specific approaches and tools to be incorporated in system design: for instance, the distribution of databases and the use of a DBMS. In contrast to a long haul network, there is no cost and no response time advantage in multiplying the file servers, since within a LAN it costs just as much and takes just as long to access one node as any other.

Hence, if the requirement for multiple servers is not obvious, then one file server per LAN should be enough. But this must be specified in the systems study. To the contrary, it is important to properly define the microfiles (at the WS level). For instance, a page of a document can be edited at the workstation to minimize network traffic.

Database/gateway coordination serves the critical function of providing the database with the ability to request subsets of central (or distributed) files for local updating and remerging. We can anticipate a need for database subsets among communicating LAN: database subset swapping is an aspect of distributed database management that, together with the existence of directories, constitutes part of a transparently distributed database.

A user or workstation issues a query, and the system is capable of going to any node that has relevant text or data to satisfy the query and formulate an answer for the user. But the technical problems associated with implementing such a system are complex and will take some time to materialize.

Still another integral part of a systems study for myriaprocessors is the decision on database management systems (DBMS). In what ways must the DBMS for a small system go beyond conventional DBMS? The answer can be given by way of solid state solutions. Where such solutions depart from conventional DBMS is in their ability to handle

- files of arbitrary structure,
- streams of text, voice/image encodings,
- extension to the data model through a very flexible pattern-search facility, and
- the means for relating such files within databases.

The silicon DBMS now emerging tend to be relational, connecting records to substrings within a stream-oriented file. The so-defined information elements can be retrieved and manipulated. The ability to relate records to text simplifies the design of a wide variety of applications.

The analyst working in a myriaprocessor environment must become proficient in such areas as these: use of records to represent the modular structure of a manuscript in a word processing system, the unified management of both keyword indexes and text in document retrieval, the ability to merge graphics information with records, the merging of text and data to produce form letters and reports, and the opportunities for enhancing classical processing applications through WS intelligence. The communications capabilities of the myriaprocessor practically force the system designer to think about DP/DB in new ways.

The whole approach to system design is slowly changing. The analyst should now be trained to see, for example, how the end product could allow the user to search for text and data, providing a way to add marginal notations. Furthermore, issues such as security, integrity, and recovery must be taken care of.

Solutions in hardware, software, and systems functionality should evidently make use of the best technology can offer. Choices are sometimes hard to make; but the trend is evident. Dedicated intelligent workstations and a single job per WS is the best choice.

Cost savings, earlier payback, manpower savings, range of capabilities—but also application imcompatibilities, implementation delays, lack of in-house expertise, resistance to improvements and controllability—should be among the key factors to be considered in a system analysis. The software package should be available for service as soon as it is tested. Design, programming, and testing should offer a considerable head start in providing benefits to the user organization.

Poor management can increase software costs more than any other factor. The following mismanagement actions are often responsible for high program development costs: assigning the wrong people to project jobs, bringing large numbers of people onto the project, creating task overlaps, demotivating people through failure to reward good performance, and failure to prepare needed resources and to validate software requirements.

Good management can promote an efficient, well-coordinated software development process and high levels of staff capability. Yet if the responsible managers do not genuinely want improved software productivity, the organization will not get such productivity, no matter which other factors work to its favor.

If the systems analyst is able to do a neat job for the end user, he should also be in a position to help himself. Promoting quality and productivity in system studies emphasizes the principles of management. The fact is that analysts/programmers of equal background or experience will display productivity rates that vary by a significant factor. These variances are attributed to their motivation but also to the tools they are working with. Other things being equal, a computer-based system design project will exhibit greater productivity.

To achieve results, factors relating both to the value of software aids and to managerial philosophy must be analyzed and properly brought into perspective. The same is valid regarding the effort to upgrade systems and programming documentation. The data dictionary provides a central repository for documentation. The availability of an online interrogation facility to retrieve information can maximize the data dictionary's role as repository.

The most vital contribution of the appropriate documentation is at the system design level, where it helps preserve the conceptual integrity of the original design. Interactively available from the development database should be the workbook as well as pages of all documents from the analysis and design phase of the project. Other pages should contain up-to-date copies with annotations, control block listings, screen generations, and so on.

Let's never forget that documentation is a major force for continuity in a project. The appropriate documentation facilities project management and control. While the tools we are describing are intended to enhance the system analyst's supporting functions, we should not lose sight of basic goal of the project: to answer the user's requirements.

4 EVALUATING THE APPLICATION

Decision support systems are a philosophy, not a product than can be bought off the shelf. The same is true of any application to which we put computers and communications.

If we really wish to do neat systems studies, both the users and the analyst should change the image they have of the current applications environment. Such images can be quite obsolete even if they date 20 years back, and some go all the way into the last century. Three examples from the office are the typewriter, the telephone and the vertical file:

> The typewriter was first mass produced in quantity in the 1870s. It became a visible fixture in offices within 20 years— that is before the end of last century. Today, typewriters are still being used as in 1890.

> Direct dialing telephones in switched local networks became available in 1899. Although improvements have been made in the service only now are voice communications really changing (voice mail, picturephone, store and forward, and the like).

> The vertical file was first introduced to the business world at the 1893 Chicago World's Fair. It has not been widely adopted until the first two decades of this century; but even so, it is 90 years old and largely unchanged.

Speaking in the most absolute manner, we should *not* use microcomputer technology to copy in the worst possible way old processes, as we did with the mainframes. We should instead orient our attention to innovative applications. The use of the PC as a marketing tool is a good example.

Over a month's time in 1982, a PC was installed in a 50-people firm for accounting purposes, but management immediately saw its potential in marketing. Prior to this implementation, each salesperson was making 35 to 40 introductory calls per week, without prior appointment or introduction. On the average, only one prospect per week turned into real customers.

A marketing package on the PC made a radical change in approach feasible. Material about the firm is now mailed to prospective customers, and follow-up phone calls are made to set up appointments. This allows the salesperson to avoid sitting in an office waiting to see a prospective client, and helps the quality of the sales call. In this case it cut down on wasted time by two thirds, and brought the average client acquisition from 1:40 to 1:8. The computer's contribution is that it permits describing each prospect in user-defined codes, following up on them. Visits are recorded in the systems along with significant remarks, using the free-form comments facility. Periodically, new mail pieces or letters are generated using output provided by the PC.

Furthermore, the PC implementation covers everything from case entry and work tickets to inventory, sales analysis, and payroll. This is a radical departure from the classical path that was followed prior to the new system. It also permitted management to see the benefits that it obtained from its computer investment.

Since the impression exists that the PC is good for the small firm, but PC *and* LAN are only of value to the bigger company, let's take an example of myriaprocessor implementation by a very small truck company. It has an owner-manager, two secretaries, some ten transport vehicles, and double that number of truck drivers.

Classically the preparation of transport orders was done by the secretaries who also answered the phone, while the manager did the scheduling. Data processing was handled through a service bureau. Then the company decided to acquire its own small business system.

The first alternative to be examined was a small business machine with 60 MBy storage essentially emulating the service bureau batch job. This would have meant another employee and it was dropped. The second alternative would have cost 50% more but given the manager and secretaries online terminals. Then came the idea of PC and LAN. The following applications have been put online through acquired software packages:

1. Receive orders
2. Give confirmation; prices
3. Schedule trucks
4. Calculate milage
5. Make bills
6. Follow-up on bills
7. Keep customer accounting
8. Keep general accounting
9. Make payments
10. Provide transport documents.

Quite importantly, not only the secretaries and the manager but also the truck drivers could now interact with the system and obtain their work schedules and bills of transport without interrupting the office personnel, who could then devote more work to customer handling. This comparison brings in perspective what an imaginative analysis can do. It also underlines the wisdom of evaluating alternatives prior to reaching investment decisions.

Applications that take a new road to implementation and come out of the routine path need imaginative people to do them. That is where their limitation lies—not in hardware, software, or costs. The hardware and software are available, and the costs are usually lower than with the often followed solutions.

If we wish to obtain good results, we should apply *the principle of top talent:* Use better and fewer people. The wide range of results obtained by software personnel (shown by different studies) confirms a well-known human phenomenon: The bulk of the imaginative solutions as well as the higher productivity comes from a relatively small number of specialists.

Therefore, training the specialists should be a major preoccupation of any project and of top management as a whole. John F. Kuemmerle, senior vice president of administration at Guardian Life Insurance Company, stated, "Because computer people realize that their skills can quickly become obsolete, the opportunity to learn new skills and *apply them* is one of their biggest reasons for moving on. To counter that, *we ask* our people to spend 40% of their time learning."

In practically every branch of human activity, the top 20% of the people produce about 50% of the output; the bottom 50% of the people produce about 20% of the output. Given this concentration of obtainable results in a relatively small fraction of people, and the additional bonus of reducing project communications overhead by using fewer, more imaginative, and more productive specialists, we would expect management to follow the principle of top talent.

A top-talented systems analyst would be qualified to properly study the workplace using the best supports technology can offer. The proper study of the workplace will necessarily involve three principal areas of activity:

1. *Fundamentals*

The study of the fundamentals includes functionality to be supported, text and data rates, text and data volumes, interactive features, response time, reliability and uninterrupted service, human engineering, and user-friendly approaches.

2. *Mechanics*

Systems analysis on the mechanics will focus on programming language(s), applications software, visualization (including the number of video units per workstation and the formats to be handled), choice of video; choice of graphic tablet; design of template(s), choice of cursor or pen, and printer or plotter (if necessary).

Part and parcel of the mechanics is the factual and documented study of database structure, database access (to be kept at minimum), authorization/authentication, journaling, and recovery/restart. But the basics of mechanics also includes choices regarding carrier and BIU, deskbottom PC, and possible add-on interfaces.

3. WS Support

Typical components include a careful examination of the growing range of office automation and decision support routines, DP/WP integration, document handling, transaction control, form control, electronic mail, voice mail, electronic meetings (teleconferencing), as well as backup and handholding.

The systems approach to be taken should center on man-information interactivity. This calls for attention to

- response time (40% at 2 sec., 30% at 3 sec., 20% at 6 sec., 10% at 10 sec.)
- uninterrupted service (99.99% uptime)
- controlled access to microfiles
- softcopy presentation
- job oriented template design.

A systems view must be taken regarding each one of these issues. Though its implementation may be timed, it must also be assured that subsequent developments will fit nicely with what has been done.

A thorough, detailed, and well documented system analysis might not have been necessary if the applications were well defined, the system's requirements cast in iron, and there were never any conflicting requests for system modifications in terms of functionality. But with computers and communications, such an ideal state of affairs is in no way a typical case.

Given even one missing statement in the code, the results may be both time consuming and expensive. They will always be so unless there is a critical appraisal by knowledgeable experts who understand what the job requires and are able to blend requirements with the tools and means offered by high technology.

5 STUDY OF THE WORKPLACE

As an example of a PC and LAN implementation, within the broader perspective of a realtime information system, let's consider the case of an airline. Up to a time, management depended on batch for day-to-day operations such as accounts handling, currency exchange, ticket reconciliation, inventory control, traffic statistics, management information—and on a sort of remote batch for reservations.

The latter area of implementation was evidently the first to be put online. Management decided on a mainframe-based *classical realtime* implementation with software packages offered by the mainframer. This involved

> passenger reservations
>
> schedule optimization
>
> freight handling
>
> inventory control
>
> personnel scheduling.

The question was then posed about the other applications that had exhausted their life cycle in the batch environment. Two solutions were feasible: crowd the newly acquired mainframes with them—and this was unwise. Or try a different possibility: PC and LAN.

The myriaprocessor presented itself well in this environment. Applications offering themselves to this solution were classified into two groups, each with its own technical prerequisites:

1. *Day-to-Day*
    - accounts receivable
    - accounts payable/fuel
    - accounts payable/other
    - ticket reconciliation
    - currency exchanges
    - general accounting.

2. *Management*
    - daily analysis
    - statistics
    - fleet planning

- component control
- management information.

Further study helped clarify and detail the characteristics of each application, thus making it feasible to locate the proper software packages. Avoiding the reinvention of the wheel in terms of applications software, the analysts were able to concentrate their attention on the study of the workplace. Both human engineering aspects and technical design issues have been considered.

Technical design primarily concerned the interactive input/output and the structure of the information elements to be stored in the local databases. The one was projected for the day-to-day operations, the other for management information.

Output media was primarily softcopy-based, with hardcopy being an exact 80-column image of the softcopy. This simplified man-information communication and also permitted the use of lower cost printers at the workplace.

The basic input medium chosen was the graphic tablet and cursor, with slightly over 250 functional keys made available to the user. Templates had thus to be designed by major applications area. In each such area, the different desks would have both *common functional areas* and *special areas* on the face of the template.

The main areas in template design for day-to-day operations were the following:

1. Suppliers.

2. Airports from/to.

3. Items, units of measurement.

4. Type of account; line of credit; discounts.

5. Aircraft identification.

6. Bank account, balance, currency.

7. Ledger chapter.

8. Line of responsibility.

Different colors were chosen to visually identify each area, thus simplifying the use of the template by the responsible clerk.

The latter reference should be underlined: It is the responsible clerk who has been endowed with the PC on the LAN and not "as usual" an intermediate data entry operator. The SA identified the number of pigeonholes and their functionality in template design.

Just as important has been the study of the response time. This is an issue on which relatively little or no interest has been paid in the implementation of mainframes and minicomputers, and the results have not been particularly good.

Response times for users on a mainframe have often exceeded the 30 second vs. the 5 second which might have been typically acceptable. With terminals online to a mini, response times of 1 and 2 minutes (even 10 minutes in some cases) are not so uncommon.

The following reference exemplifies an experiment in response time. It has been done post-mortem when the response time on a large mini configuration exceeded 1 minute on the average and in some cases reached up to 12 minutes. With experience acquired in this regard, such experimentation should be done by the analysts in the system design phase, whether for a myriaprocessor, mini, or mainframe.

It is understood that when the response time reaches the level of 1 minute, this is no longer an interactive application but a badly designed batch. This has been the situation when the response time on a fairly large size minicomputer reached unacceptably long delay levels. The machine was devoted to day-to-day accounting type applications.

The reasons thought to be the background of this result can be classified as follows:

1. *Type of Work (W)*

There exist 8 alternatives:

W1: Voucher input—without tax update

W2: Discounts, exceptions—without tax update

W3: Accounts payable—with tax update

W4: Discounts, exceptions on AP—with tax update

W5: Accounts receivable—with tax update

W6: Discounts, exceptions on AR—with tax update

W7: Different accounting updates

W8: General ledger updates

2. *With and Without Overflow (A)*

Here the alternatives are two:

A1: With overflow (nonrestructured files)

A2: Without overflow.

3. *Online only vs. online and batch (B)*

B1: Only online

B2: Online and batch

4. *Level of Archive Accumulation (C)*

C1: Minimum level—early year

C2: Maximum level—late year

5. *Number of Terminals (T)*

T1: 12 terminals

T2: 6 terminals

T3: 3 terminals

To test all conditions, a total number of 192 ($8 \times 2 \times 2 \times 2 \times 3$) cases would be necessary. As a result, the experiment was divided in two parts. Conditions 1, 2, 3 were taken first.

Through the use of Grecolatin squares, 16 rather than 32 experiments were done. The average response time per experiment is important. Overflow and batch tended to significantly increase response time.

Next, the number of archive accumulation and number of terminals were tested:

- The increase from 3 to 6 terminals tended steadily to increase response time from 18" to 30"—roughly 66%.
- More impressive has been the inclusion of past files (late year emulation).

- For the same number of terminals, the average response time increased from 30″ to 2′34″—or by 513%.

Such results help identify the weak points of a design and by consequence permit an optimal selection of design factors. In this as in other implementations, access to the database often proves to be critical. But no single correction is able to put the balance right. Interactive systems demand a long hard look in the whole range of the application. Emphasis must be placed on each and every component as well as on the total system look.

Systems analysts have been able to reproject and restructure the database to obtain a significant reduction of response time. Thus, general ledger update with value added tax was reduced from 23″-282″ to 4″-7″, depending on the number of terminals operating simultaneously.

10

STRUCTURED SYSTEM ANALYSIS

1 INTRODUCTION

Many factors contribute to the characteristics of an information system. The first is the competence of the designer. The second, the user's requirements. The third, the mandate given the designer and the time frame under which the system had to be produced. These are the positive influences. There exist also negative ones such as the number of conversions of the system, the number of modifications that are made, and so on.

To keep the information system under control, we need a structured approach from analysis and design to programming, testing and the quality control process that precedes putting any program into production. Among the basic requirements are the existence and enforcement of definitive programming standards, as well as management's understanding, support and trust—which itself is a function of the quality and timeliness of the work produced by the system's group.

Structured analysis is the activity of performing system analysis and design with a limited set of constructs. At the analysis and design level this reference is still under elaboration, but it is much more precise when we talk of programming. A key construct in structured programming is, for instance, that each program is allowed only one entry and one exit. Some basic control structures are sufficient: Do-While, If-Then-Else, Sequence, and so on.

Structured approaches are that much more necessary as the information systems for banking, business and industry are often products of less than ideal circumstances in terms of design and implementation. With the proper standards and the right management, information systems can be made to operate two, three, or four times as fast as the usual practice indicates.

The task of performing measurement and evaluation (and in that way keeping the project under control) is not very complex and does not require tremendous skills. But it does require determination and the will to get results.

Along this line of reference, state-of-the-art techniques in software design are emerging as the competitive master key to unlocking new applications developments and installation growth. This is the more important as information systems applications are handicapped by dragging timetables.

In terms of hardware, microprocessors and telecommunications foretell a future in which personal computing is a widespread reality. But software is a bottleneck. Structured approaches aim to assist in overcoming the reasons that keep applications programming expensive, time consuming, and difficult to control. To be effective we must set the priorities right, emphasize the critical parts of the system, and use a valid methodology that can assure uniform results.

Experimentation should be part and parcel of every structured design discipline. This calls for a computer-based simulator able to map the run-time environment of the system in design and test. Its sophistication should depend on the type and degree of testing to be accomplished, but in general it must be instrumented to provide test data that help polish the design results.

2 STRUCTURING AROUND THE DATA COMPONENT

A systems analysis for the implementation of computers and communications is basically oriented toward four areas of interest:

- the text and data to be handled, including storage, retrieval, and access control
- the transport (datacomm) activity for text and data
- the processing requirements
- the end user functions

In the 1950's, 1960's, and most of the 1970's, primary emphasis was placed on the processing component. Though this is always a requirement, emphasis on processing is being eclipsed by the emergence of databasing and datacomm. By the end of this decade it will be the end user functions that will command the greatest interest.

Though two distinct areas of activity, databasing and datacomm have much in common. *The bridge is the message.* A message is a record in the database, and conversely every record and file should be designed as a message.*

This is so much of a fundamental notion that it constitutes a cornerstone to a structured approach in systems design. Its impact characterizes a family of packages now emerging, the best known being *electronic mail* (teletex). Such packages place themselves

> between basic software (operating systems, DBMS, transactional routines) and applications software—but also
>
> in the middle between databasing and datacomm implementations.

Electronic mail has the competitive advantage of *decoupling* sender from receiver, thus constituting a modern and much more efficient solution than the realtime/timesharing approaches of the 1960's:

1. It is an answer to the current waste and underutilization of private lines;
2. It's a way of interleaving text, data, image, and voice—which is a coming development—but it is also the forerunner of a "further out" capability in file transfer.

It follows logically that no solution to the structured design of information systems can be effective and long lasting without considering the impact of developments such as electronic mail. This leads us to a fundamental principle characterizing design at large and computers/communications in particular.

---

*See also D. N. Chorafas: *Databases for Networks and Minicomputers* (1982), and *Data Communications for Distributed Information Systems* (1980), Petrocelli Books Inc., Princeton and New York.

Each system has a small number of critical parts. They typically comprise 1% to 10% of all its elementary components. The performance of the entire system depends to a large extent on the behavior of these critical parts. It is often possible to just about ignore the non-critical parts and still do a clean design job.

Today the critical parts find themselves concentrated around databasing and datacomm (in that order). Tomorrow, after the foregoing issues are faced in an able manner, they will be most likely concentrated around the user-friendly interface.

To make feasible the construction of an efficient database/datacomm environment and to aid in the creation of solid information systems foundations, the structured approach must provide a coherent and understandable way of expressing:

1. what the system is all about,
2. what text and data it uses, creates, and extrudes,
3. the relationship of all text/data and functional elements.

Furthermore, communication between users and designers must be facilitated. The form of the user statements about text, data, and image need must be made comprehensible to anyone with a reasonable level of intelligence in the analyst/designer profession.

Microprocessor technology can be of great assistance in this reference. What better means for user/analyst interface than a personal computer programmed as an aid to systems analysis, supporting a graphic tablet, visualizing on video step by step the user's input (preferably, in a graphic form), and able to interconnect with a *development database* stored on a local area network, mini, or mainframe?

The two pillars of software design are knowhow (the motor behind the designer's ingenuity) and documentation. Computers principally assist in the latter. A computer-aided documentation presupposes an interactive facility. If we apply it the right way, an interactive facility can double the productivity of the analyst and of the programmer.

The benefits are across the board. Computer supporting during the analysis and design phases improves performance and helps in bringing the booming software costs under control. At the same time, it assures the tool for creating the system documentation in

Structured System Analysis

a methodical and standardized way. In a computers and communications system of some size, documentation can become unwieldly. Results of interviews, design proposals, diagrams and exhibits, and use statistics soon become a major headache to file, retrieve, update, and maintain. People who have gone through this experience usually recommend that computer support be used to assist at all levels of systems requirements. The prerequisite to this implementation is formalisms. Hence, a structured approach.

The role to be played by a structured system analysis is thus brought into perspective:

1. It forces analysts and designers to consider the basic forms of plans, controls, and implementations—and their adequacy.

2. It streamlines system description and presentation, including all annotations by the end users.

3. It provides the means for automatic restructuring in a way better to assure the understanding of everyone working on the project than any manual method.

4. In the longer run, it helps improve software quality and reliability through the examination of critical linkages.

5. It leads to a reduction of complexity and therefore a greater efficiency.

6. It improves visibility, thus making it possible to place emphasis on correctness down to the level of problem specification.

7. It constitutes the best method of modularization, being particularly applicable in the programming phases. But it must be accounted for as clearly as analysis and design.

8. It promotes the employment of testing methodologies, underlying both their benefits and limitations.

9. It makes feasible the automation of validation procedure by an agency tooled for quality control.

10. It greatly assists the overall objectives of computer-aided documentation from original writing to up-to-date revisions.

User organizations who have suffered the endless complexities of unmaintained processing flowcharts, file specs, and datacomm linkages hiding innumerable logical flaws find in computer-aided solutions relief and comfort. Others with sophisticated analysis and design techniques and better-trained staff see it as imposing a discipline on the representation of a system that, without proper handling, could easily be mistaken for a design method and a short-cut code.

Everybody notices the fact that the errors made in program development are significantly reduced. The many hours spent on systems debugging are therefore being saved, and maintenance also needs less effort. Staff competence is improved, motivation and satisfaction increased, and technical coordination advanced.

3 RULES TO BE OBSERVED

Let us consider for a moment the fundamentals of information system design. The first landmark of a well managed systems project is the smoothness with which it is being accomplished. This is reflected in the analyst's productivity but also in the quality of the end product.

Speed of development is certainly enhanced by structured design. A modular approach alone would not make it possible to write the large programs needed in the amount of time allocated. Basic design goals can be enhanced through the precise definition of user requirements. These goals include:

correctness

flexibility

reliability

portability

efficiency

maintainability

Too frequently, the contents of specifications are fuzzy, inaccurate, and incomplete, resulting in systems with the same characteristics. This is largely due to a surprising majority of systems projects being undertaken with no written user specification. Delivering a quality system that meets user requirements in all respects becomes a great advantage.

The so-called conventional modes of defining requirements usually go this way. The user is rarely assisted in preparing a specification package or in describing what the system is and what it is to accomplish. Yet requirements for input, output, stored text and data, communications needs, logical processing control, testing performance, and documentation must be detailed. Without completed specifications, no one should assume project responsibility.

The challenge of the systems analyst is to transform the business specifications into system design. This is rarely accomplished in an able manner because system specifications are often inadequate. The analysts themselves resist producing written specifications; and omissions are not discovered until programming has been finished, causing costly modifications and delays.

Misunderstanding specification detail becomes more likely at each level of interface between the analyst, the designer, the programmer, and the user. If these misunderstandings are not corrected early in the development cycle, built-in errors are the consequence. These are the basic reasons that brought to the foreground the need for a formal design discipline able to describe a software entity such as a system program as an arrangement of functions to be performed.

Determining the main function of the software, decomposing it into a hierarchy of subfunctions, and naming the subfunctions is not a trivial exercise. It requires a great deal of insight, creativity, and experience on the part of the designer.

Like any and every project effort, information systems must be the object of three basic management activities:

1. Planning
2. Documentation
3. Control

These interleave with one another. Since the software is for the user, the latter must be provided with the dual ability to have a systems project recorded step by step and, at the same time, to measure the functionality of the system under development.

Top level functions on a hierarchy of system components contain the control logic. They determine when and in what order lower-level functions are to be invoked. Sequential coding statements are found predominantly in lower-level function.

The specialization of such "worker functions" is the classical foundation of data systems technology. Some are devoted to getting the input, others to processing this input, still others to producing the output. At the design stage, each of these worker functions must be examined as a prime component part and further subdivided into more elemental operations.

The reason I called attention in the introduction to the need to use simulators at the design stage can be found in this last reference. If we had to review and revise all aspects of all programs in a system, then the task would be comparable to rewiring the entire system. But when we can experiment and identify the possible bottlenecks, all that really needs to be done is to improve a very small part of the whole.

Similarly, in applying the above strategy to an entire computers and communications systems design, it becomes immediately clear that it is not worthwhile to do performance measurements on the majority of the applications components. What is worthwhile is to select a few component parts that

1. are time-critical, that is, require results a very short time after input data are supplied.

2. are run frequently and consume considerable computer resources, a subject much more important when we talk of microcomputer-based workstations.

3. consume large amounts of storage capacity, hence need to access local, regional, or central databases.

Analyzing the projected daily and monthly use statistics can be of great help in selecting the critical parts of a system. This turns the discussion back to the fundamentals: Imaginative, computer-based approaches to problem solving are required to produce good statements of requirements. Problems must be translated into goals and then into solutions, which must in turn be reduced to functional terms.

Though there is no guarantee that the functions will create the desired results, the lack of a structured approach virtually assures that the articulation of requirements will be difficult. Functions and processes will not always be properly described; tools and techniques for optimizing the definition process will not generally be available. User motivation will be lacking because reinforcement for the work is traditionally postponed until the implementation stage, by which time users have learned to expect disappointment.

Poorly defined processes lead mathematically to disappointment. In turn, to mend the fences users and analysts work on compromises that will eventually disenchant both the users and the analysts. The orderly approach inherent in a structured analysis and design has a primary goal that aims to eliminate these negative characteristics of information systems projects.

In conclusion, the difference between successful and unsuccessful systems may well lie both in the manner in which the projects were managed and the structured tool put at the project's disposal. The latter can make system implementation more successful, timely, and cost effective.

4 THE MERITS OF STRUCTURED SYSTEMS ANALYSIS

The computers and communications projects undertaken by systems analysts have been characterized traditionally by the needs to improve the procedures applied at the user's end and to better the information service that the user gets—while bettering the quality level of the analysts themselves and making their results more worthwhile.

There are two schools of thought in the structured analysis area:

1. functional decomposition, and
2. data structure approach.

The latter is more recent and helps solve some tough problems. First, it is difficult to find the best way in implementing a decomposing function. Second, it is even more difficult to reconcile a function structure with the data structure.

Still more important is the fact that we currently have available an impressive range of database management systems which can be employed as very high level languages. Quite significantly, programming through a DBMS helps in applying computer power in software developments—thus saving both labor and time.

To bring the computer into the picture as a major tool of assistance, we have to develop a structured approach for analysis and systems design. We will be reviewing what's available in the next chapter. But for the time being let's say that the tools to employ should be similar in basic concepts to that used with structured programming, and quite different from structured programming in terms of procedures and methodology.

Structured approaches do not change analysis in terms of mission. The difference lies in formalisms such as (1) the creation of a formal statement of the problem in a form suitable as input to the design method to be used, (2) formal, universally applicable file descriptions, (3) datacomm protocols, and (4) interactive video formats.

A basic difference between formal and nonformal approaches is that analysis tends to lose its highly intuitive nature. This should be valid not only in the design phases but also throughout the system's life cycle, including its maintenance. Many of the so-called "current systems" or "systems in operation" have been over the years modified to the point that they are a mockery of processing. They are prone to error and largely unintelligible even to the most experienced programmer.

To make things worse, many programs developed over the last two decades have no written specifications. The old analysis can not serve as a source of information for the new design because of the muddled documentation and the large number of modifications. This identifies a situation where analysis for new information systems projects must start from scratch.

A structured approach to design requires the use of the concept of *function* as a means of investigating and documenting user requirements. The problem is to convey certainty as to what exactly a function is. A formal way of determining the functions of the system components is first to identify them, then to document them, and after this to proceed with a series of one-to-two hour biweekly meetings with the end users, the project manager, and the analysts/programmers.

Not only a list of functions but also their description should be formed from the discussion. By focusing in-depth on one function at a time, all present could explore and absorb a small comprehensive portion of the system. Ideally, this should be done through computer support.

The best way to computer support is microprocessor-based personal workstations. For working meetings involving several participants, a menu selection type organization is advisable for the infopages to be projected on a wide screen accessible to all participants. The technology for such implementation is available; it is known as *interactive videotex*.

In terms of overall organization, the early definition of functions in structured design produces some flexibility. After such definitions have taken place, changes can be made with a minimum of effort. Furthermore, this approach allows errors to be quickly located and corrected.

In fact, a major factor contributing to system flexibility is the ability to weed out errors and make corrections at component parts without upsetting the systems structure. This suggests the wisdom of an isolation by function that is achievable by structured design.

Simplicity is another goal. Simplicity sees to it that when a problem occurs it is easy to eliminate many modules from consideration since their functions are properly delineated in terms of what they have to do with the problem.

Text and data-coupling procedures can be used in the interfacing of modules with each other. Data coupling occurs when all input and output to and from the called module are passed as parameters or arguments—as information elements. Such considerations point to the fact that a properly structured modular approach accelerates the development of the system.

The physical and logical separation of modules means that more than one person can simultaneously contribute to a program. This is further enhanced through computer-based processes. A by-product of using a modular approach is the lessening of the total learning time involved in the translation of the system specifications into code.

But there are also some disadvantages in modularity. One problem arises in the interfacing of modules. In spite of careful attention given to the flow of data to and from other modules, errors may still exist. The number and order of parameters, their characteristics, and the interpretation of their values may be in some cases misunderstood.

Another problem arises in the organization necessary for the direction of several people working on the same problem simultaneously. Modules may be developed so rapidly that coordination of testing, linking, and integrating them becomes a delicate task.

To alleviate such disadvantages, it is advisable to arrange the modules (small structures) into a hierarchy and to define controlling upper-level functions. With the completion of the hierarchy not only will system requirements be defined, but the design will be simultaneously accomplished.

The work which we are describing will be enhanced and advanced by means of design reviews and structured walkthroughs. A *walkthrough*, or mental execution of the system program by the project team, must be done for each subsystem, module, and component:

- After the analyst has compiled his module and scrutinized it for obvious errors, he sends the project leader and several other analysts involved copies of his source text.
- With time allowed for the project group to examine the text (usually a few hours or days), the team meets and collectively performs a mental execution of the program.

This is the general line of a walkthrough. Prior to seeing the details, let's add the general objectives of a design review. Contrary to the walkthrough, which goes vertically to the details, a *design review* works horizontally and has three goals:

1. To bring together users and systems specialists so that the design steps can be evaluated and comments made regarding the fit of the work in process.
2. To assure that the developing specifications integrate properly with the other different subsystems that are in production or are projected within an overall grand design.

3. To see to it that resources are properly allocated: men, money, means, material—and that agreed upon timetables are observed.

Properly done design reviews help bridge the gap between end users and system specialists. As practically all organizations have discovered, analysts and users harbor grave doubts about each other, and the origins are obvious.

Quite often users are disenchanted because information systems are often late, not so flexible, and budget overruns are the rule. Analysts blame user reluctance to participate heavily in the definition process. They also blame users for abdicating responsibility for system results.

To be successful, a design review should not enter into details. It should assume that the user is trained in his own functional field but not necessarily in systems skills. And it should work on the assumption that the user's primary objective on the project is to protect his or her own interests.

The project manager, the designers, the analysts, and the programmers—in short, the systems group—must always remember that, although responsible for the technical part of the information systems development, it has no real organizational authority over users on the project team. But it does have the responsibility to give the users its constant attention.

5 LOGICAL PATHS IN PLAYBACK

A list of errors must be made as each logical path is followed. The interface with modules either calling or called by the module being examined must be carefully checked as well. At the end of the walkthrough, the list of errors is given to the authors.

In this manner, most errors are caught before any testing has occurred. Also, team members who review the systems analysis documentation become familiar with a part of the system other than their own. This helps to establish a common base for understanding all components of the computers and communications aggregate under study.

While the members of the project team review the module and its interfaces, errors usually arising from miscommunication are spotted in other modules. However, this activity should be done fast and in a concentrated way. One of the major factors in the success of a structured walkthrough is the shortness of the time spent in testing.

Playbacks have evident advantages. In science and in technology the earlier we catch and correct errors, the better off we are. A logical playback permits that the project is examined from the top down to ascertain if all functions are present. It also makes it feasible to ascertain whether the details of input, processing, databasing, datacomm, and output are correctly interpreted. This is valid from the specifications development phase to design and all the way to the programming of the modules. The impact of the method will however be that much greater if—as underlined on several occasions—all phases characterizing a given project have been treated in a computer-based manner, the walkthrough itself is computer assisted, and the results lead to a dynamic update of the modules which themselves are computer based.

Though walkthroughs have been practiced during the last ten years through largely manual means, the advantages of computer-aided approaches are evident. The computer can help track all changes and keep record of them. Just because updating the documentation is rather difficult due to frequent alterations, computer power is a valuable tool.

Not only does computer assisted documentation make for both easier and faster design walkthroughs but it also facilitates participation by the user and programming team, beginning at the top of the subsystem hierarchy and processing downwards through each function. The latter are presented interactively to the user who must agree that all functions are present, all text and data valuable to the job are included, and all required detail is correct.

Through computer-assisted approaches, the description of a system is more complete, accurate, and easy to present. It is also more concise than any manual solutions. Updating is made easier because only the functions affected by the change require recalling.

This can be done automatically, while with manual methods one has to review the whole lot.

Having established the need, let's look into the way a structured design documentation works (though of documentation per se we will speak in a different chapter). The critical factors are always the same:

1. Stating objectives.
2. Defining and establishing specifications.

For project-oriented tasks, the logical path is the first thing to look at. As we all know so well, with computers and communications the finished product must be constructed from abstract ideas; and, all too often, both the quantity and quality of the first description (even if one takes the time to write it down) is insufficient to determine the adequacy of design. The same is true of predicting the success or failure of the outcome.

The impact of the walkthrough will be greater if from the very start of the project, the function of the module (or system) is properly described from the analyst's point of view. The analyst must produce this definition, but good practice imposes some conditions on it.

- First, the definition must be translatable into a system design, with a functional specification expressed in terms of processes and data structures.
- Second, the definition must be precise, clear and not open to misinterpretation.
- Third, the systems definition must be complete; design is optimized when all features are known and can thus be integrated neatly into databases and programs.
- Fourth, all relevant definitions and specifications are written into computer memory.

As cannot be too often repeated, a basic reason the systems effort fails is that too many systems definitions and specifications exist only orally and are not committed to writing until after programming or implementation has started, if ever. Why design information systems without applying the same standards other design efforts get? The only answer is bad habit.

That habit must now change. Design documentation must look at the user. To the user, the "system" is synonymous with the outputs:

hard copies

soft copies

graphics

audio response

The user must also be interested in the inputs. But the inputs are a resulting, not a starting consideration. At the start come the outputs which help determine user requirements and provide specifications with the aid of a systems analyst, using objectives as a guideline.

The systems analyst must study, describe, and help the user choose the database form to support this computer-based reporting capability. Since information systems are de facto distributed with text and data exchanged between them, the analyst should focus proper attention on communications and their specs. The user should participate aggressively in this database and datacomm definition activity.

Similarly, both the systems analyst and the end user must determine the input sources and timing of text and data needed to support the database, datacomm, and interactive reporting capability. Often interdepartmental or interdivisional cooperation will be required to carry out this phase. Having defined the outputs, database, datacomm, processing, and inputs, the systems analyst should be in a good position to construct through computer assistance a systems design manual.

While we will talk of documentation after we have the chance to review the different design automation packages in existence, let's add at this point that all data processing/word processing organizations have available valid software with which to work on a computer-based systems documentation program. This can be easily accomplished through any valid word processing package, and there exist plenty of personal computer-oriented WP packages.

Finally, while the subject of this chapter has been an introduction to the concepts underlying structured systems design, let's not forget that the prerequisite to adopting such methodology is of an organizational and disciplinary nature. Here are some valuable suggestions on how to go about it.

1. *Carefully select the first project.*

Since experience is the best tutor, it is advisable that the first project be of moderate size and complexity.

The estimated development period from analysis to design and programming is 6 to 9 months. More benefits can be gained from an experience limited in scope that makes the system components transparent in themselves.

2. *Expect an altered development cycle.*

Specifications development and system design will be taking place concurrently. Good functional descriptions are a complicated and lengthy process, but it will result in much less time coding and testing afterwards.

3. *Assign a project responsibility to an able and willing analyst.*

The person in charge for the first structured analysis project should be able to communicate and interface effectively with the users. Evidently, he or she should be well trained in the use of the structured analysis method to be chosen and preferably have experience in its application.

After the project and personnel have been selected, the project leader should request that the user collaborate in investigating existing manual procedures. The PL should be involved firsthand in the process to acquire an introductory understanding into the proposed system. He or she should also set up a regular series of meetings, as discussed in connection with design reviews and walkthroughs.

Such meetings should be held at the beginning every second day, decreasing in frequency to the weekly level. They should focus on one individual function at a time; determine under what circumstances the function will be performed; identify the text and data to be acted upon; and describe the processing, the interactive outputs to be produced, the databasing, and the datacomm.

For each meeting, track should be kept through a computer on both the outline and the result being obtained. As insight into the system is gained, relationships between functions will appear. They should be registered and acted upon.

Good systems practice will be helpful. Functions may take place at different levels of hierarchy. They may require further explosion. They may be determined not to be self-standing functions but rather portions of other functions. A systems analysis must be restructured to reflect the altered hierarchy.

Let's recapitulate. The first important issue is to start working with the right discipline to establish the specifications. After the specifications design phase is completed, a more exact estimate of resource requirements is possible. The computer-assisted documentation must always represent a measurable checkpoint in the development cycle of the system.

The systems documentation accumulating in computer memory should be used during structured walkthroughs and design reviews to establish a systems performance record. The project should be continued until fine tuning of the system is completed, and beyond. Problems should be noted. Attempts to correct minor problems should be discouraged. Only major disruptive system problems should be fixed immediately.

The time for a thorough checkout reconsidering even the minor issues on the problem list is when 95% of the problem-detection phase has been completed. This must be done in a valid manner without anybody involved in the analysis and design work being hurt. We no longer talk of software as a personal item.

11

TOOLS FOR A STRUCTURED APPROACH

1 INTRODUCTION

Inherent to the idea of choosing and implementing tools for a structured systems analysis is the need for training *all* analysts and programmers to work online to the computer. Admittedly, this idea has not yet taken roots. Yet it is absolutely necessary to advance toward a computer-based systems development if we wish to save the very costly manpower analysts and programmers represent.

The point that needs to be unambiguously made is the futility of following half-baked approaches. If the organization needs to adopt a structural way to systems analysis—and chances are that it does—let it be so. But it must also implement online systems development and the methodology that goes with it. If a structured solution does not support this way, then it shouldn't be chosen in the first place.

Everything concerning a project, from its conception to its implementation and maintenance, must be expressed in a computer form and stored in a database. This has the advantage that the content of the aggregate or any part of it can be produced in soft copy (or in hard copy) in various formats as the occasion requires. The presentation is neater and a system-wide update is easy.

The computer's role is extended from that of an information processor to that of a tool available to aid software development. Furthermore, different methodologies can be tested, and this can be done online.

Most computer installations have hundreds of programs and procedures and millions of program steps in operation. Most of these have never been studied in terms of possible optimization, poor human engineering factors, incompatibilities between one type of documentation standards and another, specialized nature of some procedures, and the overall unsatisfactory performance of the manual method of systems design.

Computer-aided solutions can now assist the applications development process. The computer helps the systems expert in several ways.

- It makes the documentation not only standard but also homogeneous.
- It assures that the valuable and costly time of the expert will not be spent on routine work that can be done better by machine.
- It helps observe the software system effort in its whole range (Figure 11-1).
- It makes feasible a sense of continuity and follow-up.

One of the major benefits is the service to the end user. Regardless of the approach to software development, the effectiveness of the system depends on how well it satisfies the user's real needs. The requirements that the system must meet must be available to the software developers. What better way than to handle this by computer *if* we have the proper tools and methodology.

2 WHAT IS MEANT BY THE RIGHT TOOL?

Prior to using the device, we must make it available to ourselves and to the others who are supposed to employ it. The sort of goal we just put forward in the projected usage of a tool is the first basic reference that can permit us to define its characteristics. This is valid from choosing a screwdriver to the selection of a computer-based software development system.

Formal, computer-aided approaches help the analyst in determining, recording, and examining the user's needs, which after all is the classical job of the systems analyst. What we essentially are after in selecting the right tool is the methodology and discipline it

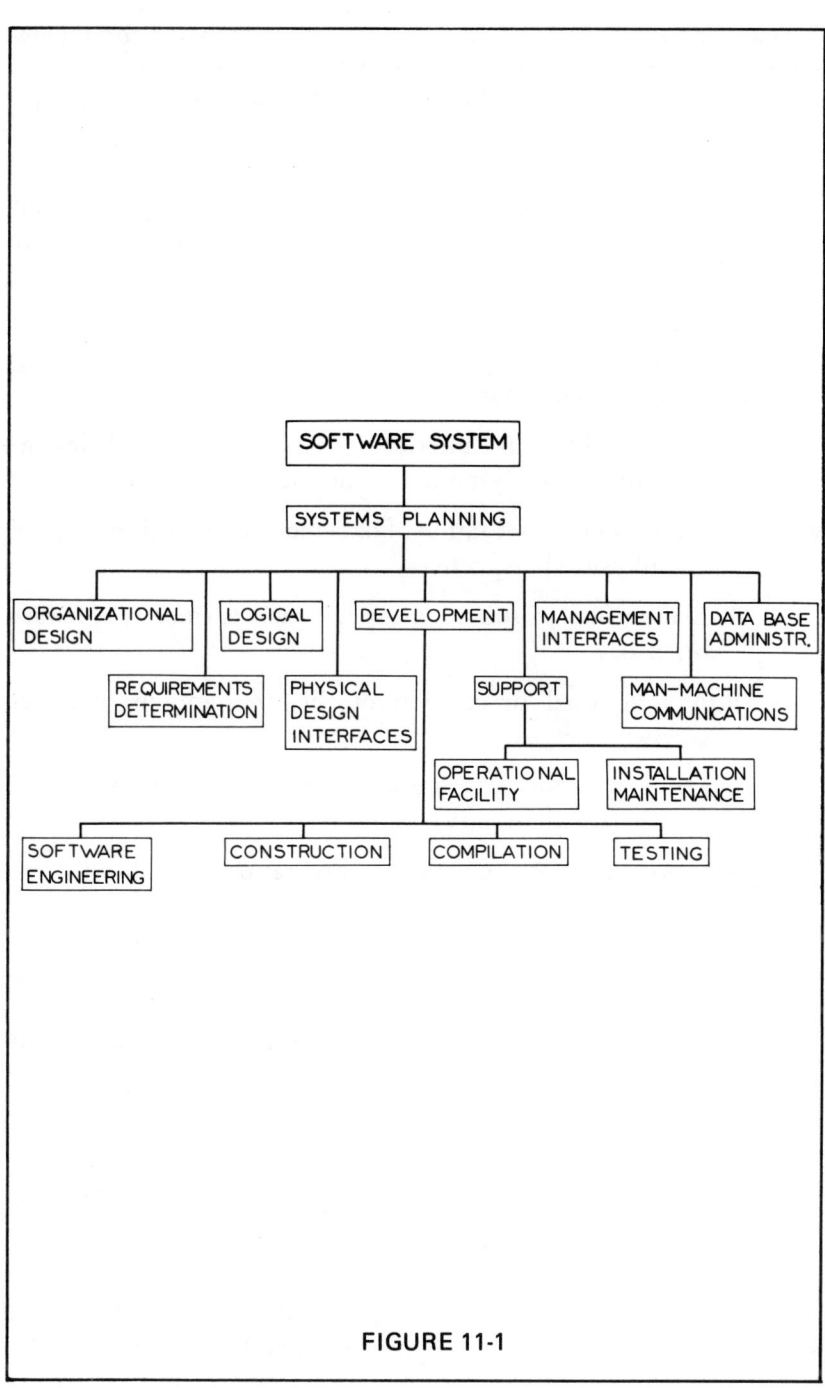

FIGURE 11-1

implies but also its kernel which can be described as a *formal language*. The tools performance should be assisted through the tremendous computer power which over the years we have underutilized in so many ways, analysis being only one of them.

Though we will be talking of interactive languages and linguistic formality in Part Three, let's briefly define at this point that a formal language for system documentation will necessarily involve the following notions:

1. A better initiation of the systems study through the observance of standard conventions.

2. An unambiguous functional description (logical design) both for the analyst and for the user.

3. An exact representation of data requirements (both logical and physical perspectives).

4. Elaboration of subsystem specifications (mostly software oriented).

5. A functional description of the programming product (software intense).

6. Datacomm and database specifications (including the role of the data dictionary).

7. A good look at the hardware integration capability (physical).

8. The possible options for developing computer-aided manuals for the user.

9. The capability to outline in concrete terms the systems test plan, to develop the test analysis report, and keep for queries the quality statistics.

10. The faculty of outlining the systems implementation plan, including conversion, introduction, baby-sitting, and hand-holding.

Furthermore, when the information system being developed passes the acid test of the implementation and is in operation, the right analysis and design tool will provide the means for preparing revised releases—helping in maintenance, the weeding out of different types of failures, and all sorts of needed updates. Some other facultative activities could also be added to this list.

Concepts, measures, guidelines and analysis techniques must be knit into a complete, formal system. Among themselves, these ten points outline the specifications and architecture for an integrated, computer-aided system for software development and maintenance.

If these are the prerequisites, admittedly none of the analysis tools fits the score. Most were originally developed to help in just one issue: documentation. No single method exists that would be the "best" in every design problem. Yet methods—even formal, computer-aided methods—*can* contribute so much to the system design effort.

The method assists the designer. It does not substitute for him or her. It is up to the individual and his or her knowhow, and not to the software development tool, to define the problem, to write the specifications, to evaluate their fitness, and to find the hidden common features. The tools are only an aid.

The question then arises: If a complete software development scheme is not to be found as a package, should the systems analyst and the designer use a currently available computer-based documentation language, or should they build their own system? The answer is simple: If one finds a structural analysis that can approximate one's requirements one should use this existing language—just like when we need a piece of hardware we buy it in the market rather than every time re-inventing the wheel.

But this is only part of the answer. While using the computer-assisted method of their choice, analysts and designers should always remember that even the best methodology assists the routine parts of the process and not the creative ones. It is up to them to use their skill and imagination in defining the representation system components and their associated relevant properties, including experimental results.

Still another question comes to mind. How many system analysis languages are presently available that uphold reasonable structural standards? Prior to risking an answer to this question, it is correct to make two statements. First, structural standards for system analysis languages do not exist. Second, an emerging conscience (not standards) suggest three basic characteristics:

1. There must be a user-friendly interface.
2. It should be reasonably simple to turn entity expressions into requirements definition and software systems specifications.
3. The analysis language should provide good prototyping and allow the flexibility to work within an architecture, distributing and recombining the system components.

One of the surprising failures with microcomputer technology, for instance, is that nobody has yet developed a microcomputer-based solution able to do structured system analysis. What is available is a series of tools. But most of these tools are not related to one another. This way a procedural analysis made with tool A cannot be mapped into a system analysis, because tool B addressing itself to it doesn't support such transition. In the same way no means are yet available to convert a structured system analysis automatically into programming.

Thus, the great unsolved problem is the transition between the different phases of an analysis, design and programming project. Figure 11-2 identifies these phases. Let's recapitulate. For *each* step there are *good* tools. But the links are missing and we lose information from step to step.

Table 4 lists nineteen alternative ways of doing a systems job with structured characteristics.* Practically all of them are handicapped by the fact that, in order to be implemented in an able manner, we need compatible processing and communications capabilities in terms of

- data structures,
- file structures,
- bits per word,
- instruction sets.

---

*However, system-level languages produce a pseudocode which is discontinuous in regard to the programming job. Thus, I suggest using a fourth generation language, particularly a relational DBMS.

Tools for a Structured Approach

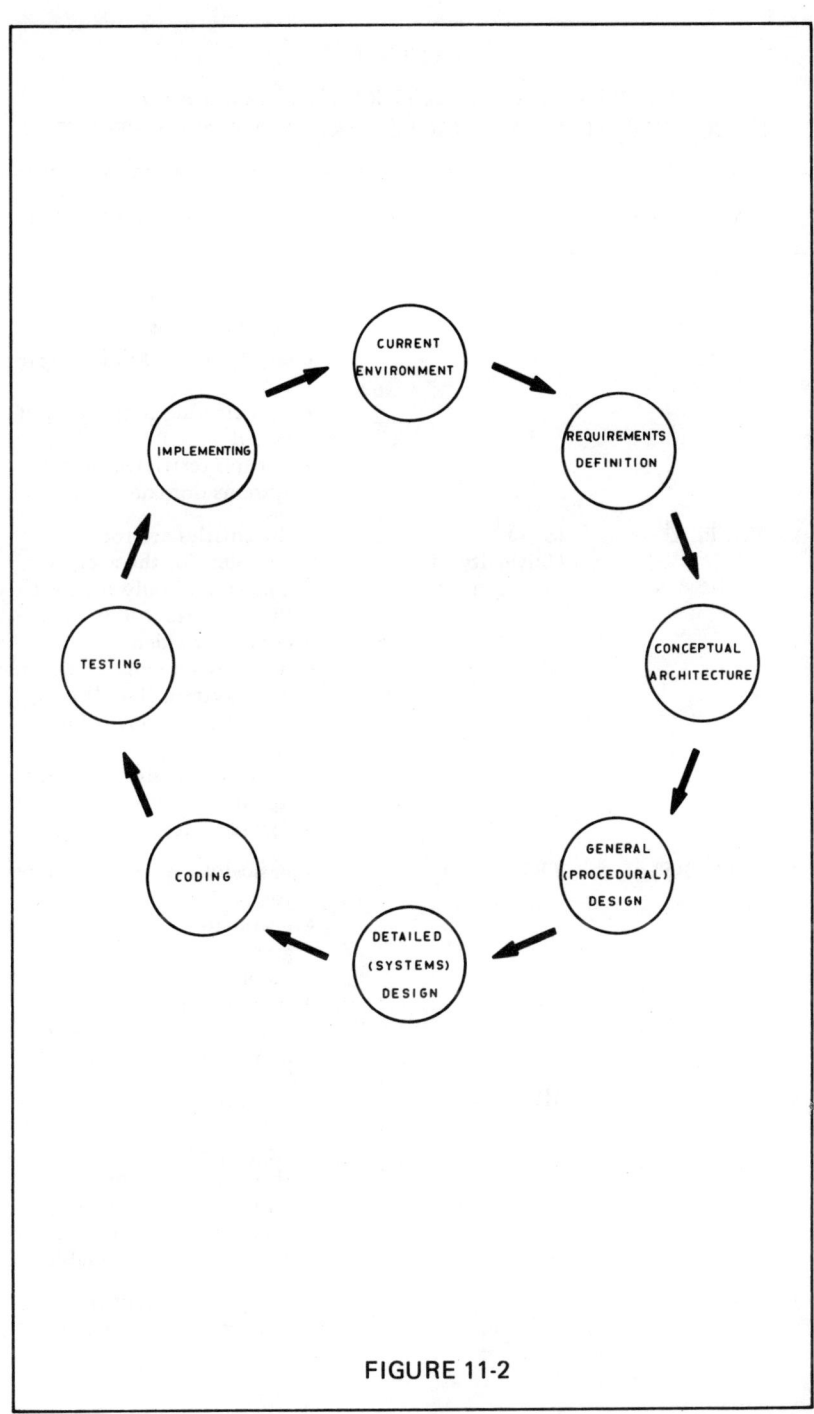

FIGURE 11-2

TABLE 4
Competitive Structural Analysis and Documentation Languages Currently in Existence

Project Name	Developed By	Strengths and Weaknesses
1. HIPO	IBM	• IBM support is available, yet the tool is • largely manual in its beginning • now starting to be computerized • but too restricted in the systems domain
2. PSL/PSA[1]	ISDOS University of Michigan	• the entities are too complex for the average analyst and only the best 20% can use it, but • computer aided • includes a database management system (DBMS) • has data dictionary facilities • provides for simultaneous update • formal texts are available
3. SREM/RSL[2]	TRW	• basically a documentation tool • automated, but programmed only on a few computers • uses DBMS • complex, needs much in computer resources
4. HOS[3]	MIT/NASA	• not yet fully computer based • developed to handle through formal means large, multiprocessing, multiprogrammed systems • no formal text available
5. MSR[4]		• not yet well defined • requires exact problem statement

Tools for a Structured Approach

			• primarily for theorectical developments
			• based on the premise that the more times you do something the better you do it
			• formal text available
6.	THREADS	CSC	• still largely manual
			• rather simple minded
			• PERT oriented
			• stimulus/result type approach
7.	SADT	Soft-tech	• manufacturer presents it as a methodology rather than as a tool
			• based on diagram explosion
			• positive procedure oriented features available
8.	Structured Design[5]	Yourdon/ Constantine/ Myers	• reliance is placed upon following the flow of data
			• special notation scheme for each data transformation
			• system specs are used to produce data flow diagrams
			• formal text available
9.	Jackson[6]		• not yet fully computer based
			• attempts to provide rational program structure—not analysis design documentation
			• input data transformed into output data
			• formal text available
10.	Warnier		• flowchart oriented
			• identifies all input data and defines files/records hierarchy
			• works on the details of the program through the types of instructions contained in the design
			• formal text available
11.	Focus	Information Builders, Inc.	• the beginning of a new generation of structural analysis tools

		• provides the analyst with an interactive environment for a formal statistical methodology
		• helps handle files in relation to shared structures
		• includes a comprehensive DBMS
		• supports plotting, graphic reporting, and query
12. Speed	The Office Manager (TOM)	• the only development system so far specifically designed for minicomputers (Wang 2200)
		• Aimed to simplify system design and control system maintenance
		• reduces applications software development time
		• provides the directory
13. IMS/ADF[7]	IBM	• Basically structured English
		• Will capture logical and physical DB structures and processing algorithms
14. IDEF	US Airforce	• A definition language
		• Main advantage, a range of HW/SW systems supporting it (IBM VSII, DEC 11/70 under UNIX, CDC 7600)
15. SDM 70		• Mainly a documentation tool
		• Helps *if* you know your problem and *if* you can state it properly
16. Metasystem 1000	Yourdon	• A spin-off from earlier Yourdon tools
		• Developed out of "Product Development Guidelines" as an approach to handling data structures
17. Superpilot	Apple	• Written as an educational tool, can be employed for prototyping

		• It is an authoring language with a series of Editors:
		   • Text
		   • Character
		   • Graphics

18. HDM[8]	SRI	• Good for capturing systems requirements • But oriented to Ph. D. and M.S. level of analysts
19. MICROSEF[9]	Softech	• A structural approach, designed to create a pilot's environment and its description—but also able to be implemented in other projects.

[1] Problem Statement Language/Problem Statement Analyser
[2] Sometimes said to mean: System Requirements Evaluation Package, and in other occasions: "Software Requirements Engineering Project"
[3] High Order Software
[4] META Step-wise Refinement
[5] also known as Composite Design, or Structured Charts
[6] The Jackson method has recently been improved to cover system analysis and design—while it originally addressed itself to structured programming. These extensions follow the data structure approach.
[7] Applications development facility.
[8] Hierarchical Development Methodology
[9] Microsoftware Engineering Facility

In short, What's the standard? Leading computer users understand the challenge. Ford, GM, Teneco, and other firms have established their own standards in systems analysis. A company may have hundreds of computers around, but without a standard the data on the one machine are not the same as that on the other.

Furthermore, the question is not only technology. There are a lot of human factors involved in this work. When we speak of system analysis we should always recall that electronic mail and interactive capabilities magnify this problem, adding a new dimension to the requirement for a homogeneous data structure design.

Let's return to Table 4.

Most of the solutions listed are not real alternatives, yet each of the possibilities the table presents has strengths and weaknesses that set it somehow apart from the others.

Significant is the fact that already more than a dozen different projects have come to the foreground. The shake-out is inevitable. Evidently, the user should employ one of the best languages the market can offer. But which is the best one?

Some other examples can be added to this list such as Sketch Code and Module Modification Language, but this will not change the reference in a significant way. Practically, most outlined tools are mainframe oriented and this limits their usefulness. Of the projects outlined in Table 4, some are oriented toward the early stages of systems analysis and design; others toward programming and testing.

- PSL/PSA, SREP, SADT are examples of the first reference.
- Jackson and Warnier of the latter.

My own preference clearly lies with the option of beginning at the earliest possible phase of the system study. Hence the former reference. In examining where and how to start, the whole system life cycle should be considered the way we have already discussed. If the ideal tool is not there, we have to choose from those available or in the last analysis make our own on a personal computer.

3 CRITICAL CHARACTERISTICS OF STRUCTURAL ANALYSIS

We said that if we can find among the market offerings a structural analysis language approximating our requirements we should use it. If not, there is no choice but building our own. In the one as in the other case, it is good to know the critical characteristics we are after, and this is what we would attempt to do in this text.

The four topmost qualities of a structural analysis project are

Consistency,

Traceability,

Completeness, and

Structural Test.

Consistency means determining whether or not an entity is internally consistent in the sense that it contains uniform notation and terminology. Also, whether it is consistent with its specification. Tools that check for consistent usage of variable names or for consistency between design specifications and code are examples that answer this requirement.

One of the structural languages to which we make reference uses for consistency reasons a statement:

```
"ASSERT    name
           attribute, attribute ... "
```

For instance:

```
              name    attribute    value
ASSERT        a1      size         27
              a2      color        green;
```

Traceability calls for the faculty of tracking the development of an entity through the software life cycle. Tools used to trace requirements from their specification to their implementation in code have this feature.

In language statements, traceability can take the following form:

```
New Object: TRACE-KEY
New Statement: TRACE-KEY
DB1        DB2
name 1     name 2
```

For traceability to be effective, all objects must accept a trace-key. Facilities must be provided that allow us to check whether the logical requirements have been met by the physical design. Notice that these are two phases of the *same* system and not two different systems.

Completeness is associated with assessing whether or not an entity has its parts present and whether those parts are fully developed. A tool that examines the source code for missing parameter values presents this feature. As an example, the following instructions help define completeness:

```
OBJECT: object type
    ATTR      attribute-name-list
    STMT      state-name-list
    WITH      attribute = value
        ATTR      ....
        STMT      ....
```

Structure checking is the ability to detect structural flaws within a program. These may be improper loop nestings, unreachable statements, statements with no successor, or unreferenced labels.

Assertion checking and *constraint evaluation* are two other examples of needed facilities. The first controls user-embedded statements asserting relationships between elements of a program. As a logical expression, the assertion specifies a condition or relation among the program variables. In this sense, checking may be performed with symbolic or run-time data. Tools that test the validity of assertions as the program is executing have this feature.

Constraint evaluation calls for generating path input constraints for determining test input and for solving such constraints where they exist. An example is tools that assist the generation of test data.

Another valuable means is *complexity measurement*. The goal is determining how complicated an entity (routine, program, or system) is by evaluating some number of associated characteristics. Instruction mix, data references, control flow, number of interconnections, size, and computations can impact complexity.

Two further examples of facilities are *comparison* and *cross reference*. Comparison is assessing similarities between two or more items. A tool that compares programs or test runs for maintaining version control has this feature. Keywords can lead to comparison.

	Keyword
Synonyms	
Entities	Keywords
.....	.....
.....	.....
.....	.....

A keywords command will see to it that all entities where a given keyword applies must be listed along with their keywords. This also could be done on a selected basis, for instance, only those that start with x.

A cross-reference facility looks after referencing entities to other entities by logical means. Tools that generate call graphs or identify all variable references in a subprogram have this capability.

Error checking helps in determining discrepancies, their importance, and cause. Examples are tools used to identify possible program errors, such as misspelled variable names, arrays out of bounds, and so on.

Tracing concerns itself with the tracking of the historical record of execution of a program. The production of trace histories permits the setting of breakpoints for tracking down errors.

The object of tuning is determining what parts of a program are being executed the most. A tool that instructs a program to obtain execution frequencies of statements is an example.

Among the supervisory features are:

- Statistics
- Transformation
- Data flow analysis
- Resource usage, and
- Cost estimating.

A statistics file is generated by the analyser. Its object is to produce statistics on commands: CPU time, clock time, size of the database, I/O to the database, and number of names and of records created or destroyed.

This can be sorted by user and provide management with statistics on work done; it can also be sorted by command to keep track of how often a given instruction is used.

A transformation feature will typically describe how the subject is manipulated to accommodate the user's needs and what transformations took place as the input to the tool is processed.

A data flow analysis will present (preferably in a graphical form) the sequential patterns of definitions and references of data. Tools that identify undefined variables on certain paths in a program have this feature.

The object of routines-oriented resource usage is estimating the resources attributed to an entity. Tools that estimate whether memory limits, throughput constraints, or input/output capacity are being exceeded are examples. Associated with them is the concept of cost estimation: assessing the behavior of the variables that impact life cycle cost.

Cost estimation also has another, management-oriented sense with particular emphasis on the human resources. Some structural analysis packages include a facility of aiding the management in controlling software development.

Tools that control access, updates, and retrievals of software; maintain data definition use; manage test data sets; and check on the analyst identification during sessions are examples of this feature. As a result they provide a documented basis for how often an analyst works on which project.

4 THE DEVELOPMENT DATABASE

A structural analysis tool follows the process of developing application software through a linear model in which the various development phases are performed sequentially till the system is completed. The importance of a computer-based approach thus comes once again into perspective: Once a given job is done its component parts can be reprocessed to produce more refined versions of the software.

In this manner, problem analysis and system planning can be interleaved, the one serving as feedback to the other. The same is true of system planning and detailed design. As a result the needs of the user (requirements specifications) and the performance of the system (including its definition) can be refined, using the outcome of the one to tune the other.

Implementation can easily go beyond this brief reference to include all aspects of a life cycle methodology, with the successful application depending much more on the support of the environment than the sophistication of the tool.

As we will see when we talk of computer-aided documentation, to assure continuing support by the user environment at the system planning level, documentation should carefully record the user requests, the result of the feasibility analysis, the conclusions, the project authorization, the costs, and the timetables. A structured analysis is much more than simply using this or that programming tool.

Tools for a Structured Approach

Time is a resource that is just as valuable as money and manpower—and sometimes even more valuable than both of them. Time and also money can easily be lost when

- Software development regards complex data processing systems involving steps difficult to control and supervise.
- The experience gained by the developer is discarded in favor of habits and prejudices.
- The procedure must be curtailed or stopped midstream to do something else (often, a maintenance job on an existing procedure).
- An overlapping of development times leads to contention for scarce resources damaging all projects involved in it.

These are generic reasons for failure and they should be kept in mind during all phases of systems planning. Particularly sensitive is the creative design job, including the logical, functional, procedural, and organizational requirements that the system *must* accomplish in order to reach its goal.

What many analysts fail to realize, whether or not they use a structured approach, is that the balance the logical design must strike is a delicate one. User needs must be expressed system-wise, in a form that would serve as the blueprint for physical implementation.

Once the logical phase is done, and done well, the physical systems design will be reasonably stable. The hardware bits and pieces with which the information system will be constructed are more resistant to mishandling. Still, here again, timeliness helps in cost reduction and in performance. After the system requirements have been described, the earlier the physical evaluation is made, the better it is.

All this is written in the understanding that a computer-aided approach must bring around the possibility of a step-wise refinement

1. providing analysts and designers with structural means to streamline and accelerate what they are doing,
2. assisting in their communication with the ultimate user,

3. helping them build the necessary documentation as the project progresses,

4. designing files and processes in a homogeneous, transportable manner by means of formalisms,

5. offering the possibility of checking the contributions each project team member is making, bringing into evidence hitherto unknown strong and weak points.

Two objectives can be met by using this methodology: First the development of a computer-based *workbook* with detailed step-by-step procedures for data preparation, error correction, and report utilization, including timetables, fault description, and statistics. This should be interactively available to all authorized persons.

Second, a reasonably detailed technical documentation for the systems analysts (and eventually the programmers) to aid in understanding the information system when he or she needs to link, review, tune, expand, modify, and maintain it.

If by design aid we mean a technique that assists the achievement of a correct system design, a structural language should do it. It should offer the designer the technical references necessary to make him think about what he is doing and the ability to illustrate his requirements. This leads to the concept of a *designer's* database.

The complex information systems we are projecting today really call for three different kinds of databasing for development reasons:

1. Databasing describing the project itself, built to assist the designer, the analyst, and the programmer in their work.

It must include schedules, status, personnel employed, planned/actual costs, and so on. A project-oriented database is important first because much of the software development undertaken today assumes that the software developer not only must be familiar with the database design and performance but also capable of using these same principles in his day-to-day work.

Second, the applications area which concerns computer aided software development itself depends very heavily on database management approaches with sufficient capability and performance to make the computer-aided aspects a reality. Let's keep this reference in mind.

2. Databasing referring to the *target* system and including input, throughput, storage, and output.

Part of the development database No. 2 are the object and source codes *after* the target runs. The available information should describe the processing functions, the filing requirements, datacomm and transactional prerequisites but also other issues such as transformation and static analysis. Using a compiler as an example, the transformation features would be translation and possibly optimization, while the static analysis features would be error checking and cross-reference.

3. A condensed database including the skeleton needed for information and update.

As Figure 11-3 suggests, the construction of the development database No. 1 must start at the early stages of the system life cycle. The same is true of database No. 2. Consequently, No. 3 comes into life shortly before the end of the development cycle and integrates into it whatever is necessary from No. 1 and No. 2.

To be of any use, this skeleton database system should be regularly maintained, computer based, and accessible in an interactive manner. And this should happen all the way till the end of the life cycle of the project, of the programs included in it, and of the database capabilities under the authority of the database administrator (DBA).

5 FRINGE BENEFITS?

The references steadily made throughout this text do suggest that effective management of information resources is the difference

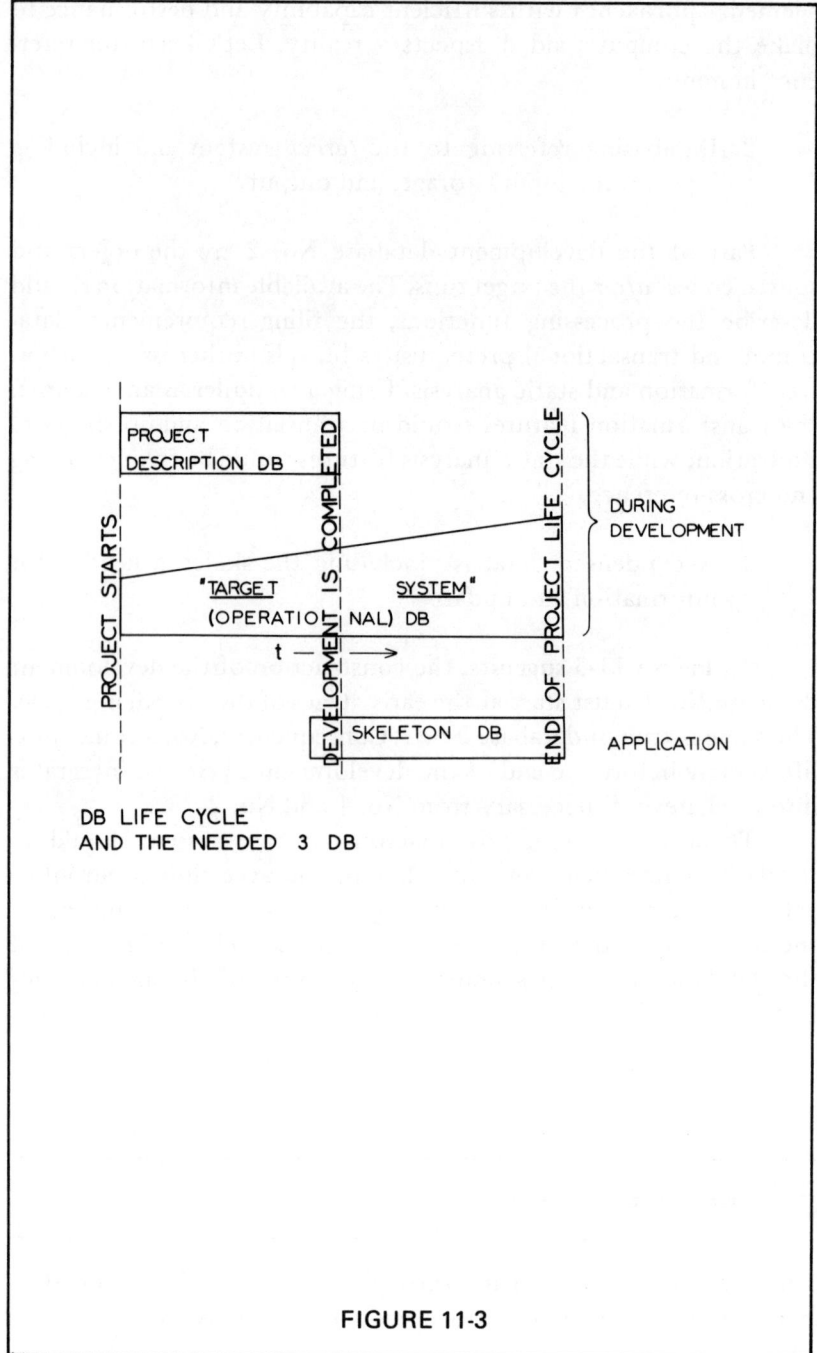

DB LIFE CYCLE
AND THE NEEDED 3 DB

FIGURE 11-3

between success and failure in today's competitive environment. Computers can analyze large volumes of data; process, store and retrieve text; and simulate cause and effect, thus influencing management decisions.

Communications media are at our disposal to transfer text and data over long distance, use increasingly efficient channels supported through satellites and optical fibers, and employ the best protocols experience makes possible. But the computers and communications gear must be programmed; and, till the state of the art makes intelligent, self-programmed machines a reality, the job must be done by humans.

That's practically all there is at issue when we talk of selecting and adopting a structured systems analysis approach. Our first goal is the discipline this can bring to the systems analysis and programming profession that for thirty years has been characterized by "I know it better" individualists. But there are also a number of fringe benefits the more recent packages can offer, such as document-handling by *Focus* (see also Table 4 in this chapter).

- Interactive data entry language, designed to provide formatted screens for transaction type applications. This offers the less experienced users the ability to manage repetitive procedures.

- Data storage structures, using both common value sharing and structural linkages. They help fully describe data as it logically exists and to present a simplified and comprehensive view of what is stored in computer memory.

- Database administration. It can be used to limit access to parts of or an entire database. To do needed processing, users may have access to particular segments of a file, being blocked from access to unauthorized areas. Through lockout, it is also possible to guard against accidental changes in the contents of the database.

- Dialogue manager facility. Working interactively, it is prompting the user on a terminal for step by step actions. It validates the answers provided before proceeding, stores repetitive procedures, and makes it feasible to access information without data-processing expertise.

- A statistical analyser contains a roster of statistical routines. The user can specify and select the variables to be analyzed from appropriate files and on an interactive basis control the sequence of the analysis.

Among the statistical operations are mean and standard deviation; correlation coefficients; canonical correlation; step-wise, multiple, linear and polynominal regression; analysis of variance; cross-tabulation; and exponential smoothing. It is true that these results can be obtained independently of the reference package through the employment of the appropriate routines. It is however handy to have to deal only with one structured package by identifying the appropriate commands.

Other fringe benefits can come from a structured system analysis solution. One major New York bank used it to create a model of all major areas of operation from the unit teller to encoding, data processing, databasing, extraction, bookkeeping, and send-out.

Here are the advantages outlined by the management of the financial institution: The structured analysis approach has helped modify bank operations involving 7,500 employees, made feasible a more fundamental examination of alternatives, assisted in creating documentation, and was instrumental in evaluating displaceable costs. The benefits were expressed in three terms:

- The biggest paybacks come when the analysts start scoping the system.
- The next, when the structural package was not used just in analysis and trouble shooting but throughout the systems study.
- Finally, experience taught the wisdom of starting a structured approach very early in the life cycle—and rather than using structured approaches with existing analyses, stressing the *new* ones.

Here are the highlights of the answers another organization has given regarding a structured analysis implementation: project organization is very important; separate responsibilities are a must; the analysts should do walkthroughs with the user and do them early; management should impose a methodology *before* the analysts start working with the package. It was also underlined that structural approaches require a great deal of forethought, thus obliging the project leader and his systems specialists to study all they want to know and how they will go about it *before* they start working with a structured analysis tool.

Still another company was to suggest that, to work well with a structured solution, project management should be careful to create the understructure: to guarantee systems integrity and permit cooperation by people of a varied background. Said a cognizant executive: "If projects don't succeed, it is because they try to do without the basic understanding. Those who take the time to THINK are a success. What's our policy? It is to use a structured approach in order to induce our people to think."

Not all reactions have been positive; not all projects handled through a structural analysis methodology were successful. Common characteristics among those that failed were

- being mainly batch oriented
- lack of experience in the implementations
- the applications were not subjected to a rigorous discipline by way of preparation
- too many miracles were expected from what one analyst called "the automatic programming piece of software."

In fact, working together with cognizant executives who saw some misfortunes with a structured solution we came to the following conclusions. I outline them to help the reader on the demands one should pose on a structured analysis project:

1. There is too much to swallow in terms of commands and procedures as the most structured analysis systems now stand.
2. These systems have more terms than they really need for 90% of applications.
3. There is a fundamental requirement to define which piece(s) must come first.

4. A new version (of structured analysis systems) should be made to cut down to basics, not to increase sophistication.

5. The "extras" (other facilities) should be organized as a Christmas tree.

6. There is an imperative requirement to make the structured analysis approach *simple* for the user.

Furthermore, the facilities included in a structured analysis package made it imperative to train the system specialists (and eventual end users) on their correct employment. For instance, in terms of the databases, the specialists should address themselves to four key questions: how to manage the data directory; implement the internal access method; follow up on the updating of the text and data files; and the problem of synchronizing the replicated files.

When we talk of challenging questions and of cases which are not success stories, let's not lose sight of our goal. The further-out aim is to achieve an order-of-magnitude improvement in the software price/performance against the current stagnation. Software productivity improves only slowly and the cost of software relative to hardware is on a steady rise. (In NASA the software/hardware ratio was about 2:1 ten years ago and in 1980 this ratio was projected at the 10:1 by the middle of this decade. On one existing program, the World Wide Military Command and Control System, the ratio is already in that vicinity—$722 million for software to less than $100 million for hardware.)

Let's not forget the goal of safeguarding ourselves against million dollar software projects going to the waste basket. Many user organizations learned the hard way the need for applying a computer-aided methodology in system analysis: ALS, the software for the U.S. Air Force Logistics system was terminated after it had cost $500 million. There were no results! No programs to be retained! The whole $500 million was written off as a loss.

PART THREE

THE ART OF LANGUAGE SELECTION

12

INTERACTIVE LANGUAGES

1 INTRODUCTION

Programming language design is an important area of research. The implementation of distributed information systems affects programming (1) by bringing to the front line the end user, (2) by implying the ability to recompile parts of the system dynamically while other parts of the system are running, and (3) by the need to handle parallelism.

As computers and communications systems start reaching the workplace, the user will increasingly specify without help the information required while the process by which it is obtained is built into the system. In the conventional sense we have been programming a series of procedural steps defining the process by which the information required is to be generated. But attention now starts being paid to a self-contained system.

Interactive programming approaches reflect a new concept of systems characteristics. The action mix and the nature of the actions permitted are a measure of the system's programming perspectives. Action mix reflects the combination of premises (or conditional statements) and action statements allowed in a use of a function. The actions may be of varying types and complexity depending on the system.

Typical actions of interest to the end user may be moves, data transfers, conditional jumps, or assignment statements. These examples reflect a procedural language. If the actions permitted are of high level implying the processing of a whole file or even of a database, then the language is more problem oriented. Interactive systems particularly suggest the latter class.

Interactive programs might execute at the workstation yet affect the global system. The model of such system becomes more complex when the user interacts with a terminal or is given the ability to create and alter procedures. Complexity increases if the user lacks the background or the desire to learn drastically different approaches to the solutions of familiar problems than those utilized in daily work.

2 WHICH LEVEL LANGUAGE?

Programming in the sense of composing instructions for a machine is the smallest part of the broader programming subject. As outlined in Part Two, we must give serious thought to the end product we want to produce. When the concepts characterizing a programming product are understood informally, it would seem to be a trivial matter to invent a language notation for them.

The problems with computer programming are not the letters of code to be employed and the system of rules they observe, but replacing an intuitive, vague idea with a precise, unambiguous definition of meaning and restrictions. Then comes the issue of choosing the notation. This should be done carefully, thinking of the elements of the problem which must be denoted.

The fact that choosing a suitable notation contributes to understanding the problem underlines the need that the concept of a programming language represents an often used general idea. But the meaning and rules of a programming language must be precisely defined.

Taken together, these two qualities make it possible that the processing, the databasing, and the datacomm concepts be represented by a concise notation that makes it easy to recognize the elements and their relationships. Added to this is the *algorithmic* approach which permits us by simple techniques to obtain a secure, efficient implementation of the concept.

Users know that computers solve problems and that any problem with numbers in it is properly a computer problem. But users should also appreciate that there is no cause and effect relationship that sees to it that any number coming out of a computer must be correct (especially if they wrote the program and failed to test it thoroughly). Nor should they believe that if they begin with a high-enough-level language, the grungy details of coding are trivial.

Believing in gossip like that is preparing oneself for deceptions. Another misconception is that computing power is becoming an almost free good, a notion reinforced by the rhetoric of computer salesmen. The facts of life are different and should be faced as they are.

Computers come in many sizes, with different price tags, features, and levels of complexity. One of the issues they support is programming languages. But not all machines address themselves to the same language solution. If the user decides to program his machine, the first thing to do is to choose the level of language he wants to work with among those provided. Classically, we distinguish three levels:

1. *Machine level* is the nearest to the way the inner machine works. Those of us old enough to be programmers in the early 50s still remember the experience. But nobody programs in machine language anymore.

2. *Assembler level* uses symbolic names for the different commands. The inner machine does not understand it. And so it needs an *assembler* (a piece of software) to translate the symbolic commands to machine level.

It is not advisable to use assembly level code unless you are a hobbyist. When programming with assembly languages, micro, mini, and even maxicomputers are about equal in challenge. The difficulty of language usage is a function of the instruction set of the microprocessor and the utility software that is available for writing programs.

3. *High-level languages*. This is a misnomer, but still an established name for languages such as Pascal, Fortran, Cobol, and the like.

4. *Very high-level languages*. These are becoming increasingly nonprocedural and easy to implement. But they also have the effect of requiring a highly structured approach to systems design (see also Chapter 22 on VHLL).

A very high-level language permits one to easily work with a number of applicative products at one time, such as screen design, procedural evaluation, applications programming and database management. The VHLL offers a well-structured, common interface to all applications needs, sees to it that man-information communications characteristics are uniformly applied to all of the users' applications, and makes sure that these applications integrate under a common work environment.

VHLL (fourth generation) programming is achieved by adding commands, entity relations, and database-oriented operations. Recovery is embedded and transparent to the user.

The new, high-productivity programming tools feature a tabular structure of the database that rests on relational concepts. The user can interactively sign-on and sign-off, add, delete, duplicate, index, find, match, sort, and so on.

Depending on their level of implementation, programming languages can provide very high level abstract objects and operations on them, as well as high level control structures. Such programming styles can simplify the programmer's task by eliminating large amounts of relatively routine detail that would otherwise have to be supplied. In general, fourth generation languages can be classified in five major groups; spreadsheet systems, database management and query, productivity oriented tools, new programming languages for artificial intelligence, graphics, and programming extensions to the OS and special software capabilities. If properly used, each of these groups assures a much greater productivity for professional systems experts while it makes it feasible for the nonprofessional to program the computer, albeit at a lesser level of sophistication.

The level of a programming language is determined by the power of the semantic primitives which it supports. Commands provided by lower level (or obsolete "high level") languages lie closer to the elementary operations implemented by the hardware. A higher level of programming presupposes primitives with storage allocation and control structures. A still higher level supports more abstract but also more powerful operations, manipulating entire arrays.

To program in a higher-level language we need compilers. A *compiler* is more powerful than an assembler. Not only does it include assembly functions but it also can call on subroutines through macro-operations, thus expanding the capabilities of the single instruction. Typically, for instance, a Cobol statement corresponds to 3 or 4 lines of assembler level code.

The compiler should be able to check that the rules governing the use of the concept are satisfied. The programmer should be able to predict the speed and size of any program that uses the concept he has elaborated by means of performance measurements of its implementation.

Traditionally, in order to use a programming language, the software specialists had to understand the notions of compile time, load time, and run time. Various other aspects were also important, such as the employment of I/O devices and memory supports.

Today the end user need not be bothered by such matters. The manager can ignore the existence of, say, a hierarchical file system if file access messages can be sent to a file server. New language developments tend to reduce the amount of information needed to program a machine.

With online operations it is, however, necessary to emphasize the network aspect of the system: the communications activity, server, nodes, workstations—as well as the requests for service, the possible contention at the server level (critical area), and so on. An extension of this is sending procedures and messages to other networks. Furthermore, features have to be added to simplify the human interface.

The perspectives that we are discussing go well beyond what the languages of the late 1950s and mid 1960s (Cobol, PL/1 etc.) were providing. The needed facilities are no longer limited to open and close files but cause transfers between levels of memory, move data from one working area in central storage to another, and equate a numeric data item to an arithmetic function.

The requirements are no longer limited to the classical statement labeling, associating statements to transfer execution control. Looping operations, to cause an action or set of actions to be repeated as long as some condition holds, are necessary but not enough. The separation between procedural actions and nonprocedural actions must be better defined for the action statements that control the movement of data between levels of memory. The trend is toward more sophisticated (higher level) statements.

Considerable attention should also be devoted to the handling of data as a self-standing activity. Data satisfying, for instance, a conditional expression may be extracted and placed into report form. For the purpose of analysis, the process of extraction should be separated from that of formatting. Extraction considers which quantities on each structure level may be included in the output file, irrespective of the process provided for formatting interactive softcopies and disregarding files for further processing.

The reference to extracting and formatting within an interactive environment is the more important as recent programming approaches for office systems have introduced the notion of expressing information flow by casting information into modules: documents and forms. The need for mechanisms to create templates for the data structures is also apparent from the time spent developing forms editors. These trends appear to be leading to the *intelligent form*.

Let's notice that the higher the level of the programming language the nearer we go to the model of the design. The goals of user-level methodologies is typically as general as possible within the scope of software development. They are intended to

- specify requirements before implementation,
- check the correctness of a design,
- be used as a design system,
- reflect the particular procedures important to end users, and
- by calling the appropriate macro-operations relieve the programming chores as much as possible.

In considering the development of modern information systems, there are compelling arguments in favor of such analytic modeling. The technology of the systems may still be in the formative stage, but these systems are quite dynamic and make the search for a comprehensive theory compelling. There are reasons to believe that the computers and communications aggregates of the future will need to lean heavily on modeling and theoretical analysis.

Since the office can be viewed as a network of highly interactive parallel processes, models employed in studies of computer systems and networks are highly applicable. Still, systems evaluation analytic needs to be augmented by simulation techinques. The latter can be transparent to the end user.

3 GREATER EFFICIENCY IN PROGRAMMING

The objective of the preceding section was to take a look at the way the programming function develops. Effective programming can be achieved through improved training, higher quality program planning, a more systematic approach to each phase of programming, and the implementation of a more efficient methodology particularly oriented to interactive programming.

Interactive programming needs its tools. At the present state of the art they include a text editor, to enter, update, and inspect text; compilers and macro-operations; link/loader facilities; and a data dictionary. Just as important are a DBMS (or at least a file system) and the ability to store programs in various formats, handle test data, and manage the development database.

The new online software development systems must support an adequate range of functions for program development. Program library managers are necessary and with them documentation aids, design aids, project control utilities. For instance, when performances are limited and compilations are slow, this will impact development time.

The quality of the programming product will be better if the programmer has easy access to the system and the facilities to perform the experimentation and tests he or she needs. The basic function to be supported is program preparation: program entry, update and inspection, program translations, compilations, link editing, unit testing, and system testing.

Another approach to providing the needed capabilities is to design new languages tailored to the interactive environment and its interfaces. It must support the use of workstations, be easy to learn and employ even by people with no previous programming experience, and have a good future in becoming a widely used one (Basic, Basic Plus, and Pascal fill this score).

User-friendly characteristics are important because, as experience with interactive systems increases, it becomes obvious that there are numerous advantages to the new computing environment for the user. Programmers can be more productive because sitting at a terminal they can work continuously on a program; the interactive features allow the users much more control over the operation.

Input data and commands can be given to the system allowing dynamic decisions during actual processing. Programmers must, however, be encouraged in the new environment to try for "better" solutions to problems rather than just the first one that worked successfully.

The problems with the programming languages of the 1950s and 1960s so prevalent still today go back to the initial concept of the digital computer put forth by von Neumann. The vision of a central processing unit, a main storage medium, and a single connector or queue between them was an elegant idea at that epoch. But times and hardware technology have changed and languages haven't.

The CPU-to-storage connector is the bottleneck in the original concept. It allows only a single word—whether data or instruction—in the conduit at any one time. Because it was the environment in which they had to function, most conventional programming languages have been built to work through this bottleneck. Mimicking the action of the bottleneck required the introduction of variables, control statements, and assignment codes.

The now developing programming technology, when it can be applied, has been mostly successful in overcoming the forementioned approach of elder languages. It tries to depart from semantics closely coupled with the state of the data and gives more expressive power to the changeable parts of the language.

Another central theme is the attempt to replace earlier hardware protection mechanisms by compilation checks. The monitor concept enables a compiler to check that *send* and *receive* are the only operations performed on a message buffer. Once the buffer monitor has been tested systematically the compiler prevents other program modules from using it incorrectly. This tends to localize errors in new, untested modules and prevent them from causing unknown effects in elder ones.

A further significant feature for an online distributed environment is probabilistic message passing. In elder approaches, the solution was deterministic. A receiving process waits until another process sends a message on a given line, each process performing a completely predictable transformation of its input to its output, in a typical situation of masters and servants.

Peer systems, however, suggest the wisdom of including nondeterministic message passing. This is a more complex problem, as the buffer process cannot predict whether the environment will ask for or send a message. Consequently, a buffer unit cannot commit itself to waiting until it receives a message on the input line, for this would make it unable to respond to a request for sending a message on the output line.

A process able to delay action until it receives a request for sending or receiving is needed. The solution would have been easy if the unit had an infinite memory and a very large number of polyvalent channels. But usually there is a finite storage capacity with a buffer process. This calls for introducing the attributes of non-deterministic statements.

As these references suggest, language facilities are rapidly changing from the rigidity of the symbol manipulation games of the 1950s and 1960s to the more natural disciplinary areas opened through the merger of computers and communications. The functional user-oriented language that may be developed by the end of this decade may present parametric faculties that permit dialects of a form more suitable to doctors, lawyers, or engineers. Other dialects of the same language might be appropriate for managers, accountants, security analysts, and so forth.

To support the handling of complex structures, facilities may be provided to permit the user to initiate data transfers between distributed text and databases. In a way transparent to the user, compilers will be exercising control over the logical flow of the program and may mix conditional statements, action statements, and loops.

Other self-contained capabilities the users of the system need not be aware of are functions of file creation and restructuring: the process of translating the user expressed data definition into its stored form, validation conditions the data entering a file must satisfy, and security prerequisites. The spread of micro-DBMS at the workstation level will accelerate and enhance this perspective.

A disadvantage of computer systems offering only self-contained capabilities today is the size of the set of applications they can handle. For applications within the set, self-contained systems offer considerably reduced setup time. The same is true of the time required to prepare a new query or database update. Hence, the suggested approach can make major economies in the end user's time and give faster satisfaction of information requirements.

Data compatibility is another problem steadily increasing in magnitude, particularly across two different software systems with several levels of data storage. The way information elements are stored within a record, logical records in a physical block, physical blocks identified as belonging to the same file, and more files on the same direct access volume are examples of the importance of data compatibility. The risk with interconnected nonhomogeneous systems is that the likelihood of data incompatibility increases greatly.

Solutions should not only be sought in the programming area. They should be largely organizational, with programmatic interfaces. One of the organizational references is the institution of a database administrator. In a user environment in which an important database is kept online for access by several workstations, there must be a single person who carries responsibility for the many aspects of its use. He or she should be responsible for

> the initial creation of the database, and
>
> the instituting of any structural modification that may be required.

The use of the system features provided by the database should be of great relevance to the applications programmer. The latter has to accept constraints and disciplines that have been noticeably absent in times past for handling business applications.

What has just been said about the system specialist is just as valid for the end user who is not a professional programmer and for whom the self-contained capabilities have been designed. The interface with the database is a matter of invoking predefined transactions, providing values to any parameters they may have.

These may not seem to be subjects directly related to interactive programming, yet they are. They stem from the increased interest in allowing end users to interact with a database. This interaction is generally online from a workstation that is microcomputer supported. Functions accomplished by a transaction program may be query or updating. The user's understanding may be limited to the types of transactions learned and the meaning of any output, including the error messages that may be generated.

4 A USER-ORIENTED LANGUAGE

The object of a user-oriented language is to ease man-machine communication, attract non-professional programmers toward the on-line interactive capability, make technical systems interfaces transparent to the end user, and provide for computer assisted documentation and its update. To understand the importance of this subject and the way in which it can affect the future of programming as a profession, let's recall that programming facilities are so named because they can only be accessed through a procedural program written in a conventional programming language (the host language).

The way man-machine communication stood until recently, the user could only invoke the programming facilities by writing and executing a program. Typically this person was a programmer. The facilities provided by a computer for the programming user represent capabilities that are distinctly different from the functions of data definition, query, and update that are the basic issues regarding the end user today.

There have also been many developments over thirty years of programming practice. The statement types used to call upon the programming facilities supported by a given computer do not constitute a complete language in themselves. Therefore, they must be embedded in a conventional procedural language, as discussed in the preceding section. In executing a program statement, the machine may perform some additional support activities such as indexing, ordering, or run-time validation. These are examples of evolution in what a language can do.

The increased power inherent in the use of evolving programming also brings

- an increased responsibility for the programmer and the program user,
- a higher risk of destroying the integrity of the database,
- but also a greater ease in programming as we move toward user oriented languages (or dialects).

Ideally such a language should be applications oriented and involve a data definition facility, easy-to-follow instructions, agile screen formats (maps), and subroutine-supported processing components. The professional can benefit from such a language by improving his applications development productivity, but the greater beneficiary is the end user.

A user-oriented language can also help in program portability, bypassing the classical systems analysis and increasing the analyst's capacity to define formats (as contrasted to the facility of taking fixed formats). Being of very high level, it can assist in getting equipment independent (the physical media don't interest the end user).

Quite evidently, a user-oriented language should assure an interactive call of stored routines of inspection, utilization, and maintenance. Given the steady drop in computer prices, such language can interface with (or convert) rich libraries developed for current equipment.

An applications-oriented user-level language should include facilities for converting the systems analysis of existing programs from remote batch to interactive. It should minimize the impact of changes on applications programs (and on their documentation) through parameters and put the user in a condition to explicitly declare the mode to be used. Common mode distinctions include input, output, and update. Random and sequential processing should be supported through keys.

Depending on the mode, certain statements may be inoperable; others may require the user to initialize communication items in advance, declaring the intention with respect to each file or area to be processed by a program. (Such declaration may be made in the "open" key, prior to initiating execution of the program.)

- With the *retrieval mode* the user would indicate that he only intends to retrieve data from some named portion of the database. The associated need for a screen format can be handled through menu. Statements calling for a modification of the database would not be executed.

- Under the *storage mode* the use declares his intention to only transfer data from the program to the database. Add-

ing entries to the end is distinct from inserting entries in the file, thus maintaining an established ordering.
- The *update mode* encompasses both retrieval and storage. Updating a sequential file requires that a new copy be created. Hence, two files can be defined: one for input, the other for output.

Standard operations regarding the workstation at the end user's desk can be supported through firmware, with the action keys actuated through a keyboard or even better a graphic tablet and cursor. The same is true of the input, output, and update modes. As discussed on another occasion, there is a need for *help* and *prompting* infopages guiding the programmer and the end user in his work. The same is true about smoothing the user's training requirements.

Application facilities necessary at the workstation level to provide the stated services include data definition, map definition, application definition, application generation, application modeling, program testing, file and database generation, file inquiry, subsystem testing, and walkthroughs. Within the broader computers and communications capability, there is need for protocols, datacomm routines, database security, and at times simulation. A workbook log will be helpful—also a complete documentation for processing, I/O, database and communications.

The way the end user may invoke a programming facility varies. One way is to incorporate statements directly into the host language. Another is to invoke the facilities through the use of a "Call" statement. By extension, we can look at the program as a single module activated through a key.

The normal sequence of host language statements may have to be explicitly interrupted by the invocation of programming facilities with a control statement. The control statement must indicate to the compiler that it must interrupt the host language to interpret a special routine. The compiler may also be important to enable the user to call upon the facilities from programs written in different host languages.

Optimally, a user oriented language will start with a

1. *Data definition.*

This must allow the complete and correct definition of the data format and its characteristics. For instance: length, data type, relation to record structure, editing characteristics of the data. The next basic need is

2. *Screen format definition.*

Reference is made to the map of the softcopy at the terminal. The I/O fields for the map must be named, but the characteristics of the data for these fields will be obtained through the data definition. Default characteristics must also be provided.

3. *Application definition.*

Its object is the definition of the relationship of data records and maps. When issuing such a statement certain information must be communicated to the system. This includes the facility desired, the data structures to be referenced, the criteria to be used in selecting data structures, the location of the user working area, and an indication of what to do upon detection of an error or exception condition. This information may be provided explicitly as part of the statement's calling sequence or it may be implicitly assumed by the system. The latter may be based upon conventions to be followed by the end user. An application definition statement would have associated with it a sequence of parameters.

4. *Process definition.*

This concerns map displays, file accesses, data record handling, and a number of associated issues. For instance: arithmetic operations, logical operations, editing, process flow, value assignments (item to item), test for special conditions, table lookup and manipulation, assignment of characteristics, and environmental constraints/facilities.

Ideally, such program development will be parametric in terms of applications and system configuration. It will also be device-independent and will separate I/O from processing proper and database access.

The operating system should interface to supported terminal(s) whether softcopy (preferably) or hardcopy. It should be capable of assuring user exits and also self-checking for errors. The latter is a requirement for providing error-free programs to the user (but with centralized audit and control facilities). The following scenario identifies a way to program conversion from elder to newer machines, with a simultaneous conversion to an interactive facility.

1. Suppose there exists an applications library.
2. Suppose it is mainly batch oriented with some realtime programs.
3. However, even batch has a structure of information elements.
4. Then the *first* thing to do for portability and interactivity is to start with a database structure.
5. The next vital issue is output and input, which can be tackled with either preformatted (standard) or variable screen structures at the user's choice.

The hand of the user should be guided from defined input to database organization and from there to a defined output. For processing purposes (say, for the 80% of all cases) it is sufficient to use macros.

The user level language must support this process, assisting the user (professional or nonprofessional) with definitions, file structures, AP processes, documentation, and tests. Experimenting with a recent user-level model, a specialist with long-standing experience in realtime through mini made this comment: It can reduce the time needed for interactive applications by 75% and the time needed for batch by 50%.

5 PROGRAMMING WORKSTATIONS

Programming workstations require two strategies: First, giving an intelligent workstation to every programmer. Second, developing online programming standards. This solution should create source and object listing along with a complete documentation automatically updatable and interactively accessible.

We have been discussing how this would work in the preceding section on user-oriented languages. Work through online workstations will involve applications-oriented programming and therefore conversational approaches that will be of a substantial nonprocedural nature. A number of generalized facilities will be required to support this approach: adding, deleting, changing files, displaying records, preparing formatted reports—but also defining information elements, allocating storage capacity, and so on.

There is nothing extraordinary in these facilities. As we have seen earlier in this chapter, they are a reasonable extension of the add-on that exists today with most of the available higher-level languages. The same is true of the *online programming* concept, whose primitives address themselves to entering code, recalling it, and making changes through an online workstation.

To help programmer productivity and software reliability, man-machine dialog models must be developed and used in systems analysis, programming, and documentation. The future is in online software, a process resembling transaction processing.

Interactive programming capabilities are instrumental in helping to solve problems and so is the use of parametric approaches. Report generators can be actuated through programming workstations and reduce by two-thirds the code to be written.

Interactive workstations will become the means of the mid and late 1980s, replacing coding sheets, pencils, paper listings, and walks to the computer room to submit and take back jobs. At the same time, computer-based workbooks will take the place of project-tracking charts and associated documentation.

If the technology is there for making interactive programming a reality, the concepts are still lacking. An earlier classification distinguished two main types: host programming workstations and standalone. This distinction is both meaningless and, if implemented, false. It makes no sense to load the expensive, batch-oriented host with online programming. Standalone approaches should be rejected off-hand.

The best solution to online programming is a local area network that can link intelligent programming workstations among themselves and to the database. A gateway should connect to the host when needed and in a way transparent to the programmer. The alternative is to dedicate a mini with host communicating capabilities.

The evident goals of such application should be to improve reliability and program quality, use structured techniques, reduce program maintenance, and substantially increase programming efficiency. Project management should be keen to look into the methodology to be established—from the concept of what a program is all the way to its development and implementation.

Chances are the principles through which to guide such policy and practice. This would be in sharp antithesis to the often found tendency in computer management to dismiss the simple program as unimportant and unprofessional. Quite to the contrary, the simple program is a valuable, discreet, controllable activity in an information systems project.

To some extent, computer literature reinforces the attitude that big system design and mammoth programs are the real thing. Other poor practices abound, and when this is so the online workstations will be ineffective. For instance, programmers are thrust into their job after only a brief course on a given language (usually the obsolete Cobol) without any guidance as to how to write a program. After some time the programmer is recognized as good if he fulfills one or more of the following requirements:

- He prints quickly, clearly, and neatly in coding forms (this is a rather rare quality but even if necessary it is not enough).
- He is very quick to have a program into a position for testing (the inordinate amount of computer time required for subsequent testing goes unnoticed).
- Every time his program fails under operational conditions, which may be rather often, he is pulled out of another job (which is delayed) and able to spot the problem.
- He writes his programs in such a complex way that his supervisor cannot help but be impressed when the program eventually runs.

These are false premises and, not surprisingly, they arrive at very poor results. Before management can expect results from the programming workstations (and from human resources working on them) it must ask itself questions similar to those that have been asked for years in like disciplines such as engineering design and management accounting. For instance:

1. *How well are we doing in programming applications?*

Four points stand out: First, though it takes quite long to get most applications programmed and tested, results often do not measure up to expectations. Much better performance is possible. This has been proved time and again at the computer center which cared enough to look for valid solutions.

Second, improvements are unlikely to come by chance and wishful thinking or by throwing some hardware at them. Results will materialize if management understands the challenge of programming computers and communications systems, and asks for both quality and performance. Experience documents that discipline can be imposed upon the programming function just as it can be placed on any other like activity.

Third, somewhat surprisingly, significant improvements are not too likely to come from the computer manufacturers. The need for improvements has been apparent to the field for thirty years. Yet the prime programming courses consist of training in the way to flowchart, that is, the symbols to be used and the syntax of high-level languages. The philosophy of the linguistic concepts is never talked about.

Fourth, if improvements are to be made, it will be up to the user organization to cause them to be made. Disciplines are needed whereby interactive processing, databasing, and datacomm goals can be achieved, together with better use of resources. It is up to management to see the programmers' technical side of the problem *before* the online workstations are implemented.

2. *Where does programming fit into the computer environment?*

In line with current trends of lower equipment costs and higher salaries, it is not unreasonable to say that the systems analysis and programming costs will eventually exceed the 80% of the total costs of the installation—if we continue to work as in the 1950s. Certainly the drop in the unit price of computing power has been more than offset by increased software costs.

Costs for system development and program maintenance are outlays subject to significant management control. They are the largest budgetary item in a computer installation today. They are also the areas that will affect future benefits from information systems.

Hence, the answer to question No. 2 is that analysis and programming fits squarely in the middle of management's preoccupations with computers and communications. Methodologies for higher quality and greater efficiency in computer programming have moved relatively slow up the steps; quite often progress is just an illusion.

3. *What is being done about the ever increasing cost of programming?*

We cannot bow to the "inevitability" of increasing programming costs only by looking about for substitutes such as packages. As we will see in the next chapter, packages are an expedient. They don't always solve the problem. The right reaction is to set standards for programming, to train, to give efficient tools, coming to grips with the real problem: What is programming?

Standards cannot be set effectively until there is agreement on what is good programming and what is a bad practice. If this is done in an able manner, the result will be reduced costs and better quality by controlling programming projects.

The activities of a programmer can be broken down into modules. Many of these modules can be automated and handled through workstations. The proportion of time spent on each of these defined activities may vary from programmer to programmer. But there is a correlation between standard times and the quality standards being produced. This is the more true today as the most difficult area to quantify and control (and which occupies the major part of programmers' time) is testing.

A good programmer—equipped with online workstations and a valid, interactive development language—if properly controlled will spend the appropriate amount of time on designing and planning his work. Management is then in a much better position to measure progress of a particular program against targets for design, coding and testing; spot weaknesses in project estimates before it is too late; make realistic estimates of completion dates; and control the overall project. We will return to these notions.

13

DEVELOPING PORTABLE PROGRAMS

1 INTRODUCTION

Getting the right machine is relatively easy today, though the right machine is not by any means obvious. Getting the right software with which to do the job effectively is much more difficult and much more costly.

The process of software development the way we have been discussing it since the beginning involves the activities of analysis, design, coding, testing, installing, and maintaining computers and communications programs. A *software package* is a specific computer program or set of programs, designed to perform one or more well defined functions that are considered useful for computer users other than the developer of the package.

The software package is a *programming product* made available to users in a prefabricated form, with associated documentation and maintenance. It is usually offered at a fixed price. Though there is an incredible variety of programming products on the market today, all of them can be classified into two basic categories:

- systems packages, and
- applications packages.

Systems packages are programs or sets of programs revolving around basic functions such as monitoring, datacomm, databasing, with the aim of making it possible to use a computer more conveniently or operate it more efficiently. Included in this broad category are operating systems and their enhancements, database management systems, report generators, job accounting systems, diagnostic routines, debugging aids, assemblers, compilers, translators, simulators, and input/output control routines.

About 30% of the currently available software packages fall into the systems category; these systems packages account for more than 55% of the total revenues from programming products. This is also the current trend as companies participating in a survey reported about 40% of funding for applications packages and 60% of their outlays for system software going to external procurement sources.

Applications packages are programs or sets of programs that perform specific data-processing tasks. After getting off to a comparatively slow start, both the computer makers and independent suppliers are now extremely active in the development of applications-oriented programming products to handle a broad range of business needs.

Payroll and general accounting packages are the best selling type of applications package to date. But packages for accounts receiveable, accounts payable, inventory control, production scheduling, and statistical analysis are selling well. It is generally expected that an increasing percentage of the applications funding will be spent to buy packages rather than modifying, updating, and expanding old software or starting program writing from scratch.

2 THE PROGRAMMING PRODUCT

Since the software package is a programming product, it is reasonable to look at it from the perspective of product planning, design, production, testing, and maintenance. Three great differences distinguish a programming product from any computer program that is written to satisfy data-processing requirements:

1. *Product Quality.*

The programming product must abide by reliability concepts, quality standards, and operational characteristics. Specific guarantees must be given to that effect by the manufacturer and vendor of the package, and they must be spelled out in the contract.

As it cannot be repeated too often, product quality is built in on the drawing board and it is certified through the appropriate

Developing Portable Programs

tests. Not only should the user look at the software market in the classic "buyer beware" frame of mind, but he should also invite the vendor of a programming product into a legal, contractual guaranty from which there is no escape. There should be a contract carefully reviewed by the user's lawyers to assure there are no loopholes.

By all means, resist the temptation to simply sign the software vendor's standard contract or order form and get it over with. As in the case of hardware, the user must be a tough negotiator to make sure that he or she is getting all the protection and support needed. The assistance of the company's lawyer is worth having. But the lawyer must also be trained in software quality assurance.

Since we have spoken to a considerable extent about quality assurance, I will not elaborate further on it. It is sufficient to note that the standards and controls that have been detailed above should be observed much more closely when the product is offered to the market.

2. *Portability*.

While the poor programming practice of thirty years has led many companies into programming one shot processing propositions, a package should be characterized by portability. "Being portable among different machines" is an issue that mostly receives lip service.

Though we will devote nearly half the text of this chapter to portability, let's immediately take notice that the transferability of a programming product implies rules both for its maker and for its user. The developer of a package must keep to standards, make it parametric, and document it properly. For his own benefit, the user should observe two basics:

> If you can find a package for your application, never write a program to reinvent the wheel—buy it.
>
> If you buy a package, never change its programming features—use them.

The meaning should be clear to the user: Adapt your own procedures rather than change the code of the package. Software is like a delicate, fine mechanical engine. By tackling, it will not get better but it can surely deteriorate.

A packaged software system rarely gives the user 100% of what he would "ideally" like to see in the system (in the rare case he knows precisely what he is looking for). This characteristic is not monopolized by packaged software. In many cases, a custom written program does not give the full 100% compliance desired either.

Quality deterioration apart, there is also a tough cost side in software alterations. People write computer programs, people tackle programs (read: mess them up), and people have become more and more expensive with the passing years. Acquiring a software package that fits 90% of the user's requirements is a good alternative to paying the people-cost to write a custom-made program that would never accomplish the 100%. What's wrong is doubling the cost of the package by messing it up through alterations.

Attention should however be drawn to the fact that not just "any package" can answer the user's needs, be portable from one machine to another, be error free, and be cost/effective. Neither will a policy of package acquisition cancel the need for systems analysis.

The analysis necessary to identify the user's need must be done *in writing*. It must also be complete and thorough as it will be used as a standard for software selection. The search for a programming product available in the market should only start *after* the fundamental step of systems analysis has been completed and the user requirements identified in an able manner.

3. *Maintainability.*

Software, like any other product, must be maintained. We devote a whole chapter to this issue. But while the right maintenance procedures are generally necessary, the way of handling this requirement should be much more formal with software packages.

Software maintenance is highly labor-intensive. Sound management principles dictate that this reason alone should force a "maintenance perspective" from the early design stages of a programming product. Ease of maintenance and completeness of the documentation should be two basic preoccupations from the start.

The user of packaged software needs manuals that he or she can understand without a specialized knowledge of computers and communications systems. But if it takes 300 pages of closely spaced type to understand and use a programming product, then this product is unusable.

Besides, user-oriented manuals should provide a series of tutorials along with trial data and sample programs. Illustrations of the video screen before and after a command can be helpful. Operations manuals should be comprehensive.

Maintenance manuals can be helpful, but wise users would leave the maintenance of packages to the vendor. Manufacturer-supported software maintenance typically costs per year between 6% and 8% of the sales price and it does three things at once:

Correct the possible errors in the preceeding release.

Adapt the package to changing legal requirements (particularly for personnel, accounting, and tax applications).

Upgrade the programming product with new functionality.

The wisdom of using the vendor's maintenance services brings up requirements. One is written assurance on the timeliness and the quality of this maintenance. The other regards a solid guaranty that, if the manufacturer of the programming product goes under, it will still be possible to proceed with maintenance—this time by the user organization itself.

Hence, when considering the purchase of a software package valid questions are: Does the vendor (or manufacturer) provide good maintenance service? Can we use a substitute in case of business failures? Is there an iron-clad warranty period? Does the vendor honor this warranty?

No matter who the vendor is, good practice suggests a security mechanism whereby the source code is deposited with a lawyer— to be made available to the user with all the documentation the day the vendor fails. Such provisions are just as important as asking whether the software is reliable, upgradable, and able to meet the user's needs.

Prior to looking once again more carefully into the subject of packages, their advantages and disadvantages, let's briefly consider what constitutes a portable computer program and where the challenges are. This will be followed by an evaluation of the development of portable programs.

3 CONDITIONS FOR PORTABILITY

One of the major problems with today's software is that it is not readily movable. Most of the applications programs appear to be designed on the assumption that only one machine will ever be utilized in any given company. As a result, it is very difficult to move libraries from one computer to another. But maintaining duplicate libraries is extremely difficult in a multi-machine shop.

The goal should be to design applications software in such a way that one machine can adequately, fully, and easily back up another in the sense that any program normally run on equipment "A" can simply be run on equipment "B":

- without stopping the machine "B"
- without performing special set-up
- without spending a fortune developing procedures and supplementary software.

A crucial factor affecting portability is the need for conversions both in terms of software and of hardware. Conversions have almost been a way of life in the computer industry since its inception. However with the growing personnel costs they result in major financial losses and in a diminution of availability.

By way of illustration, consider a company that is approaching 2,000 source modules (programs). This is by now a nearly typical case of a medium sized company, as 2,000 source modules would represent, say, some 800,000 Cobol statements. Major computer users now have in excess of 2 million statements in their libraries.

Let's suppose that within this environment a simple conversion is needed; in fact, it is so simple that it only takes 20 minutes of machine time and 10 hours of programmer's time per source module. For the stated medium sized library, this very simple conversion would require the use of 660 hours of computer time and 100 man-years of programming effort to be accomplished.

Such numbers do not appear to be at all unreasonable to expect. Even fairly small installations number more than a thousand source modules. What's more, for small computer installations the problems of conversion are becoming increasingly complex as the number of files and programs grows. Among other problems:

> Users with libraries of thousands of tapes and hundreds of discs find that a tape conversion can cost them dearly in terms of computer time.
>
> Disc conversions are unnecessarily combersome and time-consuming.
>
> Conversion to take full advantage of increased memory size can cost a small fortune with today's designs.

Let's furthermore add that the concept of conversion is applicable in varying degrees as one changes the configuration of one's computing facilities, adding or subtracting memory, major peripheral devices, new or revised software components, and so on.

Software conversion is a particularly troublesome one at today's state of the art. New software releases, new hardware features, and the drive for a better availability highlight the moving gear behind adaptations to applications software that consume available brainpower and are very costly. Hence the advice to use packages wherever possible, leaving to the vendor the care of software maintenance.

For programs made in-house, software should be designed with storage parameters that can be varied to take advantage of additional central memory (when available) and other add-on features. Particular attention is also necessary in the area of data conversion.

Technology advances or simply changes in operating systems are accompanied by changes in format, access methods, and so on. This way files created on the old system cannot be efficiently handled on the new one, but then can be converted. A simple conversion tool, capable of transforming the old files with minimum overhead, should be a part of the new system facilities.

Further, the problem of *conversion of documentation* must be solved. This applies to both hardware and software related text, but primarily its impact is felt on applications documentation.

The documentation for an applications program must often be substantially changed, for instance, when a new compiler is to be utilized and to a lesser extent when new discs are installed. Going from 300 MBy to 1.2 GBy or 2.4 GBy discs has an impact on the operations manual. This impact is all the greater since programming documentation should describe

tapes and discs to be mounted,

estimated running time,

the sort/merge routines to be used,

operational flowcharts,

record structure layouts, and so on.

This is another reason I have so much insisted in the appropriate chapter that a computer-assisted methodology should be adopted. With it, a documentation conversion can be readily done to support all hardware and software changes.

Since documentation is not an independent end item but must at all times reflect an exact correspondence with, or representation of, an end product (software), it must be changed whenever the corresponding facility is changed. Thus, even if documentation were issued in the best condition and there were no need (which there is) to test for

- errors,
- omissions,
- ambiguities, and
- misleading statements,

there would still be a need to make changes in documentation in order to keep it current.

One of the pillars of portability is the uniformity of procedures to facilitate preventive maintenance. To be both portable and easier maintainable, software must be built through a logical building block process with audit trails left by each component. Further, preventive maintenance of software implies continued testing of the product at the supplier's site.

With programming products, all copies delivered to users are exact replicas of the end item produced, not nearcopies to be continually tested in the field for conformance with the "master copy" as is the case with hardware. However,

1. Today's concepts of product testing and integration testing must be extended definitely beyond the initial release date.
2. Test scenarios must be continually expanded with more rigorous tests, both devised by the producer's test designers and derived from faults exposed in user installations.
3. Fixes to software problems should become available in a timely and clear manner to user personnel in order that the decision can be made to apply a fix to the programming product without creating upheaval in the application.
4. Software fixes should be tied more closely to logical modules, and documentation more clearly describe the problem to which they are addressing themselves.
5. Test routines should clearly identify their object, the problem they try to control, and the way in which they operate.

These issues are just as essential with software as with hardware, yet they are unavailable on most programming products, totally so with home-made software.

Software portability can be enhanced if an insistence upon standard interfaces could allow substitution with similar functions when a software component fails. This is not the case today. Statistics reported by major computers and communications users demonstrate how, every time a new application is introduced into their realtime system, there is a sharp drop in mean time of system interrupt (MTOSI).

Software reliability must be looked upon from two perspectives: the supplier developed programs, and the user developed applications programs. In both cases, it should be kept in mind that software is rarely designed for quick repair. A substantial research effort is needed to develop a methodology which can assure repair quickly and surely on the spot.

In what concerns the user's own programs major amounts of available time are lost because the user simply isn't sure whether the computer's basic software or his program is at fault. To help correct this, it is important that the basic software both protect itself and publish clear messages in the event of malfunction or improper usage.

Improved design in software diagnostics is an important factor in software repairability. We will return to this subject when we talk of maintenance.

Another of the conditions of software portability is the ability to satisfy the requirements for usability, accuracy, completeness, and currency—as well as the applicability of the programming product on different machines. In addition, there should be measures showing the nature of the failures. This is needed to improve the training of personnel, maintain tighter control over program development and implementation, and reduce the requirement for software repairs.

The time to make a repair is as important as the frequency of the failure in determining the cost to the user. Portable software magnifies this factor The more a programming product is used in different installations the greater is the wait of the mean time to repair (MTTR).

4 ALGORITHMIC CHARACTERISTICS

If we are to improve the conditions under which a programming product works at the user's site, we have to return to the fundamentals. A computer program is a formulation of the structure of a projected processing system. This formulation can be exact if it answers algorithmic characteristics by means of sequences of instructions.

Algorithms are encountered in everyday life, without us being aware of it. For example: going home, $A \times B$, the concepts of addition and subtraction. All we are asking with programming products is formality in approach, to be imbedded in the modules or subroutines.

A subroutine is a function expressed in an exact formulation such as is made feasible by means of an algorithmic expression or a wired-in circuitry. A subroutine is a black box to any end user, but for its designer it is a known function. The subroutine is also a black box to any programmer calling it by name into action.

Important to the concept of developing portable programs is the fact that algorithmic approaches do not necessarily imply unique solutions in all cases. Different algorithms may exist for the same problem just like different languages exist to say the same things. But variation is very low because mathematics is a formal non-redundant language (as opposed to the highly redundant natural languages).

Algorithmic formality requires that

1. Data belong to the same class for which the algorithm has been developed (principle of class nature).
2. The algorithm is expressed in terms of certain fundamental and known operations (principle of definiteness).

Algorithmic formality is a prerequisite to software portability. The latter demands approaches that go far away from current, "historical" solutions.

The objective is to make a software design that is *not* influenced by particular machine structures and then adapt it to the specific case of the individual machine. This is consistent with the concept of algorithmic solutions. A valid approach will proceed through mathematical expressions, bringing both the developmental steps and the tests on a mathematical level.

Software portability is more important than the optimization of processing functions. For one thing, software optimization looks like the process occupying people who do things they need not be doing *if* programming had kept up with machine technology.

Usage statistics indicate that the 46% of programs require 2% of computer capacity. With hardware prices dropping, it doesn't make sense to spend resources on the fine tuning of software, given the cost of its development and the sort of functions to be accomplished.

In terms of methodology, the problem is more fundamental than that of an implementation language. As I had the opportunity to explain in the appropriate chapter, the right methodology will

> Oblige the user to think and properly define his needs.
>
> Clarify procedural issues prior to formalizing the systems analysis.
>
> Provide the basis for thorough testing.
>
> Fully document for maintenance.

The right methodology will also see to it that the proper programming approaches are taken for the computer to which they are addressed. For instance, microcomputers should not be programmed like big machines. It is wise to keep the program simple. The personal computer hardware costs are too low and the programmer's time too expensive, whether we program a big or a small machine.

Thus, the methodology to be adopted for programming products must be viewed as a pragmatic discipline requiring a good allocation of resources. A rule valid in other business environments can find its place here. Program development should be guided by economics.

If a high-level language instruction enhances the readability and presentation of a program, it must be used in preference to an instruction that saves central memory and possibly execution time but makes a program difficult to follow. Computer running time and memory space were criteria of the 1950s and 1960s—not of the 1980s.

Furthermore, by the end of this decade software companies and the leading users will be moving away from classical coding schemes developing microcode for chips to be installed in the original hardware. And in the 1990s we will see most major computer manufacturers having just one basic type of equipment in their line. Specialization will be done through firmware and packages will be cast in silicon.

5 SOFTWARE PROCUREMENT

Many users start appreciating that it is not cheaper to write their own software. Anyone with a good accounting practice would find out that development costs can be staggering. Applications packages spread development costs over a number of users.

Commercially available programming products have further advantages. First, if properly done and tested, many of the errors in the programs would be corrected. Second, packages that sell well are constantly improved. Third, by buying its software, the user preserves some flexibility and cuts development time.

We have made reference to these issues and we have also said that a programming product must be evaluated *before* commitment is made. For the user, the best way to evaluate software is to test it at his own installation. Selecting a package could take a considerable amount of time.

Another issue that we have underlined is that even if a package is purchased after careful research, it is rarely perfectly suited to the user's requirement. However, it is extremely important to avoid changes in the existing package. Application packages that have undergone even minor changes become a nightmare to the user.

With these references in mind, let's now see advantages and disadvantages relating to the employment of programming products, starting with those issues which should have been the more obvious. It is a list based on experience, distilled from years of practice. Software packages, like computer power, can be addictive: When we seem to have a problem, we add computer power. Another problem, more power, another computer, another package; and then another and another... Many DP managers simply cannot get enough. They practically walk around with computer sizes and software packages printed on their business cards, which is self-destructive.

The immediate implication from this bad habit is that the bigger the machine and the more expensive the package, the bigger the job and the higher the salary. Just as well, standards are missing: When is it enough? And when is more too much? Yet we all know by experience that rushing out to add programming products and computer power because the procedural system is all screwed up is the worst possible justification. The same is true of "en vogue" software.

The powerful package and computer buy has become a matter of reflex rather than reflection. It's like throwing money at the problem rather than working at it: Debugging our manual system first, getting it to run as efficiently as we possibly can, understanding the applications and what benefits further computerization can provide.

This being said we also have to remember that moving ahead with technology involves risks. We have to be careful about them without being too restrictive, thus losing the possible opportunity. A specific example on this point is the indiscriminate purchase of programming products when the proper prerequisites are not being met. Any rush in this area can be costly, but the same is just as valid about remaining inactive.

The programming language in which a package is written is one of the key points of attention. The coming five years will be a period of chaos in computer languages, with DP executives under pressure to pick the ones that will survive. Cobol, for one, does not answer tomorrow's needs. As a result, its users may be in trouble. They would have to look after programs written in Cobol 68, Cobol 74, interactive Cobol, and in some other languages much more fit for the environment of the 1980s, such as Pascal.

This is another way of stating that prior to selecting a programming product we need

- First, a clear set of objectives.
- Second, the appropriate experimentation and demonstration.
- Third, an integration view: How does it fit within our operations environment?

Highly related to this specific reference is the appreciation of the preparatory work that needs to be done. Preparation is the essential first step to implementing any change. Our personnel must be trained to understand the new service supported by the programming products.

We must care to evaluate competitive products, and this must be done only after we agree on a specific set of functional specifications—writing down a document which explains how data are to be handled.

A careful evaluation of the proposed alternatives and experimentation on what the package can do demonstrate good management of the computer resources. It also demonstrates planning ability and, therefore, the proper chance to get results. These are the characteristic qualities of a progressive state of mind. They are also confirmed by success stories.

The best advice to be given to an eventual client of any vendor's programming products is that *preparation is the key to success.* This is tantamount to saying that the lack of a good standard is the source of a lot of uselessly written software. And software is written or purchased uselessly when particular attention is not paid to the end user.

Let's not underrate the possibility that software purchased from an outside source may be subject to sabotage by the analysts and programmers in the organization afraid to lose their job. Such references to sabotage are not uncommon with hardware. One, for instance, concerns a professional staff where video terminals were regularly reported as malfunctioning, only to be checked out time and again with no visible failure. "It was infuriating," said one executive. "Users kept up this harassment for months. It cost us thousands of dollars."

Another case regarded word-processing gear. The secretaries and typists had given false initial input about volumes and types of work done, files kept, and information flow. In later interviews, several of them admitted that they knew "other" secretaries had falsified data.

More direct sabotage is not uncommon either. Executives and other professional staff members can help to destroy a system's usefulness both through procedural and actual sabotage. In installing a data retrieval system, a leading company found the worst bugs were what seemed like employee attempts at undermining.

To avoid repetitions of these cases, banks and industrial companies now have a staff of full time people who do nothing but educate users on the capabilities and limitations of hardware and software. Such organizations have generally concluded that they must offer two kinds of training:

1. *Orientation.* Explain why changes are being considered, what they entail, who will be affected, and so on.

2. *Selling.* Explain the benefits of using the software system being acquired for each individual.

Rewards, such as career advancement, should be included as inducements for use, and unspoken fears and emotional reactions should be addressed in a rational way.

It is well understood that no program, no matter how good, can guarantee elimination of all negative attitudes. Yet careful preparation can go far toward defusing negative reaction and obtaining the best results from the substantial investments made in computers and communications, whether hardware or software.

14

"C", PASCAL, AND THE LISP LANGUAGES

1 INTRODUCTION

The choice of the language in which the software should be written is a function of three main variables: the purpose of this software, the applications environment, *and* life-long learning as a continuing educational perspective. Therefore a valid, documented discussion on "C" and Pascal should start with the latter issue—the more so as the reemerging LISP languages are also among the contenders.

We all know that education is the basis of law and order. But education is no longer a process concentrated in early life. Professionals who fail to keep up with technology lose their skills; their reflexes go; expertise slows down; younger challengers overtake them. This fate befalls all people: accountants, bankers, industrialists, engineers.

Prof. Louis Smulin told a 1982 MIT Symposium: "Engineers can be washed up by the time they are 35 or 40." Industry is keen in recruiting new ones from the universities. The young engineers coming in are sharper than their elders. In America, each year some 10,000, or 5% of the nation's electrical engineers, transfer out of their field, many because they feel useless or technologically obsolescent. And a study by the Bank of Wachovia demonstrated that if not recycled, in 5 years bankers lose 50% of their skill.

Our only viable strategy for coping is for industry and the banks to increase the productivity, retention, and competence of people already engaged in the profession, through a well-designed and administered professional training program.

The problems we are facing cannot be solved simply by incrementally improving and expanding current educational activities. A quantum jump is needed, amounting to a revolution in postgraduate and professional training. A 4-year long study sponsored by MIT reached the conclusion that industry stands to benefit if, on company time and at company expense, engineers would continue their graduate-level education in at least one 5-week course per year, thus avoiding professional obsolescence.

For bankers, it is suggested that as much as 5% working time be devoted to continuing education. In exchange, they will better manage their jobs, avoid the tunnel vision on the things of the past, and adapt to the new technologies. The new knowledge they will get from the course will inevitably help.

2 COMPUTER LITERACY

Computer literacy is rapidly becoming as important in modern society as reading, writing, and arithmetic. A study conducted in the United States suggests that to avoid worsening the structural unemployment some 100 million Americans will need some form of computer instruction in the next decade. Such policy is just as valid if the promise the personal computer offers for productivity gains is to be fulfilled.

In a tough job market, computer illiteracy will facilitate the replacement of the over-50 executives by their juniors. By the end of this decade, having a knowledge of computers and communications may not guarantee a job. But lacking such knowledge will see to it that the person concerned does not find employment.

Computer literacy starts with computer awareness. Computer awareness means becoming aware of the extent to which computers are a part of our lives. Computer literacy also includes the ability to use the computer: projecting its integration into workstation chores, employing packaged software, eventually programming the machine.

Such literacy can only be achieved by hands-on experience and practice. The computer is a great drill master: it never gets tired or bored; it can adjust to the level of its utilization. But effective computer usage demands exactness and patience and the will to do new things.

In many companies management takes a serious, positive stand: "We knew that personal computers were on the way in, so we could either ignore them or try to help people learn to harness them." And more often than not companies decide to follow the computer literacy course.

Manufacturers of computer gear start getting just as active in seeing training programs through. Some are worried that the personal computer market has already slipped 3 years behind its potential, the reason being inadequate user training. Training becomes a battlefield where value added clearly translates into sales.

Until quite recently, educational software consisted mostly of rather lifeless programs aimed at schools with low budgets for computer learning aids. But the explosion of the home computer market promises that the new generation of educational games will ring up annual sales of over $3 billion by 1987.

By forecasting a sharp growth in demand for educational software, top companies switch their attention out of games and into the new line. As a cognizant executive was to suggest: "The demand can only go up. Today's parents believe in education, and they know the computer is here to stay." Added another: "The rationale for the home computer will be education." The projection is for 14 million computers to be installed in American homes by 1987.

To capitalize on computer literacy needs, hundreds of independent training firms are springing up to provide seminars, classes, and on-site company instruction. They are being joined by hardware manufacturers, software experts, and retailers. Dataquest (Cupertino, CA) estimates that the training industry will capture $3 billion or 20% or the $15 billion spent on personal computers in 1986.

Computer training is fast becoming the next business frontier. At Computerland, the foremost PC trading company, a recent corporate policy mandates that all new stores, which are being opened at the rate of one a day, must have an attached training classroom and that as many as possible of the 262 old stores be retrofitted. "Training is the inducement to buy," management asserts.

A critical ingredient for success for the new training companies will be their ability to reduce labor costs for instruction. Many experiment with a combination of traditional lectures, self-instruction manuals, innovative video programs, and self-prompting software. Reassurance, called *handholding* in trade, is part of a typical introductory computer class.

Clear-eyed universities go much further. Beginning in 1986, Carnegie-Mellon will require all of its students to have their own personal computers. The Pittsburg university has installed a broadband local area network to interconnect mainframes, minis, and micros. In late 1982, CMU signed a deal with IBM to develop what will be the largest computer network in the world. This arrangement would lead to a personal computer for each of its 5,500 students and everyone else associated with the university.

This is impressive but not unique. Clarkson College in Potsdam, NY, and Drexel University in Philadelphia will begin to provide all students with computers next year. But the CMU hardware will be the most sophisticated available, and it will not depend on a large, expensive central computer, as most systems now do.

According to the CMU faculty, the LAN of personal computers will have the same role in student learning that the development of the assembly line had for the production of automobiles. When the *Integrated Computer Environment* goes on line in 1985, students will have decentralized computing power far beyond what they now get from the university's timesharing system, which already works with 800 terminals.

PC and LAN will provide instant access to local databases, to library holdings, and distant data warehouses as vast as the U.S. Census Bureau. To make this feasible, university datacomm specialists will work with IBM computer scientists on campus to lay plans for the network, which could grow to 10,000 units in a decade. In almost every aspect, this project has new ideas not completely tested anywhere else.

CMU will help IBM design a new computer tailored to the network. Though the agreement does not include a firm commitment to buy any hardware, IBM might spend as much as $25 million on all aspects of the project in order to gain the expertise.

While this reference is at the university level, let's not forget that the 7-year old attending the primary school is already being taught computer programming—and there are computer-based educational games written for the 3-year old. Control Data is rewriting Plato for the new market.

3 POSITIONING THE "C" LANGUAGE

While the discussion on "C" vs. Pascal is not made for the 3-year old (at least not for today), it is just as good to keep in mind the foregoing issue of computer literacy. This will become better evident when we talk of LISP offsprings—like Pilot and Logo—which can be of assistance both in educational and in business applications.

"C" is the basic language of Unix and the interest in its implementation has to do with the life cycle of programming products. Most critical is the issue of a coherent programming-OS environment able to maximize productivity throughout the life cycle of the programming product. This is very important to every organization.

Requirement specifications, as well as the most intimate programming phases: design, implementation, test, and maintenance, must be properly taken into account if we wish to evaluate in a valid manner life cycle efficiency. "C" can nicely stand on this score.

A problem with "C" is that not too many people today know how to work with it—or are familiar with its design structure and with what it supports in terms of:

- Step-wise refinements
- Data abstraction
- Bottom-up approaches.

Step-wise refinements are important in modern programming practice as they permit breaking up the modules into sub-modules; hence, a top-down solution able to complement the bottom-up structure of "C" programs. Data abstraction is a basic ingredient of portability, if and when we know how to handle the standards issue.

Because "C" brings forward new capabilities, it requires a mentality and discipline not commonly available. Only when these two conditions are present can we talk of life cycle efficiency and portability.

Let's now look at the specifications. The "C" language's main features can be categorized in the following manner:

1. *Structured Control Statements* introduced in Assembly/HLL level.

Typically, these are conditionals, loops, open subroutines. The open subroutines are the C-Functions and are user defined. They can be case statements for selection based on the value of an expression, or exits out of a loop.

2. *Data Structuring*, including ASCII characters, Integer, Pointers, Arrays, Records (Structures).

There is a fundamental argument on whether or not data structuring is one of the best "C" features. Many experts think it is not. Also, some programmers prefer Algol's block structure: BEGIN... END, rather than "C" symbols: , . This is a trivial argument. "C" can also employ macro facilities to introduce BEGIN, END. The hinge is that for portability, one must then take along the macros.

3. *Productivity*. A good programmer will write faster in "C". It is easier to use and needs few keywords.

To contrast to other programming systems, by being structured languages Pascal and "C" oblige us to think about what we do before we do it. Unstructured languages do not have this constraint. (If Pascal is a structured language, so is "C").

For more than one reason, the lack of structured constraints (as in Cobol) can be detrimental. The top analyst/programmer does not need them—but the average one does.

4. *Documentation* is rather a sore point in "C", and documentation is a vital issue in analysis and programming.

It is possible to write a readable program in "C", but this requires lots of discipline. The documentation need can be satisfied by macros, but then two issues pop up: (1) By leaving each programmer to his own as to the way of answering documentation needs, we don't have a standard way of expression—neither a good means of control. (2) For the same reason, as stated in a preceding paragraph, we reduce program portability due to employed macros which are not in the standard set but implemented by the users.

Thus, having examined the key variables characterizing the use of the "C" language let's now stress on the wisdom of employing it. How much truth is in the statement that it constitutes a valid vehicle for program portability?

Program portability is highly conditioned by following standards and conventions. As this was not a basic concept prior to the mid-1970s, any language written prior to that time has disadvantages to be brought under perspective. For instance, "C" does not have an I/O system as part of language standard. Vendors write and provide this subsystem but, here again, this inhibits portability.

If we wish to compare "C" and Pascal with the objective of adopting the one or the other as a DP organization's new programming language, the following observations will be in order:

- "C" is a better language in which to write system products: drivers, utilities, and so on.
- We cannot do a very efficient job with Pascal along this line; we can do more with "C".

This reference is so important that it needs to be repeated. While some programmers and DP managers believe that Pascal should be the preferred choice at the applications level—most agree that "C" should be used at the system level: drivers, processor, video, print, communications etc. Programming for these functions is more efficient in "C".

Pascal has a competitive advantage as there is a CCITT-approved higher level language with database structure, which is essentially Pascal-based. Also, users have worked out a version of Pascal with external references. (One of the developments is a proprietary compiler which runs on a 3033 mainframe and compiles for Intel -8086 based engines.) If, however, the problem is that of converting from an aged language such as Cobol, then neither Pascal nor "C" will do miracles. They both require a different state of mind. Experts with three languages express the opinion that going from

Cobol to "C" is rather difficult; and the same is true of the transition from Cobol to Pascal. The change from Pascal to "C" is easy.

Pascal presents similarities to ADA, but it is a more mature language than ADA. It features fast software implementation, facilitates the use of structured programming disciplines, and provides a measure or portability in terms of finished software.

We have spoken of program portability, but the issue is so important that we must underline it once again. Most user organizations are interested today in hardware independence. Attention has been focusing for some time on systems able to run on different hardware/software configurations—hence the interest in Pascal.

4 PILOT AND LOGO

Interactivity is one of the important references and in this Cobol, "C", and Pascal are all deficient. Neither "C" nor Pascal have built-in features for interacting with the user, and Cobol is a batch language. It was never meant to be interactive in the first place.

Systems programming languages usually lack the features necessary for an interactive implementation. The manufacturer must therefore provide forms processor, and menu routines. Let's not forget that efficiency in response time is a matter of basic software implementation and of compiler design.

It is therefore just as well to take a look at future developments, particularly in what concerns artificial intelligence. *Pilot* is an example of an AI-oriented language—and this is in LISP (a list programming structure)—not in "C" or in Pascal. LISP has a large library, but not many programmers know it. *Small-talk*, by Xerox, is another LISP-based example, but nobody else has adopted it yet.

The replacement of Basic will most likely be *Logo* (another dialect of LISP) with different syntax. Introduced in March 1982, Logo may become a development language. It's good to keep an eye on it.

The reference to Pilot and Logo is just as strong if we talk not of an applications environment but of computer literacy and education.

As we underlined in the introduction, the importance of the educational market sees to it that most personal computers are supporting highly interactive programs. The response time falls within acceptable limits for an environment in which people have little patience with waiting. What's more, Computer Aided Instruction (CAI) costs with PC are well below the cost of timeshare systems, if and when the latter meets necessary quality criteria.

Companies, schools, and educational outfits have only recently begun to explore the many ways in which computers and communications works can serve learning needs. The networking of micros creates an environment that is easily maintained on a day-to-day basis.

- The PC are turned on each morning by an attendant while the LAN units are never turned off.
- The PC automatically loads their individual program or group of programs and provide the users with a well-defined software environment in which to learn.

As the software is totally protected, an educational center can be staffed by two attendants for teaching purposes and a full time technician to keep the center's electronics running smoothly.

Software changes, when necessary, can be make quickly and easily from a network control center and downloaded. In cases where there appears to be a software problem in a particular program, changes can be made while the students are in the center. Usually, however, software modifications are made while the educational center is closed.

To help in teaching proficiency, new CAI-oriented languages are being developed and implemented. Here again, Pilot and Logo are examples. They run on Apple and Commodore, among other PC, and their hardware base is increasing.

Logo (the product of Logo Computer Systems) is a tool for learning problem solving. As an education programming language it is the result of 15 years of research on computer-based education, designed to combine ease of use with procedural capabilities.

Logo features relative or *turtle graphics*, an approach to computer graphics that makes it possible for beginners to draw complex designs the first day. Turtle geometry is based on mathematical ideas, but also on words and sentences: creating sentences, language games, and conversational programs.

Pilot is an easy-to-use system designed to support program development for computer aided instruction. It offers color graphics, sound effects, and a character set editor to allow lessons to be presented in words, pictures, and sounds.

The author can create high-resolution color graphics to include anywhere in the lesson. Simple keyboard commands draw lines, circles, and rectangles. Hand controls can be used to sketch free-form designs. Text may be written anywhere on the graphic screen. These pictures are stored on diskette. The same is valid for music sounds to be dynamically created and played back using simple menus and keyboard commands.

Pilot is a high-level language particularly suited to the needs of courseware development. Using simple commands, the author defines the flow and logic of a lesson and integrates previously defined graphics, sound effects, and special characters into that lesson.

Co-Pilot is an interactive tutorial designed to bring the first time user quickly to speed in creating computer assisted lessons. The program employs commonly used Pilot commands and provides a convenient, self-paced way to introduce trainers and educators to the Pilot language. It also gives the user a practice mode in which to test and experiment with various commands.

The SuperPilot gives trainers and educators the advantages of Pilot, plus a set of new lesson development capabilities. Features include faster execution, relative (turtle) graphics for simple creation of drawings, and options for color, character size, and external video device control.

The language allows users to add visual emphasis to selected portions of lessons with double sized characters and color text. It permits control of external devices such as videotape and videodisc players, simplifies efforts in creating geometric figures and simple objects, and provides a time-saving *immediate mode* for realtime interpretation and debugging. It also supports alternate character sets access for foreign language presentations and animation.

5 A "C" AND PASCAL COMPARISON

One of the issues treated in the preceeding sections has been a "C" and Pascal comparison. We will try to place the arguments that have been advanced in a structured form, but first let's return to the fundamentals.

The most basic notion is that in order to talk of a language's implementation we must first define the applications environment that interests us. Is it systems programming, or applications programming?

The second basic issue is the choice of the OS we will be employing. Though some UNIX lookalikes support Pascal and other languages, expert programmers suggest that within the UNIX framework it is "C" and "don't use anything else but "C". On the contrary, the same people are ready to point out that when we step outside Unix, "C" has many dialects.

In a way, "C" can be viewed as a mapping between macro assembler programming and machine language. The OS interfaces in Unix are specified in "C"—and "C" was designed so that we don't need an optimizer.

Quite often, however, an advance carries along with it constraints. Language design characteristics are a double-sided sword. For one thing, they offer "C" much of its flexibility. For another, they constitute a limitation. The language's own designer, Ritchie, implies that "C" is a non-structured language as it has an "absence of restrictions and its generality makes(s) it more convenient and effective for many tasks…" Alternatively, many programmers tend to consider Pascal as a structured language. Yet

> The "C" structure is identical to that of Pascal and "C" reflects much of the functionality embedded in PL/1.

Knowing that we are not comparing precisely equal alternatives, but still knowing that we need to establish a certain sense of measure, Table 5 contrasts the "C" language to Pascal ISO. (Design, Systems Programming, and Maintenance are the basic variables being considered.)

TABLE 5
A COMPARISON BETWEEN "C" AND PASCAL ISO

	"C"	Pascal ISO*
1. DESIGN		
1-1. Step-wise Refinement	Supports step-wise refinement through "functions"	Provides a means for top-down by defining "procedures"
1-2. Lead toward Data Abstraction	Relatively weak features for data abstraction, given present-day needs	Not fully supported data abstraction
1-3. Bottom-up	Some capability	Some capability
2. SYSTEMS PROGRAMMING		
2-1. Data Types	Low level, optional support (not part of compiler)	Better facilities
2-2. Direct Supports for Data Abstraction	Very few	weak support
2-3. Data Representation	Yes (but depends on compiler)	Yes (but depends on compiler)
2-4. Structured control	some	some
2-5. Modularization	Yes	Yes
2-6. Large Program Management	some	some
2-7. OS Interface	full	full
2-8. Foreign Language	Yes	Yes

3. MAINTENANCE

3-1. Readability (self-documented)	Fair	Good
3-2. Robustness (containing change to a given module)	Good	Good
3-3. Cross-Reference (in data types)	Good	Good

*by "Oregon Software"

Though it is a fundamental issue, *testing* is not a part of this table as answers depend on the compiler—not on the language—such as tools to support testing procedures; symbolic debugger(s); trace facility; and profiler.

It is always possible to find exceptions, particularly in dialects. But the comparison properly documents the wisdom of using "C" for systems software; "C" and Pascal for applications; while not forgetting the possible contributions by Logo and Pilot.

15

PASCAL, COBOL, AND THE MICROCOMPUTER ENVIRONMENT

1 INTRODUCTION

The choice of a programming language is of great importance to any computers and communications project. The choice may be limited by a number of factors: from specific equipments to critical issues such as portability, device independence and the facilities a given language or dialect supports.

Important in this particular connection is the message that the "ideal" programming language doesn't exist. The ideal language would be the easiest to implement but also the most efficient. It would require the least training but produce a 100% correct code. It would work at the macro and at the microcoding level. It would be equally good for business and engineering applications. But it doesn't exist. It never existed. What exists are compromises.

It is within this frame of reference that the statement can be made: Today Pascal is obviously becoming *the* programming language for personal computers (PC). After all what are our alternatives?

Eventually vendors will have to offer multiple languages. Personal computers are now used within a range of multiple applications environments and the programming needs must be addressed in an able manner. But, in terms of choice, only what is available makes sense.

When we talk of PC applications programming, the choices range between Assembler (to be avoided); Basic (good, but not so sophisticated and poor in portability); Cobol (a mainframe-oriented, heavy-in-requirements, and obsolete structure); and Pascal. Granted, like any other language Pascal has its limitations. But compared to its competitors Pascal is:

- more flexible,
- more efficient,
- better open to programmer productivity, and
- a structured technique.

Without doubt, the able use of Pascal requires *retraining* of the programmers and analysts. That much the better. We must train our people to the new computer technology anyway. Training is an opportunity, not a constraint.

The salient problem, next to training, is that of making the right choices. Decisions reached today on programming languages and OS will impact on the information systems we will be using during the next 20 years. For this reason, the priorities must be:

- Let's start by *properly* defining our applications problem in a factural, documented sense.
- Let's *first* choose the software we want.
- And only then buy the hardware that goes with it.

Let's finally never forget that we are in a profession where categorical statements show lack of knowhow and lead to blind alleys. It is wise not to commit this type of mistake.

2 PASCAL AND THE ALTERNATIVES

When we talk of new computer equipment such as PC, the choice of the programming language is first of all conditioned by the range of equipment featuring it. It is therefore of no surprise that, for instance, in 1980 the question "Which language are you using?" brought the answer "The majority of our users write in Basic."

Even if the equipment supported it, in the 1979-1980 timeframe users considered Pascal a little too complicated to use in association with the environment in which the PC were then employed. And it is also true that Pascal requires more *language skill* than either Basic or Cobol.

But in 1983, policies have tremendously changed. Today, the majority of software houses write in Pascal, and the same is true of manufacturers. Apple computers, for example, has gone to Pascal as a standard.

Still, while what happens in 1984 is of importance, much more critical is the future perspective. This calls for a distinction between

1. Basic software and applications programming.

2. The 8, 16, 32 bits per word (BPW) machines.

Figure 15-1 gives a snapshot on this reference by introducing the "C" language for Unix-oriented machines. Table 6 brings the issue further by presenting order of magnitude statistics for mini- and microcomputers.

These are, of course, estimates based on current trends and projections. So many things happen with PC that there may come some unique applications languages and compilers we don't even think of at this moment. But we have to live with what we now have available. We cannot wait indefinitely for the "miracle" to happen.

As the statistics in Table 6 indicate, the language to watch is "C". It is propelled by the Unix OS. But "C" is a rather difficult language under present day standards, particularly suited for basic and horizontal software. For applications programming the tool will be *generators*. Still these are a complement to the programming language, not a substitute for it.

Indeed applications generators are a promising way to attack the huge backlog of programs user departments want performed. They help relatively untrained persons get applications up and running quickly, by translating very high-level languages (VHLL) to intermediate or lower levels.

Another tendency that is under way, but still a long way from maturity is to turn "C" into user-friendly by surrounding Unix with a menu-driven shell to mask complexity. This is a reference, not yet an implementation.

Talking then of what currently exists, the following statement can be made: For basic and horizontal software Cobol is *out*; Pascal

BASIC AND HORIZONTAL   APPLICATIONS PROGRAMMING
SOFTWARE   (VERTICAL SOFTWARE)

 8 BPW
                PASCAL   BASIC
16 BPW
                              PASCAL

16 BPW   COBOL 74
                "C" LANGUAGE
32 BPW   FORTRAN 77

FIGURE 15-1

TABLE 6
PROGRAMMING LANGUAGE UTILIZATION FOR MICROCOMPUTERS

	Personal Professional Computers	
	1982	1986/87 (Expected)
Basic	70%	35%
Pascal	25%	30%
"C"	1–2%	30%
Cobol	1–2%	
Fortran	0.5–1%	5%
Other	2%	

is *in* but criticized; its Modula 2 version and the "C" language are growing in importance, but are still a long way from unsettling the current Pascal.

For applications programming, Basic and Pascal master the scene. The former is for simple, non-sophisticated environments with no need for portability.

The choice essentially depends on what we want to do or which capability we should be supporting. If the vertical software is *very simple*, Basic can be fine. If it is technology oriented and there is need for portability, the choice is Pascal.

3 COBOL VS. PASCAL

The senior executive who leads General Electric's information systems policy expressed his thoughts in this way: "Pascal is better than Cobol. Don't ever put Cobol on Apple computers." But let's return to the fundamentals.

Pascal was originally designed as a teaching tool. From this simple fact derive many of its capabilities and limitations. Its newer dialect, Modula 2, goes beyond these limitations. But it is still too early to have an opinion on how good it is.

Given that on the most popular microcomputer today, the IBM PC, the two languages being supported are Pascal and Cobol (by Microsoft), what about a Pascal/Cobol comparison? Here is what a cognizant computer executive had to say:

> "I have yet to see a Cobol implemented in PC that is efficient."

Another specialist added:

> "The only place of Cobol in the new computer technology is due to the fact that more people know it than Pascal."
>
> "But for PC Cobol has no place—it makes no sense."

The following reasons were given to document this statement:

1. A major area of PC implementation is decision type tasks. Pascal does them; Cobol does not.

2. Schools and universities now teach more and more Pascal, less and less Cobol.

3. Modeling can only be done in Pascal. Cobol does not lend itself to that. It is not flexible enough.

4. When it comes to PC the crashing majority of application packages is Basic and Pascal oriented. There is nothing in Cobol.

5. Cobol and Pascal could eventually coexist on some machines (e.g. Apple III) on standalone. But that requires two OS on the same PC and the need for redesign. This will be a nightmare.

6. Cobol is very inefficient in a PC environment. We shouldn't overtax the available resources.

7. Pascal is very easy to use in "what if"—even better than Fortran.

Present and coming programming requirements call for an increasing usage of "what if". This is built into Pascal. For Fortran we need extra expertise.

8. Everything coming in software will be in Pascal. *Designers are most of all interested in portability.*

If there is a single reason under current conditions for choosing Pascal, that is it. This is a major decision factor even when we talk of tradeoffs.

Time and again users have emphasized that in terms of portability across the network Pascal is *easier* than Cobol—just because it allows transport at a character by character basis.

The last few references bring us to the argument: Which language is easier in screen and file management for transaction handling? This seems to be the only issue where Cobol has an edge. But expert users have emphasized that Pascal can also have full format management facilities. To a considerable extent, these have been developed by users and incorporated into subsequent releases.

Senior people reacted this way to the argument:

"If you have screen problems in your particular environment, then write Pascal routines and use them as macros."

That's good advice. The rationale is that Pascal is a general purpose language. Heavy duty image design needs specific routines. Hence, use Pascal to design such routines on a macro basis. But be very specific.

Other experts underlined that:

"There is no character by character programming in Pascal. It is line by line.

"Cobol manages formats and so does Pascal if you know how to use the pointers, indexing the various fields."

Several senior specialists made the reference that the management of files and videopages are relatively easy to execute through Pascal once the concepts are clear. Just because Pascal is a structured language, confused concepts lead to difficulties and poor results. Let's add that, with information systems at large, if clarity is not the rule, everything is difficult.

We must be committed to structured approaches. The reference has been made in many meetings that, though Cobol makes it easier to create report generation or file management, Pascal makes it much easier to develop and manage program libraries. This is a major plus that PC Cobol does not possess.

Looking back to the fundamentals, we should appreciate that learning Pascal requires a change in the approach to developing a program. It is not sufficient to read a manual. The analyst/programmer must be exposed to the computing concepts underlying the language features.

Once this is done, the analyst/programmer will be able to benifit from language features *available in Pascal, none of which exists in Cobol*;

1. *Design Methods*
   - Top-down
   - Bottom-Up
   - Data Abstraction

2. *Systems Programming Concepts*
   - Data Types
   - Data Abstraction
   - Data Representation
   - Structured Control
   - Modularization
   - Large Program Management.

In exchange for a major programming project to be undertaken in Pascal we will be well advised to develop and make generally available to its members routines for data acquisition: database and file interface, transaction processing and datacomm—as well as report generation: editing, formating, report writer. The latter at long last are available in Cobol and are weak or still under development in Pascal.

Let's not forget that Cobol in its Codasyl origins had no video-handling capabilities. These were developed later by the vendors, and they are quite variable in what they support, depending on the vendor. With the exception of index sequential, something similar can be said of file management.

File management in fact is no typical embedded Cobol faculty since its early days. Reporting, too, had its limitations. IBM, for instance, had written report writer routines to assist the users. It is always possible to beef-up the usage of Pascal (particularly on Apple II) with specific routines able to enhance the job to be done.

Several users, including DP managers, were of the opinion that in an industrial environment Pascal is better. As one expert was to suggest in terms of Cobol vs. Pascal comparison: "It is not the language which should be brought to trial but the whole OS and horizontal software to be examined—and in the last analysis there is nothing absolute in these comparisons. Everything is relative. The basic criterion is the horizon open to the future."

This thesis goes further to suggest that the I/O is a minor issue. The major issue is the programming philosophy to be chosen. The philosophy with Pascal rests on a structured approach, and that's the way for the future.

Cognizant computer specialists have also brought attention to the fact that though with some PC it is possible to work with two languages (processing in Pascal; screens in Cobol) in the last analysis it is easier to go with *one* language. They also stressed the fact that

- Cobol has big overhead in network control.
- Pascal is both easier and more efficient for networking.

With CIS Cobol and CP/M, the solution is update the read/write (R/W) for multiple users through semaphores. With Pascal "Foundation" the application is removed from the semaphores. This leads, however, to a dialect. As with Cobol, we give up portability.

The point has also been made that "Foundation" resides on the disc and is available to all applications. It only works with Pascal. But we should program from scratch with the "Foundation" commands. This is *not* a conversion package.

Another key consideration should be brought into perspective in terms of communications. The key mechanics for 3780 (Owlsync) work with Pascal but not with CP/M nor with DOS. Hence, in a communications intense environment there may not even be a choice of Pascal vs. Cobol.

Other users expressed the opinion that for certain PC Cobol is not sufficiently sophisticated: it is a low intermediate system. For instance, for Apple III Cobol went through a very significant redesign to turn it into a high intermediate system. Still, Apple recommends Pascal.

The following three references are also significant from a managerial viewpoint:

1. Many end user customers are now migrating to Pascal.
2. A dominant trend in package design is toward Pascal.
3. What is done in other languages may end by being a wasted effort.

In conclusion, under the current state of the art and for the next 2 or 3 years, the user will be well advised to go with Pascal. The network software goes for it. And so does efficiency, the concept of structural approaches, the available packages, and the general trend.

4 THE LONGER TERM

The comparisons which we have made are valid for medium-term planning, say to 1985. User organizations that must decide on the different available alternatives have these choices to make. But for the longer term there may be so many alternatives available with PC technology that this plurality will become good news and bad news. If, as we properly documented, Pascal is preferable to Cobol, it is not necessarily the "end language." New programming languages will be introduced with the new generation of PC—some of them designed to fit the solid state software (silicon routines) solutions, which is a new and growing trend.

A guiding thought behind the languages currently in design is to get the programming facility as simple as possible. Another criterion is to see that programming languages better fit the capabilities of people. People don't think logically, yet most of the currently available languages are logical and cannot be implemented the way people think and work. This is a problem with all programming languages.

To the question which may be the prevailing programming languages by the end of this decade, some specialists have answered: Pascal/UCSD, and IDA/DOD augmented with RT/Jovial extensions. The reason given was transportability of code. (The IDA/DOD reference presupposes adoption by the majority of PC vendors, and this is still quite uncertain.)

Other specialists have contested that IDA has any future—particularly in the micro and mini classes—and have suggested ISO Pascal as a better alternative. Technically known as the SVS Pascal, this version conforms to the ISO Level "O". It provides most of the UCSD Pascal features as extensions.

We made reference to Modula 2. This new generation Pascal dialect is available on Apple II. Some organizations have received it, but the general reaction has been: "The language is not yet ready." In fact, a number of sophisticated users wait for improvments prior to going on with the tests.

In other terms, Modula 2 must be tested out prior to wider adoption. Design-wise, it relieves some limitations, but it has not settled down yet. There is also "Pascal MT" (on CP/M by Digital Research), but portability may suffer when we adopt languages that are not generalized.

Software companies go for "C". For instance Visicorp (Personal Software) programs all its new horizontal software in the "C" language. With the exception of one product, it no longer uses Pascal and it has no plans for using Cobol. But for some products it has used Basic.

An impressive reference is that in its Boca Raton, Florida, software development center, IBM uses the "C" language. This is a first class reference for other software developers.

The choice of the "C" language for basic and horizontal software will increase in the coming years, particularly in connection with a cross-compiler and Unix, as Personal Software is doing. In this and in other companies the statement was made that, as far as vertical software is concerned, the IBM PC-oriented programmers prefer Pascal, a trend that causes friction with the mainframers.

A leading user felt that Pascal gave his teams a lot more flexibility and that, once major investments are made in AP, this language will live for many years. Other users have established the policy to bypass the strictly technical issues of "which language you use" by:

- Finding out what software is available.
- What's its portability, and
- What's the machine on which it runs best.

The basic philosophy here is that users have to go the portable way. The suggestion was often made: "Don't take Basic. You will be stuck on Apple. Pascal is better than Fortran. Cobol is not available on many micros."

In terms of file handling, UCSD Pascal claims to have ISAM. Use it. It is being advertised for some time. Softech promotes it, and this is the owner of UCSD Pascal.

Other users advised: "Don't bind Pascal to UCSD. It can also be DOS." And there is a Pascal version that runs on MULTICS, made by the University of Grenoble.

As one of the leading computer experts was to suggest: "When it comes to languages for Personal Computers, Pascal is the answer today. The user gets smarter. Pascal is realistic. But if we talk of the next five years, we shouldn't loose track of the fact that we will have to support at the microprocessor level OS and languages."

This led to the discussion of language trends required to drive the integrated workstation, and the conclusion has been that the OS is just as critical. Because of its qualities Unix will be the 16-BPW and 32-BPW standard for microprocessors.

(For their work and forethought, the two designers of Unix at Bell Laboratories got the technical award of the year. And it is quite interesting to add that Unix was developed because the Bell Labs "couldn't afford" Multics.)

Today, in terms of leading contenders for a standard operating system for the 1980s on personal computers of all sorts, the choice goes to: CP/M, MS DOS, and UNIX. CP/M 80 and Pick are said to be the two really portable OS—but Pick like OASIS does not have critical mass of users. At the same time the AT&T contract to Digital

Research for porting the CP/M 80 library to Unix receives interest in an OS which was phasing out with the 8 bit microprocessor. These are the leaders in the standardization trend. In my judgment, however, the outsider that can carry the day is *silicon software*.

Let's make no mistake: solid state software is a very important trend. Intel leads in this field:

- IMX 86 OS is on a chip.
- Basic OS is on a chip.
- CP/M OS is on a chip.

Hunter and Ready (of Cleveland, OH) has written OS extensions in silicon. Applications of silicon software cross the lines of all major 16-BPW and 32-BPW processors.

The second key to success is user friendliness. Technical details must be transparent to the end user. Functions must be combined. A software package, 1-2-3 combines:

Spreadsheet

Graphics, and

Database Management.

Such functions can be cast in silicon together with the monitor routines. The Very Large Scale Integration featured in the next generation of semiconductor technology will make feasible solid state solutions that would make the discussion on programming languages resemble that of the classical Byzantine argument about the sex of the angels.

5 CRITICAL TESTS

Benchmarks provide no precise way of measurement. But if properly planned they offer good results for documenting which hardware or software system is better than another. For this reason, I searched for a Pascal vs. Cobol benchmark, but it was hard to find one. The specialists consider Cobol unfit as a language for personal/professional computers.

Instead, it was possible to locate accurate enough references on a Pascal vs. Basic comparison. The prerequisites and general perspective regarding this benchmark have been quite interesting. The specialists decided that what they really needed within a PC-based interactive environment was

1. A program with little input/output, as workstations usually go.
2. A program oriented most of the time to computations, not peripherals.
3. Program characteristics conducive to programming without constraints due to different languages.

A basic premise in this benchmark has been that when it comes to languages, speed is only one of the criteria for determining software worth. At the workstation level a more important reference is ease of use. On this count Basic wins.

The benchmark also documented that before one can do much with Pascal, one has to learn quite a lot about one's computer: how to use an editor to create a source file, how to invoke the compiler, how to run one's program after it is compiled. But that's what every programmer should learn to do—and do well.

Basic lost to Pascal on two issues:

First, portability among different computers

Second, the aftermaths of string and text manipulation.

Basic programs tended to be slow and hard to understand, though they could be set up and debugged quite rapidly.

Suppose, then, that we need a more complex program to handle calculations and lots of decisions—that is, an environment typical to workstation implementation. Which way should we follow? Which are the alternatives? What should we use?

Professor Dijkstra is often credited with inventing the notion of structured programming. Many of the issues inherent in top-down structured programming developed from original Dijkstra ideas. Here is how he characterized some of the "popular" programming languages:

- Fortran is the infantile disorder, by now 25 years old, hopelessly inadequate for whatever computer application you have in mind today: too clumsy, too risky, and too expensive to use.
- PL/1, a "fatal disease", belongs more to the problem set than to the solution set.
- Cobol, its use cripples the mind. Its teaching should, therefore, be regarded as a criminal offense.

The exact answer to the question "What should we use?" is a new *computer philosophy*. It has become evident that

1. The most important thing to do is sit down and analyze our problem.
2. Do a lot of thinking before we do any coding.
3. If we can describe our problem well, we will write a good program.

Therefore, we ought to be familiar with a variety of problem-solving devices, so that we can come up with elegant and efficient algorithms. The argument about the programming language is way down in the list of priorities, and it is often used as a smoke screen to cover people who do not wish to do a neat job.

No matter which may be the programming language to be chosen, to lessen the burden of software generation we need automated processing based on the input description of requirement specifications; we need the realization of a language capable of program verification; and we need a suitable architecture. The overall goal should be improvement in the utilization of software assets.

Beyond this, a proper programming language, such as Pascal, will help the analytical process, because the good languages force us to think in proper structures. The result is a code that is:

> readable,
>
> maintainable, and
>
> nearly self-documented.

Computer programs ought to be written after much thought and incorporate only efficient, self-documenting code. Remember that with personal computers lack of user sophistication is a constant problem.

The $100,000 payroll package will almost certainly be run by skilled people in a relatively well-managed computer center. The people running it will have read the manuals and had extensive training courses as part of the purchase. The hundred-dollar package must run or at least fail safely when handled by nonprofessionals—operating people who may never have seen a computer before.

We should not see the personal computer as merely a cheaper and smaller version of its larger data-processing relatives, with their bulky, inefficient, obsolete languages. The PC is an entirely different type of machine, shaped by a technological evolution: its exploitation can result in computers that work for people, rather than the other way around.

When this is taken as a point of departure, we will easily realize that further arguments on the advantages of one processor over another, one operating system over another, or one language over another, are wasted words unless we know how those items relate to our own problem—and to the evolutionary path of the computer industry. That's the best yardstick for measuring potential worth, and the only one that can be documented beyond doubt.

16

BETTING ON THE OPERATING SYSTEM

1 INTRODUCTION

Operational limitations imposed on computers and communications systems by hardware and software are the principal parts of an operational environment. Such factors describe this environment. They are highly interrelated and require a systems analysis on their own merits.

Software drives the hardware. Operating systems are usually designed to function on a family of computers reflecting basic hardware aspects which include both restrictions and flexibility in the way they affect the user. An operating system would address the central processor configuration, central (high speed) memory, direct access storage devices, sequential storage units, printers, and a number of terminal devices that can be accommodated by the central processor. The limitations that these impose on the operating system (OS) are also considered part of the hardware environment.

The concept of an operating system has been in evolution since first invented in the 1960s, substituting for the monitor routines and I/O processors available till then. Some of the early batch OS, such as Atlas and Exec II, were both efficient and simple. But they were not entirely reliable. Several problems remained unsolved with them.

For instance, the problem of deadlocks was not at all understood in 1961/62 when the OS in reference were designed. As a result several annoying deadlocks were programmed into the system. Quite similarly, the early timesharing routines such as CTSS were also of limited scope. Yet when faced with their availability, programmers had an irresistible urge to push them to their natural limits and beyond.

Taking notice of this tendency, the developers of the next generation of OS made them most complex for their time. In the 1965 timeframe, the multics system required 200 man-years of development effort. A year later, OS 360 called for a staggering 5,000 man-years. Because of its size, OS360 became quite unreliable over a rather significant time period.

Yet, these long duration teething problems were instrumental in introducing most of the concepts on which our present understanding of concurrent programming rests. The early experiences brought in evidence that in a multiprocessing environment all communication among processes boils down to performing operations on common data. Eventually, the concept developed that if several processes operate simultaneously on the same variables at unpredictable speeds, the result will be unpredictable.

Given the sequential nature of the von Neumann computer, experts concluded that it is essential to perform the operations on common variables strictly one at a time. If one process is operating on common variables, then the machine must delay further operations on the same variables until the present operation is finished. This concept characterized the operating systems development of the 1960s and 1970s. By now, it is ripe for change.

Two reasons weigh on this reference. The first is the explosion of the computer interest toward communications, databasing, and the end user. To handle data communications in the 1960s and the 1970s we developed the concept of the frontend or transactional routines. To answer the need for effective multiprocessor database access, the database management system (DBMS) came around. At the end user level, we now talk of online intelligent workstations.

The point often missed in this development is that the original OS environment to which in the early 1960s the first basic software efforts were oriented has changed most radically. The OS structure and functionality must accordingly change. The overriding demand is now for layered solutions, and the ISO/OSI standard (International Standards Organization/Open Systems Interconnection) is giving us the experience.

The second basic factor is the emergence of the non-von Neumann machine. Though much is being written on this subject and the Japanese-projected fifth computer generation is often taken as the guiding star, let's not forget that the non-sequential engine is alive and functioning. Local area networks with personal computers as workstations and file/printer/gateway service are the very model of nonsequential processing—when looked at a systems level. A similar though less convincing argument could also be made regarding long-haul distributed architectures.

It is therefore no wonder that computers and communications manufacturers are in the process of rewriting their OS. Not surprisingly, the new basic software structures are modular and layered. They also incorporate the datacomm and database management routines in a multifunctional setting. Designed for mainframes and minis, these may be challenged by the now evolving microcomputer-based software.

2 DEVELOPMENTS IN BASIC SOFTWARE

Since the early use of computer systems, the programming effort has constituted an integral and vital part. But *basic software* trailed other developments in programming, including that of languages. Seen under a chronological perspective, the evolution of the OS concept can be divided into distinct, well-defined periods.

Such periods have had in common a certain goal: the aim of OS has been to strike a balance between three legitimate but opposing propositions relative to the use of a computer system:

quality service

response time

good throughput

It is in relation to these goals that, looking back, we observe the chronological distinction to which reference was made. The *first period* in the 1950s, with monitors and I/O routines, emphasized processing. During this time a software standard does not exist, and users don't even feel the need for it.

However, the evolving applications oblige a reconsideration of the available facilities. This leads in the early 1960s to the *second period*. Emphasis is on capacity. The need is felt for special software, but the state of the art sees to it that it is in part answered through hardware. Still, the evolving timesharing and realtime requirements demand special software capabilities.

The use of large-scale systems throughout the 1960s accentuates this trend. The data load/resource handling requirements is another reason. At the same time, both hardware and software faculties evolute during that decade, the features of the former increasing much faster than those of the latter.

By the time the experience with operating system design accumulated, its functions included spooling, tape file management, formator facilities, disc file handling, the running of the buffer pool, and many other internal service modules. Online operations underlined the need for faculties serving security purposes: authorization, authentication, multiple system keys, and validity control (address verification, control block isolation, data movement validation, and key protection).

Special software promoted OS functionality through authorized program facility usage and through classifying the calling program in terms of files to access and calls by user. Other routines handled the integrity problems within the ranges specified by the operating environment. These issues have been further underlined in the next decade through the provision of finer programmatic interfaces.

To handle the fast growing machine faculties, by the early 1970s a new emphasis has been placed on software. The *third period*, stretching through the 1970s, underlines performance:

1. Computer work is increasingly done under a stress environment.
2. Functional specialization in timesharing and datacomm has its impact.
3. The fast increase of online terminals brings a new dimension into the software issue.
4. Users demand that the continuity of service be assured.
5. The distributed data processing capability further impacts on software development—and so do remote commands.
6. Finally, security/protection starts being taken into serious consideration.

Slowly, we come to realize that OS design must consider the data load imposed on the system, be parametric to fit the requirements of job streams and system configuration(s), and at the same time become specialized. The latter reference regards the OS proper but also the virtual storage (VS) faculties, the data communications, data entry, and query requirements.

By the end of this third period and the beginning of the *fourth period* of the 1980s, vendors and users realize the wisdom of converting into microprocessor-implemented functions. Intelligent devices dominate the scene, the distributed concept focuses on the databases, and these are changes profoundly affecting the whole OS concept.

The original operating systems were written to share resources. With "$100" intelligent machines, we don't care anymore to share. Our problem is

> the management of resources dedicated to specific applications
>
> improvements in reliability both for hardware and software
>
> flexibility and expandability

The problems to be solved center on text and data-oriented environments, involve graphics, call for user-friendly interfaces, and demand better overall organization, transparency, security, and modularity. This brings into perspective the need for error detection and correction, access at point-of-origin, authorization routines to address the database, and the fact that computer and communications systems are becoming increasingly information centered.

It may sound schizophrenic, but we are approaching the point where information must be brought in to feed the system. Satisfying the appetite of computer networks will be one of the top challenging jobs of the future. These facts bring a new orientation to the design and implementation of basic software.

Whether the objective is computer to computer, terminal to computer, or workstation communication, networks are being run with the aim of quality service. Those applications still demanding a timesharing environment promote the criterion of very short response time and the sharing of resources. Environments with heavy batch characteristics aim to obtain the best throughput under varying job mix requirements.

Batch has been the eldest application. Because of software investment, it will be around to the end of this century. Furthermore, batch processing can be of different basic types: input or output oriented, mainly of the update or job networking. Of these batch dialects some, like the input-oriented functions, are being done online (remote batch)—while output oriented batch is changing to interactive.

In this variety of applications objectives the OS and its extensions traditionally aimed to be all things to all users. Not only did it provide monitoring functions but also terminal interfaces, message routing, process control, and file handling. Yet we do know that the different examples we have taken have diverse goals, design characteristics, and implementation aspects, thus requiring a different type of approach in the software system solution and its primitives.

Still another need which became felt is standardization. This impacts on the desired sophistication and size of the OS programs.

As these issues start seeping down through the vendor organizations, there developed a drive for an increase rather than streamlining of OS routines, with a corresponding expansion of their faculties. Simultaneously, the need became evident for a decrease in the number of errors per 1,000 OS statements and for a conversion to firmware. Polyvalent capabilities must be supported while the principle is properly observed that the interfaces between applications, the database management system, transactional routines, and the operating system are explicitly defined.

A change in the environment of the operating system should not necessarily invalidate previous procedures or data. A change toward newer and more powerful OS capabilities should be evolutionary and controlled. This is what a layered approach to design aims to do.

3 THE EVOLUTION OF LAYERED SOLUTIONS

As the preceding section has detailed, the motivation for the development of a layered OS has been multifold. This included the request by customers to remove limitations in the structures carried over from the early 1960s; space availability in central memory; program size and portability; process reconfiguration; the use of enhanced hardware capabilities; the possibility for a more efficient resource sharing on a system-wide basis; and issues relative to security, protection, and isolation.

To make this discussion meaningful, we will follow the design characteristics of a new generation operating system. Introduced in 1980, this aims to substitute an elder special software for mainframes that complete a life cycle of some 17 years. For identification purposes we will call this new system LOS (for layered OS, though German-speaking readers may give to the abbreviation a totally different meaning).

The first view I had of LOS as a system left a rather favorable impression: a clear attempt to introduce a layered communications technology into the management of computer resources, following the well established layered approach (confirmed through international accords) and the guidelines set by ANSI/SPARC on session (hereby called "message management") and presentation control.

Yet, though the communications end of the coming information systems of the 1980s seems to have been streamlined, reservations should be expressed in regard to the DBMS. At the rear end of the system, the manufacturer seems to still rely on the different versions of its aging DBMS offering.

According to the specifications the manufacturer has presented, LOS is designed to support five different operating environments:

1. Transaction processing

2. Timesharing

3. Interactive remote job entry (IRJE)

4. Remote job entry (RJE)

5. Batch processing

LOS provides needed faculties for an efficient online handling, such as text and diagnostics, security, document handling, direct program access, and resource freedom.

The way the designers defined the latter reference is that with some exceptions the users can implement applications without concern for the particular physical characteristics of the system on which they run. The issue of program portability has been given its weight as it will constitute a major advantage for the 1980s, though it still remains to be seen how far the stated claims can be put into practice.

Direct program access offers a terminal user direct access to an executing batch program, making the data-terminating equipment an online peripheral. The online document-handling faculty groups up to four document handlers reading data into a single logical processor. A document handler control program provides the interface between the individual handlers and the central system making it possible for the central processor to be involved only periodically with document reading.

Security is largely assured through the implementation of a file management supervisor which controls access to the system itself as well as to files, handles the allocation and deallocation of physical file space to logical files, and maintains a catalog of all the files in the system.

The file management supervisor uses a hierarchical catalog structure to record all files in the system, providing a complete record of online and offline files and their correspondence with physical volumes. It guarantees a common file system for all processing and also performs protective and restorative functions.

- System access requires that the user supplies identification that may include a password.

- File access assumes each file has an owner who has power to grant or deny access to the file by other users (DBTG model).

LOS will initiate an abort if an activity tries to execute an illegal operation. Three subsystems come into play for diagnostic and system protection purposes. The first, error analysis and logging, has the mission to detect marginally malfunctioning central or peripheral processor and memory modules. An error-reporting program and an instruction re-try facility

- attempt recovery from transient errors,
- log detected errors in an error collection file, and
- print a summary of these errors.

The second subsystem (online testing) aims to answer both the need to ensure that all system components are functioning correctly and the requirement to minimize interference with the processing of user programs. The third subsystem is a remote testing facility permitting maintenance engineers to call up from a remote terminal and run test and diagnostic programs.

The core of the communications management capabilities of LOS is the integrated transaction processing subsystem. This is a layered structure aimed to use the available hardware resources in a way enabling the processing of a large number of transactions, permitting multiple access to programs and data from a number of remote terminals.

All configured processors can execute transactions. The transaction processor resides as an ordinary applications program and makes calls for space and resources. All configured memory can be employed with each transaction processing routine up to 1 MByte.

Buffer management permits accessibility from all processes and programs. Transaction processing routines can interact with a terminal using implicit send/receive, and one routine can call another transaction-processing routine. Among the transaction-processing routines, included in the system, we distinguish:

1. The *Executive Manager* which schedules all transaction-processing activities and allocates system resources.
2. The *Transaction Manager* which coordinates all actions during the processing of a specific transaction.
3. The *Message Handler* which activates transactions, accepts and delivers transaction messages, validates terminals, transliterates messages, and journalizes.

4. The *System Integrity Manager* which provides restart and recovery procedures.

5. The *Database Manager* which interfaces with the database management system, allowing all transaction-processing routines in executing concurrent access to the database while protecting and controlling access.

Organization-wise, the integrated transaction processor divides the central memory into seven working space registers. In simple terms, the working space is a collection of pages, a linear address space.

The following functions are assured through the programs residing in one of the working space registers:

1. Session Control

2. Buffer Management

3. Integrity Control

4. Concurrency Control

5. Tenant Management (to support a workstation concept)

6. Workstation Management

7. Shared DBMS run time subroutines

Routines outlined from points 1 to 7 are designed for system integrity. They were necessary to integrate the transaction-processing facility into the system, and they also support other functions. But the transaction-handling software must also benefit from functions described in points 8 to 10:

8. Command Executive

9. Journal Access Methods (this however can serve the whole system)

10. Global Data Management (open/close functions; packaging)

Other routines are necessary to assure save store, page tables, exception-processing entry, the segment header, the linking of segments (segment descriptions and links), code space (load and execute), and data space.

4 MEMORY MANAGEMENT

While the overall architectures and the communications part of LOS give a favorable impression, the database capabilities leave something to be desired. They carry over the old concepts distinguishing mainframes from the streamlined, efficient approaches that characterize microcomputers—as we will see in the following section.

It is exactly this integration of aging structures which is not particularly pleasing. On the other hand, it is also true that in the design of the new OS, attention has been paid to the critical issue of memory management. Transaction processing and online operations in general place particular requirements on a computer system. For instance: shared access to both data and procedures; descriptor-controlled access; and dynamic memory management. The basis for such action is a protected memory segment: the "segment descriptor." It contains

- the logical address of the beginning of the segment,
- the size of the segment, and
- the permissions that control its use.

Such functions should preferably be hardware implemented (in the case of LOS they are software based). More precisely, shared access means that segments containing fixed data or fixed procedures can be shared by two or more processes authorized to use these segments.

Through descriptor controlled access, a program can gain access only to segments whose descriptors have been placed by the

OS in the program's descriptor segment. Thus, execute-only, read-only, and read and write access can be guaranteed.

Dynamic memory management permits the development of software as though the memory were unlimited in size by instituting a logical memory faculty. This is the prerequisite for a distinction between logical and physical memory and, therefore, between information management, and resource management.

The local organization is made up of processes (programs) performing a given activity. A process can have access to a domain (a set of segments) and the access permissions. A unified file access system is being provided to assure the interface between logical data management and the physical devices. Its functions are buffer management; blocking and deblocking; record location; error checking, and label processing for sequential, relative, indexed, and integrated files.

A dynamic buffer pooling reduces the space required for data input and output buffers. From an overall structural viewpoint, the building blocks of the new architecture for memory management are

1. *The domains* that afford protection for shared software.

2. *The segmentation* that aims to increase program size and modularity.

A *Domain* is the area of addressability a process has. It may consist of compilation units. This segmentation environment supports a "multi" mode that includes native mode, shared procedures, and demand paging. The single segment mode avails accommodation mode (for programs running under the old OS), existing compilers, and utilities.

3. *The working spaces*—that is, independent memory partitions to hold separately packaged domains.

4. *The pages* that facilitate management of memory in small fixed length modules.

Instructions are provided for slave mode and system software to utilize new architecture features and, whenever possible, to promote migration. The OS controls the physical organization of working spaces of up to four million pages, each page consisting of 4,069 bytes.

Pages can be addressed as if they were contiguous in main memory, although they may be in widely scattered locations. As memory is accessed, segment descriptors and page table words translate the logical address to a main memory address.

We spoke of an accommodation mode permitting to run on a parallel basis programs written for the old operating system and for the new. This assures a migration capability to protect the current working environment and sees to it that the investment made in applications software will not become obsolete overnight.

Another goal is to provide for an evolution toward a transactional capability without massive changes in programming products. The migration toward a transactional operating environment from present day predominantly batch applications necessarily implies program translation, and file translation. To appreciate what it means to run concurrently aging applications programs which have been written in different times based on different releases of the OS, we must recall some issues that characterized the earlier years of computer usage and have since been forgotten. It will indeed be appreciated that the examples which we are taking are a long way in terms of conceptual evolution from the rather simple routines available a quarter century ago for input/output management. Being mainly peripherals oriented the I/O software of the time addressed itself primarily to signals coming in-and-out of the hardware.

What's more, the management of the peripherals was primarily done from the hardware viewpoint and concerned itself with physical handling. This found at the time its counterpart in language management. Early systems took the simple assembly/compiling approach. More than a decade passed by prior to tooling at

- Data Management (description of fields, files) and
- Communications Capability (handling messages).

The reference is relevant as an OS relates to the language by means of the compiling mode. With monoprogramming this is simple to handle. With multiprogramming (in the 1962 to 1964 timeframe) new needs came up around memory use by many programs simultaneously (TS needs), bringing new dimensions to the compiling capabilities.

As the OS became more sophisticated over the years, another need has been the implementation of diagnostics while processing. For instance, diagnostics on peripherals include restructuring the configuration to compensate failure of a processor (if more than one in the system) and of peripherals.

Over the years different concepts have developed and a significant number of solutions: hot switch, cold switch, fail slow, fail soft, and so on. Together with these solutions came the need to study drift and reliability in shared resources, doing something to improve uptime.

All this had an evident impact on the design of operating systems, but also—and this is very important—on the programs developed during different time periods and which are still around though the operating environment is being radically changed. The task of sharing and running old and new software becomes that more complex if we consider that in the typical mainframe many programs operate periodically or at prescribed times. And this is done in a way transparent to the operator.

A multiprogramming system (with or without priority switches) executes from one program to some other waiting program when the former cannot continue because of an input or output data request or the unavailability of a given resource. If all programs are not resident in central memory, transfer of control from one to another requires transfer of programs out of memory and in from disc storage.

The transfer of control from a given module to a module whose address is not known in advance requires maintenance of tables: current addresses for locations of system programs and subroutines must be maintained in appropriate transfer vectors. A program whose execution is suspended requires notification that the input or output operation has been successfully completed and the data transferred to the appropriate location so that it can resume execution.

But the concurrent operation of application programs can lead to failure of the system in case one program overwrites or destroys another. Maintenance of the integrity of the system through memory protection and error checking is necessary, and this task becomes the more complex as the applications environment lacks homogeneity in terms of the applications software.

This immediately poses two challenges. One is to evaluate the wisdom of running a dual environment against the alternative of letting the old mainframe-oriented applications die a natural death at the end of their life cycle. The other is taking the lead in the implementation of modern computers and communications systems solutions based on personal computers and networks.

5 BRINGING INTO ACTION THE MICRODBMS

If the mainframe-based data management system cannot quite get rid of its inheritence, why not examine some radical change like switching to a microDBMS?

Any organization of a certain size would be well advised to shy away from spending more money on mainframe-oriented interactive applications and on standalone micros as well. As underlined on several occasions, at the prevailing state of the art the best solution is that of communicating intelligent workstations.

Whatever the choice of the specific system may be, chances are that the local area network architecture is typically layered along the best references made on layered mainframe OS and beyond. Through file servers, software is now available for memory management which can handle not only files but databases. Once in place, this software service and the database itself may be shared by all the workstations.

Large print files might be spooled to a database server and requested by the print server when it is ready for the job. The database server can handle conventional files and access methods. It relies on distributed intelligence and is based on the separation of the human interface from the DBMS.

Though early data management engines designed for local area networks have been software oriented, there is no reason why we could not make the file server a hardware box. Such product may employ associative hardware to achieve transaction rates that even the largest mainframe cannot approach. It also can and should be viewed as a major subsystem in any computers and communications aggregate of the years to come.

Experience with the first LAN implementations documents that database contention is under control under better terms than with cluster type centralized resources. Cost is a fraction, indeed a small fraction, of similar mainframe solutions. And because the workstations are intelligent and therefore access the database less frequently than in a cluster, performance requirements are modest.

Hardware efficiency is no burning issue. The goal is achieving lower cost rather than accelerating transaction rates. The database server further acts as an autonomous node in the local network rather than a peripheral attached to a host's input/output channel.

We have said that the solution provided by the microDBMS of the server variety is a new departure. The question thus arises as to whether new products for microcomputer level engines should be clones of the earlier products. The answer is a definite "No!"

Though superficially the response seems to be that only a subset of the mainframe DBMS functionality is required, the opposite is true. The DBMS for local area networks and personal computers must provide more services than the current generation of mainframe DBMS—and there are valid reasons for this statement.

By coming very close to the end user and integrating into his desk, personal workstations must be just as agile at handling data as text and image (and eventually voice). Thus, the database server must be able to manipulate test. If so, it becomes a far more effective building block for integrated office systems. Besides, information in the office is much richer and less structured than it is in the classical data-processing environment. This, too, is a factor to remember.

In the evolving environment of intelligent workstation applications, the operating system (whose role is played by the local network architecture) must see to it that the database is

- *transparently distributed* as far as the end user is concerned,
- *supported by a data dictionary*, for directory, data definition, linkage to the processes and control, and
- *fully protected* in a text/data security sense.

System design must assure that the workstation to database relationship (and vice versa) does not result in a complex or intense interaction. System design must also account for the fact that much of the information in the office can be presented as structured records or even as streams of data, text, images, graphics and voice encoding.

Furthermore, the activities involved in database management must be invisible to the end users. Their interest is to interact with the workstations to do text or data entry, electronic mail, electronic filing, a graphics presentation, and so on. The microDBMS supporting these functions will be absolutely vital, but they must remain hidden from view.

Let's further keep in mind that many applications of interactive systems involve relatively simple, repetitive transactions of a limited set of types. The microDBMS may eventually become specialized for responding to these transactions, a task considerably more difficult and time consuming within the classical, bulky, and slow moving mainframe environment.

A layered design of the new communicating microcomputer OS generation will account for these realities both in the provision of the specialized server routines, each dedicated to the unit to which it is addressed and in terms of being supported by the appropriate availability.

The messages that a workstation sends to the microDBMS are actually encoded sequences of commands for defining, manipulating, and administering text and data. At the user level, these commands will be few and relatively well defined. Functions encoded on a graphic tablet may answer the majority of needs.

These are design considerations characterizing the new environment to which mainframes cannot offer efficient solutions. Habits are difficult to eradicate. When we talk of new information systems perspectives, it is just as good to start with new departures.

17

AN OVERVIEW OF UNIX

1 INTRODUCTION

In January 1984 Unix reached a critical mass, with almost 100,000 installations: There have been only 20,000 Unix installations in late 1982, but there are expected to be 600,000 installations in 1986. Nearly a hundred hardware vendors have endorsed Unix.

Unix frees computer users from being locked in to the proprietary hardware and software of a single vendor. This makes hardware price increasingly significant as Unix becomes a virtual standard for supermicro. Marketing aftermaths are fairly evident. A few low cost vendors will ultimately dominate the Unix market—IBM being one of them.

Unix has gone through several versions. Around 1970, it ran on PDP-7 and -9 computers. The second version ran on the PDP-11/20 (which had less power than DEC's PC); then the PDP-11/40 and /45. Many of the differences between the Unix systems come from redesigning features found to be deficient or lacking.

The PDP-11 Unix became operational in February 1971. Early applications revolved around the:

1. preparation and formatting of patents and other documents,

2. the collection and processing of trouble data from various switching machines within the Bell System,

3. recording/checking telephone service orders, and

4. for research and operating systems, languages, computer networks.

These were internal implementations at the Bell Telephone Laboratories, and the goals were projected accordingly. As the operating systems start getting commercialized, Bell releases which left their impact have been:

- PDP-11 *Version 6* (1978), still internal to Bell.
- PDP-11 *Version 7* (1979) has been the first commercialized.
- VAX *32 V* (1979/80) written to take advantage of 32-bit microprocessors, including symbolic debugger.

From the latter was derived:

- VAX *Berkeley Version* (1979/80) Release 2.1*.
- PDP 11 and VAX, Bell *PWB Version* (1980).

PWB stands for Programmer Workbench. It has been designed for software factories.

- PDP-11, LSI 11, VAX, Bell *Systel III* (1981). It integrates what was till then available.
- Bell Generalized Bell *System V* (1983). This is the latest public release. Version V.2 becomes the virtual standard.

TABLE 7
PERCENT OF UNIX LICENSES GIVEN TO FAMILIES OF USERS

Year	Family	Percent
1979	Bell System	55 %
	Universities	32 %
	Government/Military	10 %
	Business/Industrial	3 %
1983	Business/Industrial	93 %
	Bell System	4 %
	Universities	2.5%
	Government/Military	0.5%

* Release 2.1 is virtual memory;
Release 4.2 (1983) is of a different structure.

An Overview of Unix

There is finally a *System VII* as an internal Bell release whose features are to a substantial amount integrated in System V.2.

The support of UNIX has become a requirement for government contracts, and a share of the business/industrial licenses given to computer manufacturers go to government/military installations.

Further factors may alter the OS implementation perspective:

- The Microsoft/Intel effort to put Xenix on a chip, and
- The fact that Intel 80286 is optimized for UNIX/iRMX, Pascal/C/Ada instructions

2 THE MAKING OF UNIX

We have seen in a nutshell the chronological development of Unix versions. Prior to looking into some of the technical features Unix supports, it will be wise to focus on what the market needs.

With intelligent workstations (WS) dedicated to a single user being the winning proposition in system design, the computers and communications environments we are currently implementing require a good OS able to provide:

1. Concurrency in DP/DB/DC for the single user they serve.
2. Portability across different types/makes of hardware.
3. Good response time, fast turnaround, and reasonably low overhead.

Unix is weak in No. 3, particularly in what regards the low overhead requirement. It is however correct to underline that such weakness is inherent in the role of an OS as we will see later on in this section.

Portability across different types and makes of hardware is not only a technical feature but also a function of market acceptance. The DP/DB/DC market is eager to change its perspectives, actively looking for an OS which is portable across many different machines.

It really comes down to computer users having most to gain from such a system. Their investment in software is protected, and they become less dependent on a single vendor. This is propelling Unix to the foreground as users:

- gain the benefit of Unix' sophisticated and growing range of development tools,
- are able to take advantage of a growing base of third party Unix applications software, and
- become supplier independent.

For these reasons, the increasing acceptance of the Unix Operating System is likely to be a major disruptive force on the microcomputer and supermicro industries in the mid 1980s. Quite significantly, Unix provides IBM with an opportunity to repeat the success it has had with the PC, this time with a supermicro aimed at the lowend of the minicomputer industry.

The leading vendors of supermicro are also pushing Unix. At the same time AT&T and Digital Research have signed a long term commitment to support an upgrade path from CPM 80 to Unix System V. Packaging is to be standardized. New features added are:

- file security system
- interprocess communications
- networking capabilities
- datacomm protocols
- flexible disc directory.

This functionality must be seen as an evolution of the characteristics which dominated the services offered by an operating system. Let's return to the mechanics of an OS and trace them through successive stages.

In the early 1960s, operating systems were intended as automatic control programs. Their objective was to schedule work and help increase machine efficiency. There was no user interface. By

TABLE 8
UNIX ORIENTED RELATIONAL DBMS*

Year of Introduction	CM	Name	Characteristics	Environment	Other Issues
1978	1+ MB	Ingres/ Berkeley	– Born under Unix since initial version – More solid than competitor offerings	– PDP 11/Vax	
1980	1+ MB	**Ingres/ RTI	– Structural modific. – Much more powerful – Has embedded capability (EQUEL)	– Any Unix version; no dialects	– Relational host lang. – Networking – Graphics*** – OA
1979/80	0.5 MB	**Oracle/ Oracle	– Born outside Unix – Can work with SQL – Lacks embedded feature	– System V only	– Networking – Graphics*** – OA

* All written in "C" language.
** Plus 2 to 10 MBY on disc.
*** To use graphics capabilities, need intelligent WS

TABLE 8 (continued)

Year of Introduction	CM	Name	Characteristics	Environment	Other Issues
1981	0.5 MB	Informix/RDS	– Born V6, 7 Unix – Less potent	– Any Unix version; incl. dialects	– Handles C-ISAM* – *ACE* is lang. in "C"
1981	0.256 MB	Sequitur/Pacific Software	– Born V7 Unix – Works with smaller machines	– Any Unix version; incl. dialects	– QBE type – WP/screen editor*
1981	0.256 MB	Mistress/Rhodnius	– Born V6, 7 Unix Onyx, Xenix, U III	– Any Unix version incl. Berkeley	– Allows formatting*, pagination
1982	0.256	Unify/North Am. tech.	– Can work with SQL – Menu driven	– Any Unix version	– Source code is available

Another relational DBMS is RIM running under Unix, MS, DOS, GCOS, CP6

* No source code is available.

the late 1960s, operating systems began offering services that users could not supply for themselves. These included

> program libraries,
>
> file systems, and
>
> backup facilities.

But job control languages remained very difficult to use and often seemed devoid of concept. Documentation about system utilities and services could hardly be understood by skilled systems programmers, much less by ordinary users. Unix set out to correct some of these deficiencies.

The basic building block of Unix is the *process*, a program that runs asynchronously with other programs, communicating with them by means of *data streams*. In a certain sense, it is irrelevant where the input to a process comes from, or where its output goes.

- The terminal, files, or other processes may all be used.
- Processes can be configured into networks without internal modification.

This latter is the basic requirement for a configurable architecture.

Unix has a command interpreter called the *shell*, which supports a concise command language. In the latter the user can specify how data flows between processes. Two or more processes are connected by pipes from a *pipeline*.

The user can actually start several asynchronous processes just by entering one command line at his terminal. Programs connected by a pipe run concurrently, with the system taking care of buffering and synchronization. The syntax is concise and natural; pipes are readily taught to nonprogramming users.

Programs are connected with special pipe files, which have the property of passing data from a "writer" to a "reader." The implementation is flexible to the point that it is irrelevant whether a program is reading from or writing to a terminal disc file, or pipe.

Programs written in any combination of languages can be hooked together without special effort since they all use the same system calls to do input and output. The pipe files are created by the command interpreter, so that no special configuration step or precompilation is necessary.

A dictionary of commonly used words is available, along with several utility programs, a transliteration filter, a general purpose sorting program, a filter to remove duplicate lines from a file, and a utility that compares two files and reports lines found in one but not in the other.

In Unix, network specification is controlled dynamically by the user. The system supports a command language in which the user constructs and executes lists of commands (shell procedures) for frequently used functions that are more complex than a single command.

A given command list can invoke other command lists. Thus, every user builds his own personal kit of useful functions. If improved performance is desired, the user can do some performance evaluation and pick the parts of the application to be enhanced.

Furthermore, all files look like streams of data bytes. To programs it is irrelevant where these streams are coming from or going. Also, a single character suffices to specify that a process is to run asynchronously with other programs.

One of the Unix advantages is that applications are not implemented as large, monolithic systems, which would require long coding stages before any results could be observed. They are written as structures of many small, function oriented modules, which can be connected together, and tested individually or in networks of gradually increasing size.

Finally, experience with the Unix system has shown that the pipeline approach to programming can drastically reduce the effort required to program new applications. This also helps develop a tool-oriented style of programming. Each program is seen as a tool that, in connection with other tools (programs, computer equipment), can be used to get a job done.

3 THE PDP-11/45 VERSIONS AT BELL LABS

The PDP-11/45 on which a polished version of Unix was implemented is a 16 BPW machine. Unix occupied 44 KBy of the available 144 KBy of central memory. That system included a number of device drivers, I/O buffers, and system tables. There was as well 1 MBy of hard disc for file system storage and swapping.

Since the beginning, a goal in system design was to demonstrate that a powerful OS for interactive use need not be expensive in equipment or in human effort: today Unix can run on hardware costing as little as $3,000. Less than 2 man-years was spent on the main system software when it was originally developed.

Yet UNIX contains a number of features seldom offered in large systems, together with simplicity, elegance, and ease of use. Besides the OS proper, the major programs available under UNIX are

- assembler
- text editor
- link loader
- symbolic debugger
- compiler for the "C" language
- Fortran compiler
- interpreter for a dialect of Basic
- a formatting program
- Snobol interpreter
- top-down compiler-compiler
- bottom-up compiler-compiler
- macro processors
- permuted index program

This is also a lot of maintenance, utility, and other programs. Unix documents are generated and formatted by the UNIX editor and text formatter.

A distinction should however be made between versions. The relative difference that exists today between UNIX versions makes it necessary to be specific as to which one is made reference. There was no source maintenance provided with the early versions of UNIX. Still without this kind of support users did appreciate the system's consistency and elegance.

- First in terms of programming. Only the first 200 lines are written in the assembler language of the machine on which it runs. To this can be added another 800 lines for efficiency reasons. All other are in "C".

- Second, in regards to the facilities which are supported. UNIX permits a user to move freely among environments: while editing a file, he can invoke the mail program, process his mail, and later return to the editing of his file.

These are some of the features that make UNIX a system sought after by an increasing number of computer manufacturers and user organizations. The same references help document the interest a UNIX implementation starts presenting at the PC level.

The user may call an editor to create a file, then return to the mail program and mail the new file.

The user is not confined to any single environment. Instead, he or she is encouraged to employ the whole system in the solution of a problem.

- One can connect any programs together at any time.
- One can save any new modules for later use.
- One can move freely among environments.

He does not fear rejections by the operating system, because sharing is encouraged. He tends not to think of programs as personal objects; there are good reasons for this.

Let's always keep in mind that UNIX was not designed to meet predefined objectives. The first version was written when Thompson, a Bell Labs researcher, dissatisfied with the then available computer facilities, discovered a little-used PDP-7 and set out to create a more hospitable environment.

This essentially personal effort was sufficiently successful to gain the interest of other Bell Labs computer specialists and later to justify the acquisition of the PDP-11/20, specifically to support a text editing and formatting system. By the time the 11/20 was outgrown, Unix had proved useful enough to justify the acquisition of a PDP-11/45.

Throughout this effort the researchers aimed at building a comfortable relationship with the machine, exploring ideas and inventions in operating systems. As the effort continued, several considerations influenced the design of Unix:

- *First,* design concentrated on making it easy to write, test, and run programs.
- *Second,* the system was arranged for interactive use, even though the original version only supported one user.
- *Third,* the interface to the file system was built very conveniently from a programming standpoint. The lowest possible interface level was designed to eliminate distinctions between the various devices and files and between direct and sequential access.
- *Fourth,* efficiency was turned toward relieving the then prevailing size constraints on the system hardware. Such size constraint encouraged not only economy but also a certain elegance of design.
- *Fifth,* nearly from the start the aim was expressed that the system should be able to maintain itself.

The latter issue saw to it that since all source programs were always available and easily modified online, the designers were willing to revise and rewrite the system and its software when new ideas were invented, suggested by others, or discovered.

- *Sixth,* for programming convenience there are no control blocks with a complicated structure maintained by and depended on by system calls.

This reference is particularly valid if you look at UNIX as a user or application programmer. Less so, if we examine the supported facilities from a systems programmer viewpoint. The reason: though its designers were tempted to make the UNIX structure machine independent, such structure varies with the hardware implementation: VAX, PDP-11, DPS 6, different PC, and so on.

From the applications viewpoint, however, the contents of a program's address space are the property of the program, and UNIX avoids placing restrictions on the data structures within that address space.

TABLE 9

KEY FEATURES FOR UNIX AND "C" LANGUAGE

Unix	"C"
UNIX SHELL 1. I/O Routines 2. Communications Routines 3. Subroutine Library 4. Runtime Library Runtime library must support all functions in subroutine library. UNIX APPLICATIONS ENVIRONMENT Much available, most of it in "C". A reference library also exists.	• Subroutine Library • Runtime Library There is an extensive set of subroutines —including powerful mathematical subroutines. The business and professional subroutine library is under development from several sources (user organizations and software firms). User should make sure the subroutines he needs are available.

Another "plus" is the "C" language. An experienced programmer will find "C" easier than many other languages in datacomm and databasing—with a marvelous array of applicaions tools. Table 7 highlights key features for UNIX and "C". The merit of UNIX lies not in new inventions but in the full exploitation of imaginative ideas, suggested by systems experience and technical constraints and leading to the implementation of a contained yet powerful OS.

4 THE FILE SYSTEM

An originally important role of Unix was to provide a file system. There are three kinds of files to be handled:

ordinary disc files

directories

special files

An ordinary file contains whatever information the user places on it, for example, source or object programs. No particular structuring is expected by the system. Files of text consist simply of a string of characters, with lines marked by the "new line" character. The structure of files is controlled by the programs that use them, not by the system.

Directories provide the linkage between the names of files and the files themselves. Each user has a directory of his or her own files and may also create subdirectories. A directory behaves exactly like an ordinary file except that it must be written by authorized programs.

The system maintains several directories for its own use. All files in the system can be found by tracing a path through a chain of directories until the desired file is reached. The starting point for such searches is often the root. Another system directory contains all the programs provided for general use, that is, all the commands.

The name of a file, specified to the system, may be in the form of a path name. This is a sequence of directory names separated by slashes "/" and ending in a file name. The search begins in the root directory if the sequence begins with a slash. A path name not starting with "/" causes the system to begin the search in the user's current directory.

As the owner of certain files, the user can exercise control over who can read and/or modify a file or execute a program, accessing files to generate needed information. The three attributes read, write, and execute control access to a file. They may be independently defined by the owner for the world of users permitted access to the computer system. Hence, each file can be afforded personalized protection.

No large access method routines are required to insulate the programmer from the system calls. User programs either call the system directly or use a small library program (tens of instructions long), which buffers a number of characters and reads or writes them all at once. This simplifies communications.

The implementation of the file system largely rests on the directory. The entry thereby found contains the description of the file: its owner, its protection bits, physical disc (or tape) addresses for the file contents, its size; time of last modification, the number of links to the file (number of times it appears in a directory), a bit indicating whether the file is a directory, another bit identifying if the file is a special file, and a bit indicating whether the file is large or small.

Each input/output device supported by Unix is associated with at least one special file. Such files are read and written just like ordinary disc files, but requests to read or write result in activation of the associated device. A mountable file system is generated by writing on its corresponding special file with a utility program available to create an empty file system.

Unix pays attention to access control. Each user is assigned a unique identification number. When a file is created, it is marked with the user ID of its owner. There is also a set of protection bits: they specify independently read, write, and execute permission for the owner of the file and for the other users.

One of the protection bits serves to temporarily change the identification of the current user to that of the creator of the file whenever the file is executed as a program.

I/O calls are designed to eliminate the difference between the various devices and styles of access. There is no distinction between random and sequential I/O, nor is any logical record size imposed by the system. Several system entries have to do with I/O and with the file system:

- close a file,
- get the status (of a file),
- change the protection mode (or the owner) of a file,
- create a directory,
- delete a file, and so on.

To the user, both reading and writing of files appear to be synchronous and unbuffered. Immediately after return from a read call the data is available. Conversely, after a write the user's workspace may be reused. The system maintains a rather sophisticated buffering mechanism that reduces greatly the number of I/O operations required to access a file.

With Unix, an *image* is a computer execution environment. It includes:

- a central memory image,
- general register values,
- status of open files,
- current directory, and so on.

An image is the current state of a virtual computer. A process is the execution of an image. While the machine is a process, the image must reside in CM (central memory). During execution of other processes it remains in CM unless the appearance of an active, higher-priority process forces it to be swapped out to a hard disc. The user part of an image is divided into logical segments.

1. The *program text segment* begins at location 0 in the virtual address space.

During execution, this segment is write-protected and a single copy of it is shared among all processes executing the same program.

2. The *writable data segment* is not shared. Its size may be extended by a system call.
3. The *stack segment* starts at the highest address and automatically grows downward as the hardware's stack pointer fluctuates.

Except while Unix is bootstrapping itself into operation, a new process can come into existence only by use of the *fork* system call. Processes may communicate among themselves using the same system read and write calls employed for file system I/O. An interprocess channel is a pipe. This channel is passed from parent to child process in the image by the fork call.

Since a process is independent of the source of its input and of the destination of its output, a Unix process has points of attachment (or ports) that are identified by numbers: the *file descriptors*.

The latter are relative to the process itself. File descriptors 0, 1 and 2 are reserved, respectively, for the functions of:

> standard input,
>
> standard output (used by the pipe operator), and
>
> diagnostic output.

Descriptors 3 and up are available for files specific to processes. The flexibility and power of this approach should be properly underlined.

The original design effort selected and then implemented the best feature available in the late 1960s on realtime/timesharing systems. The fork operation was present in the mainframe-based Berkeley timesharing. On several points the designers were influenced by Multics. The latter suggested the particular form of the I/O system calls, the name of the Shell, its general functions, and the notion that the Shell should create a process for each command.

It is interesting to note that, though the notion of the shell was suggested by the early design of Multics, in that system it was later dropped for efficiency reasons. From there came the saying that Bell Telephone Laboratories designed Unix because they could not afford Multics.

5 FUNCTIONS OF THE SHELL

Let's examine the functions of the Shell. This is a command processor with the ability to test the results of a previous command and perform decisions (execute, terminate). Communication with Unix is carried on with the aid of this program. As a command line interpreter, it reads lines typed by the user and interprets them as requests to execute other programs. In simple form, a command line consists of the command name followed by arguments to the command, all separated by spaces. The shell splits up the command name and the argument into separate strings.

Programs executed by the shell start off with two open files that have file descriptors O and I. As the program begins execution, file I is opened for writing (standard output file). File O starts off open for reading. Programs that wish to read messages typed by the user usually read this file.

The shell also serves in multitasking:

- The shell has the ability to substitute parameters and to construct argument lists from a specified subset of the file names in a directory.
- The shell also makes possible execution of commands conditionally on character string comparisons.
- The same is true of the existence of given files.
- The shell performs transfers of control within filed command sequences.

On logging in, a user is assigned a process containing the shell. As a command interpreter the latter listens to the terminal. It handles the first word on each line as the name of a program (which it invokes with the rest of the line as input parameters) and gives the user access to the directory hierarchy of the system, in which all files are kept.

This is consistent with the Unix programming environment in which every program is a module with a single data stream input and single data stream output. Simple shell notations permit the user to reconnect a module's input or output to arbitrary files in the system and also to connect the output of one module to the input of another.

Unix detects a number of program faults, such as:

- references to nonexistent memory
- unimplemented instructions,
- odd addresses used where an even address is required.

Such faults cause the processor to trap to a system routine. When an illegal action is identified, the system terminates the process and writes the user's image in the current directory. A debugger can be used to determine the state of the program at the time of the fault. Programs that are looping or produce unwanted output may be halted by the use of the interrupt signal. It causes the program to cease execution without producing an image file.

A *quit signal* is used to force a central memory image to be produced. The hardware-generated faults, interrupts, and quit signals can, by request, be either ignored or caught by the process. For example, the editor detects interrupts and returns to its command level.

As with all procedural approaches, an interrupt signal implies that the program is still there. If an interrupt is sent to a process, this process has two options:

- Use a trap.
- If no trap is available, the process is destroyed.

Several other notions pertinent to the implementation of UNIX must be brought into perspective. A basic one is the *i-node*. It contains information on the allocation of a file and also access control:

- read access
- write access
- execute

The concept underlying file ownership in UNIX is: myself, members of my group, everybody else.

Implementation-wise, an important concept is that of *Init*. It is part of the OS, its function being to set up tables. *Fork* (to which we made reference) creates another task, such as: "make an identical copy;" "make an operation to execute another process."

6 CHARACTER SET

Unix uses all characters of the ASCII character set, but many of these characters have a special meaning in addition to their use as data. For instance: Control-D; Control-S and DC3; Control Q and DC1; Control M and FS; Control-H and BS; Control I and HT; FF; DEC; ESC; LF or NL.

Control-D is the end of file (or end-of-transmission character) used to specify an end of file to a command which takes its input from the terminal. The same character is also used to log off the Unix system. For instance, the user may receive a Shell prompt such as the % to enter another command. If he enters a Control-D, he will terminate his log in session and probably receive the prompt to log in again.

The *DC3* character is a *Control-S* on most keyboards and can be used to temporarily suspend output to the terminal. It is advisable to use this when one wishes to read lines being displayed on a video display terminal before they roll off the top of the screen.

Output may be continued by pressing the *DC1* character, which is a *Control-Q*, or by pressing the DC3 character. The *FS* character is *Control-M* on many keyboards. It is used to generate a quit signal to Unix. FS not only causes a command to terminate, but also generates a file with the high speed memory image of the terminated process. This is useful for debugging.

The backspace character *BS* on most terminals is *Control-H*. The horizontal tab character is *Control-I*, causing an horizontal tab character to be generated which may have the effect of tabbing over to the next tab stop as previously defined on the terminal.

DEL is a *delete character* (rub-out), generating an intra signal just like the break interrupt (BK) or attention signal (ATTN), causing whatever command one is running to terminate. This is employed to stop a long printout the user does not want.

LF is the line feed, and *NL* a new line character used to position the cursor on the next line. The backslash sign (\ ) can be used to escape the special meaning of the following character. This is known as *quoting*. Other quoting capabilities in Unix include the single and double quotes: ' and " .

When a sequence of characters is enclosed between a pair of single or double quotes, the special meaning of any Unix special character is escaped. Single or double quotes can be used to include spaces in a word.

and @ are the Unix default characters, though in cases, the local standard might be the backspace and the @ or some other combination.

When the user enters characters on his terminal, Unix will gather and save them until he has indicated end of the line. This may be accomplished by typing a *RETURN*, *NEW LINE*, *ENTER* or *LINE FEED*. The appropriate character to terminate a line differs from one version to another.

When a full line of characters has been received by Unix, the system will process that line. If the *KILL* character is received at any point before the end of the line, then it will kill all characters entered up to and including the kill character.

The *ERASE* character sees to it that Unix will erase the *previous* character received. If it receives two or more *consecutive* ERASE characters, it will then proceed to delete the two or more previous consecutive characters entered into the system.

7 STRENGTHS AND WEAKNESSES

Homogeneity and efficiency in command structure lead to the concept of portability. In the UNIX community, there is a feeling of portability—but this is not necessarily a fact with present releases. Though Bell insists on the capability of UNIX to sustain:

- portability, and
- upward compatibility,

there exists also evidence to the contrary. For instance, moving from V6 to V7 and then to Systems III and V.2 can be a major undertaking.

Portability is further reduced through the introduction of UNIX clones (such as Xenix, to which we will be making reference), and the need to implement supporting facilities—the database management system being an example. In commercial applications, we often need to add a DBMS (which does not come from Bell) and other, additional enhancements.

Precisely one of the arguments in the implementation of UNIX regards the wisdom of sticking to the version supported by Bell versus the alternative possibility of adopting enhancements or making one's own. Proponents of the former approach point to powerful features such as the employment of pipes as I/O channel streams and the sufficiency of the procedure which supports three standard streams:

1. input
2. output
3. error output

This serves in an able manner functions such as diagnostic output, or softcopy only.

Through pipes, we make and manage asynchronous processes. We don't need to know where the output of process "I" will be ending. It is taken up by the pipe.

As a buffer, the pipe provides *throttling*. A recipient process will *stall* (wait) till the pipe can handle its output or provide its input. This is a powerful mechanism permitting processes to work asynchronously.

A similar argument is made about the shell's ability to test the results of a previous command and perform decisions based on this test (of which we have already spoken). The shell indeed provides the flexibility to

- start another command
- write command files
- write: *If, then, else* type commands.

Proponents of the second alternative (making enhancement) base their argument on the ground that UNIX, as it comes from Bell, is not user friendly. Xenix, for instance, is more end user oriented, because it is menu based.

Another issue, along the same lines of thinking, is that there are already many hybrids—usually university made. Also not all programming languages a user may want or need are being supported by Bell. The official version features:

- "C"
- Fortran 77

- Rational Fortran
- Snobol
- DEC Assembler
- DEC Macro

But other suppliers provide Pascal, Basic, and Cobol. Critics point out that UNIX features:

1. No semaphores (for process synchronization)
2. No file recovery and record lock
3. No automatic volume recognition (AVR)
4. No back tracking (handling/create volume)
5. No "Immediate Update" feature (hence writes may be lost in a crash)
6. No file structures like ISAM, IMS, IDS, Relational
7. No volume formatting capability

In terms of argument No. 1 it is pointed out that though UNIX features an efficient pipe system, semaphores are not supported in System III. This is one of the short-comings of UNIX in a commercial environment.

Item No. 2 rests on the fact that Bell provides no journalization. Some vendors have, however, added this facility, an example being Xenix by Microsoft.

The lack of AVR is considered by many to be dangerous, in relation to the way the I/O works. If the OS crashes prior to the WRITE, we lose all that data. (Here, the counter-argument is that System III forces a synchronization). "But," the sceptics say, "one can also be unlucky."

In terms of argument No. 4, the official version supports no back tracks. It can however handle this issue by creating a dummy file that can sit in this track.

Unix has also been criticized in a number of technical areas, particularly pertaining to its suitability to commercial data processing. Some experts consider it to be archaic in file structure and user interfaces. Some specialists say: the overhead is high (three times higher than VMS which is not a good OS), and that there are too many versions and every one is building his own. (Berkeley is said to have 20 changing all the time.)

Perhaps the greatest weakness is the microprocessor on which it runs. The Motorola 68000 with a standard Unix port is barely usable in an online environment. The Motorola 68000 running at 10 MHz is soon saturated with three users running ASCII terminals at 9.6 kbps. Hence, dedicated 68000 on a LAN (MacIntosh approach) should be the preferred solution—but then you may not need UNIX.

With the exception of the last reference, the point can be made that most technical arguments find their origin in the way UNIX was originally designed. Precisely: as a program development environment where there were no removable media. Still today many users employ UNIX as a software development facility.

This can be stated in concluding the present section. While different versions of UNIX may show a variation in the interpretation of the fundamental notions we have been reviewing, as well as the addition of others, the essential design reference remains invariable. As such, it identifies a powerful OS which properly integrates vital functions—becoming, as such, the forerunner of the third generation operating system.

8 UNIX SYSTEM V

System V introduces a mechanism of interprocess communication. This is a different structure than PIPE and FIFO (named PIPE) which has been supported since early releases. PIPE/FIFO have not been adequate solutions for DATABASE/DATACOMM.

System V introduces three primitives; shared memory (segment level), semaphores and message queues (permitting data exchanges in memory which is more efficient than PIPES), but it has data sharing/record locking primitives. Other improvements have provided a stated 25% increase in overall efficiency and the electronic mail mechanism has been improved.

However, there is no official AT&T DBMS announcement yet. This poses a difficult choice between *INGRES*, which allows embedding "C" (EQUEL), but does not support SQL—the new virtual standard for QUERY, and *ORACLE*, which supports SQL, but not embedded "C".

Though by late 1984/early 1985, AT&T may have an official INGRES release, current users and prospective users must decide now on which DBMS to employ. In order to assist in this process, Table 8 identifies the available options.

9 PAYING FOR UNIX

The statement can easily be made that one of the main strengths of Unix is the large community of professionals knowing the system. It is given free of charge to universities; not so to other users. The single source license is $60,000—then it is incremental by release and installation.

Let's see how this paying proposition works (about which several sources are complaining). The following is an example of the pricing of UNIX—source program only:

- *V6, 1st Version*: $60,000. Bell delivers one source tape plus binary to run on a given CPU. The serial number of the hardware is recorded.
- *V7*, source pays an increment.
- *System III*, pay another increment.
- If another CPU is added, pay about $20,000.

The algorithms becomes more complex if the purchaser wants to resell UNIX. First, he cannot call it UNIX. Second, prior to releasing the version in his possession to a third party, he must enter into a "Binary Resale Agreement" paying a one time charge between $20,000 and $30,000.

Under this agreement, the purchaser sells binary sublicenses, at the fee the purchaser determines. But the purchaser must pay Bell $100 per user for up to 10,000 systems installed at the same user. Then the price drops to $50.

For a different number of users/log ins, pricing again varies. Pricing is a major reason, among several, why Silicon Valley companies change the structure of the OS. Some also rename the product, e.g. Xenix, and add "Derived from UNIX."

Some computer manufacturers are currently attempting to rewrite UNIX in Pascal. This will give a totally new system. There is however a fine legal point where to trace the line between the original and the revamped system.

PART FOUR

THE ART OF PROGRAM ADMINISTRATION

18

EVOLVING MICROSOFTWARE INDUSTRY

1 INTRODUCTION

We tend to stereotype our concepts and the way we look at things. The meaning of an "established" notion sharply limits the set of possible instances. Stereotypes obscure important parts of a much larger truth, make us insensitive to new developments, and lead us to miss opportunities. Such an opportunity is the breakthroughs in microsoftware.

It all started in a simple, matter-of-fact way. In 1978, during a "What-If" exercise at the Harvard Business School, Daniel Bricklin then 27 and an MIT graduate worked out with Bob Frankston the electronic spread sheet on an Apple II. VisiCalc (for visible calculator) was born out of a graduate need and spread in business—to the tune of an estimated 400,000 units, each at $200 and up.

Visicalc is probably:

- the most widely pirated software: an estimated 2.5 copies for each officially sold, and
- the most imitated: Visiclones or Calcalikes.

Yet, initially Visicalc got a lukewarm reception from computer stores. Even if backed by Personal Software—a then small software company of another Harvard graduate, Daniel Fylstra—it took some time to take off.

Visicalc is distributed by Personal Software, which has since moved to Silicon Valley and in 1982 changed its name to Visicorp. In Wellesley, a Boston suburb, Bricklin and Frankston set up Software Arts.

Such stories are typical of the developing new software industry for microcomputers. Its products are powerful, sophisticated yet user-friendly, and sell for a very low cost when compared to what's available in software for mainframes and minis.

It is wise to take notice of the fact that the microcomputer revolution is leading to an aggregate into which merge

- Programming languages
- Classical OS
- Transactional routines, and
- Database management systems.

This aggregate intends to be a new systems concept and leads toward *integrated software.*

Still, we are some time away from natural language programming. If it takes a professional programmer to develop the application, then this is not a true end-user language.

What we now have is an impressive array of end-user facilities that began becoming available in 1980 with particular emphasis on *financial models.* In this sense, Visicalc, Desktop/Plan, TK Solver, and their competitors (MicroDSS/Finance, Target, Microfinesse) employ pre-programmed financial functions, such as:

- net present values,
- internal rates of return,
- payback periods,
- amortization, and
- depreciation.

When compared function for function, the best micro modelers often have more features than the timesharing or minicomputer systems. This is particularly true of the MicroDSS/Finance, which has very sophisticated graphics that few large packages can match. And if this computing power is not the main advantage of micro modelers, price is.

Quite surprisingly, management—not the PC professionals—provides the moving gear for a change to PC and micromodels. A senior executive recounted how he had to struggle with his own DP department to get a PC installed. The department insisted on a lengthy search for mainframe software that would do the same tasks. The dedicated PC and financial package cost $1,800. The department's findings? Similar packages for their in-house mainframe cost between $20,000 and $40,000.

2 THE VISICORP STORY

Created as a small, independent software company in 1978, Personal Software changed both its name and its corporate strategy four years later. The new strategic plan rests on two pillars. First, concentrate all efforts in *generic products* for Managers, and Professionals. Such products are not designed for any specific industry: they are *horizontal*. Applications software appeals to vertical markets: steel, cement, distribution industries, banking.

Second, Visicorp reached a key decision on program portability. The "C" language was adopted as a uniform programming basis. Several personal computer lines will be followed with horizontal software developed for the leading PC manufacturers.

In 1980, four companies: Apple (II, III); Tandy (Models II, III); Commodore (896); and Atari (800) commanded 75% of the world PC market. By 1982 the share has changed. Some 105 companies are now marketing 150 PC products. But still a few makes will dominate the market. As a result of the changing market share in predominant makes, Visicorp is tuning its full line to support Apple, IBM PC, the Motorola 68,000-based engines, and probably the DEC PC. Part of the line will address itself to Tandy and other selected products. But support plans do change on a regular basis as the driving force of the marketplace alters its own orientation. It is therefore necessary to identify the leaders; this has its risks.

Horizontal software products have been reorganized along five main lines:

1. *Electronic Spread Sheet*

This includes both the original Visicalc and Visicalc Advanced Version designed for the corporate market. The latter is a producer of sophisticated templates and permits account consolidation.

Other products along this line are: Desktop Plan, for financial planning, and Business Forecasting, implemented through a series of templates.

2. Graphics Packages

The two key products are Visitrend Plot—which manipulates time series data, then charts—and Visischedule. It is employed for Pert-type project scheduling.

3. Data Management

The products are Visifile (it stores and retrieves diverse information elements) and Visidex. This is a personal filing system. It helps retrieval by keyword and also supports a calendaring function.

4. Terminal Emulation

The current product is Visiterm, while Visilink is in development. Significantly, the latest addition to Visicorp's product line is:

5. Integrated Software

A new concept developed in 1982, Integrated Software would have a profound effect both on software and on hardware makers. The fact that the new multifunction programs are being written for the newer, more powerful 16 BPW (bits per word) and 32 BPW personal computers will hasten the obsolescence of older 8 BPW machines.

Visicorp plans to do no custom programming. It is actively working to convert its own products through implementation to exploit specific PC features. There will be additional products to be released in the near future.

There is a joint product development with DRI (Data Resource Inc.) of McGraw-Hill, involving large databanks to be made available on timesharing. The new joint product Visilink will enable the PC user to gain access to DRI at very low cost with charges made through a credit card and information downloaded in Visicalc format.

A whole range of basic products can be expected during the coming years aiming to allow PC users to enter into large databases. The same is true about enhancing the ability of the PC to ride on local area networks.

The job is to insert the functionality needed for intercepting the calls of execution routines, changing the processing from local to network-wide. Such implementation calls for special visual attributes. In a user-friendly manner, PC users must actually see, drive around, and manipulate text and databases without having any specific computer expertise.

3 VISICALC

Visicalc is an end-user facility. It is the first electronic spreadsheet and modeler for PC. Initially priced at $150 and written in Basic to run on the Apple II PLus microcomputer, Visicalc put the power of the timesharing financial modelers at the disposal of any manager or analyst who could get an Apple.

Most importantly, Visicalc started a new trend in computing: users are buying the software first and then finding hardware that runs it. This both excited a responsive chord and provides advantages to managers and professionals who must frequently deal with numbers in their work. New and more powerful financial modeling programs have come around: Micro-DSS/Finance, FPL, Minimodel, Target, T-Maker, Microfinesse, Desktop/Plan II. But Visicalc is still a strong market contender.

What makes Visicalc and its clones so appealing? Fundamentally, even if the end user may not be aware of it, the background reason is a wideband calculator with the ability to drive across the screen some 20 times per second. The transmission rate to the display is about 300 KBPS (kilobits per second).

Visicalc achieves the needed level of bandwidth by eliminating the communications exchanges, putting the processor at the display in the form of a personal computer. The bandwidth lesson teaches that the more information we can display in a specific amount of time, the more inviting the display will be to users who are not trained in computer technology.

Several personal computer products have been very successful because the implementers understood the importance of bandwidth. Other office applications requiring wideband facilities are

videoconferencing and

bit-map displays, including graphics.

Full-motion videoconferencing, digitized and compressed, requires a 1.5 MBPS channel. A bit-map display with 200 pixel (points to the inch) resolution requires about 4 megabits. Adding color to that we reach 30 megabits.

On the functional side, the ability to consolidate results is one of the main reasons for using one of the Visicalc packages. Even a major corporation can bring into the PC one business line at a time without overloading the memory. Management can evaluate models for one product at a time, consolidating several to develop the structure of a product line.

Among the leading applications:

1. budgetary planning and control
2. analysis regarding mergers and acquisitions
3. sales planning and forecasting
4. material and labor requirements evaluation
5. cash-flow forecasting and analysis
6. decisions on capital investments
7. commercial load evaluation and marketing planning
8. product planning analyses
9. management performance evaluation

Financial executives and strategic planners can easily add many other specifics.

As a matter of fact, let's not forget that computer-based financial modeling did not come into its own until the mid-1960s. Prior to that time, modeling had been a laborious hand-calculation procedure. By the mid 1970s, minicomputers had provided financial modeling power for some corporations, but even more popular were timesharing systems that gave a financial analyst or planner access to mainframe computer power.

Personal computer implementation of "What-If" software contrasts and compares to centralized timesharing. It improves flexibility, reduces costs, increases ease—and permits far greater privacy. It also enhances sensitivity analysis.

After the PC-based executive experiments with the first few simple models, he wonders: "What will happen to profits if the sales growth is reduced? What about the borrowing needs? How much can sales fall and the business still break even?" Still, the way the person looks at the model is a major key to the ability to do such analysis.

With Visicalc managers can easily create preformatted worksheets (templates) for estimates, budgets, forecasts, plans: anything numerical. The PC package performs the calculations built into the worksheet and displays the answers to problems that could have taken hours to solve by hand.

Designed to serve at the executive level, Visicalc Advanced Version protects areas of a worksheet the user does not want changed. It also provides comprehensive on-screen help to assist users in completing their worksheets. Its Keystroke Memory makes it easier to

achieve multisheet consolidation,

total worksheets from various groups, departments, or divisions.

Computer requirements for the original release are an Apple III with 128 KBY and at least one external disc drive.

Visicalc's recalculation feature permits the user to change any number or formula, assuring that all numbers affected by that change are recalculated and displayed. A replicate feature duplicates any entry (label, number or formula). The window feature splits the display into two parts, either horizontally or vertically, to view separate portions of the worksheet.

A variable format sets every number to integer, floating point, dollars and cents, left or right justified, or histogram with three keystrokes. Commands include logical functions and arithmetic comparison operators. They perform simple mathematical and built-in functions (sum, minimum, maximum). Scientific notation is automatic, and eleven-digit precision is standard.

The Visicalc forecasting-model features generate the financial reports most needed for business analysis:

1. *Income Statement.*

2. *Balance Sheet:* assets, Liabilities, and Equity.

3. *Cash Flow:* cash beginning, receipts, disbursements, cash ending.

4. *Financial Ratios:* current ratio, debt to assets, debt to equity, times interest earned, profit margin, income to assets, and income to net worth.

5. *Assets & Depreciation Schedules.*

6. *Sales and Cost-of-Goods.*

7. *Salaries.*

The program's interactive display instantly shows the impact of any change, allowing the user to ask "What If?", thus investigating alternatives—and worksheets may be customized to specific user needs.

There are presently many offerings which are improvements over Visicalc. Lotus 1-2-3, an integrated software, is the most powerful of these products, with Multiplex one of the best at the spreadsheet level.

4 DESKTOP/PLAN AND MICRO/DSS-FINANCE

The Desktop/Plan programs offer structured, highly organized financial planning, budgeting, and analysis packages able to lead the user from the layout of a financial model to the final presentation of a boardroom report. It produces line charts, bar graphs, and, if necessary, tabular data. This package is particularly useful for transferring individual lines from several partial budgets into a master budget. It is also useful for consolidating identical departmental budgets into an overall company budget. It can receive information from Visicalc, permitting transfer of Visicalc files to its own required format.

On the whole, this is a simple package to use. The model size is dependent on available memory and the desired relationship of columns to rows. With Apple II and 64 KBy the user can have up to 18 columns or up to 300 rows; with Apple III and 128 KBy he can have up to 300 columns or up to 1,000 rows. With the IBM PC and 64 KBy it supports 100 columns and 990 rows. A color adapter card is needed for high resolution graphics. Two disc drives are in all cases necessary.

Applications-wise, developing a model with Desktop/Plan is fairly simple. The job begins by writing out the line items on a sheet of paper:

- sales,
- cost of goods, and so on.

Then the user must define the relationship among line items. This, too, can be simple: Gross margin equals sales minus cost of goods sold. Having written the model down, the user simply types the data into the machine.

Data entry moves easily, followed by calculation rules selected from a menu. Compared to Visicalc, Desktop/Plan gives some extra power and saves the time usually spend cleaning up the Visicalc reports. But its more sophisticated structure involves more calculation time.

Using Desktop/Plan, the chief financial officer of a conglomerate was able to construct a consolidated budget, dealing with 150 separate sheets, going back and changing one incorrect number and recalculate the whole thing. This implementation (which required some more lines of code than the package supported) has levels of consolidation:

- by subsidiary (15)

- by division: foreign and U.S.
- total company.

It features 100 rows for expense accounts, 17 columns, 12 months, 4 quarters, and annual totals. The model's formulas include conversions for different currencies and represent a consolidation for the whole company of each of 100 expense accounts.

This is a good example of what a PC can do. Other advanced features of the micro modelers include:

1. *Expanded functions,* such as minimum, maximum, average, cumulative.

2. *Line references* in which a command uses an entire line in a new calculation.

3. *Lags, leads and column referencing,* in which a user can make a current calculation using prior information.

An example is an accounts payable report in which the user must refer to previous months' bills to determine current month indebtness.

4. *Consolidation procedures* through which complete models or parts of other models can be added to a new model in memory.

Such results are achieved through sophisticated utilities for generating automatic model operations. The same reference is valid about making simple query structures so novices can use the model on a fill-in-the-blanks basis.

Quite important is the flexibility the PC and micromodelers offer. With the package, the user can do calculations by changing a few numbers, generating as much or as little information as wanted on the report. With a timesharing system, he is locked into the service's modeling format unless he wants to pay for extensive software changes. Few take this route.

Underlying this last comment are two more micro advantages:

- immediacy, and
- continuous access.

The user does not stay hooked up to a timesharing system all day long, going back and forth between the timesharing model and his desk. With micro modelers, one can leave the machine booted up and move work with it when one wants. One can test new hypotheses as they arise.

Let's look in some detail at another model. Marketed by Addisson Wesley, the Micro-DSS/Finance by Ferox Microsystems is a full-scale financial modeler that includes data entry, logical calculation, iterative analysis, and on-screen display. But it goes well beyond all this with a whole host of additional features found formerly only on mainframe decision support systems costing $50,000 to $300,000. DSS/F is only $1,500 and has the following features:

Menus and Prompting

Goal Seeking

Large Matrix Size

Report Generator

Predefined Financial Functions

Job Files

Worksheet

Consolidation

Editor, Dataview

LogOn Interface

Graphics and Slide Show

Menus make DSS easy to employ. All the user needs to do is to turn on the computer and enter the main menu. He can then move easily between eight different command level menus, create models, solve models, view/print results, ask "What If," consolidate, manipulate, do "Goal Seeking," modify the matrix, and maintain files—all by selecting menu items. Experienced users can bypass the menus and enter commands.

With the *Worksheet* facility the user can automatically generate a worksheet for data collection and show the blanks where data is needed. He can also give the worksheet to someone else for data collection.

Goal-Seeking is a backward iteration. The user is able to specify net profit figures each year for the next 5 years and then examine how much sales he will need each year to achieve these specific profit levels.

The *Report Generator* supports variable width columns; the selection of rows to be printed, changing their order and variable names; the ability to insert text, underline numbers, format numbers, and add footnotes. The *Predefined Financial Functions* handle the internal rate of return and the perpetual and multiple net present value. When it comes to calculating return on investment or discounting cash flow, these facilities are valuable. The model also evaluates periods to payback, tax loss carryforward, depreciation of all types, and loan amortization:

interest,

principal,

balance,

payment.

The *Consolidation* feature helps handling any number of entities on any number of levels in the hierarchy. Product lines consolidate into departments, departments merge into divisions, and divisions consolidate into corporate. DSS/F can add files, subtract files, and extract data from any row, column, or cell in another matrix.

The *Editor* is instrumental in creating models. Additions and changes are easily accomplished. It is general purpose so one could use it as a word processor—to create text for overhead transparencies or format text to go along with the DSS/F reports.

Dataview permits to mix the order of rows and columns on the screen, making an "What If" analysis on just the data the user wants to see in the order he wants to see it. Finally, the *LogOn Interface* is a datacomm routine written to assist in sending and receiving data from/to another micro, mini, or mainframe. This allows access to the corporate database.

Finally, in what regards the *Graphics and Slide Show* some versions of DSS/F (such as on Apple II) have color screen graphics and black/white output to a printer. It is thus possible to create pie charts, bar charts, stacked bar charts, side-by-side bar charts, and line graphs—also, a slide show of many graphic and text images for use in presentations.

Target (by Advanced Management Strategies) is a model less sophisticated than the Micro-DSS/Finance (but more complex than VisiCalc). It runs on two machines: A 64 KBy TRS-80 Model II with CP/M 2.2 and one disc drive and an Apple II Plus with 48 KBy, a Microsoft SoftCard, and two disc drives.

The TRS-80 version has a maximum matrix of 1,000 elements, that is, 100 rows and 10 columns, or 20 columns and 50 rows. The Apple II version has a maximum of 900 elements, 10 columns and 90 rows or 18 columns and 50 rows. It can recall history (previous months' values from prior columns) and uses a text editor with cursor control.

The micromodel is menu driven with one main selection that establishes and executes each model. It uses programming-like structures with line, column and heading commands. Lines are numbered sequentially and line commands can be data, operational statements, or function statements. It uses English-like program statements and combines them with match operators, which can be executed with constants.

With a price tag of $195, Target stands up in cost/effectiveness. It has logic and conditional operators. Each function, statement, and feature is clearly explained in the manual. The computer function consists of preparing a table file that includes headings, numbers, and equations. The equations calculate other numbers in the table.

The program includes trigonometric funtions, minimum and maximum values, square roots, absolute values, reciprocals, and constant value equations. As the 16 BPW PC are followed in the next two years by even more powerful 32-bit versions, the amount of internal memory available for matrix size will logically expand, and users will be able to build larger, more complex models closing the gap in capabilities with the offering of remote-computing time-sharing services.

5 TK SOLVER

The TK Solver (TK standing for tool kit) is a piece of software designed to solve problems expressed in one or more equation—as long as the keyboard supports the entry. It is also an ingenious tool for problem back-solving.

The package was studied to provide professionals in engineering and business with a personal computing tool. Its goal is a means for solving problems with mathematical calculations without knowing a programming language.

To employ this piece of integrated software, the user types in one or more equations and the known variables. The TK Solver then computes either through direct approach or interactively.

The rationale behind the TK Solver and similar packages is that their availability should stimulate interest in address business problems through interactive computer assistance. To determine the computational process, the user typically outlines his requests and best estimates in three algorithmic groups:

1. *Definitional identities* or equations with no predictive ability.

2. *Assumptions* presenting relationships that may be predicted.

3. *Hypotheses* stating predictive relationships.

The output of the model will only be as accurate as the weakest assumption or hypothesis. Still, the need for timeliness and manageability demands simplifying approaches, but the model user should at least be clear about his assumptions.

Evidently, few situations can be simplified without losing some degree of accuracy, but a model should be, in principle, simple. The benefit comes from the analysis specifying that solving the problem means deciding exactly what is desired. This should be expressed both in general terms and in detail.

Valid assumptions, the existence of computer support, and the right elements in the database will allow significant fluctuations to be detected and analyzed. Lack of historical data and no reasonable estimate of future items will bring this initiative to a stop.

The power of the method rests on the ability to identify the required input and output variables. But the database must also be designed to assure structure and integrity for the data.

Structuring the data in a formal manner allows different users and different models to share the data without risk of loss of integrity. Implementing a solution can differ widely depending on the modeling and reporting software being used. In each implementation step, the procedure being followed is converted into a concrete algorithm.

It will be helpful to recall the general problem specification, a guidepost in testing hypotheses to formulate assumptions that can be applied to the model. Implementing the reporting structure requires specifying to the software system the desired format of the output variables. Using the database involves naming information and entering the appropriate keys into the machine.

On loading the TK Solver, a two-line message area appears at the top of the screen.

1. The *status line* displays information about the status of the program.

2. The *prompt error line* displays messages.

At the *status line* the position indicator identifies where the cursor is through a row number and a letter labelling the column. The label of the contents of that field is to the right of it, showing the contents.

A *memory indicator* on the far right of the status line shows the amount of remaining memory in the work area. A message *Low* is displayed when memory capacity drops below 1 KBy. The last character on the status line is a *solution indicator*. An exclamation point appears in it when they are unsolved. It disappears upon solving a model, but it reappears if any changes are made.

The *prompt/error line* displays prompts that require a response for messages telling the status of the program. It is also used for error messages. In the prompt/error line, the user can enter either a question mark or a topic he wants to be explained by the machine.

There are eight sheets in the program, each containing different information. A model to be processed by the system can use all or only two of them:

1. The *Rule Sheet* has the equations defining the model. It is therefore a necessary ingredient of the solution.
2. The *Unit Sheet* addresses itself to conversions between units of measurement.
3. The *Global Sheet* sets limits and required constraints. They regard the program and the solver(s).
4. The *Plot Sheet* has the information needed to produce a plot of values.
5. The object of the *Table Sheet* is to produce a table of values.
6. The *Variable Sheet* exhibits the variables with their characteristics (units, values).

The user can also display subsheets: variable, list, function (Figure 18-1).

The package converts between different units of measurement; it exchanges known variables with other (unknown) variables without having to reformulate the equations. It helps solve not only for individual values for the variables, but also for lists of values. It can proceed through successive approximations to converge on a solution. Using the values such solution produces, it can display tabulated data or graphs.

The TK Solver has a menu of 22 commands used to enter formulas and data; to manipulate data and units; solve equations; and move among the sheets, windows and operations. The following are two basic control signs, followed by a list of the commands:

/	Command
⇕	Arrow Keys
	Entry mode: up, down, left, right.

Evolving Microsoftware Industry

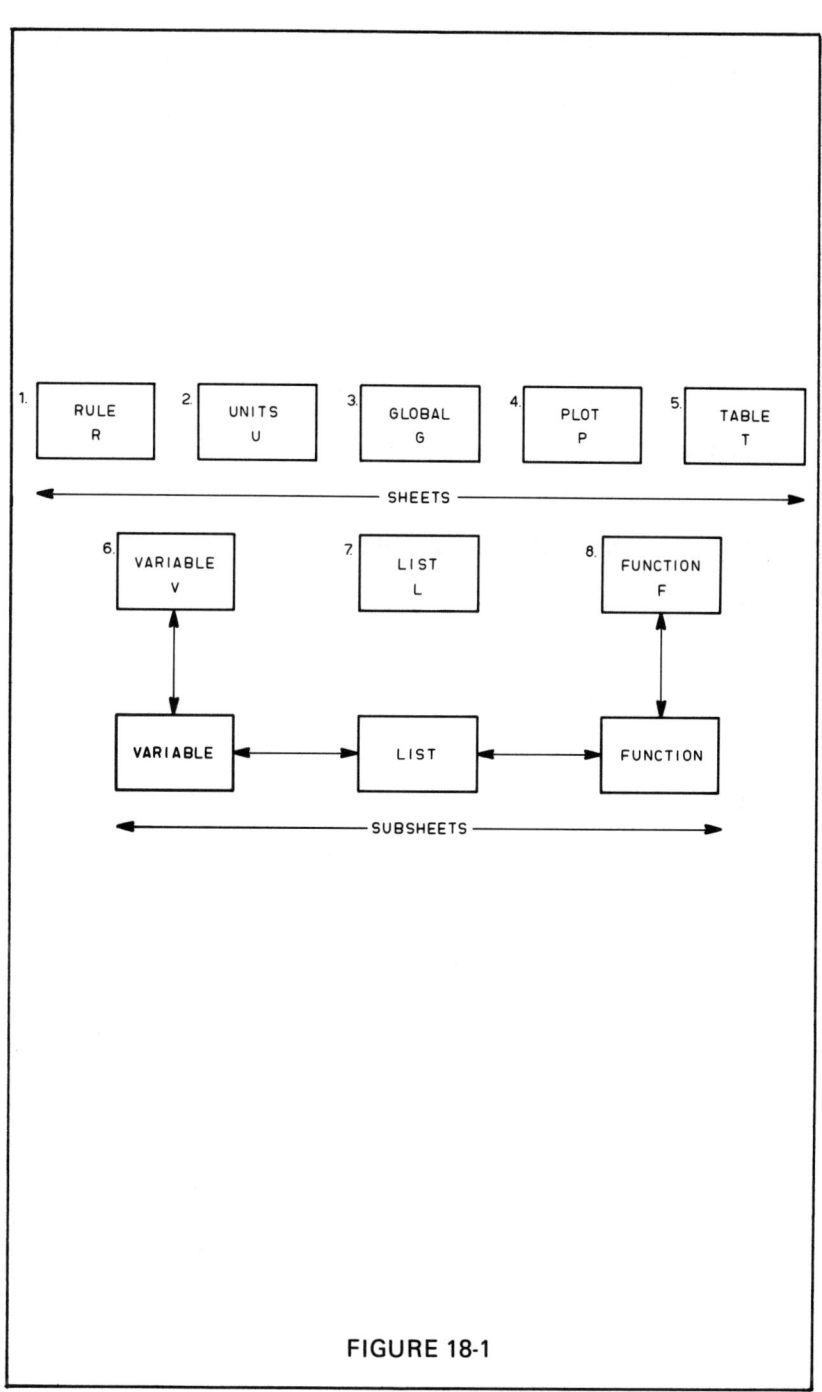

FIGURE 18-1

List of 22 commands (notice that from B to L the command stroke (/) must precede the command order):

=,	Call any sheet
>,	Push to subsheet
<,	Pop from subsheet
:,	Go to any field
;,	Switch
!,	Solve or Execute
Break,	Cancel operation
?,	Help
1E,	Edit mode (begin, end field)
B,	blank
C,	copy
D,	delete
I,	insert
Q,	quit
/!,	resolve model
E.,	Edit
M,	Move
S,	store (also save, load, delete)
W,	window (any one of two sheets)
P,	print
R,	reset (variables, sheet, all)
L,	list solver (solve, block)

These commands are executable in one or two strokes each. They can be used to present data, solve equations, convert units of measurement, make tables, and plot graphs. This permits the user to spend time creatively exploring alternative ideas and solutions.

Once he has stated his problem, he would simply enter the known values, then solve the problem with a couple of keystrokes.

If he chooses, the user can employ a graphic tablet through the *user function* sheet. The package has, however, the shortcoming that in its current release it is for standalone machines—not yet for networking—and LAN is the way to office automation.

Among the applications that can find able assistance through the TK Solver are mechanical and electrical engineering, building design and construction, units of measurement, conversion and evaluation, and educational sciences. Another evident candidate is financial management, the *"What If"* approach. But on this particular issue there are available today some 40 products, and at least one version of VisiCalc (by Hewlett-Packard) runs on networking.

The use of the TK Solver can be explained in four basic steps:

1. Formulate the equation(s) to solve the problem.
2. Input them on the Rule Sheet.
3. Enter the known values on, say, the Variable Sheet.
4. Type the Action command (!) to solve the problem.

With this command, the package gets into action, and TK Solver displays the answer. Once the user has entered the equation(s), he or she can use the program to find the values for the variables, provided the necessary precautions have been taken.

The prerequisites amount to the use of the split screen, such as:

- Variable Sheet, and
- Rule Sheet.

The Rule Sheet, for example, may display speed as a function of distance/time and mileage as distance/amount of gas. The nature of the next screen will depend on the application. In this particular instance it may be:

- *Unit Sheet*, providing for the needed conversions, and
- *Global*, for setting limits and constraints in regard to problem solution.

Once the result has been obtained, the model can be saved; and the same is true of the Unit Sheet.

The model can be used in a variety of cases, including—in a banking environment—loan evaluation and customer mirror (profit and loss by account). The same is valid in regard to the evaluation of portfolio management and foreign exchange operations.

The packages come equipped with the appropriate manual containing cross-references, a general program description and details of all the program commands and features: prompts, status messages, and so on.

19

INTEGRATED SOFTWARE

1 INTRODUCTION

The developing new generation of management-oriented microsoftware brings into focus a so far latent notion: DP managers can save their companies thousands of dollars by linking micros together through networks. Such a notion is further enhanced by the growing array of available packages, such as schedulers, file managers, and charting facilities.

Among the currently available PC packages, some programs make short work of scheduling projects and estimating costs. They give management both the overview and the details it needs to:

control projects,

meet deadlines,

level resources, and

face cost targets.

Computer-run, they instantly show the critical path among project's tasks; help allocate costs; specify earliest and latest start dates; identify slack times, prerequisites, and deadlines for each task. They also produce comprehensive summaries, calendar time charts, milestone, and other reports.

Through this kind of assistance, they make it easy to develop project control and investigate tradeoffs between manpower, costs, and time. They are reasonably easy to learn, leading step by step from start to finish. They provide interactive display showing the impact of changes in data. And they help allocate skill and cost categories per task, automatically adjusting the project schedule.

2 WHAT IS INTEGRATED SOFTWARE?

As discussed in the preceding chapter and documented by examples, PC based packages assure comprehensive electronic filing systems that make it easy to organize, maintain, and effectively use the information a business needs. They can instantly and accurately store, search, sort, retrieve, display, calculate, and print reports.

Supported features allow us to change file formats easily, without time-consuming re-entry. The user can file almost any kind of information: name and address lists, prospect and customer files, personnel records, parts lists, or merchandise inventories.

Typically, such packages sort alphabetically or numerically, in ascending or descending order; calculate formulas between fields with automatic recalculation if a number is changed; allow the user to change any file's structure, such as expanding the zip code from five digits to nine, without re-entering existing data; and merge files and create partial files for faster data entry.

For output purposes, graphics packages help the user in presenting the results of modeling: selecting line, bar, scatter, or pie charts; mixing lines and bar charts; setting the scale for both horizontal and vertical axes; inserting titles anywhere on the page; and plotting changes in, say, earnings versus changes in sales or assets.

As several of the tasks we have been discussing eventually need to be cascaded, design ideas of integrated software come as a valuable answer. This is particularly important to the user who gained experience, is ready to move to a more sophisticated environment, and looks for a *software bus* on which to hang multiple facilities.

The next generation of integrated software will include:

1. *Creation of system commands* (Shells) making all links (and other supported functions) fully transparent to the user.

2. *Encryption* capability (first SW through PASSWORD, ID; then SW/HW).

3. *Integration links:* WP to EMAIL; CALENDAR to EMAIL, etc.

4. *Voice editing* based on voice datatypes (digital encoding) and playback capabilities.

5. *Project management* incorporating automatic reporting on PLAN/ACTUAL, UPDATE, PERT Presentation.

6. *Budgetary control* capability: handling budgets, receiving financial reports, producing highlights, charts and exception items.

7. *Expert systems.* Implementing a knowledgebank (rules); presenting conversational reports; justifying the suggested course of action.

The issue to concentrate on is *added value.* To answer the requirements posed by the market, the functions involved in integrated software combine many formerly separate software packages into one program so that users can handle:

financial models,

graphics,

written reports, and other tasks.

Such integrated software packages can make personal computers so much easier to use. They are expected to become the critical element for success in this highly competitive market. Moreover, this trend toward powerful packages will undoubtedly create a powerful new industry. It is estimated that the integrated software market will grow from essentially nothing in 1980 to about $4 billion in 1987. And analysts are betting that in 2 or 3 years, integrated software will take over from standalone programs.

Visicorp, for instance, plans once again to take a leadership role in the software industry through *VisiOn*—expecting to establish an industry standard for which smaller software companies would produce add-on applications programs.

A survey of Visicorp's customers showed that 45% of them wanted integrated multipurpose software and that 73% would demand it this year. One of the targets is ease of use. Daniel Fylstra asserts, VisiOn can be learned in less than 30 minutes by using a mouse that controls the movement of a cursor on the computer screen.

The cursor on the screen is pointed at any one of the dozens of program functions listed in English, such as:

save,

transfer,

help.

The computer user can then simply press a single button on the mouse to move from one step to another in the program. The new packages also separates the computer screen into windows, in which different functions can be performed simultaneously.

The difference between separate old-style programs and such integrated software is the difference between a mainframe-hooked terminal and the properly designed, microprocessor-supported workstation. Executives who tested VisiOn estimate that it could save more than 50% from the 8 to 10 hours that they now spend with their personal computer each week.

3 A BROADER RANGE OF SOFTWARE

New approaches to the design and implementation of programming products mark a new phase of transformation taking place in the computer industry. In the sense of our discussion, integrated software means the ability to use different software packages

- over a broad range of personal computers
- for a variety of applications to hang on.

Though the concept of the *software bus* forms the common background, other developments have also to be brought into the picture. One of the most important is the observance of standard formats allowing the transfer of data between different software products.

Much in terms of this definition is due to the evolution of utility packages that permit an easy transfer of files between personal computers. For instance, one such package for IBM PC to Apple II/DOS file transfer uses an Intel 8086 and MS DOS as basic reference. It also employs the MS DOS file system.

The concept of integrated software is, however, going much further than resting on the implementation of *one set of* commands. From this spring many of the problems—as there is no single set of commands equally good for, say, spreadsheet and word processing.

Interfaces are another problem. To overcome it, at least one of the new and thriving PC-oriented software companies designed IL, a high-level implementation language. It was led to this development after having evaluated and practically eliminated "C" because of too little flexibility and the fact that it requires different interpreters for different machines.

(The company in reference, Software Arts, employs a prime computer with 1 MB of memory to serve as the main software development engine. Scores of PC are wired into this system: an Ethernet LAN allows micro-to-micro communication as well as PC-to-mainframe.)

Instrumental in IL design has been the artificial intelligence orientation developed at MIT. (This language is not in the public domain; its basic design goal and competitive advantage is portability).

If one of the pillars of integrated software is portability, the other should be communications capability. Universal protocols should enable workstation users to tap the power of large databases for convenient PC level analysis at remote locations.

The implementation of gateways between mainframe and micro software makes it feasible to apply application expertise through a broader range of facilities. It also has far reaching consequences for information management in many organizations. Thus, integrated software should not be seen from a narrow viewpoint of machine utilization but from a much broader, problem-solving horizon.

4 AN APPLICATIONS NETWORK ARCHITECTURE

Application gateways permit centralized control of company-wide processing. Yet they also allow information processing at remote sites to meet the unique needs of user stations and of individual divisions or subsidiaries. The provision of this capability can be assured through the implementation on an *Application Network Architecture* (ANA) utilizing a functional layer concept.

As shown in Figure 19-1, ANA uses a functional layer for linking application networks between mainframe(s) and PC. A layered approach is used to send data from the application software on the host to the communications link. The same layers are employed to receive data from the communications link and feed the application software at the receiving end. Layer functionality is as follows:

1. The *line discipline* handles the communications protocol and also assures verification and retry.

2. The function of *data transmission* is to assure text/data compression and if necessary data translation.

3. *Data mapping* uses a data dictionary to verify content and compatibility.

4. The *application data control* provides the facilities necessary for data security and integrity. It also interfaces between the AP and the transmission services.

A layered concept takes advantage of advancements in technology, particularly in the communications field. By interfacing between the applications software and the communications link, such architecture allows new developments to be easily incorporated into the system, as well as to replace an obsolete layer.

Furthermore, by having a mirror image of ANA on both the mainframe and the PC, it is possible (1) to provide for standards within the system; (2) to support mainframe-to-micro, mainframe-to-mini, mini-to-micro, micro-to-micro communications; as well as (3) to slowly improve the services by the functional layers in a system-wide manner.

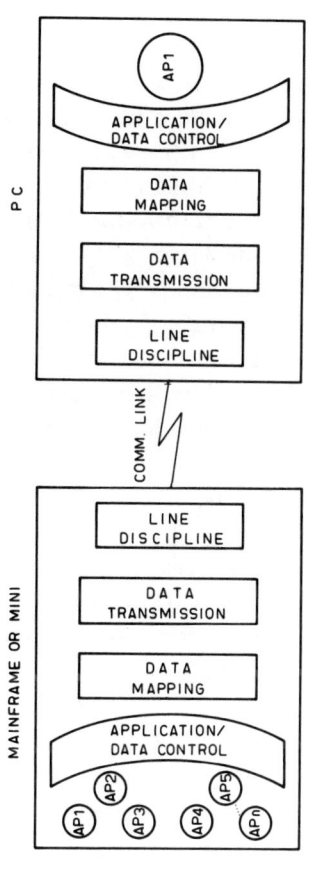

FIGURE 19-1

THE APPLICATION/DATA CONTROL PROVIDES FOR DATA SECURITY AND INTEGRITY. DATA MAPPING RESTS ON DICTIONARY SERVICES. DATA TRANSMISSION ASSURES COMPRESSION AND TRANSLATION.

In this sense, the first function of application data control is to select the appropriate information from the application program needed for conversion to a data stream. An add-on function will be to encrypt at the application level to add security—while checking data integrity and authorizing. The receiving component is part of the kernel.

At data mapping, the information being sent loses its application orientation in preparation for a physical transfer. The object is to convert text and data to a form intelligible to the transmission layer which will build the data stream and initiate data transmission. While this is a kernel activity, as an add-on data transmission will handle character stream conversion for transmission efficiency and check line speeds. Data compression and compaction are examples of add-on services, and so is data translation (if necessary).

Finally, the line discipline layer will be supportive of both hardware and software. It's function is to control the physical data characteristics for transmission through the communications link, including data integrity checks, transmission verification, and re-try. At the hardware level, this layer will use a modem to convert a digitized data stream to an analog telephone signal, and vice versa at the receiving end.

These examples of the function of an evolving integrated software concept help identify the possible extent and sophistication of the environment that is created. Supported functionality makes feasible well-rounded applications solutions. User exits promote the additions of routines specific to a given area of requirements or a single implementation.

5 SOFTWARE FOR EXECUTIVE WORKSTATIONS

While the rapid calculation facilities of the spreadsheet and the networking capabilities discussed in the last section seem to be two distinct entities—addressed to different populations—in reality they are two vital parts of the same project. Their common goal is instant information through a personal computer under every desk.

A foremost goal of integrated software is to make processing, databasing, and datacomm transparent to the end user. When non-computer people employ personal computing, the software at their disposition is always more important than the hardware that is going with it.

Under no condition should this software be too hard to use, unable to do the job, or out-of-date. The main sense of integrated software is to permit the non-computer professional to use his personal computer as a creative tool for better decisions. This means combining the foremost business functions into one easy-to use, integrated product:

1. Interactive man-machine communication

2. Spreadsheet facilities

3. Personal computing features

4. Graphics presentation

5. Electronic mail

6. Word processing

7. Report writing

8. Calendar services

9. Database management, and

10. Computer to computer communications.

Hence, only one software package is needed to make the personal computer do everything its user wants.

The spreadsheet facilities can be seen as a very high-level language, which is not only easy to learn by the end user—particularly given the integrated machine assistance through menues and prompts—but also enable him to create the formats he needs without having to depend on computer specialists. By building ten major functions into one software package, integrated software helps the user elaborate meaningful information from large amounts of data that are unique to his business.

A good example in terms of implementation comes from the hands-on experience for managers organized in the United Technologies 3-day program with the PC. Lecturing takes 10 minutes, the rest is work on the computer. PC software and hardware (particularly keyboard commands) are explained in the first morning.

Also: how to use the documentation; how to load DOS; and how to load the integrated software. The afternoon is devoted to practical examples with spreadsheet implementation:

- salary planning
- budget comparison
- sales forecasting.

In the morning of the second day, work concentrates on management graphics—made on the PC, by each participant. The afternoon is invested on word processing software. Another subject is personal scheduling routines.

The morning of the third day is devoted to communications protocols and software availability, with practice in datacomm:

- sending and receiving messages,
- electronic mail,
- connection to the company's own computer resources.

The afternoon work centers on communicating with public databases; the Dow Jones is the practical example.

Through the communications features of integrated software, the executive can connect his or her personal computer to the company's main computer center(s) to retrieve business information. This is done instantaneously and in a manner transparent to the user. The executive can store, edit, sort, and modify the information on a personal computer and use the spreadsheet to create a model of the business—or of his or her reporting needs.

Through personal computing resources mastered only by the executive, plans and forecasts can be developed in a small fraction of the time it would take to do them by hand. And one does not need to use multiple software packages to do so.

Using the spreadsheet function, one can instantly chart vital figures on the screen. One can make cost or revenue assumptions; evaluate how the result would affect the business; interrogate databases; and put words, numbers, and graphs together in a clean report.

How easy it is to learn the use of integrated software can be seen in the training stage. Throughout the United Technologies program, the instructor communicates through his PC and a LAN. The participant is taught interactively how to use his new skills. He then develops *his own personal computing* plan.

6   THE HORIZONTAL TOOLS

The usual way of looking at the spreadsheet is as the tool enabling the busy manager to answer *"what if"* questions. What should be the minimum loan period? What if this period is changed? How many sales sites are presently handled? What if they are increased or decreased? How many field engineers are employed? What may be the result on customer service of changing their number, offices, parts depots?

A model can be easily developed within the 63 columns and 255 rows of the typical microcomputer-based spreadsheet to identify how the spare parts inventory is distributed and controlled. Then experimentation can be done to establish what the optimum response time is to our present locations, our likely future locations, and so on.

We can study the availability of spares from the service company's own inventory so we don't have to keep excessive stock. We can also experiment in terms of other factors affecting sales, inventory, and production.

While this can evidently be done through big machines, it will require several months of delay, significant cost, and scarce human resources in terms of analysts and programmers. Integrated software can provide a wealth of applications possibilities through easily programmable financial models. Among supports being developed through horizontal integrated tools we distinguish:

- financial and operating projections
- cash flow evaluation (in different demonstrations)
- return on investment analyses
- capital and operating budget
- budget/actual comparisons

- make-or-buy tests
- project planning and financing
- market forecasts
- current account transactions and consolidated statements

Available software routines which come into play in a way transparent to the end user involve macro-operations, a text editor, data entry facility, matrix handler, report generators, and graphics routines.

This is a set of tools that collectively perform wanted functions. The degree of communication and interaction between the individual tools impacts on integration. Tightly integrated systems support tools transparent to the user.

In this sense, horizontal integration refers to the use of tools during the development cycle. The idea is not totally new. In some areas excellent tools have been available for years, but were not integrated. In others, more capable tools are needed, and they have been provided through integrated software.

Typically, integrated tools contain a database management system that makes integration feasible. To be effectively used, such tools should also include a common user interface and graphical input/output. Furthermore:

- It is essential that management information is captured by tools that support visibility and control.
- The horizontal integration should be addressed from within a chosen methodology, incrementally building a tool set with a common project database.
- It is important to ensure a maintainable structure for user-dependable results.

In the sense of this last reference, emphasis should be placed upon the generation of a methodology that supports integration of new tools. This structure should provide for the accumulation of knowledge.

The short history of personal computing demonstrates that the users will be demanding more and more applications software as well as changes in existing routines. Such demands will add up to more support than the information systems department can supply. It is, therefore, advantageous to enable the end user to do some of the chores.

While users will buy much of their software in the form of packages (if the computers and operating systems are chosen to take advantage of this market place), easy programming through spreadsheet facilities should be most welcome. However, let's remember that success by end users in employing their own computers is directly related to the quality of help and support they receive.

If user-programmed systems supposed to eliminate the need for programmers are neither that well designed nor that well implemented, they would not be successful. At the same time, even if users make available to themselves very efficient horizontal software, they should not push their requests beyond the limits a spreadsheet can support.

A manager might buy a micro to run a spreadsheet package that generally causes no problem. Then a word processing package is added. Then a database management system is added. And then the problems start.

The more important information systems become to their users, the more critical the integrated software's role will become. Vertical software is designed for a particular industry (a "vertical" market) and automates a firm's clerical requirements, including functions peculiar to that particular industry. Horizontal software aims to serve everybody—but none in the most detailed manner.

7 TELESOFTWARE

Integrated, horizontal software can help solve several problems connected to the programming needs for personal computing. But vertical software will still be needed. Canny software sellers have now discovered a new way to ease the shelf space squeeze at the computer stores; and that's *telesoftware*.

Tymshare, the California computer communications firm, is experimenting in four San Francisco-area stores with the electronic delivery of programs to customer. Once the buyer has selected the software he wants to buy, the salesman orders it up from a central computer and through telephone lines it is downloaded on a disc in the store. The same can apply in downloading at the user's home.

The origin of telesoftware dates back to 1979/80 in England, as part and parcel of the Videotex (Prestel) experience. Let's, therefore, look at the fundamentals.

We all know that there has been increased use of computers for sending text messages. However, leased line networks have resulted in fast growing expenses and system complexity. Videotex was designed to free users from dependence on a complex communications environment, providing a memo-and-letter distribution facility that can employ standard telephone channels.

Back in the 1960s, data communications service typically allowed attaching simple terminals to a host. As such, this facility was little more than a restricted file copy mechanism, and it was directed to the specialist.

Little or no specialized software was provided to aid in creation, projection, and final disposition of messages; what's more, the use of terminals called for specialized operators. They were not made for the end user, who was alienated.

Something similar can be said about the consumer's lack of computers and communications expertise. Yet, even with this gap, computer-based communications channels have become the veins and arteries of today's social and business life.

By using widespread devices in common use, such as telephones and TV, videotex makes the information technology user friendly. The videotex protocol is so simple that it is written on the face of the keypad used for the commands.

In this sense, videotex fills both a private and an organizational need. By providing a visual communication between people and information, it broadens the horizon of the human mind. And that is equally true of electronic mail and personal computers.

But electronic mail facilities do not open the envelope of the message being sent. Typically, today such messages are—on the average—200 characters long, with several reaching 400 characters. That is the size of a small program that can be transmitted either through electronic mail or videotex facilities to the end user's personal computer at his own request.

The automation of the delivery system is an issue of major importance to an industry whose sales are increasing at a rate of 50% a year.

- New companies are springing up almost every week.
- Big corporations are beginning to move into the market.
- New programs are being launched with heavy promotion and large advertising budgets.
- Software-only specialty stores are multiplying.

From a starting point in 1976/77, sales of software for personal computers have been on a vector that seems to be pointed straight up. Revenues reached $1 billion in 1982 and are expected to hit $1.5 billion in 1983, luring an estimated 230 companies in the U.S. alone into the business of creating software. (By 1990, industry revenues could reach $12 billion, with software equalling the size of today's household appliance industry.)

Much of this software (both horizontal and vertical in nature) is competitively priced. But many programs closely emulate one another, giving rise to large families of *clones*.

This is one of the best documentations that we are past the point where technology is all important. It is the marketing and reputation that are important now. That is why a telesoftware delivery system reaching every corner of the user population is so important to the software producers.

Programs that cost only $5 to reproduce can sell at retail for up to $500 or more—provided there is the right channel to reach the consumer. Videotex can not only do such delivery but also provide the advertising platform for brand recognition.

It is important to realize that not only are people-information communications with videotex more up-to-date (and, therefore, more efficient) than those of classical real-time, but the necessary infrastructure is much simpler.

Both electronic mail and videotex can operate as an internetwork message service. A basic reason for showing interest in this proposition (in addition to local message capabilities) is that the utility of any such service is strongly related to the efficiency of interconnection between correspondents.

Whether for message exchange or telesoftware, an electronic service is developed that has the potential to work with a variety of environments. Interactive systems are able to operate equally well in home or business. Their basic characteristics are the use of on-line terminals and the fact that untrained operators can work very efficiently.

8   VIDEOTEX SERVICES

Videotex is not exactly integrated software, but something like it. In business, applications range from telephone directories to sales prices, stock levels, parts lists, expedited items, accounts receivable, claims, and the appointments diaries of executives.

Many potential user companies already have computers, so why should they wish to buy videotex as well? The main reason is that this service is designed to be considerably less expensive than most other computer systems. It is a general-purpose, packaged offering with TV-type terminals supporting color and costing nearly an order of magnitude less than what classical computers require.

Videotex can serve a purpose in office automation. As we will see in the next chapter, the objective of office automation is to apply computer power to the costly and time-consuming paperwork problems.

Typically, whether in a public service organization or as a dedicated engine (on the company's own premises) there will be at the telephone exchange a videotex computer and viewdatabase. The end user can reach the pages in this viewdatabase either through a TV set with numeric keypad only or a business terminal with an alphanumeric keyboard.

The information sent over telephone lines can serve an unlimited number of users. This is a two-way system allowing users to select and even modify data.

Potential for imaginative applications in the broad, home-use category is even more far reaching.

- Home users can communicate directly with the computer storing the information.
- They can interrogate and get realtime answers.
- They can not only request further pages but answer questions; send messages; play games with the computer; and

do calculations on taxes and mortgages, projected utility costs, and so on.

Home banking is one of the imaginative areas with great future. It can benefit both the consumer and the bank. The consumer can pay bills, work on the family budget, have direct access to his account balance (and transactions) every time he needs to do so, contract loans, and obtain a wealth of financial information.

Through videotex the bank can automate many routine type, highly clerical operations that resisted the assault of sophisticated computers. By so doing, bank management cuts costs, reaches the consumer in the ease of his living room, improves services, and sharpens its competitive position.

It is possible for a home user to make a direct purchase by supplying a credit card number in response to an advertisement. And videotex can also be used to send bank statements to the clients of banks participating in the system.

It is a new experience, and, as such, has a lot of glamor. It is an experience that will change a person's way of looking at things, just as the auto has changed the human mode of transportation. The private user with a personal computer can attach it to the system. He or she can communicate with databases, send and receive electronic mail, and do office work remotely. Videotex is a concrete example of the imminent impact of technology on society. There is a clear link with personal computers and with software (telesoftware). There is also a resemblance to TWX and to editor/word processor equipment using video presentation with optional disc storage and printout.

The concept of telesoftware and associated downloading routines is so important that it is proper to underline its mechanics and future impact. Its implementation changes the perspectives of an industry which classically has mass produced at a central location all forms of software products.

The ability to use telephone lines for software distribution, has led suppliers to think about bypassing the retailers in getting their products to the market: Why manufacture and distribute thousands of copies of a package, not knowing how many will be bought or even if retailers will give it shelf space, when the materials can be published on demand by simply downloading the program when it is ordered?

Teledelivery presents the software industry with new opportunities. Downloading is a technology that has the potential to transform a distribution system firmly entrenched to Gutenberg's printing press. In two words, this is the whole sense of telesoftware.

20

SOFTWARE COSTS, EFFICIENCY, AND PROGRAMMER PRODUCTIVITY

1 INTRODUCTION

Computer developments in a decade tend to exhibit an order of magnitude improvement in hardware cost/performance, while software productivity changes very slowly. As a result, the cost of software relative to hardware is increasing and information processing risks becoming the most labor-intensive of all industries.

This background reason is leading recently toward a *software factory* concept that may become an important means for bringing both costs and timetables under control. So far we have not paid as much attention to the software production worker as to the hardware assembly line worker, yet we all know how highly labor-intensive software production still is.

Part of the software environment impacting on personnel, timetables, and costs is our inability to make the necessary tradeoffs between hardware and software implementation. To evaluate the strengths, weaknesses, and ensuing implications of such tradeoffs on life cycle cost and reliability, we need people with knowledge and understanding who can objectively perform and integrate tradeoffs to produce a balanced system.

Programmer productivity rather than equipment cost and performance will be the industry's chief problem in this decade. The hardware situation can take care of itself. But programmer productivity appears to be improving at a rate of only 3% per year. Software production is already a major national industry. Yet no measures exist for evaluating the product, its quality, the manufacturers or the programmers.

Software productivity is such a critical problem because the demand for new programs is increasing faster than our ability to supply software, using traditional approaches. This demand for software comes largely from pressures throughout the economy to improve commercial and industrial service through automation, while keeping the cost under control.

The problems of productivity in banking, business, and industry and that in information systems software are to a considerable extent related. If we want to achieve substantial increases in productivity in any function we must make imaginative up-front investments. We cannot increase the productivity of an assembly plant unless we re-outfit it with a lot of new and more efficient equipment—and also train our people on how to use it. Similarly, in systems analysis and programming, we cannot raise productivity simply by adding more analysts and programmers. If we do so, the result will be more of them working at less than the current productivity rate. It is up to the software development outfits and the project management effort to spend on research and development to provide for more efficient software production. But prior to doing so we must properly identify where lie the more elusive software production costs.

2 COST AND BENEFIT

There is a saying with computer systems: the devil has no greater friend than the idle hands of a coder on a new machine. If people don't stop trying to reinvent the software wheel, we cannot solve the specialists' bottleneck, nor can we improve the efficiency of programming products. Standards are part of the answer. Equally if not still more necessary is a management methodology able to allow users to plan the programming product they are about to develop or buy.

A properly projected approach to cost/effectiveness is so much more necessary as the software costs keep on growing. Back in the 1950s, the ratio of hardware to software costs was about four to one. Twenty years later, by 1973, this ratio had been reversed. The late 70s and early 80s further created a reference of legions of burned users whose request for applications software resulted in jobs that took twice as long and cost three times as much as the original estimates wanted.

When it comes to software, cost estimating is still characterized by generalities and vague approximations. Precise measurements are few and whatever exists of tools is badly used. After 30 years of computer practice, we still cannot answer the question: "Software is too expensive relative to what?"

How is the cost allocated among the different phases of software development? If we consider the following phases:

1. Overall procedural analysis emphasizing the user requirements
2. Systems analysis divided among four main functions

   - processing
   - databasing
   - datacomm and
   - end user facilities

3. Microanalysis and coding
4. The testing discipline

   - program testing
   - system testing
   - verification

5. Documentation and the production of the manuals

   - user oriented
   - operations
   - maintenance,

the latter phase (documentation) will generally absorb 12% to 18% of the whole effort, depending on how thoroughly it is done, how much computer support is used, and the particular characteristics of the programming product itself.

If accomplished in an able manner, the different aspects of testing and verification should absorb, as stated, between 40% and 60% of the total effort, with 50% an often encountered average. Depending on the way and on the detail with which it is carried out, the procedural analysis and its documentation demands 5% to 10% of the effort. This leaves roughly a third of the total investment in phases No. 2 and No. 3.

A rule of thumb to remember is that, other things being equal, 1 hour of systems analysis roughly leads to between 2 and 2.5 hours of microanalysis and coding, a ratio that tends to divide the remaining time between the two activities we have been considering. In this as in all other cases that we mentioned, ranges rather than single values should be considered, as a number of factors, particularly knowhow and project complexity, influence the finer time distribution.

In a certain sense, based on the broader guidelines given by experience, an information systems project should establish from the beginning its proper evaluation of systems analysis, design, programming proper, testing, and documentation hours for the entire project. In terms of cost considerations, due weight should evidently be given to the responsibility for project management, specification writing, program quality control, test results analysis, user training, and system inplementation.

Modular approaches can greatly help in cost estimates and their validation. By determining the number of modules in each class, it becomes feasible to forecast systems analysis and design hours, computer test hours, and computer-based documentation. Knowing the cost per hour of these resources, it is possible to estimate project costs exercising a plan/actual control at specific intervals.

A good cost algorithm and set of statistics help in costing project development through implementation. Specific costs associated with user participation during development may be omitted from the cost estimation as the contribution is part time and the user's people are not always controllable by the project manager. Oversensitivity in costing this issue can be counterproductive, discouraging user participation while the rational approach is to promote it.

Just for indicative purposes, let's note that projects that experienced a good user-level contribution have remarked that the total hours of user involvement are about 50% to 150% of the total contribution by system specialists in the procedural analysis and design hours. This can run even higher in some cases. Clerical effort required for one-shot data conversion can also be very substantial but is rather easily estimated, and its cost per hour is not excessive.

These references make evident the need for valid estimating procedures. Once a project estimate is established in terms of man-hours and corresponding cost, we will be in a position to project a master schedule. Careful evaluation can help reveal the distribution of resource consumption over project duration. Part statistics can serve as a first approximation in evaluating time, knowhow, resource, and cost requirements in future projects.

While estimates should be made about the time and cost requirements of new projects, we should also not forget that, as in all business, we can easily forego a current expense and charge it at a future date. The annual maintenance cost for changing, upgrading, or pruning applications software modules is, for all users of computers and communications facilities, a major consideration. This is the more true as software costs are steadily outpacing those for hardware.

Software maintenance is so important as an activity and its cost can be so substantial that, coupled with a high software system longevity, it may ultimately result in a 5 or 10 to 1 ratio of operation/maintenance cost to development cost when viewed over the total life cycle. Over and above the cost picture, software is finding its way onto the critical path of an increasing number of corporate systems.

The functional applications of software within company operations pervade almost every program. Software applications can be found in diverse areas and therefore the manifestation of critical faults in programming products as well as schedule slippages and delays can have severe aftermaths.

Such manifestations are symptomatic of underlying problems that originate far earlier in the development cycle. They include:

- lack of early management visibility and discipline,
- lack of life cycle perspective,

- insufficient control over timetables and expenditures,
- lack of standardization,
- failure to account for transferability,
- unawareness about possible hardware/software tradeoffs, and
- lack of response to quality pressures.

A widespread belief among computer professionals is that most user organizations have been doing a poor job managing the increasingly important resource of information systems and that they are also doing little research and development on the ways and means to improve it. Both of these shortcomings must change.

Cost and benefit cannot be treated as generalities of the type: "Motherhood is good for you." They have to be approached in a precise, specific way—with arguments that both qualify and quantify the job to be done.

3 THE SHIFTING IMPACT OF KNOWHOW

At the bottomline the problem of most computer installations is very similar: a lack of qualified people. This is a leading thought in recent considerations regarding a possible return to cottage industry.

At the supply side, programmers are now going out on their own and contracting themselves to a large company for a specific period, which may run for 6 months or a year. When the contract is completed, they often will take a months-long break before they go on to their next assignment. This practice may expand as the cost of terminals and computers continues to decline, and it becomes commonplace to put a terminal at home connected to the office.

In terms of market demand, companies where the lack of system skill is hurting development timetables are eager to tap the reservoir of housewives who are reasonably well trained and who, having raised a family, tend to stay at home.

How feasible is it to put a terminal in a housewife's home and have her do some programming? The answer to this question does not raise any unsurmountable problems. It is a solution several companies are looking at. Firms hiring people who have retired from daily work—and that put terminals in their houses—found the arrangement quite successful.

On the company premises, analysts define the specs. Remote programming solutions however call for establishing better procedures and better documentation. Nothing can be verbal; everything must be written down. But isn't this the way to go in all cases?

The cottage industry concept may not amount to much in terms of the percentage of the systems work that is done, but it is one of the stones in a mosaic of changing perspective in software development. Not surprisingly, it underlines the impact of know-how; the need for a faster, better coordinated evolution toward structured approaches; and the influence of technological issues such as remote online access to the development of computers and communications.

It is quite easy to appreciate that only some parts of the systems work can benefit from this approach, for instance, coding. The procedural evaluation and systems analysis still has to be done at the user's site. And let's not forget that there is a continuing shift of emphasis from programming to analysis.

In the decades of the 1950s and 1960s programming was the top job. Even in the early 1970s people paid a lot more attention to programming because that was perceived to be the problem. But over the past 7 years, we have begun to appreciate that the real problem is dealing with the user and finding out what he or she wants. That means we have to invest more time and energy at the beginning of a project.

The clear trend for the future is for project professionals to spend more time and place more emphasis on analysis and design. Programming should be increasingly automated, and that's what the very high level, nonprocedural languages aim to do.

If an important shift is to cut down on required programming, we must look after development tools to help from systems analysis to testing. If the analysts and designers develop better systems, the programmer's job will also become simpler.

Let's also not forget that changes in computer hardware have their impact on the software job to be done. As we are adding more intelligence to the storage products, for example, they become complete storage systems. As such, they will have their own software that must be compatible with the software of the host processor. The same is true about the need for compact, low cost, high-capacity, higher-performance peripherals and terminal workstations that greatly benefit from the nearly zero cost of the intelligence being built into them.

At the same time, the availability of good, ready-made software, specifically the applications packages, is a critical factor to consider when deciding between the alternative of homemade programming products and those available in the marketplace. Particularly, some microcomputers offer a broad range of applications software. For instance, a major difference with timesharing service is that timesharing vendors typically offer one, powerful, generalized package for any particular application. But microcomputer companies and their independent software outfits offer several different alternatives in their constellation. Users can select from among the many microcomputer packages the one which comes closest to their needs and budget.

Experience suggests that the timesharing packages often are more powerful than those available for processing on microcomputers but are significantly less user friendly. They also require thick reference manuals to take full advantage of them. Microcomputer programs are often prompting and offer simpler, straightforward solutions to many common data-processing problems. This, too, is a pointer to shifting trends of which notice should be taken.

Other trends in computers and communications with a sure impact on skills and therefore in analysis, programming, and costing are:

the personal workstation,

the local area networks, and

the graphics presentation.

A typical personal workstation includes a personal computer with one or more video screens (CRT), a keyboard (or, preferably, graphic tablet), and the ability to communicate with other workstations. This also calls for logical provisions to support resource sharing.

Local area microcomputer networks make it feasible to tie more users into the network and to one another, to share a database and a printer among connected users, and to assure a gateway to other networks. As we have already discussed, such aggregates generally serve a well defined, self-enclosed area.

The software impact from local networks can be easier appreciated if we recall that commercially available local area networks of personal computers are multiuser and multifunction systems. They do not have to be dedicated to just one application. Each user in the network gets his or her workstation with local computing power but shares disc storage and other expensive peripherals. By partitioning and sharing disc storage, it is possible for different users to run various applications simultaneously. This brings into perspective issues related to the evolving era of database productivity.

When we talk of systems analysis and programming productivity as a mental characteristic *par excellence*, we must properly appreciate that, because of the new technological developments, important changes are needed in the service provided by the systems analysts and programmers. These affect the way their services are delivered. Emphasis on the single workstation eases and simplifies the job of analysis. At the same time, global networkwide addressability brings its prerequisites and constraints. Systems analysis must consider that the workstation has more than processing capabilities: man-information communication is its main characteristic. This underlines screen formatting and editing.

The workstation addresses the common local database. A significant difference between standalone microcomputer programming and that attached to a shared resource is the incorporation of semaphores to regulate the traffic in the network. This makes more evident the characteristics of the file server.

For instance, the file server station includes a realtime clock calendar that maintains the hour, minutes, seconds, date, day of the week, and month of the year for all stations on the network. This time-stamping feature is essential in applications such as online data collection, banking transactions, reservation systems, and so on.

A more important feature of a file server is that it is a system resource that cannot be dedicated to a single workstation. Hence, the file server must coordinate current access to a given file from multiple requests, eventually also supporting file sorting, archiving, catalog management, index searching, and the like.

Systems analysis must also reflect on the shared resources of the local area network printer. Print service is provided by a station with one (or more) printer(s) interfaced to it. The print server accepts print requests from workstations, handling them in the order received; finds a file on the file server; and prints.

Given the current state of the art, an end-user-oriented study will necessarily pay due attention to graphics, whether on softcopy or hardcopy. Graphs are often essential for understanding and communicating all sorts of data. Hence, software must provide the tools for combining and plotting information stored on files.

Whether a package or homemade, software must be available to create, modify, and print automatically scaled and numbered line, bar, and pie charts from numerical data; exponential, parabolic, and other plots; best-fit curves; sums, differences, and multiple copies of existing graphs; and the like. The software that drives graphics devices has to adapt to the qualities of the final viewing medium and the way in which it will be used.

To the person accustomed to think along traditional lines, all this may seem to have little or no relation to software costs and productivity. In reality, the opposite is true. The shifting impact of the new information systems technologies is bound to change the classical views on these subjects. But the most radical change of all will be in system knowhow and the way in which it affects performance all the way to the workstation level.

4   A MORE CLASSICAL LOOK AT PRODUCTIVITY

When it comes to performance evaluation, on large programming projects productivity is often measured in terms of the number of lines of source code produced per programmer. This measure is usually independent of the level of language being used. But productivity data on programs under 20,000 lines of code is more variable and seems to depend largely upon the individuals involved. One investigator, finding that reported productivities ranged from 1 line of code per hour to 30 or more, concluded that more precise definitions of a program and even of a line of code were needed.

The implication inherent in our effort to make programmers more productive is that we know what is meant by productivity. This is not generally the case. The typical conception of programmer productivity centers on the units of output produced (for instance, lines of code) per unit of worker's time. Yet we also know that a line of code is not a proper measure of software development; it just happens to be an easy one to understand.

The lack of historical perspective in a given organization is also a handicap when we talk of improving the productivity. If we do not know how productive the software people have been in the past, how can we speak of improving their productivity? What we can do however is to improve the software development process, making it more disciplined and affecting the quality of the end result. To do so, every aspect of software and its development must be discussed, from proper selection of personnel to the management of the project; from design and coding to formal verification and proof of correctness. Only in this manner can new knowledge and new insights be found to lead us out of a state of relative ignorance.

Furthermore, though it is a valuable measure, programmer productivity is only one of the two basic pillars; the other one is quality. Software quality significantly differs from the traditional concept of machinery and other man-made objects: tolerances are almost totally foreign to software. Given the same input data, a given program must produce exactly the same results.

We know little of software failure modes and their underlying causes, except that errors causing failures are embedded from the beginning. As we had the chance to underline in the appropriate chapter, software quality is considerably more than the number of errors per thousand lines of code. It is commendable to want to deliver a software system containing no defects, but the appropriate methodology is still missing. Though software productivity measurements are no perfect art, they are more concrete than the measurement of defects in a program.

Management can positively influence software productivity if supported by a consistent measurement system. The parameters measured (and therefore managed) should include both the individual and the group. Management must also interpret and explain goals in terms of software development. The requirements for software technology advancement must be formulated in terms and measures that can be used for planning and control.

Management must feel responsible for productivity and be keen in identifying the key performers. Getting the product developed on time, on budget, and meeting performance objectives means the power to increase predictability of performance, support estimating, and make tracking feasible. Identifying key performers requires an evaluation of output, quality, and cost—but also the ability to foster creativity, initiative, and innovation.

Talking of innovation and change, since the late 1970s a leading trend in system design goes beyond the productivity issue and emphasizes *minimum risk*. The concept is related to quality assurance, the way we have been examining it in a dedicated chapter.

Risk analysis, preliminary design, hardware/software integration methodology, use of existing software modules, standardization, external interface control, security features, and life cycle system planning must be included in the design review. Correctness of software, reliability, integrity, maintainability, ease of modification, and transferability are major considerations since the initial design.

In addition, computer resource requirements should be continuously coordinated and reconciled with the company's operational requirements during the feasibility study, in project authorization, and throughout system development. Furthermore, resource planning should include equipment, software, documentation, and personnel.

A sound policy is to place economic tradeoffs, acquisition strategy, maintenance, and modification decisions on a life cycle basis. Emphasis should be placed on product definition, requirements traceability, cost, and the associated management control discipline.

I stress these subjects because to talk of productivity without placing due emphasis on all the factors that are involved is a nearsighted approach. We have to properly realize that productivity is a function of

1. the job to be done

2. the job's objectives and constraints
3. our ability to select qualified people and train them properly
4. our ability to provide an adequate, computer-based environment
5. the integration and implementation of advanced technology in information systems design
6. the user's collaboration in procedural design and system evolution
7. management's support for the effort and its ability to provide the proper planning, direction, and control.

Other things being equal, productivity will be that much higher if it is measurable. "Feeling" or "believing" that the programmers' productivity is "low", "average", "just right", or "quite high" is simply a call to irresponsibility.

The ability to measure must lead to that of planning and controlling. There is a distinction necessary when quoting man-days characterizing productive and nonproductive time.

Computer specialists are considered available for productive time somewhere between 60% and 80% of the total time. Vacations, illnesses, training, meetings, breaks, and personal allowances account for the difference. It does not serve any purpose to forget about such allowances when making a plan. It will simply make it impossible to follow a plan/actual evaluation.

For planning purposes, a measurable product must lead to economic evaluations, making it feasible for management to evaluate alternatives. At say $40,000 per man-year for analysis and $30,000 per man-year for programming, a program involving 50,000 statements will require on the average 2 man-years of analysis and 4 man-years of programming—or $200,000 in salaries alone.

This reference presupposes top performers run by an able management. Costs can hit a high multiple of what we just said if management is not iron handed and/or the analysts/programmers' skill is lower. Then we must add testing and documentation, which can double the budget we just spoke about.

We must also add social costs. The human cost component alone might exceed half a million dollars. At 15% to 20% per year maintenance, this means nearly $100,000 per year—or $1,000,000 over a 10-year life cycle of the project and $1,500,000 for a 15-year life cycle.

These costs are in no way out of line with current practices. If anthing they are conservative, as I did not include computer time and considered only wages. The prevailing cost structure for software sees to it that expenses exceed $50 per statement (with computer time) for development alone.

Furthermore, because of the very significant impact of maintenance costs over the software's useful years, the most classical sense of productivity must bring into perspective the total life cycle of the software product. A greater productivity in the maintenance work may have a significantly greater impact than a similar improvement in the development phase.

As we will see in the following section, effective software productivity improvements require a long, hard look at the whole process of making and maintaining programming products, including structured approaches and the observance of a strict discipline—which after all is the job of management.

5 THE MERIT OF STRUCTURED APPROACHES

Nobody with experience in computers and communications would argue about the need for estimating software costs and for improving software productivity. A methodology is necessary and we have it. The one means is a sound baseline for management planning and control of software projects. The other is the consistent use of structured approaches—a subject we have already treated but again review within the context of software costs, productivity, and efficiency.

Let's return to the fundamentals. The projects undertaken by systems analysis have been traditionally characterized by the needs to:

1. Better the quality level of the analysts themselves and make their results more worthwhile.

2. Improve the procedures that have been applied at the user's site and the information service which he gets.

3. Develop a way to bring the computer into the act, from the systems analysis and design process to coding, testing, implementation, and maintenance.

Items No. 1 and No. 2 have been known for years. Neither states something that has not been said before. Item No. 3 is not new to this text; we have discussed it many times. But, as I would never tire repeating, to bring the computer into the picture we have to develop a structured approach from the early phases of procedural analysis. Such approach would be rather similar in basic concepts to that used with structured programming, but quite different from structured programming in terms of procedures and of methodology. A state of modular decomposition and orderly design must reach the level of problem analysis. Analysis does not change in terms of mission, in the sense of the creation of a nonprocedural statement of the problem in a form suitable as input to the design method to be used. What is now taken as a basic factor is that methods of analysis tend to be highly intuitive and not well understood.

It is necessary to recognize the possibility of different design methods, so we must investigate the basis of these differences. We must also realize that the basic software cost drivers and origin of errors are the same: the size of the software to be developed and maintained, and the attributes that reflect complexity and therefore affect the cost of the software through commercially available products, application generators, and software reuse.

The structured design of an information system or subsystem can be *"top-down"* or *"bottom-up."* The definition of top-down is the mirror image of bottom-up, where the lower procedures are written first and the upper levels later. Top-down design breaks a large programming product into smaller parts or modules that can be dealt with individually. Such concepts can be applied to the whole range of software activity, including coding, testing, implementation, and maintenance.

The way we have treated it in the appropriate chapter, a structured design is a set of techniques for reducing the complexity of large programming products by dividing them into independent modules. Working with separate pieces permits the programmer to code, debug, test, and modify a functional module with minimal effect on other modules of the system. Concentrating effort in this way enhances efficiency and quality and reduces the origin of faults. Moreover, to the extent that the independent modules are portable, further systems can be developed with less need for new code.

This leads to the concept of *modular decomposition*. To isolate the software system into independent partitions, each module is constructed to work with others on control signals and data transfers, but to be uninvolved in the detailed internal structure of other modules. With intermodule interfaces carefully specified, the relatively independent modules become easier to code, test, and later change than more dependent modules. But we must be aware that the cost of the interfaces does not exceed that of the modules. This leads to the concept of a *step-wise refinement*.

A step-wise refinement in the design process of a programming product would typically call for the establishment of a hierarchical structure of modules to be distinguished within homogeneity in terms of functionality:

- fundamental function
- kernel, and
- add-on facilities.

Within each of these layers of software development we must care about the ordering to the sequence of decisions that are made in the division of the projected system by beginning with a simple description of the process. Through a succession of refinements of what has been defined at each level, lower levels are specified.

Within each layer, this organizational approach helps provide an expansion of functional specification to increasingly simpler functions until statements of the programming language itself are reached. As programming modules are produced in a top-down order, top-down testing can also be employed using a partially completed subsystem with programs executed in the environment in which they will actually operate. This permits an earlier integration, as testing uncovers problems sooner than conventional techniques.

Structured approaches seek to make analysis and programming productive by making each more of a discipline. This is a key part of the structured approach. For instance, among the procedural steps suggested by specialists with experience along these lines is the wisdom of finding the innermost loops in the program, locating those paragraphs and statements that are executed most often at production time.

Every program has parts that are executed only once in the beginning, or once at the end, or only in exceptional circumstances. Such areas of the program can be relatively ignored in favor of paragraphs and statements that are executed for every record processed.

The next procedural advice is to look for statements in the critical paragraphs that are superfluous or that can be moved outside the critical path. It is not uncommon to find statements that are unnecessary or ones that are executed more than once when once is sufficient. Sometimes data is moved to a field each and every pass even though it never changes, so that putting it there once would be enough.

Another suggestion along the path of establishing an efficient discipline is to look at the data types of the numeric variables used in the innermost loops. Try converting them to the types most efficient on the operating environment for which the software is intended, including the hardware characteristics. Similarly, it is advisable to look at the field sizes. Most efficient computation is done on a given computer for particular sized data fields. But overspecialization would inhibit program portability.

In complex conditional statements it is advisable to test for what is most probable first. In an IF statement with multiple conditions, efficiency can be improved by putting those conditions first that are likely to decide the result of the compound condition without testing all the conditions. Also, in a series of IF conditional statements there is no reason for repeatedly testing the same condition.

In terms of production efficiency of the object code the programmer will be well advised to watch for language interfaces and subprogram call overhead. One item to be investigated is the overhead involved in calling various subroutines and subprograms. The same is true of compiler options. Some compilers have various options that determine the efficiency of the code: there may be two or three levels of efficiency to choose from.

In data organization, beware of tables or arrays used. Many compilers will generate efficient code for table handling only if each element of the table has certain alignment characteristics. The programmer should look at the subscripts used for accessing tables, and at table-searching techniques. We should give preference to parameter tables. Can we make a table out of a file? Though these suggestions reach programming detail, they are written to imply that the entire development of a programming product from initial conception through coding, testing, and maintenance must be organized in an orderly, expert, and manageable way. Since some issues promote certain aspects of efficiency but may inhibit others, a compromise between cost, efficiency, and reliability must be achieved.

As it cannot be repeated too often, the emphasis is on discipline. Engineering development generally proceeds through a series of stages: product planning, specifications, design, documentation, fabrication, and test, with engineering change control running through the sequence. The development of any particular programming product would pass through this sequence several times, as model, prototype, and production. Furthermore, in a procedural sense, the following jobs can be instituted to enhance the software practice.

The Development Support Librarian. He or she is responsible for the programming product library, containing both machine- and human-readable material. This function helps to transform programming from a private art to public practice. This job is the more necessary as emphasis is on computer supported documentation and its upkeep. If an organization does not have a formal job definition for the "Librarian," it should institute it.

The Employment of a Program Design Language. Intended to be comparable to the blueprint in hardware, programming design languages strive to communicate the concept of the software design in all necessary detail, using a formal or structured version of English, sometimes called pseudocode. We have spoken of such approaches in the discussion on structural analysis. The outcome is often a hierarchy of charts with the corresponding input, throughput, output specifications.

The Use of Computer-based Workbooks. Design efforts inevitably produce much written material—memoranda, explanations, reports. The wise way is to treat it by computer and organize it so as to be sure that it reaches all who need to know and that it is available for later use.

We have also spoken of the structured walkthroughs, peer reviews, and design reviews. The same is true about an emphasis on *error detection*, with the identified errors becoming a critical point in the process of quality assurance.

Finally, *improved communications* as a consequence of formal, well-documented system design are a primary tool in establishing a sound disciplinary basis. There is a strong correlation between analysis/programming standards and software characteristics. Auditability, maintainability, and testability depend on them. The same issues are key features of the new systems approach taken in banking, business, and industry in regards to the development and implementation of software for computers and communications.

21

FOURTH GENERATION LANGUAGES

1 INTRODUCTION

Our discussion on Very High Level Languages (VHLL), which constitutes the Fourth Generation of programming tools, must be done within the context of Operating Systems and DBMS. The Command Interpreter of the OS and the query instructions of the DBMS have much to do with VHLL implementation and usage.

Though no formal classification yet exists for these tools, fourth generation (very high level) language offerings can be classified into 9 broad fields:

1. spreadsheets
2. integrated software
3. DBMS and query
4. query only
5. data communications-oriented
6. precompilers
7. system commands
8. graphics-oriented
9. expert systems

From the latter will eventually derive the fifth generation of programming languages.

Seven key points can be outlined with VHLL. A successful fourth generation language:

1. Produces AP at least an order of magnitude faster than HLL.

This ratio starts at about an order of magnitude and can reach 60:1 for simple routines and/or heavily database-oriented applications.

2. Employs a syntax which is typically nonprocedural.
3. Removes and automates the repetitive detail work in query, reporting, et al.
4. Acts as a control language with system commands and integrates instructions written in HLL.
5. Is database management-oriented (ideally, in a relational manner).
6. Can be learned in 3 days or less.
7. Can be understood by both the end user and systems specialist.

Add-on functions include screen support; a data dictionary; transactional, message, and file exchange; privacy and security; communicating database characteristics; and environmental recovery.

The programming tools of the new environment enable the programmer to reimpose the control that would be provided by structure in conventional practice. They achieve their effectiveness in two quite different ways:

- Some are simply agile viewers into the user's program and its state.

They permit one to find information quickly, display it effectively, and modify it easily. They include data value inspectors, editors for code and data objects, and a variety of powerful macros and report generators.

- Others address themselves directly to the issue of data manipulation with expert systems overtones.

The concept of such very high level programming structures is applicable throughout the range of computing machinery—from mainframes to microprocessors—and it has far reaching implications. Though experience with VHLL is just starting, the early results are encouraging and lead to far-out considerations.

One of these considerations is to substitute the slow, tedious job of maintaining large, complex, applications libraries by a computer-assisted reprogramming job. Though at first glance this may seem a colossal undertaking, at least one organization found that of the 2 million Cobol statements in its library only 40% had to be redone. Many were at the level where the end user facility had to do the job—not the mainframe based VHLL. And many more were dead wood. When the much greater programmer productivity VHLL effort is taken into account, at the ratio of about 40:1, the whole lot can be reduced to the equivalent of say 50,000 Cobol statements in terms of manpower requirements. This is a small fraction of what is necessary for the upkeep of an application library which often runs in excess of 10% of written code.

Other results may be just as far-reaching. The able use of the facilities provided by Very High Level Languages can make obsolete the notion of packages. Their employment is not as rewarding as it used to be, since we can obtain such impressive productivity gains through a VHLL. In this sense the clear objective should be to automate all repetitive programming operations which eat up the system analyst's and programmer's time. We should use computer power to substitute for human power; as the latter gets increasingly experienced while the cost of the former steadily drops.

In this chapter we will first examine the general perspective, then look into the spectrum of associated basic software. This will be followed by a database language classification. Thereafter will be discussed DB 2, as an example on a mainframe database oriented programming language.

2 NEW IMAGES FOR VERY HIGH LEVEL LANGUAGES

A very high level language permits us to easily work with a number of applicative products at one time, such as screen design, procedural evaluation, applications programming and database management. It offers a well-structured, common interface to all applications needs; see to it that man-information communications characteristics are uniformly applied to all of the users' applications; and makes sure that these applications integrate under a common work environment. If properly used, a VHLL assures a much greater productivity for the professional systems expert. It also makes it feasible for the non-professional to program the computer, albeit at a lesser level of sophistication.

However, to benefit from the usage of a VHLL we need to adopt new programming images. Gone are the days where the programming concept remained invariant, as exemplified by the quarter century old Cobol experience. With both the programming language developments and the microprocessor revolution, our ways of looking at 30-year old subjects must radically change. We now live in a world where 10-year old kids can be expert programmers, and 8-year olds understand their PC, including software and hardware. What's more, by being tough in primary school boolean algebra and abstract concepts, these kids can outperform *Real Programmers* of the old school who stick to the Cobol compiler. These Real Programmers have been the computer industry's software standard bearers for more than 30 years. They should now be on their way to extinction. As Ed Post aptly says in a Datamation article*: "Real programmers do list processing, string manipulation, accounting (if they do it all), and artificial intelligence programs in FORTRAN ... If you can't do it in FORTRAN do it in assembly language. If you can't do it in assembly language, it isn't worth doing... Real programmers don't need comments; the code is obvious." To Real Programmers, Post suggests, CPM is a toy operating system. Unix is a lot more complicated. The Real Programmer uses OS/370.

Is OS/370 an obsolete operating system? And is Cobol an obsolete programming language? What does it matter. The Real Programmer is an obsolete species no serious, profit oriented organization can afford. No Real Programmer, Post remarks, would ever use a computer with SmallTalk, and would certainly not talk to the computer with a mouse. The Real Programmer wants OS and languages that are complicated, cryptic, powerful, unforgiving, and dangerous. A Real Programmer wants tasks of earth-shaking importance.:

> "For this reason, Real Programmers are reluctant to actually edit a program that is close to working. They find it much easier to patch the binary object code directly, using a won-

---

*July 1983, Readers' Forum, p. 263 to 265.

derful program called SUPERZAP (or its equivalent on non-IBM machines). This works so well that many programs running on IBM systems bear no relation to the original FORTRAN code. In a number of cases, the original source code is no longer available. When it comes time to fix a program like this, no manager would even think of sending anyone less than a Real Programmer to do the job."

A must in an interactive environment is short response time. But, POST advises, bad response time doesn't bother the Real Programmer. If there is enough schedule pressure, he tends to make things more challenging by working on some small but interesting part of the problem for the first nine weeks. Then he finishes the task in the last week, in two or three 50-hour marathons. This not only impresses his manager, but creates a convenient excuse for not doing the documentation.

Poor documentation is another one of the poor habits of the past era of computer programming. Both poor documentation and no documentation at all are fully unacceptable in today's environment—and documentation can be handled in an able manner through a computer-based VHLL.

Down to its fundamentals, the level of a programming language is determined by the power of the semantic primitives which it supports.

- Commands provided by lower level (or obsolete "high level") languages lie closer to the elementary operations implemented by the hardware.
- A higher level of programming presupposes primitives with storage allocation and control structures.
- A still higher level supports more abstract but also more powerful operations, manipulating entire arrays.

Depending on their level of implementation, programming languages can provide very high level abstract objects and operations on them, as well as high level control structures. Such programming styles can simplify the programmer's task by eliminating large amounts of relatively routine detail that would otherwise have to be supplied.

The object of a VHLL is to offer a comprehensive, easy to manipulate system for answering an organization's programming needs in a highly productive manner. These languages are complete structured programming systems able to produce not only lines of code with a greatly improved programmer's productivity but, as stated, also a full documentation. Documentation is kept by the computer and is updated automatically by the machine while the programmer

- changes an instruction, redefines a table, alters its contents, or adds, modifies, or deletes

any sort of records handled by the language. Still, the original productivity-oriented languages such as Focus, may be a passing species overtaken by the database programming languages. We will return to this issue later.

3 ADOPTING A POLICY WITH VHLL

Over the first 30 years of computer usage (1953-1983) world-wide expenditures have been an estimated $400 billion in developing computer applications and supporting files. Today, an estimated 500,000 programmers are working to maintain, enhance, or replace this investment.

Including salaries, benefits, and overhead, half-a-million programmers represent $30 billion annually or, alternatively, a level of 6 billion PC including hardware, software, and applications programming.

The general implementation perspective is itself entering a totally new phase. It's a total break with past practices. During the next 5 years the professional programmers' work force will be augmented by an estimated 20 million business professionals. Typically, each of these professionals will have his own personal workstation, building databases and applications to service his own needs, and using fourth generation languages that will increase productivity by a factor of 40. This is good. But such activity, if left unmanaged, will result in chaos.

The changes which need to be done are enormous. The problem roughly divides into two areas:

1. The building of new applications oriented at the WS level and intended to serve personal and local needs.

As fourth generation languages gain in power and popularity, the management of Information Systems faces the task of installing them in place of existing centralized and obsolete production systems. The task is challenging as we have to rethink whole applications, translate old files and procedures into databases, provide on-line communications and assure user-friendly interfaces. This process must be well managed for the projects to succeed. It must also guarantee that the overall aggregate is properly thought-out so that it will be possible to implement system integration.

2. The restructuring and recasting of aging applications.

There is no DP center without a load of applications running in production mode, that are suffering from obsolescence. They were designed 10, 15, or even 20 years ago, and software typically has a working life of 10 to 15 years.

Though very few applications are designed with a specific life cycle in mind, experience indicates that after about 10 years the application begins to be outmoded and difficult to maintain. Today, obsolete applications are generally batch systems. Part of this software may have been upgraded along the way with an interactive frontend to extend its life. Yet, in essence it's batch designed for ancient hardware with old operating systems.

- Aging applications are cumbersome to operate.
- File interfaces are crude if they exist at all, and
- Emulation modes or poorly executed conversion procedures are commonplace.

There are three ways to handle this lot of aging applications:

1. One is to rewrite them on microcomputers, through professionals.

This is a most serious approach since much of the DP activity is personal or local anyway—and can be best executed at the workplace. Rewriting should not be done blindfolded. The application must first be revamped and redimensioned, then programmed in a fourth generation language—preferably a database oriented system.

2. The second, is to let the end user take care of it on his WS.

This WS will typically be a PC with spreadsheet or integrated software. The user—who is no professional programmer—can nicely work with this class of Fourth Generation languages to answer his own needs—while he may find some difficulty in manipulating the finer programmatic interfaces of database management and database programming.

3. Furthermore, a new generation of PC now being brought to the market starts presenting mainframe program portability.

A good example is IBM's PC 370. It is good, however, to remember that aging 370 mainframe applications must be of a size that can fit on a microcomputer.

There are two ways to look into this issue and two philosophies. One, regards microcomputers as small machines, but with non limiting sizes.

The IBM PC XT can be equipped with 512 KB of memory. The NCR Tower can reach 4 MB. Even with half a megabyte, the microcomputer is large enough to do real work. The 360/30 had only 65 KB of main memory; the 1401, 12 KB. By supporting the 370 applications software under VM, the IBM PC 370 opens new horizons—and also poses major challenges. To be compatible with IBM competitors in personal computer gear, it will have to either support both MS DOS and VM, or, they will have to provide up grading capabilities in their distributed information systems environment.

A key point with this compatibility issue is that many "mainframe-oriented" DP applications were originally written for machines that were smaller than current microcomputers. As a result, the latter are engines with enough memory and storage capacity to satisfy many applications programs in a DP installation—provided that portability exists.

It is only reasonable that the size of the program affects migration decisions. Large routines with thousands of lines of code are too big for a micro, though the amount of code is not necessarily an accurate calibration. Just because software maintenace is most often done with a relative lack of documentation, the tendency is that the lines of code multiply over the years. Patching, fixing, the incorporation of enhancements, and lack of knowledge on the software's inner working by those who do the maintenance work, are all factors that push in this direction. For these reasons, redesign may result in a far smaller program. It may also better support connectivity and interfaces.

When we are considering moving a piece of software, all its connections and interfaces to tiles and other programs must be assessed. With old applications, interfaces and connections have grown over the years like wild cacti. As new systems have been developed, interfaces for needed data from an older system were simply patched in. These interfaces are not sophisticated—but they can be a bother. Hence, the alternative way of looking into this same issue is to say that it is useless to carry old code into new machines, extending the heavy, costly, and slow going maintenance procedures. Better to rewrite this code through fourth generation languages, taking advantage of the productivity factor which goes up to 4,000 percent.

Companies which start following this road now find that when the code is rewritten the size shrinks. Not only does a database language compress the number of statements by an order of magnitude, but also many statements become unnecessary because they regard patches, links, and operations which are no longer needed. Most importantly, with this alternative the applications are being redesigned to exploit the strengths of the micro. For instance, the degree of user interaction that is possible.

Through fourth generation languages, it is easy to develop applications with nested menus, and user prompts. A high level of interaction should be emphasized in the system design. Data editing checks, variables, error flashes, help frames, can all be part of the user prompt activity. However, make no mistakes. Interactive systems require significantly more end user training than batch. Such training should be an important consideration in the planning process as it requires careful definition of objectives, good scheduling, proper facilities, a comprehensive program, careful attention to detail, and patience by all concerned.

Before we make a decision about moving an application, we need to weigh the costs, risks, and the opportunity. Microcomputer software often uses different file and database techniques. With a microDBMS, housekeeping functions are incorporated into the software, so the system automatically initiates backup procedures. Simple, but PC-assisted approaches result in stable software and nice user interfaces, help facilities being one example.

Whichever strategy is chosen in revamping the applications environment, it is wise to monitor the system's performance after installation. Fourth generation languages usually include a report generator that allows users to specify the reports they want. This flexibility has a price: report generators consume cycles. Frequently produced reports may be candidates for HLL programming (e.g. in "C"). Even so, the programming job is greatly facilitated as the bulk of the work is done through a very high level language with an occasional report program, and the installation of new releases—as the main detraction. Good results will largely rest on an able project management. The rules for success have always been to know what the requirements are; get management support; get the users involved; and plan correctly in terms of time, manpower, and money.

4 A VHLL CLASSIFICATION

The preceding discussion properly documented the wisdom of concentrating on a very high level language rather than just a high level language. Nobody today would project a computer with small or medium scale integration chips (SSI, MSI). All efforts increasingly focus on VLSI. Just the same, under no condition should the programming effort rest on 25-year old or even 15-year old so-called "high level" languages (HLL). As a lot, such languages are obsolete, though some of them, such as Cobol, are more obsolete than others.

Like obsolete chips, obsolete languages are non-competitive and result in spoilage of resources. Unlike semiconductor chips, they have a more far-reaching detrimental effect. *The language which we use conditions our mind and affects the way we think and do things. This is just as true of a natural language as it is of programming.* This is written in full understanding that, because of the multiplication of computer power, in the coming years the software problem will become more severe, and many companies will soon face crises. Let's always recall that the pace of technological change that has taken place over the last 20 years will be duplicated again during the following 3 years.

In software like in hardware, we should be satisfied only with the best that technology can offer. Hardware and software are means to answer, in the most effective manner, the organization's information processing requirements. The more effective the hardware and software are, the better.

A little appreciated fact in the computer profession is that the so-called "High Level" languages, with Fortran and Cobol the typical examples, are a relic of the late 1950s. They were developed at about the same time we moved out of vacuum tubes into transistors. Only in the 1980s has a really new stream of languages started reaching the applications market with names such as VisiCalc, Ingres, Focus, dBase II, Multiplan, and DB2.* Such Fourth Generation languages are "very high level" compared to Cobol and Fortran. They fall into five different classes:

1. VisiCalc and Multiplan are *spreadsheets*.

Originally designed for "what if" type calculations for decision support, spreadsheets and integrated software (a latter development) they have become programming languages of excellence, particularly oriented to the end user.

2. Ingres, dBase II and DB 2 are *database programming languages.*

This class of very high level languages evolved from database management systems (DBMS) and became prominent as we came to

---

*These languages have been listed in their chronological order of announcement.

realize that more than half the time of computer programming is spent with I/O, file design, access, and management. Database oriented VHLL appeal both to the end user and the professional programmer. The latter can do a great deal more with them than what the end user could. He also needs to treat them in an expert manner. To properly implement a database programming language it is absolutely necessary to design the Data Model. The end user cannot do that; the expert programmer should.

    3. Focus is an example of a *productivity oriented language* based on rather powerful macros—but less powerful than a database language, and much less user friendly than a spreadsheet.

Focus produces results by means of a precompiler. IBM's ADF works in a similar manner (as we will see in the following section). This class has given much better results than Cobol and other HLL on programmer productivity. Thus, if for some reason a database oriented VHLL cannot be used, this should be the preferred solution. However, Focus and its equals were at the top of the list 2 or 3 years ago when no relational databases and no command interpreters were available for programming purposes. Now they are less interesting, though still valid.

    4. New programming languages are typically VHLL oriented, designed to fit specific applications requirements. The language most discussed for *artificial intelligence* is Prolog. Among languages designed for dataflow machines are ID and Valid.

Basically a procedural programming language, Prolog attempts to solve goals sequentially. For a given goal, it searches to find a clause whose head can be made to match the goal. If the clause is an implication then it, in turn, attempts to solve the subgoals. The possible result of a goal will be failure or success, plus possible values associated with variables.

- To achieve success for a goal, all the subgoals must succeed.
- If one of the subgoals cannot be solved, Prolog backtracks and tries to find another clause whose head matches the goal.

- If no untried clauses remain, then the failure is returned for the goal.

There are similarities between this new generation of languages and database programming systems. Both have their primary goal to operate on data, with calculation becoming a subsidiary activity. Also, they both tend to show relational characteristics.

5. *Command Interpreters*, as programming extensions to the OS, and other special software capabilities should be seen in conjunction with the operating system being employed.

The first and so far best example of an OS level command language interpreter is Shell of Unix. As a command language interpreter, the Shell is a powerful programming tool. It also integrates with database level programming and HLL to form a powerful aggregate of Shell, Ingres, EQUEL (of Ingres) and "C" Language. There is so far no other offering available to match this range. As we will see in the following section, IBM's Advanced Development Facility (ADF) is a precompiler for PL/1, not a command interpreter.

The higher the level of programming for a computer within a given OS environment, the better the results will be. As this basic fact of programming science seeps in, we can expect a range of tools at the command interpreter level. Both program quality and productivity will gain from such development. Most importantly, program portability will be assured at the OS level.

5 THE ADF EXAMPLE

IBM's *Advanced Development Facility* is a programming tool. It works as PL/1 precompiler. In a certain sense, ADF-PL/1 present a similar duality like Unix-Shell, but below the database programming reference (Unix-Shell is above that level.) In a certain sense, ADF-PL/1 is like Focus. It generates PL/1 code. Its able usage makes unnecessary both PL/1 and Cobol. It can also favorably affect programmers' productivity.

ADF helps in data description and in the incorporation of generalized functions. The former can be executed much more efficiently by programming in a DBMS type language. The latter include: transaction driver; input handler; segment layout; key selection; screen formatter/deformatter; auditor; message sending/generator; and terminal writer.

In this sense, ADF is an integrated instrument of IMS, being able to develop database oriented applications. All applications can benefit from faculties ADF provides:

- *Sign-on DB* controls the mode of access.
- *Audit DB* controls the update of single fields.
- *Message DB* manages the automatic messages of those of the user.

As a superstructure to IMS/DB, DC, ADF modules permit one to: read messages from a terminal; implement segment layout rules; retrieve segments from the database; apply handling rules; update information elements in the database; provide the logic for processing segments; input transaction rules; and write messages to a terminal.

Figure 21-1 identifies the first phase of the man-information interaction. Supported options in a typical menu may involve: project message sending; project message display; session termination; transaction selection; text utility selection; project/group switch; user message sending; and user message display. The transaction modes are:

delete, initiate, remove, add, update, and retrieve.

As a senior IBM executive was to comment in the course of a meeting in New York: "Given that ADF has been available for a few years, there is *no need* for PL/1 or Cobol. And ADF is based on IMS." More precisely, ADF is working under IMS/DC for online transactions. It is a programmer's language. The recently announced DB 2 and SQL provide user interfaces, though DB 2 can also serve (as we will see) as a database programming language.

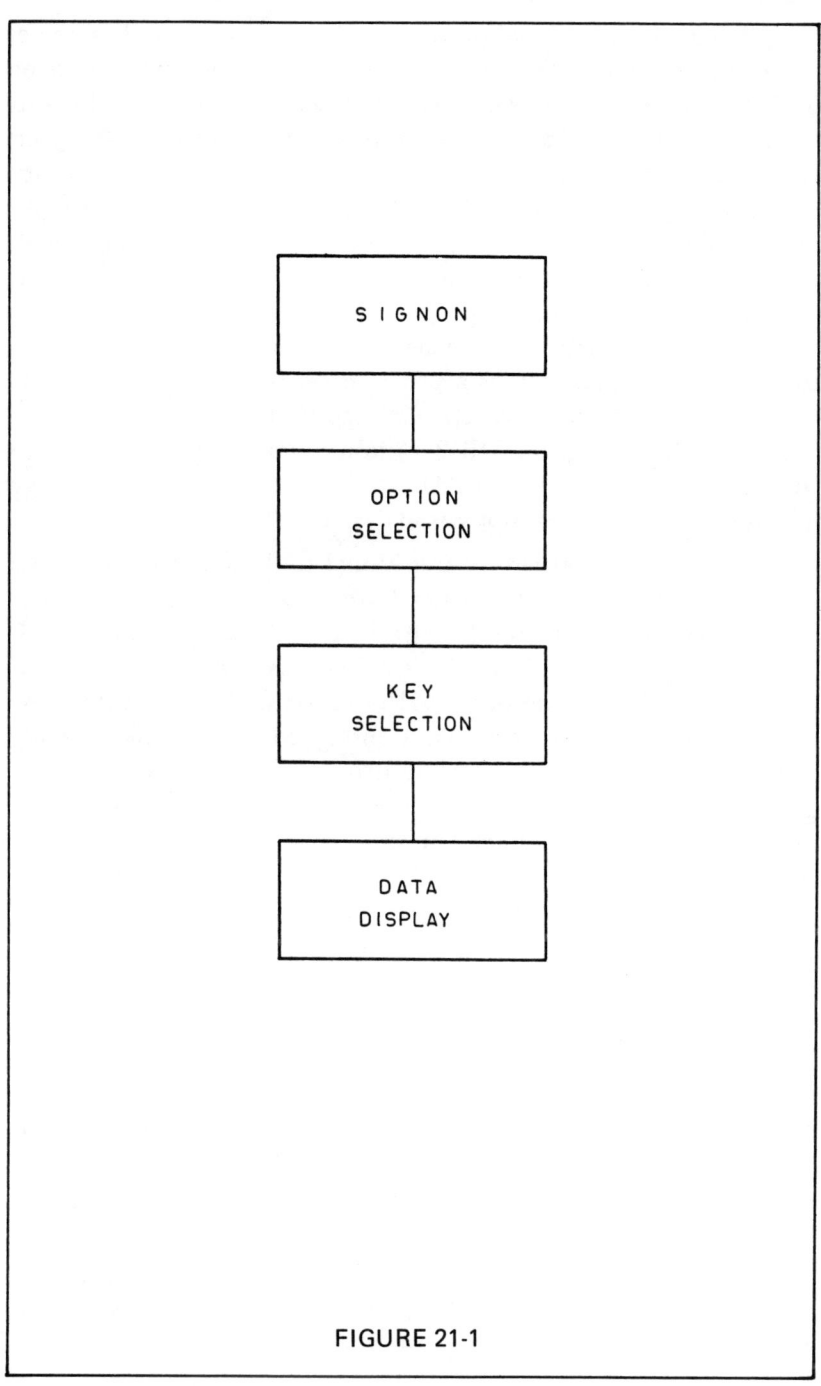

FIGURE 21-1

Being a high level add-on to the existing structure of basic software in a computer facility, ADF is also a productivity tool for professional programmers in a way that neither PL/1 nor Cobol can be. Let's underline that ADF is proposed as an advanced program structure for expert programmers—not as an alternative to, for instance, query language capability. Table 9 makes this point by comparing ADF to SQL.

Figure 21-2 identifies, within the IBM computer environment, programming languages for professionals and non-professionals. It also distinguishes between languages and supporting software structures. IBM looks at ADF as a program generator for specialists. It is not an SQL competitor. ADF links to IMS. However, tomorrow it may be developed as a DB 2 structure. (With SQL we don't do the same operations as with ADF, just like with realtime we have not done the same operations as with batch.)

The schema handled by traditional tools allows frames to be used in more than one application. Often, the resulting environment can be represented pictorally. Using their catalogs, such VHLL programming tools build executable files that implement the application. Thus, like the other VHLL currently available, this type of language works through menus and options. But while they are generally discussed as transaction drivers, they offer significantly greater capabilities to their user; one of the most vital is a great improvement in programmers' productivity.

TABLE 9
ADF Vs. SQL

ADF is	*SQL is*
A generator of transactional capabilities.	A data manipulation language with logical and arithmetic capabilities.
It is oriented to computer professionals.	SQL can provide challenging features for expert programmers.
As of today, it is not used under DB 2.	The end user oriented programming language capability is imbedded in QMF.

Fourth Generation Languages

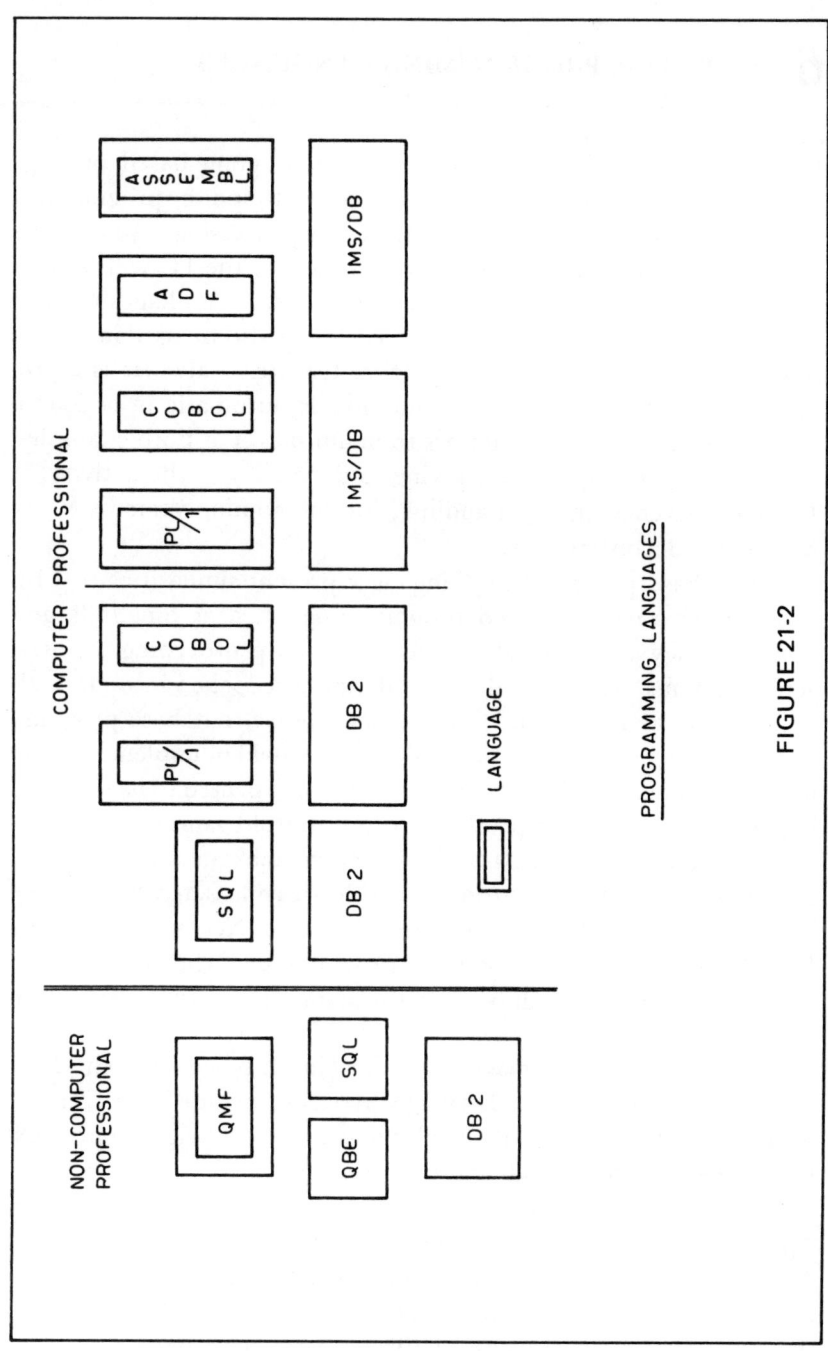

FIGURE 21-2

6 DATABASE PROGRAMMING LANGUAGES

With database languages we can write a program based on data structures—rather than the other way around—and the program will be much more efficient. Both classical data processing requirements and the modern management services—where the PC will be predominantly used—deal with file access and database handling such as query capabilities. Database languages can also be used in an able manner to provide office automation features. Calendar is a program and a file, whether this function is automatic or solicited. Electronic Mail is sending letters to mailboxes. For both examples, file creation, manipulation, saving and deleting is the activity. A further reference to file handling, for the coming years, is Voice Mail and Teleconferencing.

Database programming languages present similarities to Lisp and related object oriented programming, such as Smalltalk and Flavors. They are especially good for quick prototyping of interactive systems. This is vital before designs are locked into more efficient but far less flexible structures. Hence, database programming approaches will also find a significant field of implementation in prototyping. Lisp-based workstations are expected to have a great impact on programmer productivity, as tenfold gains are being experienced. The challenge for the hardware makers is to make the power of symbolic computing available to end users who can't be bothered to learn the intricacies of AI or Lisp. Xerox is pushing its Lisp machines as power tools for programmers. The company expects expert systems will be used for maintaining old programs not even written in Lisp.

Lisp is also the language of artificial intelligence research. Commercially available natural language interfaces include INTELLECT, SAVVY, and EXPLORER. Explorer is a natural language processing system for oil research and exploration.

Another AI language is Logo. There are many dialects such as Apple Logo by Logo Computer Systems; Apple Logo by Krell; Texas Instruments' Logo; and Radio Shack Logo. Logo is a development from Xerox' Smalltalk and other Lispoids. Some projections speak of an 80% share of the market for expert systems by Logo and the Lispoids, with Pilot and Prolog mastering among themselves the remaining 20%.

The remarkable longevity of Lisp in the artificial intelligence community is in large part due to the language having been repeatedly extended to include modern programming language syntax and constructions. These extensions were accomplished by defining source-to-source transformations that converted new constructions into more conventional Lisp. The ease with which this can be done allows each user, and each project, to extend the language to capture the idioms that are found to be locally useful. Furthermore, the accessibility of procedures to mechanical manipulation facilitates the development of programming support tools.

The Xerox Smalltalk effort solidified through the Dynabook Project and led to Smalltalk Structure and Operation; the 8010 Star; Three Rivers PERQ; Apollo Domain; Corvus Concept; Apple Lisa; VisiCorp Visi On; and Quarterdeck DESQ. Among the most notable developments in the Smalltalk reference have been the: System Browser, Graphics Editor, Cursor Forms, Object Classes and Graphic Primitive.

Lots of academic institutions and corporations are involved in the artificial intelligence (AI) field: Stanford; MIT; Carnegie-Mellon; Yale; Rutgers; University of Pittsburgh. But also Teknowledge; IntelliGenetics; Computer Thought; Smart Systems; Cognitive Systems; Machine Intelligence; Inference Corporation; Helena Labs.

Corporate in-house projects are carried on by Digital Equipment; Fairchild Camera & Instrument; Hewlett-Packard; IBM (Intelligent Interface, The Applications Expert Project, DART, Knowledge Base Programming Assistant); RCA; Schlumberger; Tektronix; TI; Three Rivers Computer; and the Xerox Palo Alto Research Center. Suppliers of Lisp computers include: Xerox Electro-Optical Systems Division; LISP Machines; Symbolics; Elite Corp; and so on. Generic AI software building blocks include inference mechanisms and knowledge representation systems.

Artificial intelligence is bringing new ways to intellectual work and computer programming. The issue with data processing in the past was the efficient use of scarce hardware resources. Because of fast developing technology, this is no more true.

An important area of AI is knowledge based expert systems. Such systems are designed to reason and infer from a set of rules how to solve particularly complex tasks.

The new generation of DBMS query facilities is typically relational in nature. These systems involve a sophisticated command file and they are reasonably fast. As they stand today, they are the forerunners of a new generation of operating systems which will integrate the classical monitor functions with databasing, query, and transaction processing.

Transactional is the system which guides the terminal and, through it, the end user, while *Query* is typical of an *interactive* environment where the end user guides the system. Through these the user can create his own menu; has the ability to write command files with conditional branching; and can access any information element in the database without knowing its address. The user can also interact with the deliverance system through a scenario simulation. He can also use various types of input as long as they are acceptable to the machine. This makes the DBMS/query system a powerful tool, though not necessarily as easy to use for non-professionals as the spreadsheet. Let's now look into IBM's DB 2 as an example of a mainframe-based database programming language.

7 IBM's DB 2

DB 2 is a relational structure. Table-type presentation is one of its relational characteristics. Another very important one is the link between the tables. Figure 21-3 exemplifies this approach to dynamic reference management. Not only does it make feasible a concatenation of tables totally transparent to the user—according to processing demands—but also the language permits user level manipulation.

Table creation is accomplished through simple statements such as CREATE, UPDATE, DELETE and INSERT.

We should recall that DB 2 was born as a relational DBMS projected in a way to interface with fourth generation languages. IBM does not look at it as a fourth generation language, but others do.

IBM says the object of DB 2 is not to substitute to DL/1 but to add to it. For instance, according to the mainframer: 1) For current accounts handling DL/1 is more adaptive. 2) DB 2 is best used in OA and in management interactive applications. The modular relationship of DB 2 to DL/1, IMS, and QMF is shown in Figure 21-4.

Fourth Generation Languages

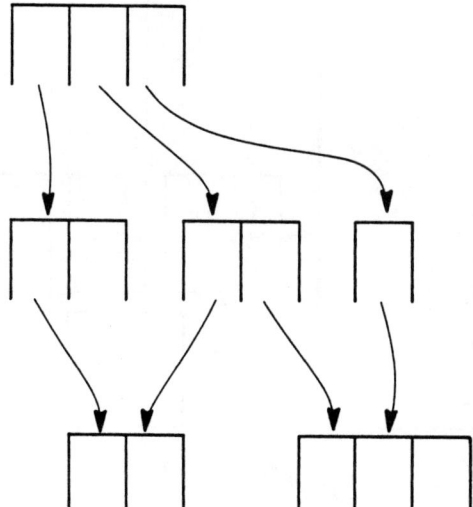

FIGURE 21-3

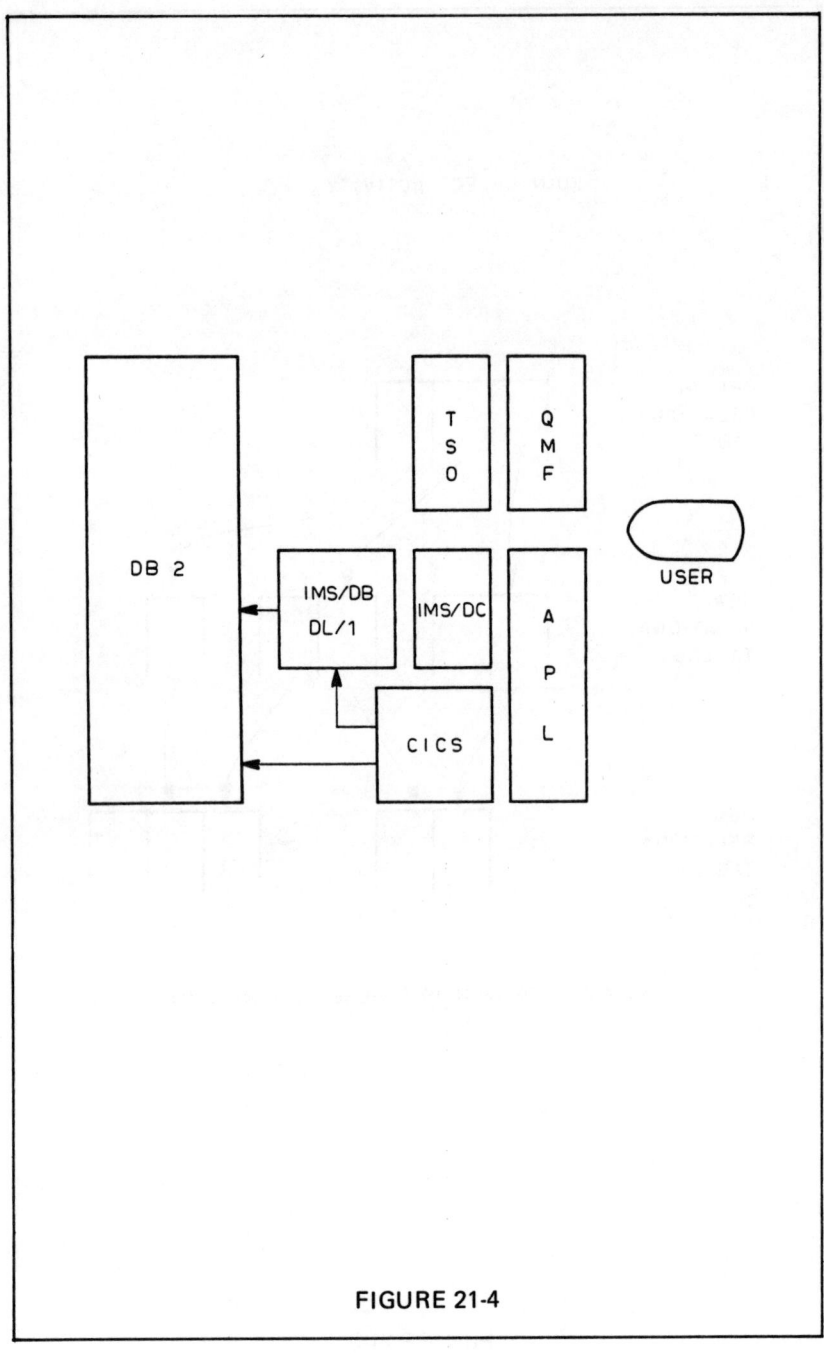

FIGURE 21-4

Fourth Generation Languages

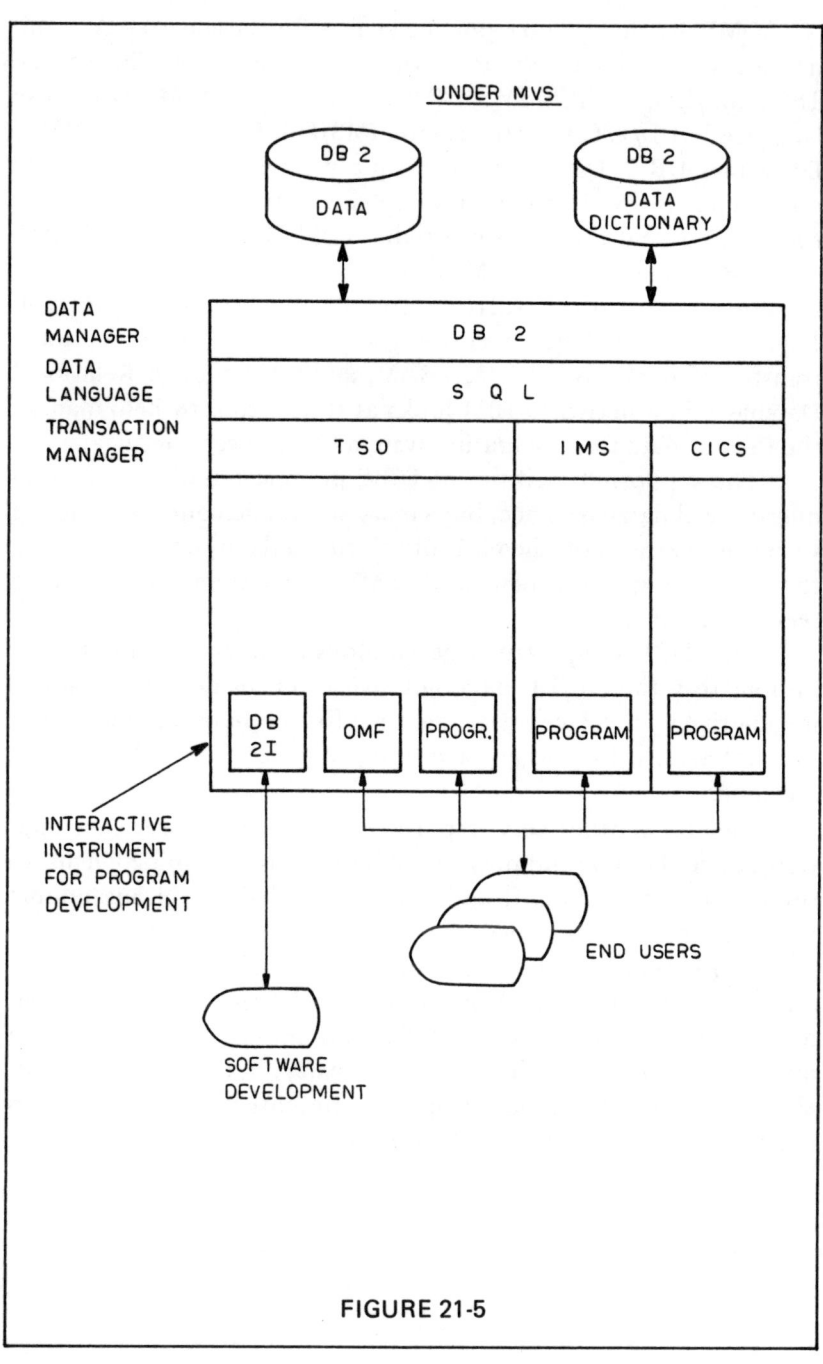

FIGURE 21-5

QMF is a query and reporting facility for the end user. A terminal needs a datacomm driver to run on a mainframe. This can be TSO, IMS/DC, or CICS. IMS/DC has in counterpart IMS/DB whose language is DL/1. CICS can also use IMS/DB. In extension to IMS/DB comes DB 2. QMF uses QBE (query by example). It operates only under MVS. For graphics implementation, for instance, the tool is QMF and the series of products: GDDM, APL, GRAFPAC.

DB 2 operates under MVS. Its exact positioning in the constellation of supporting software for IBM mainframes is shown in Figure 21-5. DB 2 has been designed for a preplanned periodic transfer of data from DL/1, VSAM, and SAM files to Relational Databases in a network. IBM looks at it as a tool to help manage the flow of data from operating system to end user query.

The supported facilities of DB 2 permit: handling extract requests: read database once, but satisfy several demands; scheduling to restrict extracts on the basis of priority and output limit; routing the extract output through another MVS subsystem; and providing security in usage.

This DBMS type language employs an operational data definition from the DB/DC data dictionary. It provides an interactive menu-driven interface, easy to use for non-programmers, but not necessarily by the average non-professional in data processing chores.

Finally, another very important reference is power consumption under the new and powerful database programming languages running at object time. It adds to the calculation of transactional throughput for given cycles.

In its calculations for client installations, IBM suggests that if a query facility is used, then the estimated transactional data load must be multiplied by two in estimating the needed MIPS on the mainframes. It sounds like a severe penalty, but it is quite acceptable if we use the database language's potential the right way: to improve productivity by 4,000 percent.

22

COMPUTER-BASED DOCUMENTATION

1 INTRODUCTION

The need for complete and up to date documentation of software systems was clearly seen as one of the most important considerations in running an efficient computers and communications service. Faced with continuing developments and changes in information systems hardware and software, many organizations are caught in the escalating problems caused by poor, unstandardized, or incomplete documentation.

The need for documentation aids is obvious. The fact that computer resources should be used to create it, maintain it, and make it interactively available is beyond question. Good documentation answers many problems, analyzing, understanding, and utilizing the programming products being the most vital problem.

As every practitioner in the computer field knows, there is a need to coordinate and update programs and files. Faster, more accurate reference to design specs, code description, and file organization is required. New programmers need help in evaluating the logic of existing programs. And there is an increasing need for security. Improving the software documentation is an activity bound to pay off.

When we know in a dependable manner how and why our program operates we will be able to quickly put our finger on the formats and the logic. We will understand how each information element is manipulated; how and when other programs are called; their specifications, past defects, and test results.

Correct documentation makes quick and economic system changes feasible. It can also serve as a planning and control aid. Software documentation has its limitations in how far it can serve as a tool. If design aid is interpreted as meaning a technique that aids the achievement of a correct program design, documentation does not do this. It merely gives the designer a computer-based recording system with which to *illustrate* design requirements.

Currently available documentation tools have no particular contribution to make to the process of establishing a correct program design, defining the functional breakdown of the project, or translating the requirements specification into compilable segments of code. What they do is to provide a coherent and understandable way of expressing what the system does, what data it uses and creates, and the relationship of all the data and the functional elements.

2 THE CONTRIBUTIONS OF A DOCUMENTATION SYSTEM

We have been speaking of the possibilities and limitations a computer-based documentation system can present. The contribution of a computer-based approach should not be underestimated. It has been found particularly useful in aiding communication between end users and designers, as the form of structural documentation statement is easily understood by anyone with a reasonable level of intelligence—particularly if presented in graphics. A structured documentation also provides, through *interactive softcopy worksheets* (video presentation) and templates, the tools for creating the transfer mechanism from systems analysis to programming in a methodical and standardized way.

In a system of any size, paper records as a documentation tool can become very unwieldy. Taking them to the lowest level of program detail, paper records result in a large volume of diagrams, statements, and statistics that are difficult to handle but even more so to

- classify,
- update,
- retrieve, and
- cross index.

What we have said on another occasion with reference to taxonomy is fully applicable in this case. Computer-based documentation needs a sense of taxonomy to be presented in a hierarchical order and in a manner able to help the basic features of software development tools. Let's always remember the many uses to which a good documentation will be put: it will serve as an aid to the specification construction, testing, analysis, management, operation, and maintenance of computer programs.

A correctly organized and taxonomically presented documentation for programming products is also important because it can be used to increase software productivity and quality. As a result, its employment evolves as an important part of software development.

Paper records cannot do that. As experience time and again demonstrates, they soon become a major headache to file, retrieve, update, and maintain. Professionals who have gone through the experiences of both paper files and interactive softcopy usually recommend that the latter method be used to specify system requirements: from design perspectives to the further levels of detail related directly to the code. (The understandability and simplicity of code using structured programming concepts usually suffices as its own documentation at the lowest levels.)

Here is a list of issues advisable to keep on a computer and access interactively by authorized personnel:

1. *Systems Analysis.* Results of interviews with end users and the resulting explanation of requirements; procedural issues and related goals.

2. *System Design* organization and structure for the information system under development; specifications regarding the text and database, datacomm, processing, and user-friendly interfaces; objectives structured in a systems approach; quantitative evaluations; statistics on data flow and so on.

In these two issues should be included information on whether or not the domain of values attributed to an entity are properly and consistently defined; the type of checks being made; a number of technical features; and the determination whether the units or dimensions attributed to an entity are properly defined and consistently used.

3. *Design Reviews.* The annotations made and the results achieved during the design reviews characterizing the software development cycle. The reservations being made; the possible bottlenecks, or inconsistencies within the current environment; possibilities for future expansion; and linkages to other procedures are examples of other information pertinent to this reference.

4. *Source Code.* Documentation relevant to the input to the machine, the program written in a procedural language that must be input to a translation process before execution can take place.

5. *Intermediate Code* (if necessary). The input to the machine between source code and machine code.

6. *Object Code.* Documentation regarding the code expressed in machine language that is normally an output of a given process.

Another issue that may be necessary is symbolic execution: reconstructing logic and computations along a program path by executing the path with symbolic rather than actual values of data.

7. *Tests and Test Results.* All tests made in modules, programs, subsystems, and the results obtained from them should be stored in the documenation of the development database. The same is true of the corrective action to be taken.

It is important to underline the precision with which this operation should be executed. Many faults found subsequently in operations have their origin both in original malfunctions and in their corrections. Tracing them in a backplay can be of a significant help to subsequent interventions.

8. *Input Features* based on the forms of input that can be provided. This documentation may include how the input should operate and of what it should consist.

9. *Database Organization.* A full description of the addressable information elements in the database (bits, bytes,

fields, records, files blocks, objects); their characteristics; description; design; use statistics; authorized access by programs and end uses; security level; location in a distributed environment; linkages; and so on.

Much of this information will be typically held in the data dictionary. The need for providing the necessary documentation remains, however, intact.

10. *Output Features.* These provide the link from the machine to the user. They describe what type of output it produces (for both the user and another machine), and the method of presentation: preferably online interactive softcopy. Formats authorizations and use statistics should be included.

Other issues can also characterize the documentation to be established. An example is *prompts:* a series of procedural primitives to interactively inform the end user who operates on the system on what to do next. In general, the object of a correct and complete documentation should be all features of software development allowing one to distinguish one element from another and to determine its characteristics.

Let's repeat what we said since the beginning of this chapter. A thorough, computer-based documentation will help in the design and programming processes. But it is neither the recipe on how to design an information system nor on how to code. There are four main advantages to a valid documentation strategy.

First, the importance of oral explanations and guesses is reduced. The main focus is on a finite, quantifiable, and written way of expression that is understandable by all concerned. Second, by putting something online quickly, the other people working on the project are enjoying the satisfaction of immediate action. Less time is spent in interlocks, and delays due to unanswered queries are eliminated.

Third, computer-based documentation means of necessity a structured approach (or, at least, nearly so). It is therefore more orderly, better organized, with the lacking features easily identifiable. The last two points lead to the fourth one. A good documentation is the prerequisite for the maintenance of the programming product and for independence (during that phase) from the original system designer and programmer.

3 WHAT ARE THE ALTERNATIVES?

An important distinction often missed is that between design methods and documentation methods. We said that even an interactive documentation scheme cannot be properly considered a design tool, since it provides no paradigm to guide the designer. However, it does assure a valid methodology for recording design characteristics and all the documentation.

This distinction is particularly important because it provides insight into the assessment of the different documentation techniques. A stepwise refinement of the documentation helps in the decomposition process of an information systems design, even if it proposes no direct assistance to guide in the creation of the specifications. The analysts and designers will still do their creative work as they have done until today. However, a computer based documentation tool will:

- provide them with means to streamline and accelerate what they are doing.
- help all the necessary recordkeeping as the project goes along.
- structure this text and data collection process in a homogeneous manner by means of formalisms.
- offer the possibility to check on the contributions each one makes, thus balancing the project and bringing in evidence till now unknown soft and strong points.

Such interactive documentation will start through an analytical *table of contents* in which the project will be planned, representing as a single entity a hierarchy of functions. From the form of an overview it will proceed to detailed diagrams, breaking the gross elements into finer ones and then into primitives.

This approach has not been "natural" with software developed for computers and communications systems. Like the computers themselves, which have known different generations, the state of the art of systems documentation has been characterized by successive epochs in its development.

Four generations can be distinguished. The first is simply identified by the expression: "Leave it to the project." For any practical purpose, this means that there will be *no* documentation.

This is the oldest, most widespread, and unfortunately still dominant approach. In Italy it is said that the "carabinieri" either know how to write or how to read. Most programmers and analysts seem to be of the species who do not know how to write.

Most surprising is the fact that management does not care to impose the preparation of software documentation (let alone the right one), though it is widely known that the systems analysts left on their own produce little or none. As a result, the software becomes eventually unmanageable (and very poorly maintainable).

The ideas behind this bad first generation of habits, and to a large measure the facts behind it, lasted over 15 years: from the early 1950s to the late 1960s. At that time a new kind of thinking started to emerge, trying to enforce some discipline.

This led to the second generation: "There shall be documentation." However, experience for setting standards was lacking—and the will wasn't there in what concerned the analysts, the programmers, and their management. It is always difficult to change a tradition (particularly a bad one). Pushed to produce more code, the system specialists left documentation for later. Usually that meant too little, too late, or never.

The motto characterizing the second generation of thoughts about the need for a documentation for programming products was enough to bring the beginning of a change to the ideas of several professionals. Management began asking for documentation, but:

- Such request has usually been made too late in the software development cycle.
- No pressure was exercised in getting the documentation done in a proper way.
- Computer-based tools were not readily available.

As a result, timeliness, quality, and accuracy have not really been better than those of the "leave it to the program" spirit. Documentation done late or after the project is over is almost as bad as that not done at all.

During the first and second generations, standards on *how* and *what* to do have been missing. It was the need for standards which brought around by the mid 1970s a change in practice. Written standards characterize the third generation, but its spirit stayed somewhat in closed quarters. It did not spread as it should.

Furthermore, while among the leading computer installations it was now said that "documentation standards shall exist" these were applied through a manual methodology. Understanding the need for standards has been a great step forward, but management found to its dismay that it is difficult to have the documentation standards enforced.

As I have underlined on other occasions, manual standards are not controllable as long as the work is in process. Sometimes they are even misunderstood. Furthermore, once again, tradition is counterproductive in enforcing a new discipline. Conviction and understanding have to come first.

To help in understanding and in observing the standards that they have developed, certain organizations packed them into a "Ten Commandments" style, and asked everybody concerned to carry them along while at work. This was the early beginning of the realization that documentation standards make an important impact on

1. the *content* of the documentation for a programming product
2. the *format* in which the content must be represented
3. the *methodology* by which the content is obtained, and
4. the best way to make this content *interactively available* to all authorized users.

The most advanced among these users identified the methods that are to be employed at each stage in the software's life cycle. However, these approaches differed greatly in the form or representation and in the methodology characterizing the employment of documentation tools.

Content, form of representation, methodology, and interactivity are not wholly independent dimensions. The choice of each can be made independently up to a point. This was not among the notions of the third generation. However, over some years, experience demonstrated both the stated interdependence of the four factors and the fact that manual documentation standards, though applicable, leave much to be desired.

Once they start maturing in the experience of management and of its senior systems experts, these reasons helped bring new approaches, the most significant of them being: "documentation by computer." It characterizes the fourth generation. Computer-aided solutions can be described as a *procedural operating system* freeing the specialists from the documentation routines, and letting them do the creative part of the systems work.

Along with other benefits, the fourth generation brought a series of concepts on how to do the proper work. Automated documentation solutions are by now an increasingly used tool in project management. But, since there are several of them on the market, it is important to weight the relative strengths and weaknesses of each.

Ease of input is a major consideration, as are the ability to produce reports with different levels of detail and to update online and to do cross-indexing. Other important goals to be served are producing the three key manuals (user's, maintenance, and operations); assuring a data dictionary facility (either directly or through linkages); and helping to construct the development database.

The computer-based approaches should guarantee that not only the production of the documentation is timely, but also that what is made available respects the desired characteristics. Which are these desired characteristics? Systems documents can only be of value if they are:

- complete (that is, include all phases of the software operation)
- accurate, consistent, and correct
- reflect a standard, and the standard *is* enforced

- regularly updatable
- observe a fixed format
- understandable by those using them at a later date; and
- controllable (possible to validate).

Users must be aware of the range of tools available and of the benefits each supports; that is, their ability to answer these prerequisites. Furthermore, not only the making of the documentation but also its proper maintenance is a critical issue.

4 COORDINATING SOFTWARE DEVELOPMENT AND DOCUMENTATION

The documentation of a computers and communications system must involve everything that is included, or to be included, in the project. Though management often controls software development through milestones, such milestones may be meaningless *if not* accompanied by the corresponding documentation.

A different way of making this statement is that documentation has to be treated as the basis of the software's life cycle from conception to functional definition, design, testing, installation, and maintenance. An examination of properly kept documentation will help flash out poor or missing standards, will make clear the contents of the files, and will reveal the intent of processes.

But software documentation has also to be kept dynamic. Regular updates and periodic reviews are necessary to maintain the right emphasis on the control of its contents.

Among the prerequisites is the availability of clear and easy standards defining the structure of the documentation and the content of the documents. The same is valid of tools: text/editors and formatters making the updating easy, interactive, and fast.

Since software design documentation is often physically separate from the programs, a synchronous updating mechanism must be made available to the analyst and the programmer, so that their updating of the design documentation together with the source statement code becomes a natural process.

One solution is a system of embedding documentation in the form of comment blocks in the program body. This implies the availability of a tool able to extract the comment blocks out of the source programs and to assemble them in organized documents.

Editing out of a documentation is often as important as inserting text. Incongruencies can be present due to the fact that the software documentation is sometimes redundant.

While under certain conditions a controlled redundancy may be necessary, the risk is that of contradicting items and of an out-of-phase update. Another problem arises from the fact that it is difficult for analysts and programmers to remember in which different documents the same information is present.

A more sophisticated approach to software documentation, its utilization, and management will incorporate tools that are capable of explaining concepts and structures in a concise and clear way. This difficulty with complexity in a computers and communications system increases when the design is not structured and when each analyst or programmer uses notations of his or her own choice.

Standards are therefore necessary which explain the content of the document (topics treated), the logical order of the topics, and the prompting necessary to clarify how a topic has been described or treated.

Among the complexities encountered in daily practice is the documentation of a software project distributed in many system components. With computers and communications networks, the documentation must be organized in a structured way, involving the taxonomical considerations to which we made reference. This is particularly important with the different source components.

Not only must the documents be taxonomically organized, but also a document can be looked at as a hierarchical structure of text in which each element refers to others through a name. It also contains information about its own organization, editing, and level of text parts. In terms of handling, a capability of document presentation and formatting is required, taking into account that the application is the production of software specifications.

In coordinating software development and documentation, text standards, comment standards, and coding standards must strictly be enforced. Each one should complement the other. This is another way of saying that documentation must be in step with system design, with programming, and eventually with implementation. It must also be a process continuing with software maintenance.

Software documentation is the inseparable part of each project and must be structured at the very beginning, reflect the interfaces, and follow the product. It must contain both file and process description, making much easier the tracking not only of the functionalities but also of structure. Just as handy is the ability to implement a parametric documentation.

5 FOCUS ON EFFICIENCY

A software documentation that is structured and computer-based relates to and promotes both the quality/reliability goals, which we have treated in the preceding chapter, and the productivity aims. It does so by promoting clarity and completeness, by making success easier, and by eliminating redundant (often misdirected) efforts.

The view that has been steadily promoted in this text is that correctness of a programming product is a legitimate concern of project management and of the designers, analysts, and programmers who are involved. Considerations such as reliability, quality, and efficiency are inseparable from one another. They must also be regarded as inputs to the implementation stage and given attention since the software project has been created.

A valid assumption is that efficiency constraints can always be met, if they are considered early enough in the design cycle. This is not necessarily true of reliability and quality—unless easily checked designs are created. It is very unwise to relegate the concern for the quality of the programming product to later stages in the software development process.

There are some points where efficiency and quality prerequisites meet. This is particularly felt on the operational side as, for instance, several programming products exhibit considerable set-up time lost with some routines—as in the case when a scheduled interruption or failure has occurred and the operation must restart from a checkpoint.

A lengthy set-up time is efficiency and design-wise a quality failure, in the sense that it is certainly inconsistent with the concept of having an online system. Only by considering the total system requirements can ways and means be found to reduce total system set-up time to a sensible amount. This is among the tasks of the software designer that should be checked at the testing level.

For instance, one of the more serious losses of availability is the time required to set up and tear down computing facilities before and after production usages and time out. Here readily accessible documentation can be of help. When we talk of a system-wide software quality *and* efficiency evaluation, testing at the specifications level should involve the establishment (in writing) of the programming product requirements from an operational viewpoint. This must include:

- reliability objectives
- design goals
- uptime expectancies
- compatibility goals
- recovery/restart characteristics
- number and size of modules
- speed of execution
- response time for a projected number of users.

As the development work proceeds, results must be evaluated in the light of this critical list. The user should definitely be brought into the picture when the plans for the programming product are established, the critical list is set up, and the design reviews take place throughout the development stages. This is synonymous to saying that the user should be a key participant in establishing the functional specifications, and he should be made aware of the test results.

The end user is, of course, most interested in total system performance. In this reference, software reliability both complements and contrasts to hardware reliability. The difference is between

- non-deterministic (software) and
- deterministic (hardware) models

With hardware we are more sure when we talk of meantime between failure (MTBF), meantime of system interrupt (MTOSI), and meantime to repair (MTTR). By now, the process of defining hardware reliability is fairly straight. But this is not so with software where we must distinguish original design/implementation malfunctions, detected and undetected errors, recoverable and non-recoverable failures.

The documenation of a computers/communications system is intimately involved in this reference. With both in terms of software and of hardware we have to understand what we are doing and what the system will and will not do—in order to be able to meet reliability and efficiency requirements, or to assure the level of protection we want to impose.

At the user site, to help the dependability of performance we can apply tools such as terminal load emulators and hardware/software monitors. The former test software behavior under simulated peak conditions. The latter analyze what goes on inside the machine. Tests and the results of test, as we have underlined, are an integral part of the documentation.

Online operations increase the demand for software reliability, raising the level of needed support. Here, again, documentation is an issue. Within an online, interactive environment we must look at all the required functions: journaling, routing, session control, and so on, to define what is the needed dependability.

To enhance the stability of the programming product after its release for production purposes, we should plan from the early design phases to co-involve the end user in field testing, when it comes. The end user has to live with the software being developed for him, and he is the best judge of its fitness.

To make the test work better understandable to the end user, also more controllable, from the original design specifications to the implementation of testing procedures we must simplify the needed tasks. This can be done

- by taking small pieces at a time,
- then creating a hierarchy of jobs

- so that modules can be used to build up complex programs, while
- taking advantage of algorithmic approaches to testing for execution by the computer.

Evidently, there exist tradeoffs to be done. We have stated that the multiplication of components, too, leads to complexity. Finally, it is not enough to develop a valid discipline. It must also "seep" down through the body of the professional analysts and programmers, and it must be understood by the users. This can be helped if we present them with the proper documents.

In conclusion, from initial explanation of objectives to the description of the user's need, the systems analysis and design, coding, testing, reliability evaluation, and final implementation the common link is a *clear, valid, computer-based documentation.* When we talk of programming efficiency, cost control, and new ways to maintenance, we will see that they are characterized by the same common link.

23

RELIABILITY AND QUALITY ASSURANCE

1 INTRODUCTION

Software is reliable if its use does not result in failure of the computers and communications system to perform as expected. Such definition can be interpreted in terms of *time* or in *number of exposures* to a unit application.

When we use a time standard, the frequency of failure is equal to the fraction of time the software is not operative (failed state). In the reference to the number of exposures, the frequency of failure is the fraction of exposures in which the software prevents a unit application from being completed as expected.

The two alternative measures we have been treating are directly related when *time* represents the operational usage time, and the *number of exposures* per unit time is specified. Whichever the chosen measure may be, software reliability manifests itself as a function of the care that has been taken at the drawing board—at the system analysis level—and of the thorough testing and certification that took place after coding the programming product.

We have spoken of structured system analysis as a valid means of procedure. The process of determining whether the programming product fulfills all requirements established at the design level, including that of quality, is known as *verification* or *testing*. This can be done at different levels, the most important being *system analysis* and *code* verification.

System design verification aims to determine whether the stated software objectives (mission requirements) have been correctly translated into the next lower level of specification. The structured walkthroughs and other detailed requirements are precisely conducted to evaluate the conceptual approaches to the automation of the procedure under study. Hence, system and subsystem relationships must be reviewed to identify:

- compliance to standards
- appropriate performance
- the observance of functional and operational requirements

To do this job in an able manner, requirements must be segmented in sufficient detail to determine whether the identified system design approaches are fully mapped into the detailed system analysis in terms of processing, databasing, and datacomm. The primary objective of this activity is to reduce the risk of deviations that always exist when we transfer a given product from one design phase to another and then on to production.

Code testing (verification) aims at determining whether the actual code (program) is compliant with the technical description of the design specifications. Testing should be detailed, seeking to identify failures, errors, or discrepancies. These may stem from:

- inconsistent use of instructions
- incorrect logic flow
- incompatible interface
- failure to meet the functionality described in the specs
- inaccuracies in scaling or calculations

The proper verification activity would distinguish unit, module, subsystem, and integration testing. It would analyze the code in detail to determine whether there are errors present; perform auditing; check the code against standards; and produce effective, quantifiable measures.

2 SOFTWARE RELIABILITY

Reliability is applicable in a whole range of the constituent parts of software engineering: languages, processors, operating systems, libraries of utilities, applied programming products, and the associated documentation. Reliability complements other software engineering aims. For instance, the care that

- the work is done on time,
- software is developed in an efficient manner,
- human resources are saved at the expense of hardware usage —not vice versa,
- the maximum transferability is assured,
- the programming products are properly documented and easy to maintain.

Its specific goal is to assure that the overall software job is reliable and that this can be measurable in a quantitative sense.

With regard to reliability, software engineering addresses itself to both the system and the user. Through quantitative measures it expresses the probability that the employment of the software being developed does not result in failure of the computers and communications system to perform as expected. As we will see, reliability is a probability.

Probabilistic (stochastic) measures can then be meaningful if we pay due attention to provide for them at the design phase. Therefore, it is important to set standards prior to analysis programming: establishing goals quantitatively, detailing the error criteria by type of error, and outlining the means for control.

A polished job will invariably reflect a great concern for accuracy that can be enhanced through the proper classification and identification scheme particularly oriented to errors and their probability. A taxonomical consideration is valuable. It must be done by experienced analysts/programmers considering all types of problems presented in the past with software—as well as their respective frequencies.

To classify errors with a taxonomical consideration in mind, we must first identify them both in an absolute and in a functional sense, describe their features, and elaborate on the damage they may cause to the programming product. Identifying error features can be a major challenge because of the past habit where most descriptions fail to provide sufficient information.

Hence, considerable effort may be required to obtain the reference necessary to identify what the error may be, what it does, and how it affects the software system. The result of classification is the hierarchical representation of the error feature (which may be abbreviated using keys), as well as of their possible impact within the software environment.

This is conforming to the characterization of the multidimensional nature of software quality in terms of a hierarchy of attributes. In this classification, reliability is one of the high-level attributes defined as the probability of failure-free operation in a specified environment for a specified time.

We have spoken of errors and failures. To fit under the perspective of this last definition, let's treat a software failure as an unacceptable departure of operation from program requirements. As in the case of hardware, *unacceptable* must ultimately be defined by the user. The program defect that causes the failure must also be identified. A failure may be

1. *Minor,* for instance a small likely acceptable deviation from the computing goal.

2. *Major*, resulting in software error.

3. *Catastrophic*—the software will never work.

(Notice that this classification is not typical of the one usually found in literature for faults and errors. But it helps in the quantitative expression necessary for reliability purposes.)

The growing number of online interactive systems increases the operational aftermaths and cost impact of failures. The same is true of the size and complexity of computers and communications networks, of the impact of distributed information systems, and of the resulting risk of failure.

By the end of this decade, the explosive growth of personal computers and associated networks will create a demand for more not less software reliability. In this as in all other cases, measurement is most important:

- In software and in hardware there can be too much as well as too little reliability.

- In both references, improvement of reliability costs money and impacts development schedules and system performance.
- Therefore, choices have to be made and there must be design tradeoffs among critical factors.

These are further reasons justifying the need for a quantitative software reliability measure. But let's look at the background reasons.

As we had the opportunity to underline, software failures can have their roots in design and coding. At production time, the processor reference is the best practical measure for characterizing the failure-inducing stress on software. Statistical measures must therefore focus on all units with processing capability: not only the CPU but also the I/O controller, disc controller, and so on—depending on system configuration.

This reference derives from the assumption that testing is representative of the operational environment and that failures can be observed, recorded, and identified. The objective should be to make software at least as reliable as hardware, especially in view of typical software repair times.

1. Much more emphasis should be placed on designing for prevention of failure, rather than repair, because of the long repair times and the possible severe impact on the user's business operation.
2. Certain applications will be so critical that no software failure can be tolerated, whereas others could stand minor failures.

One solution is two sets of software: one *very reliable*, seldom changing, with sufficient features to do a job, but with no complexity, the other *more complex*, a generalized type of software commonly used today.

Good initial system design, implementation, and testing are of paramount importance. Just as vital is the concept of *software verification*. It is defined as the process whereby six basic steps are taken:

- the verification concept is formulated,

- the functions to be tested are defined,
- the functional specification is refined by intermediate steps, including code or processes required by the previous step,
- final refinements are made on the complete procedure,
- the details of representation are settled,
- the verification tests are done.

The test and evaluation of the complete computer and communications program is aimed at ensuring compliance with the function, performance, and interface requirements. The results of verification lead to validation that involves gross tests applied to the code to assure that the requirements established during system definition are met.

The amount of testing to be applied will be a function of both the thoroughness of the design specifications and the validation procedures to be employed. In any case, successful validation requires that all verification activities are accomplished. For they provide the basis for decision in terms of software certification.

3 CERTIFICATION CRITERIA, CORRECTNESS, AND ROBUSTNESS

The process of confirming that a complete computers and communications programming product is operationally effective and capable of satisfying established mission requirements, under realistic operating conditions, is known as *certification*. This process extends the verification and validation to a real or simulated operational environment.

Through a real life test practiced on the end system (or through simulated conditions) the software can be exercised to determine with some confidence whether or not the stated design requirements are met. Endorsement of the operational capability can then be given. Hence, certification involves acceptance testing of the overall programming product.

Certification cannot be made in the abstract. To start with, it needs a precise and thorough systems design (from stated objective to handling procedures) as so often underlined. Second, it requires a complete, computer-based documentation. Third, the verification, validation, and certification must be done against concrete goals.

In this sense, it is not enough to say that software reliability implies fully operational programs, with faults weeded out through intensive testing, written for maintenance, and able to flash-out critical factors. These are general type requirements. Within a given environment, we must also state in unambiguous terms what we are after. Software quality is still elusive enough not to be subjected to a lack of precision as to the specific objective.

It is a technically valid statement that we must establish standard procedures for development, examine the maintenance costs in advance, evaluate life cycle perspectives, calculate life cycle costing, and establish built-in means to enhance reliability. But if we wish to obtain measurable results, greater precision is necessary. Reliable software means:

1. Correctness.

Software is correct if it meets functional specifications. When the inputs satisfy *dependability* (no error) criteria, the software will produce desired outputs.

2. Robustness.

Software is robust if it is fault-tolerant: that is, if it can be expected to deliver a minimum level of data-handling services, even when faced with an unexpected or hostile environment. An environment is unexpected when hardware failures occur. It is hostile when fed with bad data.

Robustness means ability to withstand demands outside the range of those planned and accounted for. This issue is so fundamental that in itself it identifies that the whole philosophy of software development has changed.

In systems design today the key criterion is *minimum risk*. To obtain this aim, the improvement of software reliability must follow rules—many derived from experience.

- *The first rule* is that computers and communications programs rarely represent the intentions of the one who programmed them.

Procedural safeguards must, therefore, be provided to guarantee the observance of original intent. What the end certificate would say is whether the design goals have been observed. This presupposes the explicit, written existence of such goals.

- *The second rule* is that testing must follow a mathematically rigorous discipline to guarantee the robustness of the program.

Since we can only test for what we design and build, robustness must first be built during software design. To assure a correct and robust software, we must provide and steadily support procedures for software validation.

Let's repeat in a nutshell what this means. In the broader sense the reference is to the process of analyzing the software in development (eventually, also in maintenance) to determine the extent to which it performs the logical functions projected in the specifications. But to validate, we must:

- test, and
- verify.

Testing is tantamount to examining a program by evaluating its response to a selected set of input data. We test by using a sample of the data. Hence, sampling is a basic procedure in software assurance.

Recently provided capabilities enable blocking of individual software modules by logical operations. High level diagnostics allow us to predict module behavior, to perform threshold monitoring, and exercise reliability control We will return to this issue.

Validation is a procedure consisting of the development of mathematical protocols. Examples are path analysis and specifications analysis. They are used to demonstrate that the logical behavior of a program is as intended; that is, it follows the original design goals.

With *path analysis* the computer program can be thought of as a mathematical object, and its properties studied in a rigorous fashion, for instance, as a *black box*. This means studying all possible outputs for a set (or more) of inputs and describe the contents of the black box.

With *specifications analysis* we study the data flow. The aim is to show that the input assertion implies the output assertion over all possible paths between *start* and *halt nodes*. Thus, implicit in the specifications analysis is the existence and observance of checkpoints.

The way we have described it, the object of validation is to assure total system fault tolerance. Correctly done, validation procedures can reveal how well the design goals are observed, or alternative modules can be added to enhance software reliability.

The major point that must however be made is that systems analysis and design should be done *defensively*. That is, the designer must assume

1. That the worst will happen.
2. That faulty or incorrect data will be presented to the system.
3. Usage not planned for will occur.
4. Modifications will need to be made.

These factors, if accounted for in the intial design, will do much to increase the overall reliability of the software. This will be the more true if programs are designed and implemented in a modular fashion—modular by end use, as seen by the user.

It is surprising how many professionals often fail to realize that proper software design is a very important factor affecting overall performance. The task is not even so demanding if the right prerequisites are observed. For example, each software module should begin with a routine that validates all data input to it.

- All data entering the system should be checked.
- Errors which can stop the software should be trapped.
- Processing of that data should be discontinued.
- An appropriate error message should be written.

The emphasis here is on the prevention of software failures. Errors must be detected, isolated, diagnosed, published, and corrected. The design philosophy must be to catch errors early enough in processing logic to prevent or localize the damage caused by them.

4   JAPANESE ANSWERS TO SOFTWARE QUALITY

We have spoken of basic criteria needed to evaluate the quality of programming products: reliability, operability, efficiency, and maintainability. The common thread in all of them is the bugs or errors that are unconsciously created by analysts and programmers.

Since the percentage of work done by humans is much greater in software production than in any other industrial product, faults may possibly occur in any part of the development processes. To better this situation, the production process must be improved in a way that allows little or no chance for analysts and programmers to make mistakes.

One solution is to use structural approaches as a means to this end. Another valuable tool is a feedback able to adjust itself to any finding upon its usage. The proper, computer-based implementation of feedback can see to it that programming products are not only free from faults but also satisfy other criteria of software quality.

Quite evidently, structured approaches and feedbacks are tantamount to introducing a new methodology and tools, rearranging the process flow accordingly. It is equally important for the software production lines to digest such improvements.

As a means for the acceptance of new tools and of new standards, the Japanese computers, communications, and software firms have introduced the Quality Control (QC) Circle solution. A QC is a small group performing voluntarily quality control activities within the same workshop.

This small QC group carries on continuous self-development and mutual development control. The result is improvement within the workshop utilizing quality control techniques. The important reference is that all members are participating.

Typically, in a Japanese QC Circle, *the faults are treated as precious information sources.* Through the group discussion, the real reason (or root) is tracked back and isolated. The objective is to find out a defect of the software development and production process, not to fix the fault per se.

Significantly, in Japanese software production prior to establishing this methodology a fault was shame. It was detected in secrecy and fixed the same way. But since nobody else knew the real reason why it happened, the mistakes repeated themselves. Now, when a software fault is found, every member of the development team gets the information. Its members use a set of tools to isolate the origin of the problem. Statistical methods are also included in the tool set, the way we have been discussing this issue in the preceding sections.

Incidentally, in Japan a number of different approaches have been tested since the early 1970s. An original method was *draft documents review* (applied since 1973). It aimed at clearer insights into assigned projects. In 1976, the next method, *acceptable specification development* was initiated. Its objective was to obtain the user's view in the product specification.

A third solution, known as *product redevelopment procedure,* has been introduced since 1980. This is based on the observation of abundant program reserves of computers and communications power.

A fact of the methodology followed by the Japanese is the *draft document review.* Its original intent was productivity rather than reliability. Document drafts are taken as the evidence of development jobs done at the time of predefined milestones. That allows managers to freeze design specification and to obtain better insight.

The basis of this employment is the experimental Japanese finding that there is a positive relationship between

- the quality of documents and
- the quality of the resulting programming product

Along this line, major draft documents under control are system design concepts, configuration and functional description, system test specifications, the users manual, the maintenance manual, and the installation manual.

A cornerstone of the Japanese approach is the attention in establishing since the beginning an acceptable specification development for programming products. The formation and promotion of *user review groups* is a crucial condition. The approach has been successful in some Japanese computer environments.

Finally, still another interesting Japanese software initiative of which to take good notice is the *programming redevelopment procedure.* Leading firms see the redevelopment of existing programs as a short cut to a better quality software, accounting for the fact that most computer users have accumulated large investments in software assets.

Redevelopment approaches rest on four pillars:

- Practical quality improvement studies using old programming products
- The establishment of "usage proven" specifications
- Accurate project costing and quality evaluation approaches
- Thorough program testing, followed by systems integration and verification.

This can be said in conclusion: the great quest for software quality is spreading and the approaches being taken are reflected in a wide variety of solutions. Differences in managerial procedures, company standards, specification techniques, and design strategies may make each methodology unique, but the underlying trend is for a strong emphasis on verification.

Like reliability, the concept of a valid verification either starts from the drawing board or it will not be present in any phase. "At the drawing board" means that along with the requirements definition we should establish what functions are to be implemented by the target system. These functions should reflect the user's needs and be the basis for the implementation.

For the sake of clarity let's recall that the requirements definition stage consists of interviews with the end user, the formulation of a functional model, and an evaluation of the same. This should assure that the functional model is complete, precise, relevant, and can lead to a reliable programming product.

A basic statement I would like to make in conclusion concerns formalisms. As the chapter on structured systems analysis should have made evident, the methodology to be chosen and its formalisms lead to a permanent record that is computer-based, complete, unambiguous, and user friendly. The iteration of the different methodologies that took place in Japan has in the background the search for a compromise between competing aims.

5 STRUCTURED TESTING APPROACHES

Studies performed during the last few years in the United States, Western Europe, and Japan help document that testing accounts for an average of 40% to 60% of the total software project effort—with 50% a good average. Testing consumes expensive resources that could be put to more productive use by the introduction of improved testing methods. Many companies search to decompose the testing problem by identifying the generic structure of a programming product.

This policy of steady search for new testing approaches has placed considerable interest on *structured testing techniques*. Its goal is improving design methodologies and bettering the means not only of testing but also of test data construction.

Both the techniques and the management of testing activities can be improved to avoid common absurdities that account for much of the wasted effort in testing today. Some of the problems relating to testing techniques are:

- How to find and correct faults before productions, or build error tolerant systems?

- What is the effect of the programming language on the error rate?

- What are the comparative advantages of top-down and bottom-up testing?

- What is the effect on error rate of structured design and coding techniques?

- How many test cases do we need to try in order to achieve a satisfactory level of confidence in a software system?

- What are the minimum quality requirements for test data?

- What is the correct volume of test data?

- How can the project manager know whether testing is complete?

More specifically, the following issues must be examined within the framework of the main reference: the role of testing in the development process of computers and communications software; the phase in which it should be inserted; the cost of testing versus the obtainable results; the different approaches which exist to reach the goal such as design for fault-tolerance and for reduced error rates.

Among the better known testing approaches is *path testing*. It derives test data according to the program's internal structure to test every statement, branch, and logical path in the system. Automated testing tools are available to monitor path coverage.

The trend in specialist opinion seems to be that path testing can achieve higher reliability than functional testing. On the other hand, path testing approaches require detailed knowledge about the program's internal structure, which is not true of functional testing. The latter is easier to perform, but a valid approach should systematically and comprehensively verify the system functions.

This is written in the realization that the methodology for effective testing is as important as that for system design and coding. When testing programming products, the number of conditions can be very high. How we can organize these testing conditions into a structured plan in order to systematically and comprehensively test the software system becomes an important issue.

Several structured design methodologies have been proposed (and used) for system design and programming, but this reference is not necessarily valid when it comes to testing. Current research in testing methodology mainly concentrates on how to select test data, though the issue of how to organize test data has not received much attention.

Under these circumstances, a reasonable approach would derive testing conditions from the functional design documents, organizing them into a structured testing plan. This will involve the correct identification of functionally important classes of input and output. It will also involve a functional decomposition of data structures into design substructures and of design functions into processing elements.

To proceed in an orderly manner we should employ programming structures that are easy to design and that help avoid the accumulation of errors. We also need a test model able to do three things:

- lead to the avoidance of faults
- provide a means for error detection
- assure a means for effort allocation

Typically such a model would define a structure composed of nodes (in the program's framework), arcs (mainline of code), and cycles (iterations). A selection will be done probabilistically, allowing however the user to specify the path. The model's complexity will be a function of:

1. the number of paths (distinct start to end),
2. path length, and
3. program coverage.

The task will be the easier if we have followed structural systems analysis and structured programming principles.

The error distribution will be expressed in paths and locations, with particular attention to errors versus input, complexity, and coverage. Models of this type tend to classify the input domain into *commands* (deletion, updates, and so on) and *objects*. The latter include a set of primitive data structures.

Users can construct complex objects using these primitives. The test design problem is to develop a set of test programs to thoroughly evaluate the command functions against all possible data structures.

One of the critical questions is when to stop testing. Though no general rule can be stated, the leading thinking is that, once the defined level of coverage has been reached, continuing testing does not pay off.

Much has been stated about a modular approach in system design, and similar statements have been made about testing. Undoubtedly, as we had the opportunity to underline, modular approaches have many merits. But the relation is not an ever increasing function of benefits due to modularization. In this sense, it is correct to keep in mind the following references:

1. The average module size must be 3 to 5 times the average module overhead (combined).

2. With modules, memory overhead ranges from 20% to 35% and execution time 10% to 15%.

3. The program overhead (linkage) for a higher level language is about 10 instructions.

4. The combined overhead, increased time and more memory due to linkages, is a variable to watch.

There is a saying in our profession that software costs triple as modular size is cut in half. Thus, while structured design provides guidelines to develop simple independent modules, there are limits to be observed. Table 10 reflects certain considerations linking together the type of programming, the relevant characteristics, and the benefit to be derived.

Let's observe in this connection that the so often criticized monolithic programming has its advantages. A rarely appreciated fact is that modular and monolithic programming become synonymous we talk of personal computers. Machine size introduces beneficial constraints. Large program size for the sake of it is avoided.

All these references are being made in the understanding that the user organization properly appreciates the role of program proving, the use of formal methods, and the need to have proofs implicit in a constructive approach to system building. The difficulty of program testing is magnified if we attack a vague or meaningless program structure. Testing is simplified through the use of a correct structure.

Another understanding that is necessary regards the system testing problem and its relation to program testing. A further reference is the specification necessary to allow the checking of results. Here, attention should be placed on testing modularity and on matching system, program, and problem structure to permit effective modularity.

Testing problems may be posed by hardware/software obscurities, the relationship of the testing environment to the program-

TABLE 10
CHARACTERISTICS AND BENEFIT AS A FUNCTION OF TYPE OF PROGRAM

Type of Program	Characteristics	Benefit
Structural Design	• Use of structure charts • Total system design prior to implementation	• Improved system design • Better communication between designers and programmers • Fewer backtracking problems • Way open to structured programming
Structured Programming	• Modules perform ONE function • Small modules: 60 to 20 instr. • Structured walkthroughs	• Improvement in software development cost • Better documentation • Greater tendency toward modularity
Modular Programming	• Functional allocation • Top-down design • Bottom-up implementation	• Easier chance and maintenance • Higher programming productivity • More accurate processing • Greater cost of linkages
Monolithic	• Interrelated functions • Imbedded I/O Control	• Minimal time and cost

ming language, and the avoidance of checking the completeness of a test. A meaningful testing procedure would force designers, analysts, and programmers to consider:

- The basic forms of the control structure (motivation, adequacy, expected results).
- Effective control by means of a computer-based restructuring and means of documentation.
- A balance between software costs, reliability, quality, and the reduction of complexity.
- A concern with correctness, from specifications to the suitability of design approaches and the solution to be given.
- Effective methods of modularization (particularly applicable in the programming phases, but which must be accounted for early in analysis and design).
- The benefits and limitations of structural testing methodologies.
- The vital issue of correctness in proving software quality, including validation procedures and certification.

Software-producing organizations that have suffered the endless complexities of unmaintained flowcharts and lines of code hiding innumerable logical flaws find structured testing a blessed relief and comfort. Others with sophisticated analysis and design techniques and better-trained staff see structured testing as imposing a discipline on the evaluation of a system that, without proper verification, could easily become mistaken for a programming product, which it is not.

6 RELIABILITY WITH ONLINE SYSTEMS

It's an old saying in engineering that no chain is ever stronger than the weakest of its links. In an online system the reliability is a function of hosts, nodes/switches, long distance, local network, concentrators, multiplexors, modems, terminal workstations—their hardware and software. If correctness and robustness is a general software requirement, this is so much more with realtime interactive systems.

All types of system interrupts create a prejudice, but their effect on usage varies. Hence, we must classify *prejudices* as minor/major/catastrophic for *our* system, and within *our* operating environment. Usually, short and long interruptions are software oriented. Medium term interruptions are due to hardware. Short interruptions have a disproportional amount of "recovery" time.

With an online system, remote diagnostics (telediagnostics) are necessary. This involves data collection (on classified failures) and the ability to screen for failures; the localization of failures and failure reasons; and the proper, timely maintenance action to be provided on a documented basis. Telediagnostics must help in fault finding, fault isolation and removal, installation checkput, direction for a documented repair, supply support action, program reruns, remote recovery, remote dumps, and remote restart.

Because the reasons for failure multiply, with a distributed information system the software must be simple in its origin. Preferably there should be no "multi" (access, programming, processing) on the same workstation but one application on one machine. Most important is the careful language choice proper for this equipment. No sophisticated or complex kind of solution is needed. Software design must assure unattended operations in the periphery. That's another reason why logical and physical solutions must always be simple.

Within a given organization, analysis and design should observe from the beginning homogeneous procedures. It is a serious error to multiply by orders of magnitude the needed software support. For, say, 200 workstations there must be *one* release, centrally supported. The software must be designed for online diagnostics.

To gain insight on the basic reasons for software failures, it is advisable to study in detail the quality history records of online operations. (We will return to this when we talk of maintenance.) The types of failures with computers and communcations have always been a function of the technology that is used.

Sometimes malfunctions and technical problems that have been prominent for a certain period disappear with the new technologies. Then they reappear as still newer technologies come into play. Spillover was prominent in the early to mid-50s, with Williams

Tubes. We have not heard of spillover for a quarter century. Now super VLSI presents a similar reaction to data patterns.

"Pattern sensitivity" has not been a problem with magnetic core nor with small-scale to medium-scale integration. But with large-scale to very large-scale integration the memory chip is pattern sensitive (effect of alpha radiation on ceramics).

Environment variations such as temperature, humidity, and dust, present problems of their own. Though these are basically hardware issues, they do affect the software and have to be accounted for.

There are many unknown or lesser known situations with systems reliability. Parameterization is an example. After years of work, a machine that worked satisfactorily presents defects within a given applications environment. It then becomes necessary to define the parameters and to keep them dynamic within the changing job stream of the applications environment.

Finally, we are confronted with apparent and latent software failures—particularly bothersome in regard to the operating system, virtual storage, DBMS, and communications software. In the general case, software failures fall into two classes:

- Those creating short machine interrupts and requiring a disproportional amount of recovery time.
- The long-term error tracking category which is in the background of successive software releases.

Each class has its own problems. These problems call for different approaches in terms of solutions and of control actions. Effective management requires the careful recording and analysis of resource utilization associated with system hardware and software.

This should provide detailed runtime statistics on resource usage and on failures of all types. A careful data organization able to lead to simulation representing the critical features of system behavior is a prerequisite. If we wish to develop more reliable on-line systems we must be able both to simulate and replay the environment under which operational programs are executed.

24

NEW THINKING ABOUT SOFTWARE MAINTENANCE

1 INTRODUCTION

One of the worst notions the computer industry has sold to users is the idea that it is good to be able to tinker with software. Even after 30 years of computer practice the erroneous concept still persists that frequent changes in software mean improvements in processing. In fact, exactly the opposite is true.

Software maintenance entails costs, risks, and quality problems. A rule of thumb suggests that every time one change is made in a small area of a programming product some ten errors are introduced, to be weeded out later. Software should therefore be altered only when it is absolutely necessary. This should be done under rigid conditions, and any change should be documented so that it is always possible to find the origin of the change and roll back. Quite often, the supposed improvements are less than satisfactory. Even when it is satisfactory it is very costly and time consuming. Typically, in an established computer installation, an estimated 70% to 80% of the programmers work on maintenance jobs. As more software manpower goes into maintenance, less is available for new development.

There are many excesses in terms of doing unnecessary maintenance work since people don't realize what it really involves and ask for noncritical changes. But it is also true that in most organizations a great deal of software is already in existence, some of it of low quality.

If we are to change the prevailing procedures of heavy maintenance work, we must improve software development practices from conceptual design to documentation. We must furthermore establish a policy of easily maintainable software and guarantee its execution. A software product is easily maintainable to the extent that its design accounts for and facilitates changes to satisfy new requirements or to correct deficiencies.

Which are the characteristics able to indicate the extent to which a software product is maintainable? The first and foremost is the ease of modifying its documentation. This reference includes insertions and deletions to be made without renumbering all the pages and the possibility for the revision of records. Evidently, computer-based documentation—the way we have been discussing it—can best meet this requirement.

A second characteristic concerns the program statements. Code modifications must be traceable to any previous state. Hence, source code lines should be sequentially numbered. Comment marks should be used to convert previously executable source code statements to comments which remain in the listing as a change record. At this point, the function of code statement and of documentation tend to merge. To make effective maintenance possible:

- Documentation should include cross-references of variable names with subroutines in which they are used.
- The proper subroutines calling sequences must be established.
- Comments must be used to locate subroutines calls and entry points.

Furthermore, source code format should be such as to facilitate visual search for locations of branching statement and their targets. Up-to-date flowcharts must be available and the program properly designed to fit into available computer resources to avoid major restructuring.

In a different sense, the characteristic of being easy to modify implies controlled change. In this change some parts remain the same while others are altered so that a desired new result is obtained. Furthermore, the ability to repair a programming product is a subclass of maintainability. The implication is that software becomes norepairable when the effects of a proposed code structure are not understood with sufficient confidence, owing to previous poor maintenance practices.

One of the poor design and maintenance practices is the lack of traceability in the program code. A state of nonrepairability is reached when it can be concluded that it is cost/effective to redesign a significant portion of the program. Computer-based approaches provide significant assistance in reaching this objective *if* the original design has been accomplished in a structured, easily defined way.

2 FACILITATING THE MAINTENANCE TASK

The maintenance of a programming product can be facilitated if provisions have been included in the original design for the addition, repair, update, and general modernization of components. Whether changes are made to enhance function and respond to new equipment technology or to adjust to a changing legislation or user desires is not important. What is important is to foresee the possible need for changes and adjust accordingly the design and structural perspectives.

On the other hand, the amount of changes to be done in a programming product should be strictly controlled. While legal requirements and program efficiency can and do lead to a change, the most frequent reason is that users and analysts did not put enough forethought into design and subsequently users ask for alterations. Here, the best answer is applications discipline. Modifications induced by new customer requirements and by the desire to alter overall performance should be kept to a bare minimum.

It is better to plan ahead than pay the cost thereafter. But what does it mean to plan ahead? Two answers can be given:

1. An end-user–oriented approach is one in which the objective is to obtain a solid understanding of the job to be done. Project, say, a 10-year life cycle, and cover this life cycle in terms of user requirement in data processing, databasing, and datacomm.

This might have been unfeasible 30 or even 20 years ago when computer experience was thin. It is possible today because we have so many aging applications which should be redone to change from batch to interactive, using the best of available technology and answering in a valid way user requirements.

Even if the overriding requirement is to do many of the existing applications all over again to benefit from the advantages presented by third generation online systems, it is no less true that their existence and the problems we have experienced in their maintenance present a good basis for new departures. Such experience, furthermore, can and should be used in the development of other applications that did not exist earlier.

2. The alternative answer is a software design approach, properly organized, rational, modular, computer supported, and projected for maintenance.

It should be expected that, with this approach, for every generic functional component there will be a structured implementation, offering a solid basis of departure for software designers. How can the designer identify the best alternative against a given environment? The only sensible basis is experimentation.

Let's return to the reference we just made about our experience with the current software. To make rational approaches feasible, increasingly more empirical evidence must be collected about the system-level behavior of a great variety of generic components. Organized information based both on observations and on experiments is the only valid method for making intelligent design choices.

We must organize the whole operation from the design of programming products to their maintenance in the sense of a component factory. The last phase of the production process should consist of full scale testing and careful documentation of test results, which then accompany the delivered programming product to aid in maintenance. Software should become engineered like a hardware product.

The formal, properly structured testing procedures that we are suggesting should also reflect the fact that software maintenance, in addition to correction of problems, includes updating and revision of applications programs caused by changes or expansion of the operational mission. Every computers and communications organization needs to take a strong look at the life cycle approach to software. This includes the formulation of design and management principles to assure in the software life cycle cost models, maintenance, and program update.

This being done and provided that it is executed in an able manner, the cost of program maintenance can be further reduced in any of three possible ways:

- Reduce the amount of changes users require. This can have a good effect, yet some changes are inevitable and it is the duty of the software people to ensure that the information system provides what is required.
- Improve the systems documentation, making very explicit the applications aspects and the results. This has its limitations with manual solutions, but computer-supported approaches can be very effective.
- Assure modularity, legibility, and the logical presentation of programs. Few people have tackled the problem from this direction; however, this is an area in which maintenance time can be reduced dramatically.

This advice can go a long way if its implementation starts at the design and maintenance level. A logically laid out programming effort, properly presented and executed in an able manner, will reduce not only the time eventually necessary in changing the program but also development proper and testing. A Rand Corporation study showed that when a single instruction is changed in a large program, the program has less than 50% chance of working the first time, after the change.

Such known facts must be accounted for and remedied by using better methods in programming, including the development of the right methodology for efficient testing. Many programmers compare the testing phase of a program with entering a very large, very dark tunnel of indeterminate length. The program is completed when one emerges into the light from the end of the tunnel. Here is a mentality that must be radically changed.

This analogy can be extended to depict the rather common occurrence of the programmer who emerges from one tunnel, only to disappear into a larger, longer, darker tunnel when he discovers a major logical error after having spent considerable time in testing. The situation can not and should not be regarded as acceptable.

If we wish to facilitate the programming task, emphasis should be placed on methodology. As many programmers know, most maintenance problems are associated with: error handling; improper data structures; ill defined input/output operations; repetitive loops and associated decisions; less than clear logical expressions; excessive subscripting; and, at the end of the list, with numerical operations. For each of these areas, a number of specific "what-to-look-for" guidelines can and should be given.

As far as the user organization is concerned, the maintenance task can be facilitated through the use of packages assigning their vendor the maintenance responsibility. Still for homemade software it is wise to keep the maintenance in-house, observing the strict rules we are discussing rather than going for third party software maintenance.

Finally, whether we talk of in-house programming product development or of packages, we should be prepared for some radical changes as microcomputers increasingly become as self-contained as pocket calculators. No one may consider repairing them. No one repairs a pocket calculator costing $10. We throw it out and get another.

Not only may software in this environment come in a microprocessor-based firmware form; but also, if it stays microprocessor-based, it will be much easier to repair. As with packages, the hardware vendor may be offering a reasonable maintenance contract on these systems. This, too, is a reason things may be getting easier.

3 TESTING AS A PREREQUISITE TO SUCCESSFUL MAINTENANCE

If preventive maintenance is a prerequisite to the correct functioning of many hardware systems, the thorough testing of programming products can be seen as preventive software maintenance. Testing must have a dynamic character. When we are dealing with items that require preventive maintenance, they cannot be considered in static terms.

Software is dynamic by definition. Applications programs respond differently to changes in the operating system or in the machine itself; as a result, they need to be tuned.

To properly tune a programming product we must identify at the design and testing level measurable program properties that influence maintainability. We need to examine the effect of various software characteristics on the subsequent frequency and magnitude of program errors, and project the necessary measures accordingly. Such characteristics fall roughly into four categories:

- high level control action,
- numerical/text processing,
- database management, and
- datacomm requirements.

Correspondingly, we can characterize the maintenance performance of a program by two values:

1. The total maintenance time spent on the programming product
2. The number of maintenance changes made to it.

For measurement purposes, it is wise to consider a module in maintenance from the time it leaves the development stage and enters system testing. Maintenance performance data can come from either informal time records that include time "spent on" and cause of maintenance activities or from a formal maintenance activity database, recorded automatically when a program is changed. The latter is the preferable solution.

Among the issues impacting on the maintenance requirements we can distinguish the complexity of the program control flow, the clarity of the program control structure, and the procedures characterizing the program data usage. A valid maintenance policy will be searching to avoid problems before they occur, being concerned with preventive measures to protect continuity—detecting and correcting faults which may result in failures.

Such careful approach to the issue of maintenance should not be looked at as an alternative or substitute to testing at the end of the development phase. The stages of testing a program are usually:

1. Module by module.
2. Subsystem level—integrated with the programmer's data.
3. Systems testing with the user's data.

Maintenance will be so much more simplified if item No. 3 includes operational acceptance testing and makes it a specific requirement. Beyond the system testing comes the need for interface testing with other applications where there is a data path connection. Then, there will be parallel or pilot running before cut-over.

Test results should be part and parcel of the maintenance manual. The most significant testing will be in the systems, operational, and interface phases. All three involve both operations personnel and the systems people responsible for the development. They should also co-involve the maintenance people.

If there are programmers dedicated to the maintenance phases, they must both take a keen interest in the tests and be particularly aware of what tests have achieved. Not only should they be concerned that:

- the data presented to the system is processed properly,
- the invalid routines are checked out, and
- the correct files and reports are obtained,

but they should also be concerned that the modernization permits easy maintenance; restart and recovery procedures are properly established; incorrect responses by operators are treated; incorrect responses by operators are trapped; all error messages are unambiguous and can be actioned; terminations are correctly carried out; and files are not left unclosed, undated, unlabeled, or unified.

Both for the sake of a clean developmental job and for that of an easier maintenance, the label checking procedures must be accurate. The continuation files must be properly dealt with; data files passed from other applications must be correct in content and structure. To be quite blunt, it should be the endeavor of the maintenance personnel to "break the system" before it receives the stamp of quality assurance.

Thus, in a certain sense testing and maintenance planning merge in the process of verification. This needs to be understood as meaning nothing more than a convincing demonstration that a certain formalization describes the subject of validation as we have discussed it in quality assurance. In this sense, the immediate objective of verification is to provide guidelines for the various stages of the development, testing, and maintenance procedures.

In the process it is wise to establish a unique error detection strategy capable of significant impact upon the overall system performance. The time to think about these issues is after the requirements definition is completed, while the software architecture is selected, but also when the program design is finished and the testing phase starts. It is perhaps needless to add that the verification techniques must be self-consistent and in accordance with the standards prevailing in the organization.

During the maintenance design stage, programs, flow of control, input/output, throughput, and relations between programs and data must be identified. The system specs should specify the manner in which the functions considered in the requirements definition stage are to be implemented. The narrative that is required to accompany this procedure should account not only for processing requirements but also for the data structures.

Again, for maintenance planning reasons, it is necessary to split the development of large or complex programming products into several modules that can be implemented serially or in parallel. This method can also be advisable for smaller systems, and it can be just as helpful in development, testing, and subsequent maintenance.

The satisfactory verification of a programming product involves science and some art. The art can be compensated to some extent by a thoroughly disciplined approach, which is instrumental in separating the good programmer from the average programmer. Through it, the programmer assures himself and his superior that his software will solve the problem he started out to solve and will continue to solve it.

The beginner approaches this phase with a casual air—a chore to be performed after the supposedly real challenge of design and coding has been conquered. His approach to the problem is to throw together some test data—any data—and then laboriously check the file dumps and output results. This is wrong.

For reasons of making the eventual maintenance action more linear, program acceptance testing must include data validation routines, output files and reports, file generation controls, identification of continuation files, and labeling of the interchange of data files with other systems. Among the valuable components are bulk data tests, unambiguous messages for maintenance reasons, idem for operators with checked operator responses, as well as correct file closure and reporting procedures including all termination conditions.

It is well known that any conditions under which the system cannot recover from failure must be specified in advance and corrected. Less appreciated is the fact that all such corrections along with their background reasons should be in the documentation. We should remind ourselves that the majority of productive work is run on a computer after the programmers have gone home—and the same is true of maintenance.

It is not very practical to call back the original programmer to sort out conceptual or operational difficulties caused by bad design every time they occur. But being rational in the approach requires changing the mentality of the people. Hence, steady training and a lead time to implement new directions is desirable.

The good programmer is always suspicious of his program. The experienced software specialist becomes adept at inventing procedures that test his own logic as fully as possible. When a difficult error is found, he runs over the elements of the problem several times until a pattern emerges which encompasses them all. And it is always sound to suspend judgement till all results are in. A person who jumps to conclusions is less sensitive to the symptoms he encounters.

In conclusion, the following points are worth noting. First, start thinking of testing and maintenance in the design phase. Then make sure the design and coding up to this stage facilitates testing and subsequent maintenance. Further, each time a difficult module is coded, data should be written to test the intricacies of the logic. If this verification is kept until later, the sections of code likely to cause problems will be forgotten.

Efficient solutions do not rest on printing out masses of data to be examined by human eye. Instead, exception reporting should be used to allow all important information to be seen at a glance. It is just as wise to know when to stop testing. Many poor tests do not equal one good, carefully thought out procedure. The same is true of maintenance activity.

Though much time may pass till the new maintenance-oriented directives seep down through the organization, the important thing is to begin right. Any progress in the area of applications development and their maintenance—hence in the growth of computing—must come through discipline rather than the miracle of certain (or uncertain) breakthroughs.

4 PREDICTION TECHNIQUES

The emphasis which is placed on testing in a chapter dedicated to the maintenance of programming products is justified by the role proper software validation procedures may play within a life cycle approach. Testing is not only part of the software development process; it also has a life cycle impact. As the computer program is subject to specific conditions to show that the program meets its intended design, it also reveals internal inefficiencies and sources of faults.

Looking at the fundamentals, what we do in a testing process is to feed sample input data into a program, execute it, and inspect the

- the output and
- the program behavior for correctness.

This is at the same time the cornerstone of a reliability methodology. As such, it goes well beyond the traditional view whereby testing is the development phase during which the largest quantity of errors is detected and corrected.

We have said that testing by the software development agency usually accounts for about 50% of the software development cost. Though this tends to be a near standard, the results to be obtained can vary greatly. With the classical means for program testing, in spite of this expenditure, the software developer has no real assurance of getting error-free programs. The testing cycle only demonstrates the presence of errors.

We must go beyond this state. Among the techniques and tools developed to improve the outcome of the testing cycle we can notice: analyzers, test drivers, intentional failure, procedures, regression testing, environment simulators, symbolic interactive execution, and the like. The common ground is to stress the major functions to be accomplished, then proceed from there to an identification of the lesser functions that derive from the major ones always recording the outcome.

In this process a functional modularity would facilitate the matching of requirements to specific modules of a program. The capability of providing diagnostics (through use of conditional assembly to invoke macro generation of code) would bring many faults under control. Comments indicating unacceptable values and the recommended default action must be a standard, fully observed discipline.

The use of test drives is recommendable. These are tools that provide the facilities for executing the test article by loading input files with data values, the objective being to yield recorded data for evaluating purposes against expected results. The outcome of test drivers is more meaningful when the latter are restricted to operation in the same host environment as the program under test article.

The drivers can operate in a static or dynamic mode. Static test routines may be one-shot or repetitive, providing the facilities for reading test input data into specific database locations, passing control to the test article or its associated operating system, and resuming control after each execution (storing test results, visualizing them, or printing them).

The difference with dynamic test drivers is that these operate in realtime to assure a more realistic environment than is possible with static solutions. The facilities available to a static driver are usually part of the dynamic test driver as well. Furthermore, a test executive is provided to sequence test and data transfer operations unless the operating system interfaces with the dynamic test driver in an able manner.

The broader possibilities opened by this approach within the testing and maintenance frame of reference is that such drivers can be designed to work with a variety of offline utilities and support programs. For instance: test generators/distributors, text editors, scenario generators, data reduction, and fault analysis software. This can help automate the current manual tasks in a maintenance situation but also it can significantly improve the perspective for software control.

Such action both improves the dependability which can be placed on the maintenance of programming products and promises a swamping of costs. The latter is a necessity as studies made in the data-processing industry indicate that user expenditures for maintenance are expected to increase at the rate of 22% per year until 1985, the growth in the user maintenance costs exceeding the growth rate of user expenditures.

As cannot be too often repeated, in the long run, the only real hope of reducing maintenance costs is to build maintenance considerations into the design of the software system. The idea is to develop new software designs to provide for computer-based diagnostics as well as self-diagnostic and self-sealing hardware and software architectures.

Self-sealing approaches aim to assure a fail-safe capability and allow future systems to run with their faults isolated and sealed while the maintenance specialist schedules his response time and the corrective action which follows. But in the short to medium term the only valid answer to this subject is the account to be taken of software maintenance since the design stage all the way through the testing procedures, with quality histories a basic part of this effort.

A formalized testing and maintenance discipline is inevitable, if we wish to obtain results. One of the methodological approaches leading installations are implementing reflects the catastrophic, major and minor fault classification to which we have made due reference. This would allow minor bugs to accumulate, minimizing the disruption caused by frequent changes, some of which result in additional problems.

Such premises can be just as valid in software maintenance as in development. If quality can be assured through testing, by bringing the situation under control through the observance of a valid methodology, we enhance this project. But once again a new philosophy must be applied since the design stage. Not only must programming specifications define the function of a program module but they should also be required to include variables to be manipulated solely for the purpose of making meaningful tests.

One effective technique, for instance, is using an activity variable in each module. Initially, this activity variable is set up as inactive, but as the module is invoked the value of the activity variable is changed to indicate that it is active. When control is relinquished, the variable returns to the inactive state. This way it is easier to trace the path of active modules by identifying the activities that have occurred.

Another useful technique is to display the parameters of a module at the time of invocation. Because of data coupling, the complete set of relevant data is available for determining the state of the module.

An additional technique that proves to be useful is the gathering of statistics internally by each module. Typically, a module would keep track of how many times it had been invoked, the parameters it had been called with, what type of internal results it had generated, and the like.

Data of this type makes reconstruction and analysis of program activity a relatively easy task. They also help identify areas of code that have never been tested and to locate issues critical in the efficient running of the program. These are examples of prediction techniques which are both part of a comprehensive testing methodology and of a maintenance policy able to assure software quality and reliability.

Let's recapitulate. Whether done at the end of the development process or as a maintenance discipline, testing consumes expensive resources that could be put to more productive use by the introduction of improved methods and computer-assisted solutions. This is the basic reason why leading organizations start showing great interest in *structured testing techniques* with the single goal of improving program correctness.

The management of testing activities can be bettered to avoid some of the common absurdities that account for much of the wasted effort in testing today. Some of the questions relating to testing techniques are:

- How to find and correct faults before production to build error tolerant systems?
- What is the effect of language on error rate?
- What's the effect on error rate of structured design and coding techniques?

- How many test cases do we need to try to achieve a satisfactory level of confidence in a system?
- What are the minimum quality requirements for test data?
- What's the role of testing in the maintenance of programming products?
- How can the results of testing be used to ease and improve the maintenance effort?
- What are the comparative advantages of top-down and bottom-up testing?
- How can the project manager know whether testing is complete?

If we wish documented answers, the following issues must be examined within the framework of the main reference: First, the role of testing in the system development process and in the subsequent maintenance testing task. Second, the cost of testing within a life cycle perspective and in consideration of the goal of designing for fault-tolerance and for reduced error cost.

This makes evident the need for research on the role of program proving: formal and informal methods, proofs implicit in a constructive approach to system building and its maintenance. It also underlines challenges such as the difficulty of testing with a formalized structure. Can testing be simplified by the use of structured approaches? The answer to this question leads to the system-testing problem and its relation to program testing.

The next issue is the development of early specification to allow checking of the results to be obtained in production. Such a subject can find able answers through the use of modularity in testing, matching program/system structure to permit effective approaches.

There are also questions relating to the relationships of the testing environments to the programming language, and vice versa. There are quality problems posed by hardware/software obscurities which will surface during program maintenance.

Finally, it is proper to recall the development of the proper documentation and even of a specialized software for the comparison of the results being obtained. This is a prerequisite to procedures needed for checking the completeness of the software tests and the ease of subsequent maintenance of programming products.

5   THE ROLE OF REMOTE DIAGNOSTICS

A discussion of the new thinking about software maintenance would be incomplete without reference to remote diagnostics. The reason why this subject was kept for last is preparedness. Without the different aspects of computer-based support from the definition of the maintenance task to testing, prediction techniques, and quality histories, it is not possible to speak of remote diagnostics in an able manner.

Remote diagnostics is done online and involves *loopback* tests. Whether for hardware or software, this is a different way of running a maintenance function than we usually are familiar with. For hardware, the idea is to have every line within a system turned around and send back to itself. This is done by system component since failures do occur and we must be able to isolate the location.

What we just said is the essence of diagnostic tests. Data entered at one part of the network, typically through control center, pass through the transit portion of a terminal to the modem interface. The modem's output data flow is connected to the terminal's input or receive station. Test data are then turned through the terminal equipment to be stored on a quality database, projected on a video display, or presented in hardcopy.

This is the hardware story of remote diagnostics, but the same concept is extended into software. Once the hardware units have been tested and found conforming to standards, we can remotely call on software modules and exercise a testing procedure. This must be prearranged along the lines discussed in the preceding sections, in order to give meaningful results.

For instance, in one application of remote diagnostics provided by the equipment vendor, to be able to take advantage of malfunctions users have to provide a dedicated, voice-grade telephone line and a data access arrangement. This remote computer-based diagnosis program is composed of three elements:

- An electronic console, which is a microprocessor controlled unit that performs system diagnostic procedures and communicates with the remote host computer;
- The service response line, a 24 hour toll-free telephone service;
- The digital diagnosis center where the host computer, communications equipment, and engineering staff are located.

The electronic console is projected to permit users to initiate operating commands through the system terminal. When a unit malfunctions, the user dials the toll-free number to contact the service response group, which then arranges for remote diagnosis and reaches the appropriate field service office to schedule a service call.

Configuration files are used to determine proper parameters and diagnostic procedures for specific systems. The console also allows the remote host system to log problems for each installation so trends can be identified and flagged.

These solutions are becoming fairly standard and are now practiced by computer equipment manufacturers, value added networks, and company operated and maintained distributed architectures. They are, however, in large measure hardware oriented. Software faults are still predominantly handled through human intervention using a toll-free software service.

Along this reference, a coast-to-coast facility established by a computers and communications manufacturer enables customers to phone toll-free at any time for software assistance. Online software support centers are the first point of contact for many customers seeking help with:

1. programming problems
2. information on preventive service, or
3. assistance in programming installation.

Such support centers are staffed by expert personnel, familiar with the most frequent problems of programming products. They are operated around the clock, 7 days a week. The software specialists take customer calls directly, working at display terminals linked to a database of programming information. This database contains software problem descriptions and solutions previously received from hundreds of computer locations worldwide.

Testing with a significant sample of computer users shows that many inquiries can be handled quickly by telephone, often with information available in the support center. This should be seen as a first step. *The goal is to automate the process. For when we talk of computers and communications, it is inexcusable to leave the software on a manual basis.*

INDEX

algorithm, 240-242
Apple, 138, 139

"C", 251-254, 263, 271
   see also Pascal
Cobol, 275, 384, 391
   see also Pascal
compiler, 214-215
computer
   literacy, 248-250
   philosophy, 275-276
cost
   hardware and software, 148-153
   in a system study, 153-157
critical region, 39

Desktop/Plan, 330-333
documentation, 58-62, 405-419
   advantages, 410
   formal language of, 188
   languages, 192-195
   system, 406-410
   value of documents, 413-414

end user, 152, 182
   responsibilities, 25-26
   and software, 92
   and Unix, 302

information system
   databasing, 202
Ingres, 391, 393

Japan
   software quality, 430-432

LAN, 112, 113, 120, 147, 150, 151
   and student learning, 250

and system analysis, 148
language, computer
   levels, 213
   user-oriented, 221-225
LISP, 254
local area networks, *see* LAN
Logo, 254-256

maintenance support, 110
management information system, 111-116
   basics of, 173
medium range planning
   cost calculations, 71-72
   documentation, 84-86
   questions, 70
   and software, 72-73, 75-78, 82-83
Micro-DSS/Finance, 333-336
microsoftware, 141-146
milestones, 29
MIS, *see* management information system
myriaprocessor, 43-45
   applications, 162-163

online system
   reliability, 438-440
operating system, 37, 123, 125
   layered (LOS), 282-287
   memory management, 288
   and microDBMS, 291-293
   new releases, 37-38
   segment descriptor, 287

Pascal, 134, 217, 271, 272, 319
   advantages, 262
   compared to Basic, 274

460 THE SOFTWARE HANDBOOK

    compared to "C", 253–254, 257–260
    compared to Cobol, 265–270
Pilot, 254–256
PL/I, 135
productivity, 370–374
program
    fault, 101
    maintenance, 443–446
    package benefits, 205–206
programmer, 55–56, 101
    productivity, 55
programming
    practices, 120–123, 125
    workstations, 225–230
project
    basic concepts, 4
    basic problem areas, 21–22
    control, 27–30
    goals, 6–9
    information, 50–51
    organization, 15–16, 49
    planning premises, 18–20
    resources, 3
project manager
    and personnel, 33
    profile of, 14
    purpose of, 4–5
    responsibilities, 5–6, 8, 44–45, 76
    roles and responsibilities, 46–47
project personnel, 10–13, 33
    see also project manager

response time, 164–165

semaphores, 40–41
silicon, 103, 155
Small-talk, 254
software, 421–422
    certification, 426
    cost, 362–366
    design, 170
    developments, 279–282
    engineering, 90–93
    environment, 107–108

    failure, 440
    life cycle, 96–100
    online applications, 159
    packages, 139–141, 162, 231–236
    portability, 236–240
    procurement, 243–246
    quality, 371
    reliability, 422–426, 427–429
    security, 119
    SQA, 73, 75
    strategy requirements, 135–136
    subsystem applications, 95
    see also software, integrated; testing
software, integrated
    added value, 345
    ANA (application network architecture), 348, 350
    bus, 346
    defined, 344–346
    interfaces, 347
    telesoftware, 355–358
    tools, 353–355
    videotex, 358–360
    for workstations, 350–353
structural analysis
    benefits, 206
    failures of, 207
    major qualities, 196–198
structural design
    bottom-up, 375
    data organization, 377
    modular decomposition, 376
    step-wise refinement, 376
    top-down, 375
system analysis, 374–375
    basic areas, 168
    design review, 178
    playback, 180
    procedure, 183–184
    role of, 171–172
    schools of thought, 175–176
    walkthrough, 178, 181
system design, 52, 78, 161, 172
    desirable characteristics, 81–82

systems analyst, 57, 173, 201
   and workplace analysis, 160-161
systems designer, 429
   responsibilities, 25-26
   tools of, 24-25
testing, 62-66, 451-456
   acceptance test, 63
   baby-sitting, 64
   life cycle costing, 65
   parallel runs, 63-64
   and remote diagnostics, 456-458
   and software maintenance, 446-451
   structured, 433-436, 438
TK Solver, 336-338, 340-342

Unix
   character set, 312-314
   data streams, 301
   file system, 306-310
   influences on, 305
   major programs, 303
   new features of System V, 298
   PDP-11/45, 302, 304
   pipeline, 301, 302
   process, 301
   shell, 301, 302, 310-312
   strengths and weaknesses, 314-317
   System V, 317-318
   versions, 295-297

VHLL, 213-214, 263, 381-404
   ADF, 393-394, 396
   classes, 391-393
   database languages, 398-400
   DB 2, 400, 404
   general fields, 381
   key points, 381-382
   policy, 386-390
Visicalc, 327-330, 391
Visicorp, 325-327

DATE DUE

GAYLORD   PRINTED IN U.S.A.